Gender in the Middle Ages

Volume 9

RELIGIOUS MEN AND MASCULINE IDENTITY
IN THE MIDDLE AGES

Gender in the Middle Ages

ISSN 1742-870X

Series Editors
Jacqueline Murray
Diane Watt

Editorial Board
Clare Lees
Katherine J. Lewis

This series investigates the representation and construction of masculinity and femininity in the Middle Ages from a variety of disciplinary and interdisciplinary perspectives. It aims in particular to explore the diversity of medieval genders, and such interrelated contexts and issues as sexuality, social class, race and ethnicity, and orthodoxy and heterodoxy.

Proposals or queries should be sent in the first instance to the editors or to the publisher, at the addresses given below; all submissions will receive prompt and informed consideration.

Professor Jacqueline Murray, Department of History, University of Guelph, Guelph, Ontario, N1G 2W1, Canada

Professor Diane Watt, School of Literature and Languages, University of Surrey, Guildford, Surrey GU2 7XH, UK

Boydell & Brewer Limited, PO Box 9, Woodbridge, Suffolk IP12 3DF, UK

Previously published volumes in the series are listed at the end of this book.

RELIGIOUS MEN AND MASCULINE IDENTITY IN THE MIDDLE AGES

Edited by

P.H. Cullum and Katherine J. Lewis

THE BOYDELL PRESS

© Contributors 2013

All Rights Reserved. Except as permitted under current legislation
no part of this work may be photocopied, stored in a retrieval system,
published, performed in public, adapted, broadcast,
transmitted, recorded or reproduced in any form or by any means,
without the prior permission of the copyright owner

First published 2013
The Boydell Press, Woodbridge
Paperback edition 2019

ISBN 978 1 84383 863 0 hardback
ISBN 978 1 78327 368 3 paperback

The Boydell Press is an imprint of Boydell & Brewer Ltd
PO Box 9, Woodbridge, Suffolk IP12 3DF, UK
and of Boydell & Brewer Inc.
668 Mt Hope Avenue, Rochester, NY 14620–2731, USA
website: www.boydellandbrewer.co.uk

A CIP catalogue record for this book is available
from the British Library

The publisher has no responsibility for the continued existence or accuracy of
URLs for external or third-party internet websites referred to in this book, and
does not guarantee that any content on such websites is, or will remain,
accurate or appropriate

CONTENTS

List of illustrations	vii
Contributors	viii
Acknowledgements	x
Introduction *P.H. Cullum and Katherine J. Lewis*	1
From salve to weapon: Torah study, masculinity, and the Babylonian Talmud *Michael L. Satlow*	16
Gender and hierarchy: Archbishop Hincmar of Rheims (845–882) as a religious man *Rachel Stone*	28
The defence of clerical marriage: Religious identity and masculinity in the writings of Anglo-Norman clerics *Jennifer D. Thibodeaux*	46
Writing masculinity and religious identity in Henry of Huntingdon *Kirsten A. Fenton*	64
'The quality of his *virtus* proved him a perfect man': Hereward 'the Wake' and the representation of lay masculinity *Joanna Huntington*	77
Episcopal authority and gender in the narratives of the First Crusade *Matthew Mesley*	94

Contents

'What man are you?': Piety and masculinity in the *vitae* of a Sienese craftsman and a Provençal nobleman
  Marita von Weissenberg — 112

'Imitate, too, this king in virtue, who could have done ill, and did it not': Lay sanctity and the rewriting of Henry VI's manliness
  Katherine J. Lewis — 126

John of Bridlington, mitred prior and model of the mixed life
  Catherine Sanok — 143

Why men became monks in late medieval England
  James G. Clark — 160

Feasting not fasting: Men's devotion to the Eucharist in the later Middle Ages
  P.H. Cullum — 184

Index — 201

LIST OF ILLUSTRATIONS

Figure 1: St John of Bridlington, parish church of St Laurence, Ludlow. Photograph: the author. 146

Figure 2: St John of Bridlington, Beaufort Hours: London, British Library, MS Royal 2 A XVIII, fo. 7v. © The British Library Board. Reproduced by permission. 156

CONTRIBUTORS

James G. Clark is Professor of History at the University of Exeter. He has published widely on monastic and clerical life in later medieval and pre-Reformation England. Recent books include *The Benedictines in the Middle Ages* (2011), *Ovid in the Middle Ages* (2011) and *The culture of medieval English monasticism* (2007). He is currently completing a study of the Dissolution of the Monasteries for Yale University Press.

P.H. Cullum is Head of History at the University of Huddersfield. She has written widely on religion and gender in the later Middle Ages and particularly on clerical masculinity. She is co-founder of The Bishop's Eye, a research network based at the Universities of Huddersfield and Lincoln focused on medieval masculinity, high status men, and interactions between *clerici* and *laici* using the archival and material resources of the diocese of Lincoln.

Kirsten A. Fenton is a Teaching Fellow in Mediaeval History at the University of St Andrews, UK. She is the author of *Gender, nation and conquest in the works of William of Malmesbury* (2008) and co-editor, with Cordelia Beattie, of *Intersections of gender, religion and ethnicity in the Middle Ages* (2010); she has written a number of articles that focus on ideas of medieval masculinity.

Joanna Huntington is Senior Lecturer in Medieval History at the University of Lincoln. Her current and forthcoming publications focus on masculinities in twelfth-century histories, hagiography, kingship, and rulership, and she is working on a monograph, *Heroes from histories: Shaping male virtue in post-Conquest England and Normandy*.

Katherine J. Lewis is Senior Lecturer in History at the University of Huddersfield. She is the author of *Kingship and Masculinity in Late Medieval England* (2013). She has also published a number of works on saints' lives and cults in later medieval England (especially St Katherine of Alexandria), considering the operation of both femininity and masculinity within these.

Contributors

Matthew Mesley was awarded an MPhil at the University of Cambridge, and his PhD at the University of Exeter. He is currently a Postdoctoral Research Assistant at the University of Zürich and is working on a SNF-funded project exploring clerical masculinity and the episcopal office.

Catherine Sanok is Associate Professor of English and Women's Studies at the University of Michigan. Her book, *Her life historical: Exemplarity and female saint's lives in late medieval England*, was published in 2007. She is currently completing a monograph that explores forms of affiliation and community in vernacular Lives of English saints.

Michael L. Satlow is Professor of Religious Studies and Judaic Studies at Brown University. He has written widely on the social and religious history of Jews and Judaism in Antiquity and issues of method and theory in the study of religion. His most recent books are *Creating Judaism: History, tradition, practice* (2006) and *Jewish marriage in Antiquity* (2001); he is the editor of *The gift in Antiquity* (2013).

Rachel Stone is a Postdoctoral Research Associate at King's College London, working on the project 'The making of Charlemagne's Europe, 768–814'. Her book, *Morality and masculinity in the Carolingian empire*, was published in 2011. She is currently preparing a translation of Hincmar of Rheims' treatise 'De divortio Lotharii regis et Theutbergae reginae' with Charles West of Sheffield University.

Jennifer D. Thibodeaux is Associate Professor of History at the University of Wisconsin-Whitewater. She is the editor of *Negotiating clerical identities: Priests, monks and masculinity in the Middle Ages* (2010), and the author of numerous essays on the Norman clergy and masculinity. She is currently working on a monograph provisionally titled 'The manly priest: masculinity, the clergy and Anglo-Norman reform'.

Marita von Weissenberg is Visiting Assistant Professor of History at Xavier University, Cincinnati, Ohio. She was awarded her PhD by Yale University in May 2013. Her dissertation is titled 'Men in the family – Husbands in society: Men, marriage and masculinity in late medieval hagiography 1100–1500'. More broadly, she is interested in the intersections of religion, society, culture, and gender.

ACKNOWLEDGEMENTS

We would like to thank all those who gave papers at the conference 'Religious Men in the Middle Ages' at the University of Huddersfield in July 2012, and those others who attended, for ensuring that we all enjoyed such an inspiring and thought-provoking weekend. Particular thanks are due to Sarah Bastow, Victoria Bielby and Margaret Bullett for helping to ensure that everything ran smoothly; and to Krista Cowman and Joanna Huntington of the University of Lincoln for arranging sponsorship of the reception which launched 'The Bishop's Eye' research network. We are extremely grateful to Jonathan Gledhill for his invaluable work in putting together the final manuscript of this collection. Thanks also to Nicole Harding for research assistance. Finally we would like to thank Caroline Palmer at Boydell for her support of and encouragement with this project.

P.H.C. and K.J.L.

INTRODUCTION[1]

P.H. Cullum and Katherine J. Lewis

Medievalists are fortunate to be able to draw on a great deal of insightful scholarship that has uncovered the devotional practices of medieval women (both lay and religious). There has been much fruitful discussion of the representation and veneration of female saints, and the ways in which lay piety was informed by ideals and practices that can be identified as 'feminine'.[2] Indeed, 'femininity' has often been presented as the dominant discourse through which late medieval religion was both envisaged for and experienced by lay people, alongside discussions of the development of an individualised affective or Christocentric piety and the female readership for vernacular devotional works.[3] This scholarship forms part of a wider project to uncover the lives and experiences of medieval women, a crucial corrective to traditional accounts which focused almost exclusively on men.[4] However the comparative lack of studies of medieval men and religion informed by gender means that the impression sometimes given is that the devout person at this time was either female or feminised, that male religious (monks or clerics) were motivated by career considerations rather than

---

[1] We are grateful to Joanna Huntington for commenting on an earlier draft of this introduction and helping to improve it.

[2] The website 'Feminae: medieval women and gender index' offers an invaluable compendium covering the vast range of scholarship published in this area which can be searched by subject [http://inpress.lib.uiowa.edu/feminae/Default.aspx accessed 9 November 2012].

[3] The work of Caroline Walker Bynum has been extremely influential, *Jesus as mother: studies in the spirituality of the high Middle Ages* (Berkeley, Los Angeles and London, 1982); *Holy feast and holy fast: the religious significance of food to medieval women* (Berkeley, Los Angeles and London, 1987); *Fragmentation and redemption: essays on gender and the human body in medieval religion* (New York, 1991). On women and devotional literature see for example Felicity Riddy, '"Women talking about the things of God", a late medieval sub-culture', in *Women and literature in Britain: 1150–1500*, ed. Carol M. Meale (Cambridge, 1993), pp. 104–27; Jocelyn Wogan-Browne, *Saints' lives and women's literary culture: virginity and its authorizations* (Oxford, 2001); Mary C. Erler, *Women, reading, and piety in late medieval England* (Cambridge, 2002).

[4] For the continuing necessity of undertaking historical studies informed by feminism, and the importance of studying medieval women, see Judith M. Bennett, *History matters: patriarchy and the challenge of feminism* (Philadelphia, 2006).

spirituality and that lay men, while engaging in parochial and devotional practices actually felt 'left out' of religion and used the Reformation as a way to regain control of it via a more theological and patriarchal version.[5] This alleged lack of male religious vocation fits neatly into the long-standing historiographical model of later medieval monasticism as an institution in terminal decline, both in terms of the quality of its practitioners and its relevance to the spiritual lives of the laity.[6] Religious belief and devotional practices have been identified as crucial to certain notions of the feminine and also, on occasion, of great value to women in mitigating patriarchal restrictions on their spiritual potential.[7] But until relatively recently the consensus seemed to be that religion had nothing much to do with men *as* men.

Over the last two decades there has been an increasing tendency for medievalists to employ theories of masculinity as a tool of analysis to complement and amplify existing understandings of medieval gender identities.[8] The words 'masculinity' or 'masculinities' are generally used to refer to the social construction of certain properties and behaviours as being appropriate to men, or understood as naturally possessed by them.[9] Much scholarship on the subject explores the means by which manhood was achieved in different contexts and entails a sense that masculinity was often hard work for men both to attain and to maintain. In contrast to femininity, whose ideals remained broadly the same for women across the social spectrum, both lay and religious, there was a wider range of

---

[5] For discussion of men feeling 'left out', see R.N. Swanson, *Religion and devotion in Europe: c. 1215–c. 1515* (Cambridge, 1995), pp. 306–8.

[6] The work of David Knowles has been enormously influential in this respect, *The religious orders in England*, 3 volumes (Cambridge, 1948–59), especially volume 2, *The end of the Middle Ages* (Cambridge, 1955). This negative characterisation has now been challenged, see James G. Clark, *A monastic renaissance at St Albans: Thomas Walsingham and his circle, c. 1350–1440* (Oxford, 2004), Martin Heale, *Monasticism in late medieval England, c. 1300–1535*, Manchester Medieval Sources Series (Manchester and New York, 2009). See also James G. Clark's essay in this volume for the continuing attractions of monastic profession in late medieval England in terms that shed light on vocation and personal identity.

[7] Work on Margery Kempe provides a good illustration of these issues, e.g. Lynn Staley, *Margery Kempe's dissenting fictions* (University Park, PA, 1994); *A companion to the Book of Margery Kempe*, ed. John H. Arnold and Katherine J. Lewis (Cambridge, 2004).

[8] The field was established in the 1990s, which saw the publication of four important collections of essays: *Medieval masculinities: regarding men in the Middle Ages*, ed. Clare A. Lees (Minneapolis, 1994); *Becoming male in the Middle Ages*, ed. Jeffrey Jerome Cohen and Bonnie Wheeler (New York and London, 1997); *Conflicted identities and multiple masculinities: men in the medieval West*, ed. Jacqueline Murray (New York, 1999); *Masculinity in medieval Europe*, ed. Dawn M. Hadley (London and New York, 1999).

[9] For discussion of the limitations of the term 'masculinity' for approaching the Middle Ages and the importance of exploring contemporary language and its associations, see Christopher Fletcher, 'The Whig interpretation of masculinity? Honour and sexuality in late medieval manhood', in *What is masculinity? Historical dynamics from antiquity to the contemporary world*, ed. John H. Arnold and Sean Brady (Basingstoke and New York, 2011), pp. 57–75. This collection is particularly valuable for the wide chronological range of its contributions, it is unusual to find medieval masculinity discussed alongside masculinities of earlier and later periods. The journal *Gender & History* has a special edition on gender and religion forthcoming in 2013 which will also cover a wide chronological period, including contributions by medievalists.

Introduction

potential versions of ideal masculinity.[10] Both the theory and performance of these varied depending on other aspects of individual and collective identity, such as age, social status, profession, location and ethnicity.[11]

Our own particular interests lie in the intersection between medieval manliness and religious identities and, as a result, we organised a conference on 'Holiness and masculinity in the Middle Ages' at the University of Huddersfield in 2001. This resulted in an edited collection of the same name, published in 2004.[12] We wished to discover what work was being done in this area and to add to the then relatively small body of published material on medieval masculinity. Ten years later we decided to explore what difference a decade had made, so we organised another conference which took place in July 2012.[13] Our earlier conference and collection, by virtue of its focus on holiness, tended to make saintliness the centre of attention, so on this occasion we chose the broader topic of religion and religiosity, naming the conference 'Religious men in the Middle Ages'. We sought to examine and re-evaluate medieval men's relationship with religion, both professed religious men and laymen. We invited papers from scholars working in any relevant field, across the medieval period, which considered the experiences, self-perception or depiction of individuals or groups from any faith or religious tradition (monotheistic, pagan, or heretical), or considered men who rejected faith and religion altogether. Not all of the papers offered or delivered at the conference used gender as a tool for analysis, but many did explicitly focus on issues of masculinity. From these we were able to create a coherent collection of essays which, between them, address common themes and methodological issues in relation to a range of different types of evidence. Some uniform conclusions have emerged about the ways in which men understood and responded to gendered ideals and, in part, this is because all but one of the essays engage with narratives and other sources that were produced by male religious.[14] But there are revealing contrasts too, some chronological or geographical in nature, others testament to the varying experiences and objectives of different authors. Types of religious manliness were revised and refined in response to wider devotional and socio-cultural trends and could also play a role in shaping them.

---

[10] See for example Kim M. Phillips, *Medieval maidenhood: young women and gender in England 1270–1540* (Manchester, 2003) for the prevalent influence of the ideology of 'maidenhood' on women from a range of social backgrounds and occupations.

[11] This is not to suggest a clear cut division or one-way train of influence between 'theory' and 'practice' – the relationship between the two was dynamic; social practice could affect the creation and representation of idealised gender identities.

[12] *Holiness and masculinity in the Middle Ages*, ed. P.H. Cullum and Katherine J. Lewis (Cardiff and Toronto, 2004).

[13] For useful surveys of the field and its development see Derek G. Neal, *The masculine self in late medieval England* (Chicago, 2008), pp. 1–11; Jennifer D. Thibodeaux, 'Introduction: rethinking the medieval clergy and masculinity', in *Negotiating clerical identities: priests, monks and masculinity in the Middle Ages*, ed. Jennifer D. Thibodeaux (Basingstoke and New York, 2010), pp. 1–15.

[14] The exception is Michael L. Satlow's essay. Rabbis of the late antique and early medieval periods were not professional religious in the Christian sense. They had religious expertise but their role was more marginal to their communities than it was for Christians.

In the interim between our first and second conference there has been an increase in publications focussed on medieval masculinity and a few monographs on the subject have appeared.[15] The studies by Ruth Mazo Karras and Derek Neal both address men of clerical status, and in the last ten years there has been a marked emphasis on the gender identities of professional religious men in much published scholarship. Studying men whose profession dictated that they could not experience such rites of passage to adult manhood as marriage and fatherhood provides fruitful material for understanding contemporary representations of masculinity, as well as responses to these. There has now been some detailed consideration of the ways in which the assumption of a professional religious life (whether regular or secular) could both support and contradict contemporary understandings of manliness, and the differing ways in which men responded to these ideals as a result.[16] An important contribution to the field is the collection of essays edited by Jennifer D. Thibodeaux.[17] This focuses on three themes: the bridge between aristocratic men and monks and the use of military imagery in the monastic context, celibacy and sexuality, and contested identities. The idea of clerics negotiating their way between different, and sometimes starkly competing, versions of masculinity has formed a common focus for much scholarship in this area. Although there was still an interest in 2001 in a proliferation of genders (especially 'third gender') as a way of conceptualising difference in gender identity, this approach, although intellectually interesting, has largely been replaced by 'varieties of masculinity' as a way of engaging with different types of adult male identity.[18] This 'masculinities' approach is more flexible and seems better able to cope with ambiguity, with men whose role changed over their lifetime, and with difference related to chronology, status and geography.

Clerical masculinity was generally formed in relation to other masculinities, not in relation to women, and for many clergy women were irrelevant.[19] Several

---

[15] Ruth Mazo Karras, *From boys to men: formations of masculinity in later medieval Europe* (Philadelphia, 2003); Christopher Fletcher, *Richard II: manhood, youth, and politics 1377–99* (Oxford, 2008); Neal, *The masculine self*.

[16] P.H. Cullum, 'Clergy, masculinity and transgression in late medieval England', in Hadley, *Masculinity in medieval Europe*, pp. 178–96; Jacqueline Murray, '"The law of sin that is in my members": the problem of male embodiment', in *Gender and holiness: men, women and saints in late medieval Europe*, ed. Samantha S.J.E. Riches and Sarah Salih (London and New York, 2002), pp. 9–22; Jennifer D. Thibodeaux, 'Man of the church or man of the village? Gender and the parish clergy in medieval Normandy', *Gender & History* 2006 (18), pp. 380–99; Ruth Mazo Karras, 'Thomas Aquinas' chastity belt: clerical masculinity in medieval Europe', in *Gender and christianity in medieval Europe*, ed. Lisa M. Bitel and Felice Lifshitz (Philadelphia, 2008), pp. 52–67; Neal, *The masculine self*, pp. 89–122.

[17] *Negotiating clerical identities*, ed. Thibodeaux.

[18] E.g. contrast Jacqueline Murray, 'One flesh, two sexes, three genders?', in *Gender and Christianity in medieval Europe*, ed. Bitel and Lifshitz, pp. 52–75, with Karras, 'Thomas Aquinas' chastity belt', in the same volume.

[19] Although some clergy were deeply involved in the direction and care of religious women, which raises important questions about the fluid nature of both gender and authority within a professed religious life. See for example *Gendered voices, medieval saints and their interpreters*, ed. Catherine M. Mooney (Philadelphia, 1999); *Partners in spirit: women, men and religious life in Germany, 1100-1500*, ed. F.J. Griffiths and J. Hotchin (Turnhout, 2013).

Introduction

studies have focussed on the process of Gregorian Reform in the eleventh and twelfth centuries as particularly revealing of changing and developing forms of clerical gender because of the imposition of celibacy upon secular clergy which this entailed. In an influential essay, JoAnn McNamara argued that the reform therefore inspired anxiety and subjective crisis in members of the secular clergy, who could no longer consider themselves to be 'real men' as a result.[20] More recently it has become apparent that this process was not simply a top-down imposition of papal authority on a reactionary lower clergy, or even the attempted imposition of a hegemonic form of monastic masculinity: instead it was more of a battle between competing forms of masculinity. However, Thibodeaux cautions against the assumption that sexuality was always the most important marker of manhood in this context and notes the range of masculine roles that could be employed to express clerical gender identity, including those of father, warrior and husband.[21] Two recent studies of the apparently unique 'marriage' of the bishop of Florence and the abbess of the convent of San Pier Maggiore further emphasise the disparate uses that could be made of sexual and marital imagery in different contexts. This ceremony symbolised the bishop's marriage to his diocese, which suggests something of the richness of this imagery and the ways in which it could be deployed to establish and change relations between the bishop, his diocese, the convent and the city.[22] Here the symbolism of marriage was both the product and guarantor of clerical celibacy. Celibacy as a form of sexuality for men in itself has received less attention than it has for religious women, but there is an increasing consensus that within clerical discourse (which was also influential upon laymen) it came to represent a superior form of manliness, rather than one that signalled assimilation to the feminine.[23] There is now much

---

[20] Jo Ann McNamara, 'The *Herrenfrage*: The restructuring of the gender system, 1050–1150,' in *Medieval masculinities*, ed. Lees, pp. 3–29. Essays in this volume by Jennifer D. Thibodeaux, Kirsten A. Fenton, Joanna Huntington and Matthew Mesley all consider the impact of reform on masculinity. Rachel Stone's essay (also in this volume) reminds us that these debates were not new, see also C. Leyser, 'Masculinity in flux: nocturnal emission and the limits of celibacy in the early Middle Ages', in *Masculinity in medieval Europe*, ed. Hadley, pp. 103–20.

[21] Thibodeaux, 'Introduction', *Negotiating clerical identities*, ed. Thibodeaux, pp. 5–7. For detailed discussion of the different gendered roles adopted by bishops, see M. McLaughlin, *Sex, gender, and episcopal authority in the age of reform, 1000–1122* (Cambridge, 2010).

[22] Maureen C. Miller, 'Why the bishop of Florence had to get married', *Speculum* 81 (2006), pp. 1055–91; Sharon T. Strocchia, 'When the bishop married the abbess: masculinity and power in Florentine episcopal entry rites, 1300–1600', *Gender & History* 19:2 (2007), pp. 346–68.

[23] The case for virginity as a gendered identity for women has been made persuasively by Sarah Salih, *Versions of virginity in late medieval England* (Cambridge, 2001); for discussions of virginity ranging across a variety of subjects and sources see *Medieval virginities*, ed. Anke Bernau, Ruth Evans and Sarah Salih (Cardiff, 2003). For examples of work on male virginity/celibacy see Maureen C. Miller, 'Masculinity, reform, and clerical culture: narratives of episcopal holiness in the Gregorian era', *Church History*, 72:1 (2003), pp. 25–52; Anthony Perron, 'Saxo Grammaticus's heroic chastity: a model of clerical celibacy and masculinity in medieval Scandinavia', in *Negotiating clerical identities*, ed. Thibodeaux, pp. 113–35; Cassandra Rhodes, 'What, after all, is a male virgin? Multiple performances of male virginity in Anglo-Saxon saints' lives', in *Representing medieval genders and sexualities in Europe: construction, transformation and subversion, 600–1530*, ed. Elizabeth L'Estrange and Alison More (Basingstoke and New York, 2011), pp. 15–32.

less interest in gender as a source of anxiety for professional religious men than there was a decade ago, and much more sense of confidence in the superiority of a masculine religious identity, even if that had to be negotiated in relation to lay authorities. Moreover, flourishing scholarship in the area of medieval sexuality more widely has allowed for more sensitive readings of medieval debates revolving around sex and the gendered implications of these.[24] Articles by Thibodeaux, Michelle Armstrong-Partida, Laura Wertheimer and Janelle Werner have begun to establish both a chronology and geography of clerical sexuality, suggesting clear cultural differences, with some places such as Normandy and Spain having a normalised culture of clerical marriage and family life, irrespective of episcopal intention.[25] This suggests that these phenomena have to be understood not simply as resistance or disobedience, or even as some kind of innate male sexuality which could not be repressed. Rather they reveal deep-seated regional and cultural practices and a coherent expression of a particular type of clerical masculinity dominant within its own cultural context. England, by contrast, seems to have embraced clerical celibacy with more limited resistance and breach of vows was seen as rare and transgressive by the later Middle Ages.[26] Geo-cultural specificity is thus a vital area of study and, as noted above, the call for papers for our conference sought exploration of non-Christian traditions or the interaction of Christian and other faith traditions. Only a minority of papers offered to us considered these areas, and of these we could include only one in this volume.[27] Hence the focus here is overwhelmingly on Christian styles of religious masculinity, but Michael L. Satlow's contribution enables comparison with a form of Jewish religious masculinity constructed by rabbis from inherited traditions in the late antique period. Comparisons between different faiths and ethnic groups are so intellectually stimulating and informative that we hope more work which considers a diversity of religious traditions and communities will appear in due course.[28] A related area is the development of 'gender aware' scholarship on the crusades, first presented in S.B. Edgington and Sarah

---

[24] Two useful general surveys are provided by Ruth Mazo Karras, *Sexuality in medieval Europe: doing unto others* (New York, 2005); Kim M. Phillips and Barry Reay, *Sex before sexuality: a premodern history* (London, 2011). See also *Representing medieval genders and sexualities*, ed. L'Estrange and More.

[25] Thibodeaux, 'Man of the church, or man of the village?'; Michelle Armstrong-Partida, 'Priestly marriage: the tradition of clerical concubinage in the Spanish church', *Viator* 40:2 (2009) pp. 221–53.

[26] Laura Wertheimer, 'Illegitimate birth and the English clergy, 1198–1348', *Journal of Medieval History* 31 (2005), pp. 211–29; Janelle Werner, 'Promiscuous priests and vicarage children: clerical sexuality and masculinity in late medieval England', in *Negotiating clerical identities*, ed. Thibodeaux, pp. 159–84. Fenton's essay in this collection explores evidence for earlier English resistance to clerical celibacy.

[27] Other papers delivered at the conference which explored non-Christian traditions were John Jenkins, 'Mendicant masculinity: a comparison of the treatment of gender in the lives of St Francis and the Buddha Gautama', and Elisa Pulido, 'Rabbi Gershom's ban on polygamy and Jewish accommodation in the Middle Ages'.

[28] The fruitfulness of such comparisons is demonstrated by a number of the essays in *Intersections of gender, religion and ethnicity in the Middle Ages*, ed. Cordelia Beattie and Kirsten A. Fenton (Basingstoke and New York, 2011).

Introduction

Lambert's volume *Gendering the Crusades*, published only a few months after our first conference.[29] Consideration has now been given to the influence of gender ideology on the representation of the crusades in contemporary sources, and to the ways in which crusading modified or even changed the gender identities of the men who participated.[30] It is to be hoped that such studies will stimulate further work on the range of masculinities observable among crusaders, and within Frankish society in the Middle East, as well as among the other communities and states with which the Kingdom of Jerusalem interacted. Crusading against communities within Europe, whether monotheistic, heretical or pagan remains relatively impervious to gendered analysis, but provides another potentially rich area of investigation.

To return to the topic of professional male religious, central to a nuanced understanding of clerical celibacy and sexuality is developing work in the area of queer theory and sexuality, leading to reconsideration of the nature of same-sex attraction and 'homosexual' acts, and their implications for gender identity.[31] Professional religious have formed the focus of a number of studies, but the 'homosexual' activities and potential identities of monks and clerics have not yet received the same treatment as their 'heterosexual' counterparts.[32] We are mindful here that some work in this area may well lead to significant reconfiguration of the understanding of all kinds of sexual orientation, both in the past and the present.[33] Relationships between religious men which can be identified in homosocial terms is a related and overlapping topic that needs further exploration, although its importance to twelfth-century monasticism in particular is

---

[29] *Gendering the crusades*, ed. S.B. Edgington and Sarah Lambert (Cardiff, 2001); see also Natasha R. Hodgson, *Women, crusading and the holy land in historical narrative* (Woodbridge, 2007).

[30] Anne Dunlop, 'Masculinity, crusading, and devotion: Francesco Casali's fresco in the Trecento Perugian contado', *Speculum* 76 (2001), pp. 315–36; Kirsten A. Fenton, 'Gendering the first crusade in William of Malmesbury's *Gesta Regum Anglorum*', and Simon Yarrow, 'Prince Bohemond, Princess Melaz, and the gendering of religious difference in the *Ecclesiastical History* of Orderic Vitalis', both in *Intersections of gender, religion and ethnicity*, ed. Beattie and Fenton, pp. 125–39, 140–57; Andrew Holt, 'Between warrior and priest: the creation of a new masculine identity during the crusades', in *Negotiating clerical identities*, ed. Thibodeaux, pp. 185–203. See also Matthew Mesley's contribution to this volume.

[31] See for example *Queering the Middle Ages*, ed. Glenn Burger and Steven F. Kruger (Minneapolis and London, 2001); William E. Burgwinkle, *Sodomy, masculinity and the law in medieval literature* (Cambridge, 2004); *The Boswell Thesis. Essays on Christianity, social tolerance, and homosexuality*, ed. Mathew Kuefler (Chicago, 2006); Robert Mills, 'Male-male love and sex in the Middle Ages, 1000–1500', in *A gay history of Britain: love and sex between men since the Middle Ages*, ed. Matt Cook, Robert Mills, Randolph Trumbach and H.G. Cocks (Oxford, 2007), pp. 1–44.

[32] Although there is some important work in this area emerging, see for example Michelle Sauer, 'Uncovering difference: encoded homoerotic anxiety within the Christian eremitic tradition in medieval England', *Journal of the History of Sexuality* 19 (2010), pp. 133–52; Robert Mills, 'Gender, sodomy, friendship, and the medieval anchorhold', *Journal of Medieval Religious Cultures* 36:1 (2010), pp. 1–27.

[33] Karma Lochrie, *Heterosyncrasies: female sexuality when normal wasn't* (Minnesota, 2005); James A. Schultz, 'Heterosexuality as a threat to medieval studies', *Journal of the History of Sexuality* 15 (2006), pp. 14–29.

becoming clearer.[34] Associated with the issue of sexuality and sexual conduct is the symbolism of bodies and clothes. Study of this has also come to prominence in the last decade as indicative of varying reflections and constructions of both masculinity and religiosity.[35] Control of the body was fundamental to authoritative forms of masculinity and so inappropriate sexual activity, which was in breach of moral and religious codes, could be used as an excuse to challenge the authority not only of clergy but also of royalty.[36] Similarly acts which impinged on or damaged another's body, or even their clothes, demonstrated contestation or sometimes removal of the target's authority, and might be used to police boundaries between lay and clerical estates.[37] Illness too might suggest a failure of control and indicate both sinfulness and a defective gender identity, which, in the case of high status men (both lay and religious), could have very worrying implications for those over whom they ruled; yet these failures and problems could be recuperated by a good death.[38] Death itself, or at least the disposition of the dead body, could be a way to establish or re-establish particular forms of masculine and religious identity.[39]

As noted above, in 2001 much of the emphasis in our conference and collection was on issues of sanctity. This reflects the fact that questions of gender, or the gendered experience of life-cycle, have formed the focus for a number of important studies of medieval hagiography and saints' cults, virtually all of which relate to female saints and female devotees.[40] André Vauchez's *Sainthood in the Middle Ages* has done much to establish the interactions of chronology,

---

[34] E.g. Julian Haseldine, 'Friendship, intimacy and corporate networking in the twelfth century: the politics of friendship in the letters of Peter the Venerable', *English Historical Review* 126 (2011), pp. 251–80. See also David Clark, *Between medieval men: male friendship and desire in early medieval English literature* (Oxford, 2009).

[35] E.g. Allison Fizzard, 'Shoes, boots, leggings, and cloaks: the Augustinian canons and dress in later medieval England', *Journal of British Studies* 46 (2007), pp. 245–62.

[36] Conrad Leyser, 'Episcopal office in the Italy of Liudprand of Cremona, c.890–c.970', *English Historical Review* 125 (2010), pp. 795–817; Megan McLaughlin, '"Disgusting acts of shamelessness": sexual misconduct and the deconstruction of royal authority in the eleventh century', *Early Medieval Europe* 19:3 (2011), pp. 312–31.

[37] Danielle Westerhof, 'Deconstructing identities on the scaffold: the execution of Hugh Despenser the Younger, 1326', *Journal of Medieval History* 33 (2007), pp. 87–106; Andrew G. Miller 'To "frock" a cleric: the gendered implications of mutilating ecclesiastical vestments in medieval England', *Gender & History* 24:2 (2012), pp. 271–91.

[38] Jonathan Hughes, *Arthurian myths and alchemy: the kingship of Edward IV* (Stroud, 2001); David Green, 'Masculinity and medicine: Thomas Walsingham and the death of the Black Prince', *Journal of Medieval History* 35 (2009), pp. 34–51; Katherine J. Lewis' essay in the present volume discusses the recuperation of Henry VI's gender identity after his death.

[39] Roberta Gilchrist, 'Rethinking later medieval masculinity: the male body in death', in *Mortuary practices and social identities in the Middle Ages: essays in burial archaeology in honour of Heinrich Harke*, ed. Duncan Sayer and Howard Williams (Exeter, 2009).

[40] E.g. Gail McMurray Gibson, *The theater of devotion: East Anglian drama and society in the late Middle Ages* (Chicago and London, 1989); Karen A. Winstead, *Virgin martyrs: legends of sainthood in late medieval England* (Ithaca, NY, 1997); *St Katherine of Alexandria: texts and contexts in western medieval Europe*, ed. Jacqueline Jenkins and Katherine J. Lewis (Turnhout, 2003); Catherine Sanok, *Her life historical: exemplarity and female saints' lives in late medieval England* (Philadelphia, 2007).

Introduction

gender, status and style of sanctity in the medieval period.[41] Donald Weinstein and Rudolph M. Bell's study pioneered a thematic sociological approach which considered the relative experiences and representations of both male and female saints.[42] Given the extent and sophistication of available work on female saints' lives and cults we had hoped to find the development of a similar body of work on male saints. But although male saints have been the subject of study in the last decade, this has rarely been from a gendered perspective.[43] There is obviously still much to be said about how the lives of saints engaged with contemporary notions of manliness, and the extent to which the cults of male saints informed both piety and masculinity.[44] This is part of a wider question about the operation of gender in devotion and religious practices. It has been well established that women often showed a marked devotion to female saints who were believed to have a special connection to fertility, childbirth, and motherhood, such as the Virgin Mary, St Anne, and St Margaret.[45] But male saints could also function as enablers of female fertility, with implications for the representation of their gender and potency.[46] Moreover, the popularity of female saints with male patrons has received little attention; for example St Katherine of Alexandria could be represented both as a model of demure womanhood, and as a model of masculine intellectual authority, which may well explain her popularity as a focus of clerical devotion.[47] In order to understand the extent to which the choice of a favoured saint was

---

[41] André Vauchez, *Sainthood in the later Middle Ages*, trans. Jean Birrell (Cambridge, 1997; orig. pub. 1988).

[42] Donald Weinstein and Rudolph M. Bell, *Saints and society: the two worlds of western Christendom, 1100–1700* (Chicago and London, 1982).

[43] One of the few collections to address the issue is *Gender and Holiness*, ed. Riches and Salih. This was in production simultaneously with our own first volume and with many of the same contributors. Danna Piroyanski, *Martyrs in the making: political martyrdom in late medieval England* (Basingstoke, 2008) and M. Cecilia Gaposchkin, *The making of Saint Louis: kingship, sanctity and crusade in the later Middle Ages* (Ithaca, NY, 2008) both include some consideration of the operation of gender in their subjects' sanctity. For a study that takes gender as a more central focus to understanding a male saint's representation see S.J.E. Riches, *St George: hero, martyr and myth* (Stroud, 2000). Thomas Becket remains remarkably impervious to gendered analysis despite the wealth of narrative and documentary sources relating to his cult which would benefit from such a reading. However, the doctoral work currently in progress by Eilidh Harris assesses Becket's gender in relation to that of other twelfth-century episcopal saints.

[44] As argued by Katherine J. Lewis, 'Male saints and devotional masculinity in late medieval England', *Gender & History* 24:1 (2012), pp. 112–33, and P.H. Cullum, '*Virginitas* and *virilitas*: Richard Scrope and his fellow bishops', in *Richard Scrope: archbishop, rebel, martyr*, ed. P.J.P. Goldberg (Stamford, 2007), pp. 86–99. This is further explored by Katherine J. Lewis, Marita von Weissenberg, Catherine Sanok and P.H. Cullum in the present volume.

[45] Susan Signe Morrison, *Women pilgrims in late medieval England: private piety as public performance* (London and New York, 2000); Wendy L. Larson, 'Who is the master of this narrative? Maternal patronage of the cult of St Margaret', and Pamela Sheingorn, '"The wise mother": the image of St Anne teaching the Virgin Mary', both in *Gendering the master narrative: women and power in the Middle Ages*, ed. Mary C. Erler and Maryanne Kowaleski (Ithaca, NY, and London, 2003), pp. 94–104 and 105–34.

[46] As discussed in Lewis, 'Male saints and devotional masculinity', pp. 121–2.

[47] See Karen A. Winstead, 'St Katherine's hair', and Sherry Reames, 'St Katherine and the late medieval clergy: evidence from English breviaries', both in *St Katherine of Alexandria*, ed. Jenkins and Lewis, pp. 171–200 and 201–220.

actually informed by gender and life-cycle (as opposed to other considerations) we need to consider both female and male devotees, otherwise we have only one side of the picture. Instructive here are the contrasting interpretations of the rite of churching presented by Gail McMurray Gibson and Becky R. Lee.[48] The former argues for it being, essentially, a 'women's ceremony' in which women could take on quasi-clerical status, whereas the latter claims that it revolved primarily around male, patriarchal interests of potency and inheritance. The two explanations are not mutually exclusive, but it is extremely useful to have studies which allow us to contrast feminine and masculine in the evaluation of such rituals and their significance.

When it comes to the relationship between piety and gender there is still a dearth of work on medieval men, whether religious or lay. While there is an abundant wealth of scholarship on women's piety, the devotional lives of men have not been systematically explored from a gendered perspective.[49] In particular, the role of religion in the negotiation of lay masculinity remains largely unexplored.[50] An exception is provided by Christina Fitzgerald's study of English guilds and the mystery plays, which explores the interplay between urban mercantile and artisan manhood with religious practice.[51] She argues that Christ offered a model for men struggling, not always successfully, to reconcile various competing models of masculinity, particularly the roles of householder with responsibility for family, and the guild member who should prioritise homosocial relations with his fraternity. This contrasts revealingly with the emphasis on Christ as a feminine figure that we find elsewhere.[52] More work of a similar nature would help us to gauge the extent to which religious and devotional practices currently identified as inherently 'feminine' should accurately be labelled so, and, moreover, whether there are comparable strictly 'masculine' practices.[53] If men sometimes adopted 'feminine' modes of devotion, can we also see women, on occasion, adopting 'masculine' ones, and, if so, why? These are questions that we hope others will feel moved to give far greater attention than we are able to here.

In attempting to understand how men perceived their own gender Neal advises that 'we have to think about masculinity as something that mattered to

---

[48] Gail McMurray Gibson, 'Blessing from sun and moon: churching as women's theater', in *Bodies and disciplines: intersections of literature and history in fifteenth-century England*, ed. Barbara A. Hanawalt and David Wallace (Minneapolis, 1996), pp. 139–54; Becky R. Lee, 'Men's recollections of a women's rite: medieval English men's recollections regarding the rite of the purification of women after childbirth', *Gender & History* 14:2 (2002), pp. 224–41.

[49] John H. Arnold does provide consideration of both women and men in a section on 'Gendered Christian identities' in his *Belief and unbelief in medieval Europe* (London, 2005), pp. 143–53.

[50] Neal explicitly left discussion of piety out of his monograph, *The masculine self* (p. 246) but many of his methodological observations on the relationship between piety and masculinity for clerics are also applicable to a consideration of lay men, Derek G. Neal, 'What can historians do with clerical masculinity?', in *Negotiating clerical identities*, ed. Thibodeaux, pp. 16–36.

[51] Christina M. Fitzgerald, *The drama of masculinity and Medieval English guild culture* (Gordonsville, VA, 2007).

[52] As discussed influentially by Bynum in *Jesus as mother*.

[53] See Cullum's essay in this volume.

individuals – as an aspect of identity, in other words, not just as a set of metaphorical meanings that cultural powers could manipulate to serve rhetorical or disciplinary ends'.[54] This is a difficult undertaking for the Middle Ages, given the nature of the source materials and the lack of explicitly enunciated reflection on selfhood and manliness within them. Moreover, much of the evidence focuses on prescriptive formulations of gender and the consequences for those who did not adhere to these, which can distort our understanding of the subjective experience of masculinity.[55] Despite these methodological problems the essays in this collection all strive to offer insights as to just how masculinity mattered to certain individuals, and also to groups of men who shared common professions or experiences. There is evidence here of subjectivity, of men making sense of their own and others' identities as men, in relation to vocation and circumstances. The essays have been arranged in rough chronological order to highlight the tenacity of certain ideas of and responses to masculine ideals across the centuries, and within different settings. But although certain themes and elements persist that does not mean they were always essential to notions of manhood. This collection demonstrates clearly that although some elements of medieval masculinity may seem 'universal', none the less it was not handed down unchanging through the centuries. Masculinities were always, to some extent, contingent on their settings and thus we find some versions specific to particular times and places, or types of men, or to particular genres and discourses. The arrangement of the essays also allows those moments witnessing the emergence, waning or regeneration of contrasting versions of manhood to emerge more clearly. For example, overall the essays both explore the establishment of distinct lay and clerical masculinities in the twelfth century and suggest the blurring of those boundaries in the fifteenth, which may help to explain the attack on a clerical masculinity founded on chastity in the sixteenth. This reminds us that it is important not to install such processes as Gregorian Reform or the later Protestant Reformation as simple one-way turning points for masculinity, whether clerical or lay. Debates around the difference between lay and clerical masculinities, and particularly sexuality, have been revolving within Western Christendom since its inception and continue in some contexts to the present day. The early medieval wrestling with problems which some historians of later periods regard as specific to post-Gregorian reform shows that issues of celibacy and the boundaries between clerical and lay estates and privileges were constantly revisited and never finally settled.

In the opening essay Michael Satlow argues that the rabbis of the late antique and early medieval period used the study of the Torah and Talmud to explore conceptions of masculinity which continued to have influence on Jewish understandings into the later medieval period. In some respects the rabbis made radically different choices about the context for male religious and religious study from those that became dominant in the Christian tradition, such as the rejection of asceticism and celibacy. But in other respects they faced similar problems about

---

[54] Neal, 'What can historians do with clerical masculinity?', pp. 25–6.
[55] Neal notes that this inevitably involves a certain amount of informed speculation, but argues for the value of this, ibid., pp. 29–30.

how to 'make masculine' the practice of religious study. Satlow shows how the conceptualisation of the Torah changed over time, with the initial wholesale dismissal of warrior masculinity and its conventions as a possible model eventually replaced by an acceptance of the idea of the spiritual warrior. This demonstrates how hegemonic discourse could reshape its challengers but could also itself be reshaped by that challenge. Satlow's essay is thus an excellent starting point for its consideration of a group of men engaged in 'working out' masculinity in relation to existing ideas and ideals, and to their own setting and experiences. This is a theme that runs throughout the collection as a whole and which Rachel Stone explores with the close study of a specific individual: Hincmar of Rheims. Hincmar (d. 882) was one of the most influential men in Francia for nearly forty years, and his copious writings in many genres have helped define our image of the late Carolingian empire. This essay explores Hincmar's works to understand his difficulties in applying theoretical models of clerical masculine superiority in contexts where lay men and even laywomen might hold significant power. In so doing it emphasises the role of status and hierarchy within Hincmar's understanding of gender, a relational view which assessed clerical men almost exclusively in comparison to other men. It also demonstrates that a concern with celibacy for the clergy was not just a feature of the Gregorian reform movement, the phenomenon which forms the focus for the next four essays.

Jennifer D. Thibodeaux, Kirsten A. Fenton, Joanna Huntington and Matthew Mesley all discuss the repercussions of the eleventh- and twelfth-century reforms, focussing on sources which reveal the opinions of individual authors, but which also reflect the mores of the wider social settings in which they lived, and for whom they wrote. All four provide evidence for the expression and renegotiation of masculinity during a period in which there was considerable tension and disagreement revolving around its proper nature for secular clerics. They also discuss the employment of these debates as the manifestation of attempts to establish clerics as superior to laymen. The Gregorian reform movement's imposition of celibacy on the secular clergy has often been seen as a pivotal moment in the construction of the late medieval gender regime, but while the motives and success of the reform movement have received some attention, those who resisted it have generally been dismissed as reactionaries swimming against the historical tide. Thibodeaux's essay on the clergy of twelfth-century Normandy reveals a sophisticated and articulate defence of the tradition of a married clergy, which constructed a model of clerical masculinity that allowed for a combination of sacramental efficacy and marital domesticity. The Norman clergy had a well established culture of marriage which was accepted within the wider community and which related masculinity to sexuality and virility in ways very similar to contemporary laymen; they were unwilling to accept the promulgation of a new definition of masculinity based on monastic asceticism and celibacy. This suggests that the success of the Reform movement was not inevitable, as has often been claimed.

Kirsten A. Fenton's essay also considers the response of married clergy to the fiat that they should eschew their wives and family for the celibate life, this time with reference to an individual author: the English historian Henry of

Introduction

Huntingdon (c. 1088–c. 1157). She traces the extent to which Henry's own status as a married man affected his depiction of contemporary reform. His formal role as an archdeacon made him responsible for policing the behaviour of other clergy at parish level, which gives an additional dimension to our understanding of his opinions. Henry was clearly not comfortable with the reform movement's insistence on clerical celibacy and saw both marriage and violence as endemic to a masculine religious vocation. Henry was forthright in his opinions, but also knew that he was waging intellectual war on behalf of a cause that was already lost. Joanna Huntington further illuminates the impact of reform through a close reading of the mid twelfth-century *Gesta Herewardi*, which describes the exploits of the famous English outlaw, Hereward, later known as 'the Wake'. She traces its response to reform both in general terms, and in relation to its place of origin: Ely abbey. This is a well known narrative, but not one to which a gendered reading has frequently been applied before. Huntington explores the status of the *Gesta* as history not in terms of its 'factual accuracy' but as an excellent guide to the dissemination of clerical ideas about masculinity. The *Gesta* constructs its hero as a model of lay masculinity and, in so doing, employs contemporary conceptions of the means by which a man could acquire adult masculinity, demonstrating the extent to which these rested on rites of passage such as knighthood, marriage and inheritance. But, crucially, all these are viewed through a clerical lens to provide an exemplary but subordinate version of lay masculinity, which acknowledges the superiority of the clerical version.

Like Huntington Matthew Mesley's focus is the narrative representation of a particular individual: Adhémar of Le Puy (d. 1098) appointed by Pope Urban II to lead the First Crusade. In common with Huntington's attitude to Hereward, Mesley is less interested in the 'real' Adhémar, and more concerned with the changing depiction of the bishop in a range of early twelfth-century chronicles. He explores both similarities and differences and accounts for these in the varying intersections between discourses of crusading, leadership and gender. Mesley notes that the versions of masculinity that Adhémar embodies are partly a product of narrative context, genre and authorial intention. But they also suggest something of the extent to which bishops themselves could 'play up' or 'play down' specific characteristics deemed appropriate to the episcopal office depending on circumstances. In common with Huntington he argues that they seek to categorise men and their behaviour in certain ways in order to valorise clerical authority as the 'natural' basis for social and religious hierarchies. Within this discourse Adhémar's portrayal varies between texts; it was elaborated and updated, yet always his manhood is constructed in ways that underline the superiority of clerical over lay, both metaphorically and actually. The crusaders are shown to submit to clerical authority, just as Hereward does in the *Gesta*, and this mirrored the philosophy of the reforms, thus providing validation for the clerical readers who would have formed the bulk of the audience for these narratives in the first instance.

Marita von Weissenberg's essay is the first of three that investigate male sanctity and its hagiographical representation. She examines the nature of lay male sanctity in the thirteenth and early fourteenth centuries. This historical moment saw men such as Pietro Pettinajo (d. 1289) and Elzéar de Sabran (d. 1323) recognised as saints by dint of the exemplary execution of secular duties; thus their laity was an intrinsic part of their sanctity, not something that needed to be explained or excused. These men still embodied qualities we might describe as emblematic of clerical masculinity (especially self-mastery) but von Weissenberg prefers the term 'spiritual masculinity' precisely because these men were not clerical. The development of specific lay forms of male sanctity may have been, in part, a result of the ideological division that reform created (or sought to create) between clergy and laity. As with Huntington and Mesley, von Weissenberg considers clerical versions of lay masculinity, but the superiority of clergy to laity is not observable here. Moreover von Weissenberg invites consideration of the relationship between representation and reality in these saints' lives by observing that the saints in question were influenced by hagiographic discourse, not just described by it, and thus helped to reinvent notions of male sanctity. This point also informs Katherine J. Lewis' discussion of the posthumous representation of Henry VI, king of England, as a saint. She argues that there was a more complex dynamic between ideas of holiness and perceptions of Henry as a saint than has previously been acknowledged. Once again, this involves interpretation of a clerical construction of an idealised version of holy lay masculinity, as authored around twenty years after Henry's death in 1471 by John Blacman, who had known the king personally. Blacman's representation of Henry as a saint owes much of its substance to established notions of lay sanctity, but in contrast to von Weissenberg's saints, by the fifteenth century lay saints had become, effectively, quasi-clerical saints. Their sanctity derives not so much from the exemplary exercise of office, but from their fundamental desire to leave the world and devote themselves wholly to an inherent religious vocation. This serves to restore the hierarchy between religious and lay manhood. The contrasting versions of sanctity thus described reveal changing notions of holy masculinity and their intersection with other aspects of the male experience. This suggests something of the continuing tensions revolving around the dynamic between holiness and masculinity: how were they best to be made compatible?

These questions and concerns also inform Catherine Sanok's essay on England's last formally canonised saint before the Reformation, St John of Bridlington (d. 1379), prior of the Augustinian house. His cult and representation suggest something of the difficulties in negotiating the gap that had developed between clerical and lay forms of masculinity by the fifteenth century. Sanok argues that the common practice of religious devotion was a route by which a bridge between the two forms could be constructed. The complex and unstable depiction of John of Bridlington in both literary and visual sources is explored to argue for a model of piety that was in some contexts undifferentiated in gender terms precisely to appeal to a wide audience which might include both clergy and laity. Sanok argues that both clergy and laity shared a form of the mixed life, and suggests that the concept of the active life was no longer meaningful even for laymen. In other contexts however it emphasised clerical status in a way that undercut some aspects of John of Bridlington's actual piety. Thus Sanok contends that the unspecified form of masculinity presented allowed men

Introduction

otherwise divided by status and occupation to see themselves as a commonalty and was thus a preparation for the development of humanism.

The lived experience of religious devotion either as professed monk or as an expression of piety, whether clerical or lay, is the focus of our final two essays. James G. Clark argues that, far from being a creature of decline, the post-Black Death monk was in good health. The cloister proved more attractive than the parish and even up until months before the Dissolution men were making their profession as monks. This essay accounts for the continuing attraction of the monastic community to young men who thereby acquired both an adult status and masculine authority earlier than they would have done in the outside world. They also joined a community that represented security, stability and tradition. He argues that the monastic life came to be seen less as a vocation than as a learned profession with a robust sense of its own manhood, which increasingly borrowed from the assertive and status-conscious masculinity of elite laymen. A small but significant group of laymen and secular clerks who chose to live within the monastic precinct and sometimes even the cloister, and to share its homo-sociability, suggests the appeal of a common professional and spiritual identity, and supports arguments made in Sanok's essay.

Finally P.H. Cullum's essay explores evidence for a distinctively masculine piety, particularly in late medieval England. It is twenty-five years since Caroline Walker Bynum published *Holy feast and holy fast: the religious significance of food to medieval women* and despite critiques it has remained highly influential in the field of lay piety, as well as a major landmark in the historiography that argues for a distinctive feminine piety. The absence of much significant study of specifically masculine piety means that it remains difficult to evaluate how far we should continue to accept the central thesis of the book: that devotion to the body of Christ in the Eucharist was actually a specifically feminine form of piety in the Middle Ages. This essay addresses evidence of men's, especially laymen's, devotion to the Eucharist and the body of Christ. It argues that eucharistic devotion was not necessarily specifically feminine, although men tended to focus more on the embodied figure of Christ on the Cross, with whose suffering but also sacramental body they could identify, and indeed on the cross itself as the instrument of that suffering. While women may, as Bynum argues, have imitated Christ through the self-denial of food, men were able to imitate Christ through the provision of food to their household and the wider community, as feasting re-enacting the Last Supper. A final case study explores the experience of Sir Piers Legh, who appears at the end of his life to have sought to encompass and hold in tension the various identities that religious men had explored and differentiated during the medieval period: a husband and father, who became a celibate, a layman who became a priest but retained the status and trappings of knighthood while claiming humility, and a devotee of the Eucharist, but as celebrant rather than recipient.

FROM SALVE TO WEAPON: TORAH STUDY, MASCULINITY AND THE BABYLONIAN TALMUD

Michael L. Satlow

'Who is a [real] warrior?' the ancient Jewish sage Ben Zoma rhetorically asked, 'He who conquers his desire, as it is written, "Better to be forebearing than a warrior, to have self-control than to conquer a city."'[1] If there has been one central insight from the last two decades or so of the study of masculinity in Antiquity and the Middle Ages, this short maxim, probably dating from the third century CE, encapsulates it. Whether they were Roman philosophers, ancient rabbis, or medieval monks, cultural producers and religious specialists went to extraordinary lengths to transform the discourse of masculinity and masculine identity. These men may have rejected the wider, hegemonic understanding of what manliness meant – almost always some form of physical strength, power, and domination of others – but they by no means rejected their own sense of themselves as men. Ben Zoma, like so many others of his type, assumed that 'conquest' and domination were essential components of masculinity, but he directed that conquest inward. To be a man meant to control oneself rather than to control others. It was, to turn a Nietzschean phrase, a strategy of the weak, useful for powerless men who nevertheless could not stand to think of themselves as women.[2]

The rabbis of late Antiquity and the early Middle Ages shared with the better studied Roman philosophers and Christian clerics a desire to see themselves, and perhaps to be seen by others, as men, despite their rejection of the dominant cultural paradigms of masculinity.[3] Yet, I argue in this essay, that redefinition had longer term unexpected consequences. In short, I argue that the early rabbinic gendering of Torah study as a masculine activity that stood in contrast to traditional masculine characteristics led to a later rabbinic conception that

---

[1] Mishnah Avot 4:1, citing Proverbs 16:32. Translations, unless otherwise noted, are my own.
[2] 'Whatever the specific forms of holy masculinity under discussion, throughout there is a strong emphasis on the masculine ability to exercise self-mastery', P.H. Cullum, 'Introduction', in *Holiness and masculinity in the Middle Ages*, ed. P.H. Cullum and Katherine J. Lewis (Cardiff, 2004), p. 6. Cf. *Masculinity in medieval Europe*, ed. D.M. Hadley (London, 1999).
[3] Michael L. Satlow, '"Try to be a man": The rabbinic construction of masculinity', *Harvard Theological Review* 89 (1996), pp. 19–40; Michael L. Satlow, 'And on the earth you shall sleep: Talmud Torah and rabbinic asceticism', *Journal of Religion* 83 (2003), pp. 204–25.

valorised precisely those same rejected masculine characteristics in its practice. That is, Torah study begins as a way of escaping the hegemonic discourse of masculinity, but that very redefinition causes that hegemonic discourse to shape its later institutional practice.

Before proceeding with this argument, a few preliminary comments about the rabbis are in order. The rabbis began to emerge as an identifiable group in Palestine after the destruction of the Jerusalem temple by the Romans in 70 CE. The early rabbis, it seems, were relatively wealthy, thus enabling them to find the time necessary for the intensive study that was at the heart of their praxis. They formed themselves in small disciple circles for the study of Torah. Torah, in their understanding, meant not only the first five books of the Hebrew Bible or Old Testament, but more widely the entire Hebrew Bible, its exegesis, and the oral traditions and practices of the Jews of their time. Torah was seen as God's revelation, and they saw their task as engaging and expanding it as a form of service to God, or worship. This is a very important point that has only begun to replace prior scholarly views of the rabbis and their role in the wider Jewish community, which saw them more as communal leaders than as isolated religious specialists. The rabbis were thus largely marginal within the Jewish community. When they spoke and functioned as rabbis, they tended to address each other. Despite their occasionally grandiose claims to antiquity and authority, in reality they wielded very little power, be it through compulsion or persuasion.[4]

Classical rabbinic literature – the primary focus of this essay – is comprised, without exception, of redacted texts. These redactions began around 200 CE. The earliest rabbinic texts, the Mishnah and various collections of interpretations of the Bible, or midrash, primarily concern themselves with legal issues. Later texts, most notably the Palestinian Talmud, redacted around 400 CE, and the sprawling Babylonian Talmud, redacted a century or two later in Babylonia, anonymously combine what appears to have been a wide variety of texts, edited and sometimes changed to create a unique voice.[5]

Classical rabbinic literature, which through the Middle Ages would become the central textual authority for most Jewish communities, is thus a diverse literature composed over centuries in very different geographical locations, somewhat ruthlessly edited by anonymous editors at an indeterminate place and time. Also, unlike many contemporary and later Christian writers, the rabbis by and large rarely discuss issues that we might call theological or cultural systematically; there are no rabbinic tracts from this period, for example, reflecting on God, Torah, women, men, or modesty. Coherence is thus elusive.

Yet even with those strong caveats, we might, I believe, point to a loosely shared understanding of masculinity throughout this literature. To get at this

---

[4] Cf. Seth Schwartz, 'The political geography of rabbinic texts', in *The Cambridge companion to the Talmud and rabbinic literature*, ed. Charlotte Elisheva Fonrobert and Martin S. Jaffee (New York, 2007), pp. 75–96.

[5] For an overview of rabbinic texts, see H.L. Strack and G. Stemberger, *Introduction to the Talmud and Midrash*, translated by Markus Bockmuehl (Minneapolis, 1992).

understanding, it is necessary to first take a step back to consider rabbinic anthropology.

RABBINIC ANTHROPOLOGY

As the opening quote of this essay illustrates, the rabbis largely believed in the constitutional existence of 'desire', called in Hebrew the *yetzer* or more descriptively, *yetzer ha-ra*, the evil desire. This 'desire' was seen as created by God, and its theological necessity is readily apparent – it can explain why it is that we, as creations of a good God, nevertheless sin, and with startling regularity at that. Even by the rabbinic period, some notion of an 'evil desire' had long been part of Jewish thought.[6] Renewed scholarly debate has just begun over two particular aspects of this desire. First, is it part of the self or external to it? I have argued that the rabbis largely equated the evil desire with what contemporary philosophers called the 'irrational soul'; this is the seat of our unreasoning appetites.[7] In recent publications Ishay Rosen-Zvi has challenged this understanding, claiming instead that, as in earlier Jewish literature, the 'desire' should be seen as a demonic force external to the self that lodges in the individual.[8] The second debated aspect of the evil desire is its nature. Is it to be seen as generating physical appetites, especially sexual, or instead is it quite literally a desire to do evil?[9] While it is important to mention these debates, there is no need here to adjudicate them. It is enough to observe that the rabbis largely believed that the *yetzer* existed in all human beings and generated desires that, at minimum, also include sexual desire.

The rabbis thus also believe that our task, as both men and women, is to resist the *yetzer*. Interestingly, the rabbis almost never discuss the possibility of actually killing or extirpating it; it will always be part of or lodged within the self. Here, though, is the gendered and ethnicised nub: women, children, and non-Jews are not truly capable of battling their desire. They lack the strength and resources to fight it. Men, particularly Jewish, rabbinic men possess this ability. In turn, the ability to resist desire is itself gendered as male; it is a masculine act, to be contrasted with the natural, gendered female, state of being at desire's mercy.[10]

This rabbinic anthropology roughly parallels developing Christian ideas. The presence of a permanent force or urge within the self toward sin and its strong connection to sexual desire – the problematicisation of sexual desire – enters Christian thought early on.[11] For some Christians, the answer to this problem

---

[6] For an overview, with review of past scholarship, see Ishay Rosen-Zvi, *Demonic desires: Yetzer Hara and the problem of evil in late Antiquity* (Philadelphia, 2011).

[7] Satlow, 'And on the earth you shall sleep'.

[8] Rosen-Zvi, *Demonic desires*; idem, 'Two rabbinic inclinations? Rethinking a scholarly dogma', *Journal for the Study of Judaism* 29 (2008), pp. 1–27.

[9] Rosen-Zvi, *Demonic desires*.

[10] Cf. Satlow, '"Try to be a man"'.

[11] The literature on this is vast. Cf. Peter Brown, *The body and society* (New York, 1988); Susanna Elm, *'Virgins of God': The making of asceticism in late Antiquity* (New York, 1994).

was asceticism.[12] Throughout late Antiquity and the early Middle Ages Christian ascetics withdrew from sex and society in order to fight these internal forces. Although women too became ascetics this activity was largely gendered as 'male' – to fight the forces effectively some of these women were said to have 'become male'. Even for women, fighting desire – whether one locates it in the self or the body – is a gendered activity.[13]

The rabbis have at best an ambivalent approach toward asceticism, as we normally understand the term. They almost completely reject sexual renunciation, with the one notable exception of a rabbi who reportedly forewent marriage in order to focus on his true love, the study of Torah.[14] They approve of some mild forms of ad hoc ascetic behaviours for a variety of different purposes, including self-formation and repentance. At the same time, however, they reject 'asceticism' as a lifestyle.[15]

Thus, instead of turning to asceticism as a defence against unruly desire, the rabbis adopted a different strategy against the *yetzer*, the study of Torah. A rabbinic text from around 200 CE illustrates how this works:

> 'And you will place these words on your hearts' – this says that words of Torah are compared to a life-giving drug. A parable: [It is to be compared] to a king who was angry with his son and gave him a powerful blow. He then put a bandage on his wound and said to him, 'My son, as long as you keep this bandage on your wound, eat whatever pleases you, drink whatever pleases you, and wash either in warm or cold water, and no harm will come to you. But if you remove it immediately a sore will arise.' Thus the Holy One, blessed be He, said to Israel: 'My children, I created for you an evil inclination from which is no evil, 'Surely if you do right there is uplift' [Gen. 4:7], when you are occupied with words of Torah it will not rule over you, but if you separate from words of Torah behold it will rule over you, as it is written, 'sin couches at the door, its urge is toward you.' [Gen. 4:7][16]

The analogy is a little puzzling: why did God, in anger, afflict Israel with the evil desire? Perhaps this is a reference to Adam and the expulsion from the Garden, or maybe – as suggested by the use of Genesis 4:7 – to Cain's murder of Abel. It is just as possible, though, that the analogy simply does not fully work. Since the point of this interpretation is to assert that Torah is the antidote to the evil desire,

---

[12] Cf. David Brakke, *Demons and the making of the monk: spiritual combat in early Christianity* (Cambridge, MA, and London, 2006).

[13] Elizabeth A. Castelli, '"I will make Mary male": Pieties of the body and gender transformation of Christian women in late Antiquity', in *Bodyguards: the cultural politics of gender ambiguity*, ed. Julia Epstein and Kristina Straub (New York, 1991), pp. 29–49; Brakke, *Demons and the making of the monk*, pp. 182–212.

[14] *Tosefta Yebamot* 8:7.

[15] Cf. Satlow, 'And on the earth you shall sleep'; Eliezer Diamond, *Holy men and hunger artists: fasting and asceticism in rabbinic culture* (New York, 2004); Daniel Boyarin, *Carnal Israel: reading sex in Talmudic culture* (Berkeley and Los Angeles, 1993), pp. 134–66.

[16] *Siphre ad Deuteronomium*, ed. Louis Finkelstein (1939; reprinted New York and Jerusalem, 1993), pp. 103–4.

the rabbis just needed to get that desire into the analogy, and to do so in a way that somehow confirms its origin in the one true God.

The analogy is also gendered. It compares God's relationship with Israel to the relationship between a father and son. This was not the only analogy that describes Israel's relationship to God available to the rabbis, and the gender here really does matter – 'son' cannot be replaced with daughter or wife. The reason is that study of Torah was itself gendered as a male activity. Women learned in Torah almost never appear in rabbinic literature, and when they do, they appear to have acquired their knowledge from domestic contexts rather than any formal study.[17]

Other rabbinic texts address more directly the connections between Torah and gender. According to one tradition in the Babylonian Talmud:

> Why are the idolaters polluted? Because they did not stand on Mt Sinai. When the snake came upon Eve, it placed upon her pollution. Israel, when they stood upon Mt. Sinai, their pollution ceased. Idolaters, because they did not stand on Mt. Sinai, their pollution did not cease.[18]

This tradition plays upon the ambiguity of the term 'came upon', which in Hebrew is frequently a euphemism for sexual relations. The 'pollution' becomes here natural and ontological, an inherent part of the human condition. Like the wound of the previous tradition it can be treated. The treatment here seems located in the past, but I think that the tradition at least implicitly exhorts proper behaviour for the present.

On Mt Sinai Israel received the Torah, which cleansed them of their ontological defect. There are two ways of understanding this cleansing. First, it was a one-time historical event that affected Israelite men and women alike. Read in this way, the tradition would say little about the connection of Torah to gender.

In contrast, I would like to suggest that this tradition is deeply informed by and encodes gender expectations. Following Sherry Ortner's classic if dated suggestion, this tradition reflects the gendered division between nature and culture.[19] 'Nature' is what Eve gives us, an ontological state of pollution. 'Culture' is what happens at Sinai and is connected to Torah. It is the masculine, Jewish activity that fixes the defects of nature. Those who are not part of Sinai – the idolaters in this tradition – remain part of nature. They thus also remain feminised. Sinai and Torah are not necessarily promoted here as a one-time historical

---

[17] David Goodblatt, 'The Beruriah traditions', *Journal of Jewish Studies* 26 (1975), pp. 68–85; Michael L. Satlow, 'Fictional women: a study in stereotypes', in *The Talmud Yerushalmi and Graeco-Roman Culture III*, ed. Peter Schäfer (Tübingen, 2002), pp. 225–43. Cf. Boyarin, *Carnal Israel*, pp. 166–96.

[18] Babylonian Talmud, *Shabbat* 145b-146a. The parallel in Babylonian Talmud, *Avodah Zarah* 22b attributes the tradition to Rabbi Yohanan. There is another parallel at Babylonian Talmud, *Yebamot* 103b.

[19] Sherry B. Ortner, 'Is female to male as nature is to culture?' in *Women, culture, and society*, ed. M.Z. Rosaldo and L. Lamphere (Stanford, 1974) pp. 68–87.

Torah study and masculinity

event. This tradition reinforces a distinctly masculine, Jewish identity rooted in Torah. To engage in Torah study is to continue to defeat nature with culture, and thus to reinforce the gendered nature of Torah study and the identity of the student as a man.

Rabbinic discussions of circumcision and the covenant display a related web of cultural and gender associations. The rabbis understood Jewish women to share in the covenant of Israel, but to the extent that that covenant was marked by circumcision and enacted in Torah study, they were excluded. Discussing the rabbinic treatment of circumcision, Shaye Cohen writes: 'the absence of circumcision from women will have confirmed for the rabbis their deeply held conviction that only men were the "real" Jews and that, while women certainly were "Israel" and part of the Jewish people, their Jewishness was inferior to that of males, the real Jews.'[20] The tradition cited above on the ontological effects of revelation reflects the general ambiguity with which the rabbis understood women, and can be equally applied to the study of Torah. Like circumcision, the Torah is an exemplary sign of God's covenant with Israel, which for the rabbis essentially meant Jewish men. Some rabbinic passages explicitly link circumcision, Torah, and masculinity, debating whether it is allowed to teach Torah to gentiles.[21] Non-Jews remain on the 'nature' side of the divide.[22]

While these rabbinic texts clearly gender the activity of Torah study as male, it is a kind of 'masculinity lite'. Salve or cure is the dominant metaphor for understanding the relationship of Torah study to the *yetzer*. Given that such constructions of masculinity are frequently thought to serve, as Daniel Boyarin has stated in the case of the rabbis, as 'an instance of opposition to the representation of masculinity as activity and dominance', the metaphor is particularly worthy of note.[23] That is, more aggressive metaphors that allude to hegemonic masculine values, such as the image of 'athletes of virtue' that frequently appears in Christian writings, are almost entirely absent from the earliest collections of rabbinic literature.[24]

The opening quote in this essay provides a signal example of precisely this kind of value transformation. The 'warrior' – a term always used to denote a man of physical war – is revalued to mean one who fights his desire. This image, however, is uncommon in Palestinian literature. Outside of the Babylonian Talmud rabbis rarely use aggressive or martial metaphors to describe the relationship between Torah study and the *yetzer*.[25]

---

[20] Shaye J.D. Cohen, *Why aren't Jewish women circumcised?: gender and covenant in Judaism* (Berkeley and Los Angeles, 2005), p. 136.

[21] Babylonian Talmud, *Sanhedrin* 59a.

[22] Cf. Christine Hayes, 'The "other" in rabbinic literature', in *The Cambridge companion to the Talmud and rabbinic literature*, pp. 243–69.

[23] Daniel Boyarin, *Unheroic conduct: the rise of heterosexuality and the invention of the Jewish man* (Berkeley and Los Angeles, 1997), p. 5.

[24] Cf. Gregory E. Sterling, '"Athletes of virtue": An analysis of the summaries in Acts (2:41-47; 4:32-35; 5:12-16)', *Journal of Biblical Literature* 113 (1994), pp. 679–96.

[25] The martial metaphor, though, is not completely absent. See Ruth Rabbah 4:3 (King David is transformed into a 'warrior' in study).

In sum, Palestinian rabbis in late Antiquity began to develop a gendered understanding of Torah study. Torah study, a masculine activity, was linked to self-control, a masculine virtue. This understanding was similar to, and undoubtedly in complex ways connected to, models of masculinity used by Roman philosophers and early Christian ascetics, although the nature of these connections is beyond the scope of this essay. It is worth emphasising here that the earliest rabbis, in the second and third centuries CE, developed an alternative model of masculinity, not necessarily an oppositional one. The texts provide no evidence of tension, anxiety, or ambivalence about the prevailing understandings of masculinity. There were alternative, equally good, ways of being a man.

FROM PALESTINE TO BABYLONIA

This changes in Babylonia. The Babylonian Talmud approvingly refers to Ben Zoma's notion, which other Palestinian rabbinic literature never cites. More importantly, the Babylonian Talmud begins to portray the study of Torah as aggressive, fraught, martial and competitive. The rabbis self-consciously smuggled the 'traditional' masculine values back into Torah study, and reflected on the tension thus created.

For Ben Zoma, the character of 'desire' remains undeveloped – it is a defect or power that needs to be conquered. In Palestinian rabbinic literature, this largely remains the case; desire does not aggressively fight back.[26] The Babylonian Talmud, on the other hand, turns desire into a much more formidable opponent. Desire is said to 'attack' both men and women.[27] Several traditions reflect on desire's extraordinary power. One tradition, an atomised commentary on Joel 2:20, attributes all of Israel's woes to desire, particularly sexual desire:

> Our rabbis taught:
> 'But I will remove the hidden one far off from you' (Joel 2:20) – this is the evil desire which is hidden in the human heart;
> 'and will drive him into a land barren and desolate means' – to a place where there are no humans for it to attack;
> 'with his face toward the eastern sea' – that it set its eyes against the First Temple and destroyed it, and killed the sages therein;
> 'and his hinder part toward the western sea' – that it set its eyes against the Second Temple and destroyed it, and killed the sages therein;
> 'That his foulness may come up and his ill-savor may come up' – that it leaves the other nations and attacks only Israel;
> 'because he has done great things' – Abaye said: [Desire attacks] sages more than anyone. As was the case when Abaye heard a certain man saying to a woman, 'Let us arise early tomorrow and go on our way.' [Abaye] thought: 'I will go and keep them

---

[26] Rosen-Zvi, *Demonic desires*, pp. 65–84.
[27] Babylonian Talmud, *Kiddushin* 63b; Babylonian Talmud, *Ketubot* 54a. Cf. Rosen-Zvi, *Demonic desires*, pp. 108–11.

Torah study and masculinity

away from transgression.' He followed them for three parsangs in the meadow. When they parted they said: 'Our way is long and our company is pleasant' and they went each to their own way. Abaye said, 'If it were me, I could not have restrained myself,' and so he went and leaned against a doorpost in despair. A certain old man came up to him and taught him: 'The greater the man, the greater his desire.'[28]

This text combines a reputed exegetical tradition about the strength and danger of desire with a story that links it to sages in particular. This story – produced by rabbis and for rabbis – reinforces the sense that desire is a powerful adversary particularly for those who are 'great'.

If desire is a strong adversary, the scholar has an even stronger weapon: Torah and its study. 'It was taught in the School of Rabbi Yishmael, "If this wretched one [i.e., desire] wounds you, drag it to the house of study. If it is stone it will dissolve; if it is iron it will shatter."'[29] The language is here more violent, and points to a shift in the metaphor used in later Babylonian literature to indicate the role of Torah. Torah is no longer a cure or a salve, but a weapon. The Torah scholar is the new warrior, brandishing Torah as a weapon against the enemy, the *yetzer*.

Another extended exegesis in the Babylonian Talmud, this time of Isaiah 3:1–3, illustrates this new transformation:

> 'For lo! The Sovereign Lord of Hosts will remove from Jerusalem and from Judah prop and stay, every prop of food and every prop of water: Soldier and warrior, magistrate and prophet, augur and elder; captain of fifty, magnate and counsellor, skilled artisan and expert enchanter . . .' (Isaiah 3:1–3).
> 'prop' – these are the masters of Bible;
> 'stay' – these are the masters of Mishnah . . .
> 'every prop of food' – these are the masters of Talmud . . .
> 'every prop of water' – these are the masters of homilies (*aggadah*) . . .
> 'soldier' – this is the master of traditions;
> 'warrior' – this is one who knows how to give and take in the war of Torah . . .[30]

This rabbinic tradition transforms the biblical verse, which clearly means simply to include all the various roles and classes upon which a functioning community depends, into one entirely about scholars. The soldiers and warriors now are those who engage in the 'war of Torah'. Elsewhere the Babylonian Talmud uses the term 'a warrior in Torah'.[31]

This transformation of the traditionally masculine values of physical aggression and domination to the study of Torah appears in several relatively late stories in the Babylonian Talmud. One in particular encodes an extended

---

[28] Babylonian Talmud, *Sukkah* 52a, modified translation from Rosen-Zvi, *Demonic desires*, pp. 105–6.
[29] Babylonian Talmud, *Sukkah* 52b, with parallel at Babylonian Talmud, *Kiddushin* 30b. The tradition is not paralleled in any tannaitic source and I take it to reflect Babylonian values.
[30] Babylonian Talmud, *Hagigah* 14a.
[31] Babylonian Talmud, *Sanhedrin* 106b.

reflection on the meaning of masculinity. It is somewhat long, but worth quoting in full:

> One day, Rabbi Yohanan was bathing in the Jordan. Resh Lakish saw him and thought he was a woman. He crossed the Jordan after him by placing his lance in the Jordan and vaulting to the other side. When Rabbi Yohanan saw [Resh Lakish], he said to him, 'Your strength for Torah!' He replied, 'Your beauty for women!' He said to him, 'If you repent, I will give you my sister who is more beautiful than I am.' [Resh Lakish] agreed. [Resh Lakish wanted to cross back to take his clothes but he couldn't.] [Rabbi Yohanan] taught [Resh Lakish] Mishna and Talmud and made him into a great man.
>
> Once they were disputing in the Study-House. 'The sword and the lance and the dagger, from when [in the process of production] can they become impure?' Rabbi Yohanan said, 'From the time they are forged in the fire.' Resh Lakish said, 'From the time they are polished in the water.' Rabbi Yohanan said, 'A brigand is an expert in brigandry.' [Resh Lakish] said to [Rabbi Yohanan], 'What have you profited me? There they call me Rabbi and here they call me Rabbi!' [Rabbi Yohanan] became angry and [Resh Lakish] became ill [due to Rabbi Yohanan's curse]. [Rabbi Yohanan's] sister came to [Rabbi Yohanan] and cried before him. She said, 'Look at me!' He did not pay attention to her. 'Look at the orphans!' He [quoted] to her, 'Leave your orphans, I will give life' [Jeremiah 49:11]. 'For the sake of my widowhood!' He [quoted to her], 'Place your widows' trust in me' [Jeremiah 49:11].
>
> Resh Lakish died, and Rabbi Yohanan was greatly mournful over him. The Rabbis said, 'What can we do to comfort him? Let us bring Rabbi Elazar the son of Padat whose traditions are brilliant, and put him before [Rabbi Yohanan.]' They brought Rabbi Elazar the son of Padat and put him before him. Every point that he would make, he said, 'There is a tradition which supports you.' [Rabbi Yohanan] said, 'Do I need this one?! The son of Lakish used to raise twenty-four objections to every point that I made, and I used to supply twenty-four refutations, until the matter became completely clear, and all you can say is that there is a tradition which supports me?! Don't I already know that I say good things?' He used to go and cry out at the gates, 'Son of Lakish, where are you?' until he became mad. The Rabbis prayed for him and he died.[32]

Daniel Boyarin has called attention to this passage 'as a paradigmatic story of the formation of the Jewish male subject'.[33] While my own reading of the passage differs in focus from Boyarin's, it follows his insight that the connection between gender and Torah study are the heart of the story, and this in turn reflects certain real tensions for the community that produced it.

Not coincidentally, in my opinion, this story is located immediately after a series of comments on male appearance and beauty. This discussion – which

---

[32] Babylonian Talmud, *Baba Metzia* 84a, slightly modified translation from Boyarin, *Unheroic conduct*, pp. 127–8.
[33] Boyarin, *Unheroic conduct*, p. 128.

Torah study and masculinity

includes mention of some rabbis with exceptionally large sexual organs – eventually winds its way to this story, which is triggered by mention of Rabbi Yohanan's beauty. The first paragraph emphatically links gender, sexuality, physical power and Torah. On the one side of the river stands the brigand, Resh Lakish, with (not coincidentally) his lance. On the other side is the beautiful Rabbi Yohanan (and, although not physically, his sister). The beauty seduces Resh Lakish. Once on the other side, both literally and metaphorically, Resh Lakish 'repents', an act that saps his physical strength. The medieval commentator on this passage, Rashi, clarifies this connection: 'Since he accepted upon him the yoke of Torah his strength weakened'. Now truly weak and vulnerable, Rabbi Yohanan builds him into a new, 'great' man, a scholar like himself.

The rest of the story portrays a friendship whose primary bond is competition. Rabbi Yohanan and Resh Lakish are related by marriage and bound by an aggressive, intellectual back and forth. This is emphasised in the character of Rabbi Elazar ben Padat, who will not engage Rabbi Yohanan in the competitive dialectics he craves. Yet this competition also proves to be the undoing of their friendship. Intellectual debate quickly descends into ad hominem attack, as Rabbi Yohanan publicly reminds his friend of his base origins. Resh Lakish calmly throws the retort back at him: since he is a great man in both contexts, who needs Rabbi Yohanan and his Torah anyway? For Rabbi Yohanan this was too much, and he knowingly and deliberately killed his friend, widowing his sister and orphaning their children. Only later did he come to regret his act.

The story is an almost classic tragedy; two friends are drawn together only to destroy each other. Like many such rabbinic stories, however, the narrative is so sparse and enigmatic that it is difficult to pin down with certainty the tragic flaw. Is it Rabbi Yohanan's hubris and sensitivity, or Resh Lakish's questioning of whether this path – the one that sapped his strength – really is worthwhile? The tragedy is unresolved, posing and never answering Resh Lakish's question. Torah, and the fierce competition that is intrinsic in its study, is a story about the 'formation of the Jewish male subject'. But it is a subject that remains contested at the end, one that is bound in complicated ways to the values of physical strength and competition that it is sometimes seen as opposing.

The characters in the story are from third-century Palestine, but the story itself was almost certainly composed by the later editors of the Babylonian Talmud. It is also within this context that the story makes the most sense. Jeffrey Rubenstein has noted that the late strata of the Babylonian Talmud is far more likely to thematise the dialectics involved in Torah story as violent than are either earlier strata or Palestinian rabbinic sources. Throughout the Babylonian Talmud, as in our story of Rabbi Yohanan and Resh Lakish, the study of Torah is portrayed as highly competitive, aggressive, and violent.

Rubenstein argues that the institutionalisation of Torah study in Babylonia in the fifth and sixth centuries accounts for this thematisation.[34] This

---

[34] Jeffrey L. Rubenstein, *The culture of the Babylonian Talmud* (Baltimore and London, 2003), pp. 54–66.

institutionalisation, which replaced the informal network of small disciple circles in which rabbis were traditionally trained, led to a strongly structured and hierarchical academy that prized oral dialectical debate. The late, redactional layer of the Babylonian Talmud provides a snapshot of or window into the values of this academy, along with a reflection of the cultural tensions present within it.

Rubenstein's compelling social historical explanation can be further enriched by incorporating the issue of gender. There is nothing particularly natural or inevitable about the emergence of aggressive, violent, and competitive tendencies in an all-male academic institution, even one based on oral argumentation. Once those tendencies are encouraged and unleashed, however, such an institutional context could certainly help to fuel them.

I would like to suggest here that the seeds for these tendencies can be found in the earlier, Palestinian literature, particularly the gendering of Torah study as masculine. This gendering arose, I have argued, from a conception of self-control; the active force – of which Torah was one tool – that allowed a man to subdue his desire was seen as male. The Babylonian rabbis inherited the gendering of Torah study as masculine, but the reasons behind it were ignored, perhaps as a matter of transmission but more likely of cultural difference. Self-control as denoting male power was, perhaps, distinctly Greco-Roman.

This basic equation of Torah study as a masculine activity helped to inform the development of the peculiar culture of the Babylonian Talmud. For Babylonian rabbis, masculinity meant violence, power, aggression, war, and competition. These became the values of the academy. The ability to argue aggressively proved one's masculinity within the academy, and was rewarded by moving up the academy's hierarchical ladder. The transfer of masculine values from the realm of true physical violence to the intellectual realm, though, was by no means transparent and clean. As in the story of Rabbi Yohanan and Resh Lakish, the rabbis themselves acknowledged their adaptation of traditional masculine values to the academy, and reflected on that very tension. They were not necessarily sold on their own creation.

CONCLUSION

While specific to the rabbis of late Antiquity, the argument made in this essay raises a more generalisable and nuanced way of thinking about religious men. Rabbis created an alternative model of masculinity that was quite distinct from the hegemonic discourse without actually opposing it. Yet this very alternative would later lead to the development of institutional practices that reincorporate these same aggressive, competitive and dominant values. One question that this thesis raises is whether such a dynamic can be seen among other religious men, Jewish and not, throughout the Middle Ages.

At the same time, this essay raises questions for future research specifically on Jewish men in the Middle Ages. For the Jews of medieval Europe, particularly central Europe, the Babylonian Talmud would become the cornerstone of

Torah study and masculinity

their religious curriculum.[35] It became not only a central text of study, but also a wellspring that authorised Jewish practices and ideas, whether religious or cultural. Rabbis in the Middle Ages inherited a conflicted and complex discourse on masculinity in a text that they revered. How they brought that discourse to life – how they performed it – in their own environments, though, must await further research.

---

[35] Talya Fishman, *Becoming the people of the Talmud: oral Torah as written tradition in medieval Jewish cultures* (Philadelphia, 2011).

GENDER AND HIERARCHY: ARCHBISHOP HINCMAR OF RHEIMS (845-882) AS A RELIGIOUS MAN

Rachel Stone

In 881 the clerics and laity of the city of Beauvais in Picardy were electing a new bishop. Beauvais had long been vulnerable to attacks by Vikings on the Carolingian Empire. The city was burned by raiders in the early 850s; in 859 a previous bishop, Ermenfrid, was killed by the Danes.[1] The archbishop of the province in which the diocese of Beauvais lay, Hincmar of Rheims, sent the citizens a letter about the election, advising them of the procedure they should follow and the qualifications they should look for.[2] Hincmar is clear that the right sort of man has to be chosen:

> Let him not be approved who has no dignity of birth nor morals, or he who is held bound by hereditary or other condition. No neophyte from the laity, that is newly tonsured and without discipline, or not promoted to ecclesiastical grades at the constituted times. This we therefore specially designate, since when the canons say: 'Let no one be ordained from the laity', they show that this does not refer to all laymen. For clerics cannot be born and cannot be made [from those who are already clerics], but the varieties (*genera*) are designated from which they [laymen] cannot attain to clerical office.[3]

---

[1] *Annales Bertiniani*, ed. George Waitz, Monumenta Germaniae Historica. Scriptores rerum Germanicarum in usum scholarum separatim editi (hereafter MGH SRG) 5 (Hanover, 1883) s.a. 851, 859, pp. 41, 52.

[2] Henry G.J. Beck, 'Canonical election to suffragan bishoprics according to Hincmar of Rheims', *Catholic Historical Review* 43 (1957), pp. 137–59, summarises Hincmar's view of correct procedure, and in 'The selection of bishops suffragan to Hincmar of Rheims, 845-882', *Catholic Historical Review* 45 (1959), pp. 273–308, he analyses the evidence for actual elections: pp. 302-6 discusses the Beauvais election, which became controversial when several candidates were rejected. Cf. Gerhard Schmitz, 'Hinkmar von Reims, die Synode von Fismes 881 und der Streit um das Bistum Beauvais', *Deutsches Archiv für Erforschung des Mittelalters* 35 (1979), pp. 463–86.

[3] Heinrich Schrörs, *Hinkmar Erzbischof von Reims: sein Leben und seine Schriften* (Freiburg im Breisgau, 1884), pp. 518–88, provides a numbered register of Hincmar's writings, still useful for identifying specific letters. Hincmar of Rheims, *Epistolae*, I-LV, *Patrologiae cursus completus, series Latina*, ed. J.-P. Migne, 221 vols. (Paris, 1841-64) (hereafter PL) vol. 126, cols. 9–280, at cols. 259–260, Epistola XXXIX (Schrörs, no. 501): 'Non eum, cui nulla natalium, nulla morum

Hincmar of Rheims as a religious man

Hincmar goes on to list unsuitable types of men, including soldiers, those who have done public penance, those who have married twice and the illiterate. Instead, the chosen candidate should be a man who, if a barbarian attack occurred, 'would know to offer help to you with prudence, would be strong with manliness, would reflect with temperance'.[4]

HINCMAR THE MAN

Hincmar's text allows us to begin an exploration of how one prominent ninth-century man could understand gender as it related to religious men.[5] Hincmar, archbishop of Rheims between 845 and 882, was one of the most influential men in Francia for nearly forty years, and his copious writings have helped define our image of the late Carolingian empire.[6] He advised Frankish kings, writing 'mirrors for princes' as well as compiling the first surviving coronation *ordines*.[7] He played a prominent role in theological disputes, combating Gottschalk's views on predestination.[8] His expertise as a canonist led to decisions that were crucial to the development of the canon law of marriage.[9] He also played a key role in

---

dignitas suffragetur: vel qui originali, aut alicui conditioni obligatus detineatur. Neminem ex laicis neophytum, id est noviter attonsum, et sine disciplina, vel non per tempora constituta ad ecclesiasticos gradus provectum. Quod ideo specialiter designamus, quia cum canones dicant: "Nullus ex laicis ordinetur", demonstrant quod non de omnibus sit laicis constitutum. Neque enim clerici nasci, et non fieri possunt; sed designata sunt genera, de quibus ad clericatum pervenire non possunt.'

[4] Ibid., col. 260: 'et contra barbaricam infestationem, si quod absit, acciderit, vobis ferre auxilium prudentia sciat, virilitate valeat, temperantia consulat'.

[5] Julia M.H. Smith, 'Introduction: gendering the early medieval world', in *Gender in the early medieval world: east and west, 300–900*, ed. Leslie Brubaker and Julia M.H. Smith (Cambridge, 2004), pp. 1–19 at pp. 4–11, provides a useful introduction to the changing meanings of the term 'gender' in English. Smith comments (p. 4): 'At its simplest it [gender] refers to the disparities in all societies between the social roles permitted to men and women together with the wider cultural meanings associated with masculinity and femininity.' On gender as an analytical tool for historians, the classic article is Joan W. Scott, 'Gender: a useful category of historical analysis', *American Historical Review* 91 (1986), pp. 1053–75.

[6] Jean Devisse, *Hincmar, archevêque de Reims 845–882*, 3 vols., Travaux d'histoire éthico-politique 29 (Geneva, 1975–76) is fundamental on Hincmar's overall career.

[7] Hans Hubert Anton, *Fürstenspiegel und Herrscherethos in der Karolingerzeit*, Bonner Historische Forschungen 32 (Bonn, 1968), pp. 281–355; Janet L. Nelson, 'Kingship, law and liturgy in the political thought of Hincmar of Rheims', *English Historical Review* 92 (1977), pp. 241–79; Richard A. Jackson, 'Who wrote Hincmar's ordines?', *Viator* 25 (1994), pp. 31–52.

[8] Devisse, *Hincmar*, pp. 115–279; David Ganz, 'The debate on predestination', in *Charles the Bald: court and kingdom*, ed. Margaret T. Gibson and Janet L. Nelson (2nd revised ed., Aldershot, 1990), pp. 283–302; *Gottschalk and a medieval predestination controversy: texts translated from the Latin*, ed. Victor Genke and Francis X. Gumerlock, Mediaeval Philosophical Texts in Translation 47 (Milwaukee, WI, 2010), pp. 37–54.

[9] See e.g. Jean Gaudemet, 'Indissolubilité et consommation du mariage: l'apport d'Hincmar de Reims', *Revue de droit canonique* 30 (1980), pp. 28–40; Catherine Rider, *Magic and impotence in the Middle Ages* (Oxford, 2006), pp. 31–42; Rachel Stone, 'The invention of a theology of abduction: Hincmar of Rheims on *raptus*', *Journal of Ecclesiastical History* 60 (2009), pp. 433–48; Karl

the development of the cult of St Remigius, the baptiser of the Merovingian King Clovis.[10]

Hincmar's status as a religious man was fundamental to his identity from his earliest years. He had been raised 'from boyhood' in the monastery of Saint-Denis, and as a young man accompanied his abbot Hilduin to Louis the Pious's court, when Hilduin was made archchancellor by the Frankish emperor. Hincmar then went into exile with Hilduin in 830.[11] He soon found favour and returned to become a court chaplain. Hincmar was rewarded for his loyalty to Charles the Bald by being given the bishopric of Rheims in 845, but his life as a bishop was no less chequered.

Indeed, Hincmar's episcopal status itself was challenged. His predecessor, Ebbo, had been deposed in 835 in the aftermath of a rebellion by Louis the Pious's sons, Lothar I, Pippin of Aquitaine and Louis the German. Ebbo had been briefly restored to his see after Louis's death, when Lothar had controlled Rheims, but had then had to flee again. He was still in exile but maintaining his claims to the see when Hincmar was consecrated in 845.[12] Even after his death in 851, Ebbo continued to haunt Hincmar's imagination.[13]

How did Hincmar's own experiences affect his views on gender? In an important recent overview of research on clerical masculinity, Derek Neal has argued that:

> we have to think about masculinity as something that mattered to individuals – as an aspect of identity, in other words, not just as a set of metaphorical meanings that cultural powers could manipulate to serve rhetorical or disciplinary ends.[14]

Neal also calls for us to 'take account of the religious side of being a clergyman'. Yet as he makes clear, it is often difficult to find suitable evidence,[15] and the problems for the early Middle Ages are even more acute. This was not a time before 'individualism', as it sometimes suggested, but the evidence for authorial

---

Heidecker, *The divorce of Lothar II: Christian marriage and political power in the Carolingian world*, trans. Tanis M. Guest (Ithaca, NY, 2010).

[10] Marie-Céline Isaïa, *Remi de Reims: mémoire d'un saint, histoire d'une église* (Paris, 2010), pp. 417–546.

[11] Flodoard of Rheims, *Historia Remensis ecclesiae*, ed. Martina Stratmann, MGH Scriptores 36 (Hanover, 1998) 3-1, pp. 190–1.

[12] On the deposition of Ebbo and its subsequent effects, see Steffen Patzold, *Episcopus: Wissen über Bischöfe im Frankenreich des späten 8. bis frühen 10. Jahrhunderts*, Mittelalter-Forschungen 25 (Ostfildern, 2008), pp. 315–57.

[13] See below, p. 40.

[14] Derek Neal, 'What can historians do with clerical masculinity? Lessons from medieval Europe', in *Negotiating clerical identities: priests, monks and masculinity in the Middle Ages*, ed. Jennifer D. Thibodeaux (Basingstoke and New York, 2010), pp. 16–36 at pp. 25–6. On earlier calls by modernist historians for exploration of the subjective side of masculinity, see John Tosh, 'What should historians do with masculinity? Reflections on nineteenth-century Britain', *History Workshop Journal* no. 38 (1994), pp. 179–202 at p. 194; Michael Roper, 'Slipping out of view: subjectivity and emotion in gender history, *History Workshop Journal* no. 59 (2005), pp. 57–72.

[15] Neal, 'What can historians', at pp. 30–1.

Hincmar of Rheims as a religious man

identities is particularly problematic.[16] Hincmar's works fill one and a half volumes of *Patrologia Latina*, but these texts are overwhelmingly public and polemical. Can we use them to explore both Hincmar's conceptions of the sex/gender system and the more personal aspects of what it meant for Hincmar to be a man, and specifically a religious man?

GENDER AND THE CAROLINGIAN WORLD

As Neal points out in the introduction to his article, the concept of 'clerical masculinity' comes with much baggage for the secular, modern, Protestant-influenced world in which the study of masculinity first developed.[17] Yet if the Middle Ages 'seem in some inescapable way cut off from the present day',[18] the early medieval period in turn sometimes seems remote to historians of medieval masculinity.[19] Implicitly or explicitly, the period between late Antiquity and the Gregorian reforms is often regarded as static and unimportant. Two of the most influential studies of clerical masculinity, those by Jo Ann McNamara and Robert Swanson, see its distinctive features as essentially created by those reforms.[20]

This ignores, however, the extent to which the Carolingian reform movement was also influenced by the 'singularly powerful ideal of differentiation which defined the separateness of those who mediated between God and mankind'.[21] Participation in warfare and public marriage are repeatedly shown as the defining characteristics of (male) lay life in Carolingian Francia, as opposed to that of

---

[16] On this topic, see *Ego trouble: authors and their identities in the early Middle Ages*, ed. Richard Corradini et al., Forschungen zur Geschichte des Mittelalters 15 (Vienna, 2010).

[17] Neal, 'What can historians', at pp. 16–24; John Tosh, 'The history of masculinity: an outdated concept?' in *What is masculinity? Historical dynamics from Antiquity to the contemporary world*, ed. Sean Brady and John H. Arnold (Basingstoke, 2011), pp. 17–34 at pp. 17–25, gives an overview of the origins of masculinity as a topic of interest for historians.

[18] Neal, 'What can historians', at p. 18.

[19] Essay collections include *Medieval masculinities: regarding men in the Middle Ages*, ed. Clare A. Lees, Medieval Cultures 7 (Minneapolis, 1994); *Becoming male in the Middle Ages*, ed. Jeffrey Jerome Cohen and Bonnie Wheeler, Garland Reference Library of the Humanities, New Middle Ages 4 (New York, 1997); *Conflicted identities and multiple masculinities: men in the medieval west*, ed. Jacqueline Murray, Garland Medieval Casebooks 25 (New York, 1999); *Masculinity in medieval Europe*, ed. D.M. Hadley (London, 1999); *Gender in the early medieval world: east and west, 300–900*, ed. Leslie Brubaker and Julia M.H. Smith (Cambridge, 2004); *Holiness and masculinity in the Middle Ages*, ed. P.H. Cullum and Katherine J. Lewis (Cardiff, 2004); *Negotiating clerical identities*, ed. Thibodeaux. Only the collections edited by Hadley and by Brubaker and Smith have much to say on continental Europe before the year 1000. See also Smith, 'Introduction', at pp. 10–11, on the important role that studies of sexuality and of the early Church's attitudes to women had in driving the study of gender in the early medieval world.

[20] Jo Ann McNamara, 'The *Herrenfrage*: the restructuring of the gender system, 1050–1150', in *Medieval masculinities*, ed. Lees, pp. 3–29; Robert N. Swanson, 'Angels incarnate: clergy and masculinity from Gregorian Reform to Reformation', in *Masculinity in medieval Europe*, ed. Hadley, pp. 160–77. See the essays by Jennifer D. Thibodeaux, Kirsten A. Fenton, Joanna Huntington and Matthew Mesley in this volume for further discussion of these reforms and their impact.

[21] Mayke de Jong, 'Charlemagne's Church', in *Charlemagne: empire and society*, ed. Joanna Story (Manchester, 2005), pp. 103–35 at p. 124.

religious men.²² Ninth-century kings and bishops were eager to enforce abstinence on both monks and secular clerics;²³ Hincmar himself spent much time demanding that the clerics of his diocese avoid all contact with women.²⁴ In theory, married men were not prohibited from becoming clerics, as Hincmar indicates in his letter on the Beauvais election, although marriage subsequent to ordination was specifically banned.²⁵ Post-ordination celibacy, however, was expected of all, even if there are hints that some educated clerics may have queried this doctrine.²⁶ Carolingian bishops were in practice drawn from an elite, who, like Hincmar, had entered religious life in childhood.²⁷

Expectations of clerical celibacy were common both to the Carolingian world and to the post-Gregorian one; Hincmar's terminology also suggests a basic understanding of gender similar to that of later in the Middle Ages. There is no sign of the 'third gender' sometimes said to be characteristic of this period.²⁸ Hincmar's wish is not for an angelic bishop for Beauvais, but a manly one.²⁹ Such manliness was a characteristic shared by both religious men and laymen: Hincmar describes his king Charles the Bald in 873 as besieging a Viking army 'manfully and energetically'.³⁰ Hincmar's usage of the term reflects the more general Carolingian usage of *virilitas* for situations involving Christians showing strength and determination, whether in military or religious activities.³¹

Hincmar's own use of such specifically gendered terms is very limited, but one final quote does raise another issue: implicitly such Christian manliness could also be demonstrated by women. In a passage from *De cavendis vitiis et virtutibus exercendis*, a mirror for a prince sent to Charles the Bald, Hincmar cited Gregory the Great on how one should seek help from the saints:

---

[22] Rachel Stone, *Morality and masculinity in the Carolingian empire*, Cambridge Studies in Medieval Life and Thought, 4th series 81 (Cambridge, 2011), pp. 7–8.

[23] Mayke de Jong, '*Imitatio morum*: the cloister and clerical purity in the Carolingian world', in *Medieval purity and piety: essays on medieval clerical celibacy and religious reform*, ed. Michael Frassetto, Garland Medieval Casebooks 19, (New York, 1998), pp. 49–80.

[24] See below, p. 39.

[25] Michel Dortel-Claudot, 'Le prêtre et le mariage: évolution de la législation canonique des origines au XII siècle', *L'année canonique* 17 (1973), pp. 319–44, summarises the legislation.

[26] de Jong, 'Charlemagne's Church', pp. 123–4.

[27] de Jong, '*Imitatio morum*', p. 51.

[28] See e.g. Jo Ann McNamara, 'Chastity as a third gender in the history and hagiography of Gregory of Tours', in *The world of Gregory of Tours*, Cultures, Beliefs and Traditions 8, ed. Kathleen Mitchell and Ian Wood (Leiden, 2002), pp. 199–209; McNamara, '*Herrenfrage*' at pp. 6–7. The claims by Swanson, 'Angels incarnate', and Jacqueline Murray, 'One flesh, two sexes, three genders?', in *Gender and Christianity in medieval Europe: new perspectives*, ed. Lisa M. Bitel and Felice Lifshitz (Philadelphia, 2008), pp. 34–51, of a third gender existing later in the Middle Ages seem equally unconvincing to me; I prefer the formulation in Ruth Mazo Karras, 'Thomas Aquinas's chastity belt: clerical masculinity in medieval Europe', in the same volume, pp. 52–67 at p. 53: 'Rather than speak of third (or fourth or fifth) genders, it is more useful to speak of multiple variations on the basic two'.

[29] Compare Maureen C. Miller, 'Masculinity, reform, and clerical culture: narratives of episcopal holiness in the Gregorian era', *Church History* 72 (2003), pp. 25–52, on eleventh-century narratives of the manly bishop.

[30] *Annales Bertiniani*, s.a. 873, p. 124: 'viriliter ac strenue'.

[31] Stone, *Morality*, pp. 317–19.

Faithful men are there whom the desires of the world were not able to soften from the firmness of their virility. Holy women are there, who vanquished the world and their sex. Boys are there, who here transcended their years by their morals. Old men are there, whom age made feeble here and yet the virtue of work did not leave them.[32]

As his quotation from Gregory the Great suggests, Hincmar's understanding of gender was only one aspect of wider social hierarchies, hierarchies which had specific moral duties attached.[33] In 874, for example, he wrote the judgment of the Synod of Douzy on a transgressing nun, Duda; the text included instructions for her abbess on how Duda should be punished.[34] Duda had failed to live up to the standards imposed by her position of religious privilege; others, however, like the holy boys mentioned by Gregory the Great, could exceed society's expectations of them.

The quotation, however, also raises a more troubling possibility: the existence in Carolingian society of a 'gender continuum'. Carol Clover has seen this as characteristic of early Norse society, in which 'there was finally just one "gender", one standard by which persons were judged adequate or inadequate, and it was something like masculine'.[35] She argued that the existence of such a continuum contributed to the 'frantic maschismo' of Norse society, in which all men inevitably became 'effeminate' with age.[36]

Such a one-gender system has already been suggested for the early medieval West.[37] More generally, hierarchical systems of gender have often been seen as inherently unstable. Jo Ann McNamara saw the twelfth century as marked by a 'masculine identity crisis',[38] and claimed that '(a)n important class of men institutionally barred from marriage raised inherently frightening questions

---

[32] Hincmar of Rheims, *De cavendis vitiis et virtutibus exercendis*, ed. Doris Nachtmann, MGH Quellen zur Geistesgeschichte des Mittelalters 16 (Munich, 1998) 2-6, p. 203: 'ibi fideles viri, quos a virilitatis suę robore voluptas sęculi emollire non potuit. Ibi sanctae mulieres, quae cum saeculo et sexum vicerunt. Ibi pueri, qui hic annos suos moribus transcenderunt. Ibi senes, quos hic aetas debiles reddidit et virtus operis non reliquit.' The citation is from Gregory the Great, *Homiliae in Evangelia*, ed. Raymond Étaix, Corpus Christianorum Series Latina (=CCSL) 141 (Turnhout, 1999), Homilia XIV, c. 5, p. 101, on the Good Shepherd.

[33] Cf. Kim M. Phillips, 'Masculinities and the medieval English sumptuary laws', *Gender & History* 19 (2007), pp. 22-42 at p. 33: 'It was not being "a Man" which mattered so much as expressing legitimate claims to a place in the hierarchy of men.'

[34] Council of Douzy 874, *Die Konzilien der karolingischen Teilreiche 860-874*, ed. Wilfried Hartmann, MGH Concilia 4 (Hanover, 1998), no. 13B, pp. 587-96.

[35] Carol J. Clover, 'Regardless of sex: men, women and power in early northern Europe', *Speculum* 68 (1993), pp. 363-87 at p. 379.

[36] Ibid., at pp. 380-5.

[37] See e.g. Julia M.H. Smith, 'Gender and ideology in the early Middle Ages', in *Gender and Christian religion. Papers read at the 1996 Summer meeting and the 1997 Winter meeting of the Ecclesiastical History Society*, ed. R.N. Swanson. Studies in Church History 34 (Woodbridge, 1998), pp. 51-73 at pp. 58-9; Lynda L. Coon, 'Somatic styles of the early Middle Ages', *Gender & History* 20 (2008), pp. 463-86 at p. 468.

[38] McNamara, *'Herrenfrage'*, p. 3.

about masculinity'.[39] She enquires: 'what does it mean to "act like a man" except to dominate women?'[40]

John Tosh, among others, has gone further, arguing for masculinity as inherently insecure:

> Masculinity is insecure in two senses: its social recognition depends on material accomplishments which may not be attainable; and its hegemonic form is exposed to resistance from both women and subordinated masculinities.[41]

Tosh also sees masculinity as tending to insecurity from its psychic constitution, with the need for boys to separate from identification with their mother.[42]

More recently, however, some scholars have objected to the 'increasingly programmatic masculine crisis' and others have argued against early medieval masculinity, specifically, as being 'in crisis'.[43] In the remainder of this chapter I will explore both how Hincmar conceptualised the sexual and religious hierarchies around him, and also how he responded to the gap between this ideology and lived experience. Did this necessarily result in anxiety or crisis on his part?

HINCMAR'S HIERARCHIES: THE THEORY

Hincmar, like the other Frankish men whose voices we hear in the sources, believed that men were fundamentally superior to women. He describes Duda as being of 'fragile sex';[44] and instructing her to read the Fathers on monasticism, adds: 'And when she should read the word of St Augustine about the fall of a monk, let her know, that although unequal by sex, she is equal by profession'.[45]

In this, Hincmar follows standard biblical patriarchy: the man is the head of the woman and she is the weaker vessel.[46] Such subordination extended

---

[39] Ibid., p. 5.
[40] Ibid.
[41] Tosh, 'What should historians', p. 192.
[42] Ibid.. p. 195.
[43] Bryce Traister, 'Academic Viagra: the rise of American masculinity studies', *American Quarterly* 52 (2000), pp. 274–304 at p. 297; Stone, *Morality*, pp. 323–6; Andrew Romig, 'The common bond of aristocratic masculinity: monks, secular men, and St. Gerald of Aurillac', in *Negotiating clerical identities*, pp. 39–56. Ruth Mazo Karras, *From boys to men: formations of masculinity in late medieval Europe* (Philadelphia, 2003), p. 9, looking at the fourteenth and fifteenth centuries sees 'no "crisis of masculinity" in the sense of broad social trends that threatened all men'.
[44] Council of Douzy 874, c. 8, p. 595.
[45] Ibid., c. 7, p. 592: 'Et cum sermonem beati Augustini de lapsu monachi legerit, sciat se, licet imparem sexu, parum professione.'
[46] Hincmar of Rheims, *De divortio Lotharii regis et Theutbergae reginae*, ed. Letha Böhringer, MGH Concilia 4, Supplementum 1 (Hanover, 1992), Responsio 5, p. 143 (hereafter *De divortio*): 'Sed et ipsi viri, qui, ut ostendimus, pari legis iudicio sicut et mulieres apud deum tenentur, si adulteraverint, et tanto etiam graviori poena damnentur, quanto capita et rectores sunt mulierum, fragilioris scilicet sexus et vasis infirmioris' (drawing on 1 Corinthians 11:3 and 1 Peter 3:7).

throughout all ranks of society, as shown in the anointing formula used by Hincmar for the coronation of Charles the Bald's first wife Ermentrude in 866. The prayer, adapted from a nuptial blessing in the late eighth-century Gregorian sacramentary, begins:

> O holy Lord, Father almighty, eternal God, who by the power of your *virtus* ... having made man [*homo*] in your image, created the inseparable helper of woman, and you gave the beginning to the female body from male flesh ... Look down upon this your servant ... may she marry in Christ, faithful and chaste, and may she remain an imitator of holy women. May she be lovely like Rachel to her husband, wise like Rebecca, long-lived and faithful like Sarah ... May she be fertile in offspring pleasing to you, may she be approved and innocent.[47]

Even a crowned queen remained fundamentally a wife, a woman put firmly in her correct place.

Alongside this gender hierarchy, Hincmar also saw a hierarchy of religious status, in which clergy had a more exalted place than laity. (Although raised as a monk himself, he says little about where monks fitted into such a hierarchy.) This superiority was reflected in priests' ability to perform acts beyond those of other men or indeed of religious women. For example, Hincmar quotes a story of Bede in which a priest tried to cure a nun from a demon and the ulcers it had caused, but was only partially successful.

> And he [the priest] asked her whom he wanted to cure for advice on how she might be cured. She said, 'If you sprinkle me with oil consecrated for the sick and anoint me in this fashion, I will be at once restored to health ...' And he did as she suggested, and at once the ulcer ... took the remedy.[48]

The nun might know what action was required, but only a man with priestly authority could heal her.

Such authority carried a particular moral responsibility. As Hincmar puts it, discussing the case of a misbehaving priest: 'Since a priest is higher in grade

---

[47] Coronatio Hermintrudis reginae, *Capitularia regum Francorum*, ed. Alfred Boretius and Victor Krause (Hanover, 1883–97), vol. 2, no. 301, pp. 454–5: 'Domine sancte, pater omnipotens, aeterne Deus, qui potestate virtutis tuae ... homini ad imaginem tuam facto inseparabile mulieris adiutorium condidisti, ac femineo corpori de virili dedisti carne principium: ... respice propitius super hanc famulam tuam ... Fidelis et casta nubat in Christo, imitatrixque sanctarum permaneat feminarum. Sit amabilis ut Rachel viro, sapiens ut Rebecca, longaeva et fidelis ut Sarra ... Sit foecunda in tibi placita sobole, sit probata et innocens.' On this text see Jackson, 'Who wrote' at pp. 34–6; Julie Ann Smith, 'The earliest queen-making rites', *Church History* 66 (1997), pp. 18–35 at pp. 27–34.

[48] Hincmar of Rheims, *De divortio*, Responsio 15, p. 213: 'ab eadem ipsa, quam sanare volebat, consilium, quo sanaretur, accepisse. Si, inquit, oleum pro infirmis consecratum eidem medicamento asperseris sicque me perunxeris, statim sanitati restituar ... Fecit, ut illa suggesserat, statimque ulcus remedium ... accipere, consensit' (citing Bede, *In Lucae evangelium expositio*, ed. David Hurst, *Bedae venerabilis opera. Pars ii, 3: Opera exegetica*, CCSL 120 (Turnhout, 1983), pp. 5–425 at III, 8, 30, pp. 184–5).

than whatever Christian layman, his fault is the more serious.'[49] In particular, Hincmar saw bishops as ultimately superior to kings. He declares this most explicitly in the *acta* of the Synod of Fismes in 881:

> The dignity of bishops is so much greater than kings, since kings at the summit of the kingdom are anointed by bishops, but bishops cannot be consecrated by kings. And priesthood is a much heavier weight than kingship, in as much as they are also going to render account for the kings of men themselves in the divine examination.[50]

In turn, bishops were not all equals. Hincmar was a metropolitan and had firm views on the need for his suffragan bishops to be obedient to him.[51] More than that, he was archbishop of Rheims, successor to St Remigius, for whom Hincmar invented the title 'apostle of the Franks'.[52] Hincmar made repeated attempts to identify himself with the saint; indeed he saw himself as in some ways Remigius' vicar.[53]

In the last years of his life, Hincmar completed a *vita* of Remigius, drawing on earlier material he had collected. The work is a radically new form of hagiography, using Remigius' life as the basis on which to hang an encyclopaedic collection of liturgical, theological and homiletic material.[54] Marie-Céline Isaïa describes the work as a double mirror for both princes and bishops, with autobiographical overtones; Remigius is a model for every bishop of Rheims.[55] One of the ways in which Hincmar shows his exemplarity is by his stress on Remigius' role as a holy *man*:

> O man worthy for God in all things. He stood out by beauty in the habit of the soul itself ... he was terrible in appearance to the irreverent ... to be feared for severity, to be venerated for kindness. The gentleness of humility used to temper the judgement of authority.[56]

---

[49] Hincmar of Rheims, *De causa Teutfridi presbyteri*, PL, vol. 125, cols. 1111–16 at c. 5, col. 1113: 'Et presbyter, quanto gradu quolibet Christiano laico est celsior, tanto culpa illius est gravior'.

[50] Hincmar of Rheims, *Capitula in synodo apud S. Macram ab Hincmaro promulgata*, ibid., cols. 1069–86 at c.1, col. 1071: 'Et tanto est dignitas pontificum major quam regum, quia reges in culmen regium sacrantur a pontificibus, pontifices autem a regibus consecrari non possunt: et tanto gravius pondus est sacerdotum, quam regum, quanto etiam pro ipsis regibus hominum in divino reddituri sunt examine rationem'. See Nelson, 'Kingship, law and liturgy', at p. 247; Janet L. Nelson, 'Kingship and empire in the Carolingian world', in *Carolingian culture: emulation and innovation*, ed. Rosamond McKitterick (Cambridge, 1994), pp. 52–87 at pp. 66–7.

[51] Devisse, *Hincmar*, pp. 635–69; Nelson, 'Kingship, law and liturgy', at p. 248; Peter R. McKeon, *Hincmar of Laon and Carolingian politics* (Urbana, IL, 1978), pp. 88–98.

[52] Isaïa, *Remi de Reims*, p. 448.

[53] Ibid., pp. 436–9.

[54] Ibid., pp. 465–500, discusses the form of the text in detail.

[55] Ibid., pp. 491, 500.

[56] Hincmar of Rheims, *Vita Remigii episcopi Remensis auctore Hincmaro*, ed. Bruno Krusch, MGH Scriptores rerum Merovingicarum 3 (Hanover, 1896), pp. 250–341 at c. 4 p. 264 (hereafter *Vita Remigii*): 'O virum per omnia Deo dignum! Eminebat in ipso habitu animi pulchritude ... Erat

Hincmar of Rheims as a religious man

Hincmar recounts how Remigius desired God, sighing and weeping day and night.

> Glorified, he found the grace of God, since he did not seek the glory of the world ... Manfully holding the helm of faith, now he settled the anchor of hope in a calm anchorage. He held the shield of God so unwearyingly against the devil that he came to victory. We have in him a doctor from heaven.[57]

Indeed Remigius transcended all categories of sainthood:

> the innocence and power of the first Adam, before he sinned ... were understood to be reformed in that holy man, through the second Adam, our Lord Jesus Christ.[58]

Even if Hincmar was not himself the holy Remigius, as a religious man and Remigius' vicar he was theoretically at the top of a hierarchy that was both social and moral. It is easy therefore to read Hincmar simply as full of himself, self-important. Yet the question arises of whether he protests rather too much? In practice, the hierarchies of ninth-century Francia were rather messier than Hincmar's theories allowed.

HINCMAR'S HIERARCHIES: REALITIES

In Hincmar's actual dealings with women, for example, we can see a rather different picture from their theoretical subordination. We have only one fragmentary letter of Hincmar to a female correspondent, but Flodoard of Rheims also summarises twelve other letters of Hincmar to women. These summaries often provide enough detail, especially from the verbs used, to give not only a sense of Hincmar's message, but also of his tone.

Hincmar could be confrontational, even to royal women. Flodoard refers to a letter from Hincmar to Charles the Bald's second queen, Richildis, after she had imposed a new abbess on the convent of Origny:

> He [Hincmar] showed however by sacred authority how much danger the queen was in from that and that he sent her someone to instruct her to avoid this evil; she indeed not only did not amend her action, but made it much worse, against divine

---

 irreverentibus terribilis aspectu ... metuendus severitate, venerandus benignitate. Censuram auctoritatis temperabat mansuetudo humilitatis.'
[57] Ibid., p. 265: 'qui ideo gratiam Dei glorificatus invenit, quia mundi gloriam ... non quaesivit; qui gubernaculum fidei viriliter tenens, anchoram spei tranquilla jam in statione composuit; qui contra impetum diaboli, scutum Dei ita infatigabiliter tenuit, ut ad victoriam perveniret. Habemus in eo medicum e caelo.'
[58] Ibid., p. 266: 'ut innocentia et potestas primi Adae, antequam peccaret ... in isto sancto viro per secundum Adam Dominum nostrum Iesum Christum, reformata intelligerentur.'

authority, by placing as ruler a neophyte new in religion because of the worldly goods she had received from her.[59]

According to Flodoard, Hincmar also claimed in the letter to have admonished (*commonuerit*) Charles the Bald himself about Richildis' actions, and Charles' failure to correct them. Yet in letters to other queens, Hincmar is far more circumspect. He may have consecrated Charles the Bald's first wife, Ermentrude, but twenty years earlier, in 845, he sent one of his first letters as archbishop to her, requesting (*petens*) about the bishopric of Beauvais:

> that she advise the king lest his spirit be unsuitably influenced by someone in some direction about the disposition of this church, until he [Hincmar] coming into his service, can reveal to his ears what things are necessary to it.[60]

Hincmar could be equally deferential to non-royal women, such as Bertha, the wife of Count Gerhard of Vienne, a man controlling estates belonging to the church of Rheims in Provence. Hincmar requested (*petens*): 'that she might be a vigorous intervener with her husband for the same properties'.[61] At some unknown time during his long episcopate, he wrote to a *matrona* called Irminsinde who had allegedly forced a deacon into servitude, after he had legally been made free and ordained. Hincmar warned her (*monentque*) that he wanted to hear no more of such 'presumption' from Irminsinde, before concluding rather bathetically: 'since, if she presumed to do that, he himself would take care to avenge this legally and regularly'; adding that he warned (*commonere*) her thus, 'since he used to hold her familiarly dear'.[62] There is no trace here of his normal readiness to threaten excommunication of those attacking the church;[63] Hincmar knew enough to take some women's power extremely seriously.

---

[59] Flodoard of Rheims, *Historia Remensis ecclesiae*, 3–27, pp. 350–1, from 877–82 (Schrörs, no. 557): 'Ostendit autem ex auctoritate sacra, quantum inde regina periculum habeat, et quia miserit ad eam qui moneret illam hoc evadere malum; illa vero non solum non emendaverat, sed malo peius superaddiderat, contra divinam auctoritatem, neofitam scilicet in religione novellam provehendo ad regimen propter res terrenas acceptas ab illa.'

[60] Ibid., p. 348, from late 845 (Schrörs no. 4): 'Irmintrudi reginae pro Belvacensis ecclesie dispositione in pastoris electione, petens, ut suggerat regi, ne a quocumque in quamcumque partem animus illius indebite possit inflecti de huius ecclesiae dispositione, donec ipse in eius servitium veniens, que ipsi necessaria fuerint notificans ipsius auribus pandat.' Translation adapted from one by Joan Ferrante on *Epistolae* website [http://epistolae.ccnmtl.columbia.edu/letter/1000.html, accessed 22 September 2012].

[61] Ibid., p. 352, from 861–874 (Schrörs no. 343): 'Item Berte, uxori Gerardi comitis, pro rebus ecclesie sibi commisse in Provintia sitis, quas eidem Gerardo tuendas atque ordinandas conmiserat, petens, ut ipsa strenua sit interventrix apud coniugem suum pro rebus eisdem.'

[62] Ibid., p. 352, from 845–882 (Schrörs no. 524): 'monentque, ut talem presumptionem ulterius de ipsa non audiat, quia, si haec illa presumeret, ipse hoc legaliter atque regulariter vindicare studeret; adiciens eam se taliter commonere, quia caram familiariter ipsam habebat.'

[63] Devisse, *Hincmar*, pp. 544–6.

UNHOLY RELIGIOUS

Hincmar was conscious of powerful women using that power both for good and evil ends; he was also aware that it was not only women who could be 'fragile'.[64] The clerics of his province certainly showed all kinds of moral defects; Hincmar wrote an entire treatise on the procedure for dealing with criminal priests.[65] Both the statutes he wrote for his diocese and other letters also give us an unusually detailed view of religious men behaving badly.

Hincmar highlighted two particular problems: the misuse of money and the failure to keep a suitable distance from women. The priests of his diocese had to be firmly taught to maintain proper boundaries about church property. In 852, Hincmar told them: 'No priest must presume to give the chalice or paten or altar-cloth or priestly vestment in pledge to either an innkeeper, a trader, or whatever layman or a woman.'[66] He wanted inquiries made as to whether priests were supporting their relatives from church funds or buying up land and setting up buildings where women might carry out wool-production. Were they frequenting taverns or showing undue familiarity with women?[67] These were not purely theoretical concerns. Priests in Laon were practising usury.[68] The priest Teutfrid had stolen gold and other church valuables, including 'a tunic from Queen Emma'.[69] Hincmar's own nephew and namesake, whom Hincmar appointed as bishop of Laon, was later accused by him of simony and misusing church property, amongst many, many other faults.[70]

Indeed Hincmar saw the sins of Frankish men as extending to the highest levels of both secular and clerical hierarchies. In about 877 he had a vision written down, which a man called Bernold had supposedly seen.[71] Like many

---

[64] PL volumes 125 and 126 include more than sixty references to *fragilitas* in Hincmar's work, but apart from the reference to Duda, only one other passage specifically refers to *female* fragility (Hincmar, *De divortio*, Responsio 5, p. 143).

[65] Hincmar of Rheims, *De presbiteris criminosis. Ein Memorandum Erzbischof Hinkmars von Reims über straffällige Kleriker*, ed. Gerhard Schmitz, MGH Studien und Texte 34 (Hanover, 2004).

[66] Hincmar of Rheims, First capitulary, *Capitula episcoporum*, ed. Peter Brommer et al., 4 vols (Hanover, 1984–2005), vol. 2, pp. 34–45 at c. 11, p. 39: 'Ut nullus presbiter presumat calicem vel patenam aut pallam altaris vel vestimentum sacerdotale aut librum tabernario aut negotiatori aut cuilibet laico vel femine in vadimonium dare.' On Hincmar's episcopal capitularies, see Carine van Rhijn, *Shepherds of the Lord: priests and episcopal statutes in the Carolingian period*, Cultural Encounters in Late Antiquity and the Middle Ages 6 (Turnhout, 2007), pp. 139–70.

[67] Hincmar of Rheims, Second capitulary, *Capitula episcoporum*, vol. 2, pp. 45–70 at c. 17–21, pp. 50–9; Janet L. Nelson, 'Making ends meet: wealth and poverty in the Carolingian Church', in *The Church and wealth. Papers read at the 1986 Summer meeting and the 1987 Winter meeting of the Ecclesiastical History Society*, ed. W.J. Sheils and Diana Wood. Studies in Church History 24 (Oxford, 1987), pp. 25–35 at pp. 32–3.

[68] Gerhard Schmitz, 'Wucher in Laon. Eine neue Quelle zu Karl dem Kahlen und Hinkmar von Reims', *Deutsches Archiv für Erforschung des Mittelalters* 37 (1981), pp. 529–58.

[69] *De causa Teutfridi presbyteri*, PL, vol. 125, c. 3, col. 1111; *De presbiteris criminosis*, pp. 10–11. Another priest, Trisingus, had a relationship with his brother's stepdaughter, and then killed a relative of hers in a quarrel (pp. 7–8). On this case see van Rhijn, *Shepherds*, pp. 201–4.

[70] McKeon, *Hincmar of Laon*.

[71] Maaike van der Lugt, 'Tradition and revision: the textual tradition of Hincmar of Reims' "Visio Bernoldi" with a critical edition', *Archivum latinitatis medii aevi* 52 (1994), pp. 109–49;

Carolingian dreamers, Bernold saw souls tormented in the afterlife because of their sins; unlike some such texts, this was all-male suffering.[72] Of the specific figures mentioned, Bernold saw forty-one bishops (including Hincmar's bête-noir, Ebbo), Hincmar's former lord, the emperor Charles the Bald, as well as a nobleman and a count. Hincmar may in theory have seen men as morally stronger than women, but in practice he had no illusions that men were necessarily good.

MINDING THE GAP

How did Hincmar cope with the reality of a world where kings had power over bishops, a *matrona* might be able to enslave a cleric, and a successor to the holy Remigius might be in hell for his sins? Was the result either personal crisis or claims of a society in crisis? Hincmar's writings bear witness to the numerous difficulties suffered by Carolingian society, beset by heretics, pagan attacks, invasions by Carolingian rulers of their relatives' kingdoms and oppression of the poor.[73] He is keen to denounce sinful actions by sinners at all levels and sound dire warnings about God's punishments. Yet amongst his many dissections of the faults that had led to such disasters, a lack of masculinity is never mentioned as a factor.

Hincmar moved in a world in which both social structures and ideology helped maintain his elite position. Though women could be described as 'manly', there are very few examples of men being called effeminate, and the majority of these refer to marginal men, such as heretics or Jews. Rather than a 'gender continuum', the Carolingian evidence suggests more of a one-way gender barrier, with men unlikely to slide down into (social) womanhood.[74] In particular, unlike Carol Clover's Norse men, doomed to become unmanned with age, Hincmar could claim, on patristic authority, that royal counsellors should be 'old and wise and sober men'.[75]

The early medieval religious elite also had their celibate status supported by both ideology and practice. In the west, from the sixth century onwards, the 'battle for chastity' characteristic of late antique male asceticism had been

---

Paul Edward Dutton, *The politics of dreaming in the Carolingian empire* (Lincoln, NE, 1994), pp. 183–94.

[72] Dutton, *Politics*, pp. 63, 68: both the *Visio Wettini* and the *Visio cuisadam pauperculae mulier* (*Vision of the Poor Woman of Laon*) refer to female sinners in hell.

[73] On the invasions of the west Frankish kingdom by Louis the German in 858 and 875, see Janet L. Nelson, *Charles the Bald* (London, 1992), pp. 181–91, 239–41; on Hincmar's concern for the poor, see Jean Devisse, '"Pauperes" et "paupertas" dans le monde carolingien: ce qu'en dit Hincmar de Reims', *Revue du Nord* 48 (1966), pp. 273–87.

[74] Stone, *Morality*, pp. 319–22.

[75] Hincmar of Rheims, *De regis persona et regio ministerio*, PL, vol. 125, cols. 833–56, at c. 2, col. 835: 'Justitia vero regis est . . . senes et sapientes et sobrios consiliarios habere'. The quotation is from Pseudo-Cyprian, *Pseudo-Cyprianus: De XII abusivis saeculi*, ed. Siegmund Hellmann, Texte und Untersuchungen zur Geschichte der Altchristlichen Literatur 3. Reihe, Bd. 4, Heft 1 (Leipzig, 1909), p. 51. On the *De duodecim abusivis* see Rob Meens, 'Politics, mirrors of princes and the Bible: sins, kings and the well-being of the realm', *Early Medieval Europe* 7 (1998), pp. 345–57.

Hincmar of Rheims as a religious man

replaced by a new form of monasticism, structured around the corporate chastity of groups of enclosed male and female virgins. As Albrecht Diem puts it, 'sexuality transformed from an attribute of human sinfulness to a manageable opposite of virginity'.[76] Hincmar's own celibate gender identity had probably been formed in his monastic childhood, rather than the more troubling process of having to acquire it as an adult.[77] He also had no need for the female domestic service that made lesser clerics vulnerable to scandal. As Mayke de Jong puts it, Hincmar was 'a powerful bishop who could afford to stay away from women'.[78]

Hincmar's more personal responses to discrepancies between his ideology of religious male status and the realities of clerical life are also visible. They show ways in which he could draw on religious tradition to understand and assimilate disconcerting experiences of (relative) powerlessness or moral failure. One important tool was humility. As we have already seen, Hincmar praised Remigius' humility; he was also keen to display it himself. The first complete letter we have preserved from him begins:

> Hincmar, bishop of the holy church of the metropolis of Rheims and the poor servant of all the servants of the Lord, greetings to the simple beloved sons of this holy see, whom I serve diligently by God's command, under the care of the pontificate of St Remigius, highest and glorious archbishop.[79]

Similar tropes recur repeatedly: Hincmar is 'by name, not merit, bishop of Rheims'.[80] In 860 the synod of Tusey asked for his advice on the marriage problems of Count Stephen of the Auvergne; Hincmar, before literally laying down the law, insisted:

> And therefore, not as if to those not knowing these things which follow ... nor as claiming special authority of knowledge for myself, or boasting audacity of

---

[76] Albrecht Diem, 'The gender of the religious: wo/men and the invention of monasticism', in *Oxford handbook of women and gender in medieval Europe*, ed. Judith M. Bennett and Ruth Mazo Karras (New York, forthcoming). There was a revival of the concept of chastity as a battle in the twelfth century: see e.g. John H. Arnold, 'The labour of continence: masculinity and clerical virginity', in *Medieval virginities*, ed. Anke Bernau, Sarah Salih and Ruth Evans (Cardiff, 2003), pp. 102–18; Jacqueline Murray, 'Masculinizing religious life: sexual prowess, the battle for chastity and monastic identity', in *Holiness and masculinity*, ed. Cullum and Lewis, pp. 24–42.

[77] This contrasts with the tendency later in the Middle Ages for males to become (celibate) clerics only as adults: see e.g. Patricia H. Cullum, 'Clergy, masculinity and transgression in late medieval England', in *Masculinity in medieval Europe*, ed. Hadley, pp. 178–96; Jennifer D. Thibodeaux, 'From boys to priests: adolescence, masculinity and the parish clergy in medieval Normandy', in *Negotiating clerical identities*, ed. Thibodeaux, pp. 136–58.

[78] de Jong, '*Imitatio morum*', at p. 59.

[79] Hincmar of Rheims, *Epistolae* 1–206, ed. Ernst Perels, MGH Epp. 8 (Berlin, 1939), Epistola 37, p. 12, from 849–850: 'Hincmarus sanctae metropolis ecclesiae Remorum episcopus et omnium servorum Domini exiguus famulus dilectis filiis simplicibus huius sanctae sedis, cui auctore Deo deservio sub cura pontificatus beati Remigii summi et gloriosi archiepiscopi, salutem.'

[80] See e.g. Hincmar, *Epistolae*, nos. 99 (to Charles the Bald), 132 (to Bishop Adventius of Metz), 169 (to Pope Nicholas I) (pp. 44, 74, 144, Schrörs, nos. 103, 137, 174).

decision, but as a servant of the Church and your servant, namely of all the servants of God and servant to the Lord's people, I have taken care to collect anything, not as I ought, but as I could, from obedience of devotion.[81]

Such protestations of humility are, of course, entirely conventional, but we also need to take them seriously. Hincmar's humility was potentially an internal buffer against adversity, a reassurance of a brighter future. If he did not crave the glory of this world, he would be glorified in the next, like his model Remigius.

And indeed, in the *Visio Bernoldi*, this glorification was already almost visible to Hincmar and his audience. In Bernold's dream, Charles the Bald, with worms gnawing at his body, tells Bernold that his punishment is because he did not listen to the advice of Hincmar and others of his faithful men. Bernold must go to Hincmar and ask for his help. In the dream, Bernold does this and sees Hincmar about to say mass with his clerics. He passes on the emperor's message to Hincmar and is immediately returned to Charles, now with his body restored and clothed in royal garments.[82] As Paul Dutton comments: 'the living Hincmar saw in the *Vision of Bernold* not only a demonstration of his blessedness, but also of his immense intercessory power.'[83]

For Hincmar, then, a religious man, however humble he might be, controlled potentially cosmic powers via the sacraments. Yet what if he himself fell from grace, like the forty-one bishops in Bernold's vision? One last, strange story from the *Visio Bernoldi* explored how even a fallen bishop might be restored. The story discusses St Genebaudus, whom Remigius made bishop of the newly-created see of Laon. Genebaudus had left his wife, St Remigius' niece, in order to enter the religious life, but 'confident in the loftiness of his grade', continued to allow her to visit him frequently.[84] Hincmar goes on:

> Whence it happened that repeated visits and frequent and tempting conversations with the woman softened the heart of the bishop ... with chaff, that is the material of female flesh, moved by fire, and diabolical persuasion, like a furious wind, exciting the fire of lust, the ardour of luxury erupted into flames, and sleeping with his former wife, the woman conceived.[85]

Genebaudus called his son Latro (Robber); he and his wife later also had a daughter, whom he called Vulpecula (Little Fox). At that point, 'recalled to

---

[81] Hincmar, *Epistolae*, no. 136, p. 90 (Schrörs, no. 142): 'Et idcirco non quasi nescientibus haec, quae sequuntur ... nec ut arrogans mihi auctoritatem specialis scientiae vel iactans diffinitionis audaciam, sed ut ecclesiae ac vester omnium videlicet servorum Domini servus et plebis dominicae famulus, quamquam non ut debui, tamen ut potui, devotionis oboedientia colligere ... procuravi.'

[82] *Visio Bernoldi*, c. 3, in van der Lugt, 'Tradition and revision', pp. 143–5.

[83] Dutton, *Politics*, p. 187.

[84] Hincmar, *Vita Remigii*, c. 16, p. 301: 'Genebaudus plus quam necesse fuerat de anteacta vita et gradus sublimitate confidens.'

[85] Ibid.: 'Unde contigit, ut crebre visitationes et blanda ac frequentia mulieris colloquia ... mollitiem cor episcopi emollirent ... admota igni palea, id est carnis muliebris materia, libidinis ignem suasione diabolica, quasi vento vehementi, exagitante, ardor luxuriae in flammas erupit, et concumbens cum eadem quondam uxore sua, mulier concepit.'

himself', Genebaudus confessed to Remigius, who told him that nothing was impossible for God and that he must do worthy penance. Genebaudus then spent seven years in a small hut doing this penance, while Remigius administered the see for him.[86] Genebaudus' penance was so sincere that in his seventh year, an angel of the Lord came to release him, but he refused to leave his hut until Remigius himself confirmed that his penance might end. The angel then appeared to Remigius, who came to Laon and restored Genebaudus to his office. Genebaudus spent the rest of his life in sanctity and justice, preaching how much the Lord had done for him;[87] he was succeeded in his see by his son Latro, 'himself holy'.[88]

Marie-Céline Isaïa, the most recent researcher on Remigius and his legend, is sceptical about this story, especially given the suspicious parallels to Hincmar's own insubordinate nephew, Hincmar of Laon.[89] Yet as a story essentially created by Hincmar, it provides interesting insights. Firstly, it reminds us of the difficulties of interpreting language as gendered. Lynda Coon has argued for *mollitia* (softness) and its cognates as being early medieval code words for effeminacy, following in a classical Roman tradition that valued the 'hard' bodies of upper-class men.[90] Yet although Genebaudus' 'soft heart' is clearly a sign of his weakness here, hardness of heart was certainly not desirable for a Christian. Attempting to impose simple gender binaries on such metaphors may obscure more than it reveals.

This is particularly the case because the story implies the ultimate unimportance of women to Hincmar.[91] The form of the narrative owes much to Hincmar's wish to show that any bishop of Laon must be subordinate to the archbishop of Rheims. That may explain why we hear nothing of the fate of either Genebaudus' wife or Vulpecula. Yet it is still noticeable that, unlike authors from other eras, Hincmar does not indulge in extended misogynistic rhetoric, beyond a passing reference to female flesh as 'chaff'.[92]

Women as temptation are not the important issue here; two other moral messages are. One is again about humility: Genebaudus falls because he is over-confident in his own 'loftiness', but is redeemed by his humility, as shown by

---

[86] Ibid., pp. 301–3.
[87] Ibid., pp. 303–4.
[88] Ibid., p. 305.
[89] Isaïa, *Remi de Reims*, pp. 151–6, 437–40. She notes the existence of a Bishop Genebaudus of Laon in 549, but that it is unlikely that he was a relative of Remigius or consecrated as bishop in Remigius' lifetime.
[90] See e.g. Lynda L. Coon, *Dark Age bodies: gender and monastic practice in the early medieval West* (Philadelphia, 2011), p. 77.
[91] Cf. Karras, *From boys*, p. 11: 'The sheer insignificance that women held for men struggling over their masculinity in some cultural contexts forms as much a part of the complex history of medieval misogyny as do discourses that overtly critique women ... The subjection of women was always a part of masculinity, but not always its purpose or its central feature.'
[92] Compare e.g. Dyan Elliott, 'The priest's wife: female erasure and the Gregorian reform', in *Medieval religion: new approaches*, ed. Constance Hoffman Berman (New York, 2005), pp. 123–55 at pp. 127–40 on successive re-writings of the *vita* of St Severus of Ravenna.

his obedience to his uncle. The second message is about the power of sincere penance, combined with clerical authority, to redeem any sin.

Frankish reformers in the eighth and ninth centuries had developed a complex discourse and practice of confession and penance.[93] Hincmar himself had repeatedly become involved in arguments about distinctions between 'secret' and 'public' penance and their aftermath. This was a key issue raised during discussions of King Lothar II's attempts to divorce his wife Theutberga and remarry, but it had far more personal resonances for Hincmar.[94] Had Ebbo's regaining of his position as archbishop of Rheims in 840–41 after doing penance been lawful, and were the clergy he had ordained then validly ordained? The answer depended on contested accounts of the exact form and contents of Ebbo's confession in 835.[95]

Hincmar, protective of his own episcopal status, had always firmly resisted the possibility of a bishop being able to retain his position after doing penance.[96] Now, however, with Ebbo long dead, he was prepared to say that the church was able to loose or bind *anything* on earth.[97] The story of Genebaudus, he claimed, showed that 'the truly humble and penitent' could be returned to their former position at the altar, just as David remained a king after penance and Peter an apostle.[98] Remigius' behaviour demonstrates a transcendental option beyond the church's normal rules.

Here, the humble religious man's status is secure both in this world and the next. If he should ever fall from grace, confession and penance allow him once again to be restored to his rightful position in the social and moral hierarchy. Nor is a man necessarily feminised by such failure;[99] Hincmar's parallels to Genebaudus are the Biblical heroes David and Peter. There could be little room for crisis in a conceptual world such as this.

Our access to Hincmar's subjective view of his identity as a religious man is inevitably limited, yet we can gain some insights. Hincmar used the resources of Christian texts both to build up an ideal of social and gender hierarchy, and also to cope when reality failed to match that image. He could still take for granted women's overall God-given subordination; clerical masculinity related primarily to other men, rather than to women. Such masculinity also remained ideologically secure, even when clerics themselves might lapse temporarily or be

---

[93] See e.g. Mayke de Jong, *The penitential state: authority and atonement in the age of Louis the Pious, 814–840* (Cambridge, 2009); *A new history of penance*, ed. Abigail Firey, Brill's Companion to the Christian Tradition 14 (Leiden, 2008), especially the chapters by Meens and Firey.

[94] Stuart Airlie, 'Private bodies and the body politic in the divorce case of Lothar II', *Past and Present* no. 161 (1998), pp. 3–38 at pp. 26–7; Heidecker, *Divorce*, pp. 82–5.

[95] Patzold, *Episcopus*, pp. 316–23; de Jong, *Penitential state*, pp. 252–9.

[96] See e.g. Hincmar, *De divortio*, Responsio 2, pp. 125–9.

[97] Hincmar, *Vita Remigii*, c. 16, p. 306: 'In eo enim, quod dicitur: "Quaecumque solveritis, erunt soluta", nihil excipitur, nihil non comprehensum relinquitur. Igitur omni electorum aecclesiae iuxta modum culparum vel penitentiae ligandi ac solvendi quantorumcumque vel qualiumcumque peccatorum datur auctoritas.'

[98] Ibid.

[99] Cf. above, n. 74.

subordinated to others. Hincmar's gendered religious thought was clearly a tool for advancing his own status; it may also have been an important consolation for him at times when, despite his power, he was not able to make other men conform to his views.

THE DEFENCE OF CLERICAL MARRIAGE: RELIGIOUS IDENTITY AND MASCULINITY IN THE WRITINGS OF ANGLO-NORMAN CLERICS

Jennifer D. Thibodeaux

A poem of unknown provenance from the late eleventh or early twelfth century shares what must have been the perspective of a married priest at a time of changing laws on clerical marriage. The writer tells us:

> We married clergy were born to be made fun of, to be ridiculed, to be criticised by everyone ... you draw up harsh laws, bitter statutes, and make things generally impossible for us. You deny it is right to touch a woman's bed and to consummate the marriage rite in the bridal chamber. But it is the natural right of a man to enjoy his wife ... this response rightly takes account of the laws of nature: if no one propagated, if no man procreated, everything would come to an end ... a half man, an effeminate, you steal the prostitute's joys ... you are driven by a lust which all of nature abhors.[1]

This writer, clearly a married cleric, touches upon the prominent beliefs on clerical marriage held by those who defended it as a right. He points to the ridicule, the shame, and the dishonour created by laws banning clerical marriage. He suggests that such laws are new and severe, that such decrees do not consider the real effects on clerical families. He points to the importance of procreative sexuality and its place in the 'natural order'. Finally, he lashes out at the perceived instigators of such laws: sodomite reformers.

In short, the unknown writer of this poem touches upon all of the major points used by clerical writers for the defence of clerical marriage in the late eleventh and early twelfth centuries in Normandy. These clerical writers were

---

[1] Translated by John Boswell, *Christianity, social tolerance and homosexuality* (Chicago, 1980), pp. 399–401. This poem is titled 'We married clergy' (*Nos uxorati*). Boswell pinpoints the writing of the poem to the twelfth or thirteenth century, but I would suggest an earlier time period, before 1150, due to the language of the poem, which suggests that married clerics could still identify as such, and due to the commonalities of the poem with the polemical treatises defending clerical marriage from the same time period. Boswell's dating of the poem is likely due to its placement in a thirteenth-century manuscript, housed in Munich (Bayerische Staatsbibliothek, clm 17212). All translations are my own unless otherwise noted.

Defence of clerical marriage

clearly defending the right to take a wife, but they were also reacting to the ideology of clerical manhood, an ideal that took shape concurrently with ecclesiastical reform. This ideology was part of an agenda to 'masculinise' religious life, characterising ascetic self-denial and the struggle against sexual desires as performances of manliness.[2] Clerical manhood elevated the monastic ideal of self-restraint and chastity as a standard for the secular clergy. In short, proponents of this ideal changed the nature of religious life for secular clerics by waging a campaign effectively to deny them wives and legitimate children.

Married clerics did not remain silent as celibacy legislation was introduced and gradually enforced. Celibacy laws, which sought to impose a new standard on the male body, prompted the creation of a resisting discourse, one that not only defended clerics' right to marry, but also defended the necessity of procreative sexuality. As the discourse of clerical manhood increased in its frequency and dissemination by the reformist party, there was a concerted effort on the part of some writers to defend a traditional form of manliness, one based on marriage and procreation. In some cases, these writers did not deny that celibacy was a higher, even more desirable, state; they did, however, defend marriage as an alternative and legitimate performance of manliness.

While some scholars have explored how ecclesiastical reformers sought to civilise the nobility with their messages on marriage and procreation, only Jo Ann McNamara has studied how this message potentially affected the secular clergy. Reformers advocated legitimate, indissoluble, and monogamous marriage for the laity at the same time as insisting upon celibacy for the clergy; this posed a dilemma for priests and other clerics, what McNamara called the '*herrenfrage*', a crisis in male identity. McNamara argued that clerics were forced to choose between their ingrained cultural notions of masculinity or risk loss of manliness by embracing celibacy, a path which would offer them no standard by which to define their gender identity. They could either accept the propaganda of legitimate marriage intended for others of their social status, and face censure; or adhere to the reform ideal of clerical celibacy, a rule that could provoke what McNamara called gender confusion.[3]

The McNamara theory is plausible, yet a crisis in masculine identity assumes an abrupt, literally automatic cultural transformation of a group that historically, at least in Normandy, had always engaged in publicly-recognised marriages. Documentary evidence from the eleventh to the thirteenth century in this region shows the continued practice of marriage or marriage-like unions among the secular clergy. If marriages for the Anglo-Norman clergy were a subject of

---

[2] Jacqueline Murray, 'Masculinizing religious life: sexual prowess, the battle for chastity, and monastic identity', in *Holiness and masculinity in the Middle Ages*, ed. P.H. Cullum and Katherine J. Lewis (Cardiff, 2004); Ruth Mazo Karras, 'Thomas Aquinas's chastity belt: clerical masculinity in medieval Europe', in *Gender and Christianity in medieval Europe: new perspectives*, ed. Lisa M. Bitel and Felice Lifshitz (Philadelphia, 2008), pp. 52–67. For continence as a performance of manliness, see John Arnold, 'The labor of continence: masculinity and clerical virginity', in *Medieval virginities*, ed. A. Bernau, R. Evans and S. Salih (Cardiff, 2003), pp. 102–18.

[3] JoAnn McNamara, 'The *Herrenfrage*: the restructuring of the gender system, 1050–1150', in *Medieval masculinities*, ed. Clare A. Lees (Minneapolis, 1994), pp. 3–29.

contention before the twelfth century, that is, if the local communities did not accept married priests, the sources certainly do not indicate this. There are, of course, limited sources for understanding the perspective of married priests, and most of what we draw from this time period is from monastic sources which were typically hostile to clerical unions. But the limited, anecdotal evidence that comes to us from the twelfth century, from such monastic authors as Orderic Vitalis and William of Malmesbury, suggests that Normans supported the tradition of clerical marriage and even staunchly defended the tradition in the face of eradication. How common this support for clerical unions was in twelfth-century Europe as a whole is unknown. Thus, a real 'crisis' could only have occurred if celibacy mandates were truly immediate and revolutionary in sweeping away, overnight as it were, the marriages of the clergy. As long as Anglo-Norman bishops took wives, and appointed married clerics to elite positions, clerical marriage was still permissible and the preaching of a few monastic reformers would have hardly caused alarm. For instance, Bishop Roger of Salisbury attended the 1102 Council of Westminster, where Anselm first legislated against clerical marriage, ordering that clerics could not marry, and if they were already married, must separate from their wives; yet there is no evidence that he experienced any 'crisis' over his marriage to Matilda of Ramsbury, and may have even married her after he became bishop.[4] The chroniclers from this time period never suggest that clerics were in 'crisis' over their gender identity because of the 'new laws'. Even in their strictest condemnation of these unions, monastic writers still portray Normans defending clerical marriage as a long-held tradition, intricately tied into their views of manliness. The message of ecclesiastical reformers on masculinity, marriage and procreation which had been intended primarily for the laity undoubtedly affected the clergy's defence of their own marriages.

The Norman treatises that defended clerical marriage were authored before the year 1123, when the ecumenical council Lateran I took the unequivocal step of dissolving all marriage contracts of clerics in major orders.[5] Anglo-Norman reform efforts prior to Lateran I had failed to separate these men from their wives. At the time these treatises in favour of clerical marriage were written, clerical marriage was still *legally valid*; Anglo-Norman decrees had never declared these unions invalid, but had only stipulated the separation of clerical husbands from their wives, and the cessation of sexual relations. The language used to describe these unions had already changed, however, and references to 'concubine' instead of 'wife' were soon being utilised in legal discourse. In this case, discourse did affect practice as regional reformers began the process of socially invalidating clerical marriages by their emphasis on these unions as concubinage. In the currency of reform-era language, clerical marriage no longer existed. But in the mindset of clerical advocates, these marriages were not only valid, but had always existed with social and ecclesiastical acceptance.

---

[4] Eadmer, *Historia novorum*, trans. Geoffrey Bosanquet (London, 1964), pp. 149–50.
[5] Norman P. Tanner, *Decrees of the Ecumenical Councils, vol. I: Nicea I to Lateran V* (Georgetown, Washington DC, 1990), p. 194, for Lateran I (1123), canon 21.

Defence of clerical marriage

Scholarly treatments of clerical marriage have generally focused on the legislative history behind the imposition of celibacy, without considering the lived experiences of married priests. The documents under examination here have been studied by other scholars. Anne Barstow's *Married priests and the reforming papacy: the eleventh-century debates* has examined the debate over clerical marriage in Europe as a whole, focusing on this debate as the most pressing issue of the reform agenda. More recently, Erwin Frauenknecht's *Die Verteidigung der Priesterehe in der Reformzeit* analysed in great detail the origin of several pro-clerical marriage documents, including the ones under discussion here, and produced new editions to replace those appearing in the *Monumenta Germaniae Historica*.[6] What has not yet been examined is how these pro-clerical marriage documents reflect the debate over the intersection of religious identity, sexuality, and masculinity. The Anglo-Norman realm makes an excellent case study of gender identity and the clergy precisely because it provides existing treatises written by clerics in support of clerical marriage at a pivotal moment in the late eleventh and early twelfth centuries.

The voices that supported clerical marriages, while passionate and polemical, do not appear to have had doubts about their gender identity. The Norman texts in favour of clerical marriage allow us to hear an educated, clerical voice on the subject, one that links manliness to marriage and procreation, as well as to social status. The clerical writings examined below show that at least among the elite clerics there existed a conception of masculinity that fitted the lay model better than the monastic one. It also illustrates that the authors of this discourse made use of some of the same language and ideas that ecclesiastical reformers deployed for the reform of lay marriage. Additionally, these authors show that the clerical community in this region supported marriage and saw legitimacy in what reformers claimed was impure and illegal. They defended marriage using a rhetoric tied to an essentialist definition of manliness, one based on virility and sexuality. These authors do not link manliness to asceticism, but they do implicitly tie marital sexuality to the sexual control of the male body. In this manner, the discourse of clerical marriage responds to the ideology of clerical manhood with similar concepts.

THE CLERICAL WRITERS BEHIND THE DEFENCE OF CLERICAL MARRIAGE

It has been argued previously that the authors of these pro-clerical marriage tracts derived their ideas from a common source, the so-called *Rescripta* attributed at different times to both Ulric, bishop of Augsburg (923–73), and Ulric,

---

[6] Anne Barstow, *Married priests and the reforming papacy: the eleventh-century debates* (Lewiston, ME, 1982); Erwin Frauenknecht, *Die Verteidigung der Priesterehe in der Reformzeit* (Hanover, 1997). All of these documents were first printed in *Monumenta Germaniae Historica, Libelli de Lite*, III (Hannover, 1891–7), pp. 588–96, 645–55. They were also discussed by Augustin Fliche, in *La réforme grégorienne*, vol. III, *L'opposition antigrégorienne* (Louvain, 1937), pp. 13–38.

bishop of Imola (1053–63). It has more recently been argued that this letter originated in the German diocese of Constance.⁷ The *Rescripta* was thought to be a response to the celibacy decrees of Pope Nicholas II (1058–61); those harsh statutes which had shocked so many within the medieval Church, severe measures against clerical marriage, with a mandate for the laity to avoid the church services of married priests. Under these decrees, married priests who did not separate from their wives faced excommunication if they continued to preside over Mass. The *Rescripta* may equally have been written in response to similar reform efforts by Gregory VII at his 1075 synod.⁸ The *Rescripta* has already been discussed in detail by Anne Barstow, who has accepted Augustin Fliche's assertion that the document influenced the writers of two other pro-clerical marriage tracts, both living in Normandy.⁹ Erwin Frauenknecht has instead demonstrated that the Pseudo-Ulrich *Rescripta* was not the basis for these other writings, but that the common source was Cassiodorus.¹⁰ If this theory is correct, then the pro-clerical marriage texts discussed below are more culturally relevant than previously thought; they are more indicative of a Norman cultural attitude to clerical marriage, and less a simple rendition of another pro-marriage tract. The *Rescripta*'s emphasis on the scriptural and patristic foundations for clerical marriage, along with the idea that the enforcement of celibacy would force priests to commit more heinous sins, are all ideas found, to some extent, in the Norman texts, the *Tractatus pro clericorum conubio*, the *Treatise on Grace*,¹¹ and the writings of the Norman Anonymous. The *Rescripta* may have been a response to the Roman celibacy decrees, but the use of similar ideas by Norman writers shows that a resisting discourse had developed in this region as well. Furthermore, the texts, while similar in many ways, also emphasise different key elements in the defence of clerical marriage. When examined together, they reveal a very strong cultural outlook on masculinity and sexuality; they also illustrate a common resistance to the destruction of clerical marriages and clerical families. It is perhaps the only time that the collective voices of married clerics can be heard, and it is resoundingly a strong, gendered defence of the clerical right to marry.

The texts to be discussed here were written within a relatively short time span, although the precise dating and even the geographical origins of these tracts are not conclusively determined. The four primary writings on clerical marriage for Normandy are the *Tractatus pro clericorum conubio* (c. 1077–78), the *Treatise on Grace*, and tracts J22/26 and J25 written by the Norman Anonymous

---

⁷ See Frauenknecht, *Die Verteidigung*, p. 70, for this assertion.
⁸ Ibid., p. 70.
⁹ Barstow, *Married priests*, pp. 107–20. She asserts that the *Tractatus pro clericorum conubio* and the *Treatise on Grace* were both influenced by the *Rescripta*. The original document, *Pseudo-Udlarici epistola de continentia clericorum*, is published in *Monumenta Germaniae*, vol. I, pp. 244–60, and in Frauenknecht, *Die Verteidigung*, pp. 203–15.
¹⁰ See Frauenknecht, *Die Verteidigung*, pp. 12–34, for an extensive discussion on this subject.
¹¹ For the sake of simplicity, I have adopted Anne Barstow's title for this work, for which the incipit is 'cum sub liberi arbitrii potestate creati simus', as shown in Erwin Frauenknecht's edition.

Defence of clerical marriage

(c. 1102–10).¹² These writings were influenced by the resurgence of celibacy legislation and enforcement in this region. The authors of these tracts were likely associated with the cathedral chapters of Normandy, where they would have obtained significant education and experience in environments where clerical marriage flourished. Their use of scriptural and patristic writings demonstrates their access to a library of some kind. While scholars have assumed that the *Tractatus* was a response to either of the ecumenical councils at Poitiers and Autun, it is as likely that the more geographically relevant 1072 Council of Rouen, held under the archbishop, John d'Avranches, and/or the 1076 Council of Winchester, held under Lanfranc, archbishop of Canterbury, prompted the creation of this text; and that the *Treatise on Grace* along with the Norman Anonymous J22/26 and J25 tracts, written almost a generation later, were more likely responses to the anti-clerical marriage legislation of Anselm, archbishop of Canterbury, in 1102 and/or 1108. Thus, all of these texts were influenced to some degree by Anglo-Norman ecclesiastical reform. The ecumenical decrees which would unequivocally dissolve clerical marriages were not to come until the second and third decades of the twelfth century with Lateran I (1123) and Lateran II (1139). These councils destroyed clerical marriage, at least in theory.¹³

These texts functioned as a response to local and regional efforts to destroy clerical unions. The authors of these documents direct their polemics to a group they hold responsible for the celibacy campaign in the Anglo-Norman Church: monastic reformers. These texts share some common arguments, but also focus on distinct issues that each author found most disturbing. In this manner, we can see the personal perspective of a cleric defending his right to marry, along with his conception of masculinity. The identity of the author who wrote the *Tractatus pro clericorum conubio* was probably a cathedral canon or cleric, possibly even an archdeacon.¹⁴ The date and geographical origins of the writing are in dispute; at the very least, we know that the document originated somewhere in northern France (including Normandy) sometime between 1075 and 1078. While there are many plausible theories of origin, I believe there is strong evidence for locating the document within the archdiocese of Rouen.¹⁵ The cleric who wrote the

---

[12] The dates and authorship of the *Treatise on Grace* and the *Tractatus* have recently been questioned. Barstow has provided a date of 1075 for the *Treatise on Grace*, while Frauenknecht has argued for a later date in the 1120s. I place the document within the range from 1102 to 1110, due to its common elements with the Norman Anonymous tracts. I consider these documents to be a part of Anglo-Norman clerical culture, and I examine their origins more fully in my current project, 'The manly priest: clerical marriage, masculinity and Anglo-Norman reform'.

[13] Tanner, *Ecumenical Councils*, pp. 191, 198. Lateran II, canons 7 and 21; Lateran III, canons 6 and 7.

[14] Brigitte Mejins, 'Opposition to clerical continence and the Gregorian celibacy legislation in the diocese of Thèrouanne: *Tractatus pro clericorum conubio* (c. 1077–1078)', *Sacris erudiri* 47 (2008), p. 281; Barstow, *Married priests*, p. 116, claims, as does Fliche, that he was an Italian cleric living in Normandy.

[15] Erwin Frauenknecht and Brigitte Mejins have both posited theories of origin. Frauenknecht has allowed for the possibility of the document being produced in either the archdiocese of Sens or Rouen, while Mejins has offered a radically different theory that it was produced in the diocese of Thèrouanne.

Treatise on Grace was familiar with the theological work of Anselm of Bec, and drew upon that work in his defence of marriage.[16] The Norman Anonymous authored many tracts and has still escaped conclusive identification, although there are strong reasons to believe he was William Bona Anima, abbot of St Stephen's of Caen (1070–1079) and archbishop of Rouen (1079–1110), and the son of a Norman bishop.[17] If Bona Anima was the author of these texts, then he would be one of the few monastic proponents of clerical marriage. His tracts J22/26, *Apologia pro filiis sacerdotum et concubinarum*, and J25, *Scire velim quis primus instituit*, concern clerical marriage and the ordination of priests' sons. Tract J25 shares common elements with the *Treatise on Grace*, and this suggests that one of the authors had read the work of the other. What is notable about tract J25 is that it too utilises Anselmian language, even taking direct passages from Anselm's *Cur deus homo*. Thus, the Norman Anonymous was well versed in Anselm's work and his tract was more likely a response to Anselm's conciliar legislation against clerical marriage than a reaction to the Council of Rouen in 1096, as has been previously argued.[18]

These writers created arguments that reflect an Anglo-Norman clerical identity. They offer proof that Norman clerics strongly resisted clerical celibacy and could offer logical, well-constructed arguments for the legitimacy of clerical unions. These texts, then, were composed in a crucial time period in which the battle over clerical marriage was quickly becoming a war.

THE JUSTIFICATION OF CLERICAL MARRIAGE AND THE CONTROL OF THE MALE BODY

Masculinity and religious identity had not been traditionally regarded as separate experiences for the Anglo-Norman priesthood before the introduction of celibacy legislation. A cleric in the major orders of priest, deacon and subdeacon could reasonably expect to preside over a household in the same manner as a layman of the same social stratum, and thereby achieve the same degree of masculine status. These pro-clerical marriage texts illustrate the common concerns of their authors on the changing norms of masculine social identity as it related to their religious vocation. One of the central ideas that they refuted was the reformist belief that clerical marriage was unlawful and impure. In order to counter this claim, the advocates of clerical marriage justified such unions on the basis of historical precedent, showing with a deep knowledge of scripture that the Bible permitted priestly marriage.

All of these authors begin their defence by arguing that clerical marriage had always had a place in both scripture and ecclesiastical tradition, and that the laws

---

[16] See Frauenknecht, *Die Verteidigung*, pp. 138–43, where he argues for a later dating of the tract, as late as 1129.

[17] George Williams, *The Norman Anonymous of 1100 AD.* (Cambridge, MA, 1951).

[18] See *Married priests*, pp. 157–61. The Electronic Norman Anonymous Project (ENAP) has offered a different interpretation, one that I accept. See http://normananonymous.org/ENAP

against such marriages were new inventions. Their response and the language used in this response are very telling of their perspectives as married clerics. For example, the *Tractatus* emphasises the ideas that legitimate marriage had always been permitted to priests, and such unions were neither adultery nor fornication (*adulterina vel fornicaria*), as the 'architects' of the new laws (*novi dogmatis*) suggest.[19] The author then insinuates that, because such laws were not traditional, the 'foreign hypocrites' who promoted these laws were 'adulterators of the canons and the creators of new traditions'.[20] Elsewhere, he quotes the book of Job, to claim once again that reformers were 'creators of lies and cultivators of perverse laws' (*fabricators esse mendatii et cultores perversorum dogmatum*).[21] Over and over again, the *Tractatus* author places the reformers in a suspect category, attacking their honour with accusations of mendacity. In a manner of speaking, he further suggests that enforced celibacy was a perverse condition. Reformers, he argued, went against societal tradition with these laws, even defeating what has been firmly established through scripture.

The Norman Anonymous also utilised a polemic that refuted any notion that celibacy decrees were biblical. In his tract J25, the writer began by questioning whose ordinance it was to institute celibacy. He decided that it was a 'tradition of man' not 'an institution of God.' Such decrees could not be found in either the Old or the New Testament, or in the writings of the apostles. The author used the same line of thinking as did the *Tractatus* author, by offering the same biblical support for his argument. If the apostle (Paul) did not intend priests to marry, he would not have stated that a 'bishop should be the husband of one wife' (1 Tim. 3:2). The Norman Anonymous extends his discussion further than the *Tractatus* author, by attacking the traditionally used nuptial imagery of the reforming Church. The writer denies the validity of the frequently used motif of 'bishop as bridegroom' (of the Church), a term used in other regions of Europe, particularly the Holy Roman Empire. Nuptial imagery such as this was generally used in investiture ceremonies, to underscore the marriage of a bishop to his church.[22] The writer argues that 'the Holy Church is not the wife (*uxor*), nor the spouse (*sponsa*) of the priest, but of Christ'. He further points out that not only is this the true relationship but that it was legal, by apostolic tradition, for this 'bridegroom' [Christ] to marry this Church.[23] Christ married the Church not as priest, but as king. The writer's use of this analogy was indeed reflective of his royalist theology; but this rhetoric also had useful conclusions for married clerics. If a bishop was married to the Church, and the 'husband of one wife', he would have been rendered either a bigamist or adulterer. The Norman Anonymous here presents

---

[19] Frauenknecht, *Die Verteidigung*, p. 254.
[20] Ibid., pp. 254, 265.
[21] Ibid., p. 263.
[22] See Megan McLaughlin, 'The bishop as bridegroom: marital imagery and clerical celibacy in the eleventh and twelfth centuries', in *Medieval purity and piety: essays on medieval celibacy and religious reform*, ed. M. Frassetto (New York, 1998), pp. 209–29, for further discussion of this imagery.
[23] Norman Anonymous, J25, at ENAP, http://normananonymous.org/ENAP/index.jsp?view=edition&p=256. The author also refutes it in J24, a treatise on episcopal and royal consecration.

scripture alongside the reform agenda to fully illuminate the problem of the priest being a husband to two wives.[24]

As further proof that laws against clerical marriage were against tradition and ungodly, the Norman Anonymous points out that marriage is a sacrament (*sacramento*) and indissoluble (*ut coniugium non separetur et dimissus aut dimissa*). In this manner, the author seemed to be responding to celibacy legislation with the same language and concepts used by reformers to regulate lay marriage. Although the indissolubility of marriage was first proposed by Augustine of Hippo, here the author is clearly responding to the resurgent drive of reformers to define marriage as both monogamous and indissoluble.[25] The sentiment that such laws against clerical marriage are new is also found in other writings from the region, including the early twelfth-century Serlo of Bayeux's *Defensio*, which rails against the 'new laws' and 'harsh statutes' of the reformers, and the late eleventh-century letter of the Cambrai clergy, discussed below.[26]

The impurity of clerical marriage is refuted as the impurity of illicit sexual unions is highlighted. Aside from their biblical defence of clerical marriage, the authors also tap into the view of self-restraint that reformers had focused on as necessary to demonstrate manliness, in order to justify such unions. The *Tractatus* author points out the outcome of enforced celibacy when he writes that 'all clerics will be either continent or married or fornicators' (*omnis vero clericus aut continens erit aut coniugatus aut fornicarius*). The author clearly does not approve of fornication. He emphasises that all clerics are forbidden to have concubines (*mulieres subintroducta*) but may have legitimate marriages; he offers a contrast between the legitimate conjugal union and the taint of fornication when he quotes Paul, 'he who unites himself with a whore becomes one with her in body'.[27] Furthermore, he views clerical marriage as a form of continence, stating that such unions are 'chaste and pure' (*casta esse et sincera*).[28] The Norman Anonymous also makes a similar point when he defends his position in his J22/26 compositions. Here the writer, after appealing in J22 for debate on the subject of clerical sons and their rights, offers an addendum (J26) in which he states clearly that his position is not a defence of sexual immorality (*ut nec fornicationi feramus patrocinium, ne peccatis hominum faueamus*).[29] More clearly, it appears that these writers were very concerned with sexual purity and aware

---

[24] Anonymous of York, *Monumenta Germaniae, Libelli de Lite* III, p. 646: 'Sed quod Deus hoc instituerit, nec in veteri testamento nec in euangelio nec in apostolorum epistolis scriptum repperitur, in quibus quicquid Deus hominibus precepit, insertum describitur. Traditio igitur hominis est, non Dei, non apostolorum institutio. Quoniam et apostolus instituit, ut *oportet episcopum esse unius uxoris virum* [1.Tim. 3:2].' The *Tractatus* author also uses the same passages; see Frauenknecht, *Die Verteidigung*, p. 258.

[25] James A. Brundage, *Law, sex, and Christian society in medieval Europe* (Chicago, 1987), pp. 95, 183.

[26] Serlo of Bayeux, *Defensio pro filiis presbyterorum*, in *Monumenta Germaniae*, vol. III, pp. 579–83, here at p. 580.

[27] Frauenknecht, *Die Verteidigung*, p. 258.

[28] Ibid., p. 255.

[29] See the ENAP for J22 and J26 editions with commentary on added passages.

that their defence of marriage would incite critics to accuse them of supporting concubinage and fornication, or any kind of illicit sexual relations.

These authors discussed sexual desire in a way that implied the necessity of marriage. The author of the *Treatise on Grace*, once again relying upon Pauline authority, makes use of the biblical passage from Corinthians which states that 'because of the present crisis, I think that it is good for a man to remain as he is' (1 Cor. 7:26). 'What is on account of the present crisis?' the author asks, 'unless a weakness is present?'[30] The author goes on to suggest that such a 'weakness' leaves one vulnerable to commit fornication if not married. The Norman Anonymous similarly makes a statement on sexuality in J25. In describing sex as the 'ruin of filthiness' (*ruinam turpitudinis*), the Anonymous makes the case that it is redeemed by the 'honour of marriage' (*honestate nuptiarum*). Referring to Augustinian concepts once again, the Anonymous states that the good of marriage is threefold: the fidelity (*fide*), the offspring (*proles*) and the sacrament (*sacramentum*) which belongs to that institution. The fidelity of marriage, it is implied, prevents fornication with others.[31]

The three authors all point to the outcomes of male sexuality if marriage is denied to clerics; they all acknowledge that some clerics will be continent, but also point to the impurity that will occur from the ban on marriage: fornication, incest, bestiality and sodomy are all possible consequences of mandated celibacy. In this perspective, marriage is the proper vehicle for sexual expression, and allows a man to enact a form of continence. Self-restraint was an important aspect of manliness, especially within the ideology of ascetic masculinity. The authors speak to this ideal by addressing this concern over bodily purity.

FREE WILL, CONTINENCE AND HONOUR

The cultural construction of the male body played a pre-eminent role in the defence of clerical marriage. Both the *Treatise* author and the Norman Anonymous constructed the male body as innately and sexually vulnerable, and this vulnerability could only be relieved through divine intervention. For the male bodies left uncorrected, marriage was prescribed. While arguing for this necessity, these authors highlighted the role of chastity in relation to free will and grace in a manner that not only legitimised clerical marriage, but deemphasised the manliness of celibacy. Both the *Treatise* author and the Norman Anonymous connected free will and grace to the achievement of continence. Their use of common ideas can be traced back to the works of Anselm of Bec, archbishop of Canterbury. While such ideas on free will and grace were employed by others outside the Bec school, only these two writers used it in conjunction with the defence of clerical marriage. Both authors agree that continence is a gift from God, without which it would be impossible to live up to the standards of celibacy.

---

[30] Frauenknecht, *Die Verteidigung*, p. 277: 'Quid est propter instantem necessitatem? Quae est necessitas instans, nisi infirmitas presens?'

[31] Anonymous of York, p. 646.

Since celibacy was the cornerstone of the ideology of clerical manhood, the implication of these arguments extends towards the reform ideal of ascetic masculinity. In the *Treatise on Grace*, the author says:

> Since therefore the good of continence, indeed every good, is the gift of divine grace alone, capable of being embraced neither through mandate, nor through one's own free will, they not only err but indeed they labour in vain, who attempt to force chastity on these men.[32]

In the perspective of this writer, it was futile to hold clerics to celibacy when achieving it lay not in their power, but was bestowed upon them by God. There are many, he comments, who because of their own 'infirmity' (*infirmitatem*) cannot attain the celibate state. Using the biblical example of Lot's sin of incest, the author asserts that, likewise, priests may commit worse crimes if forced into chastity; without the blessing of divine intervention, sexual transgressions such as sodomy, fornication and incest could all occur from forcible celibacy. The author allows that continence is a better and higher state than marriage, but not for everyone.[33]

In the J25 composition, the Norman Anonymous, employing the same argument as the *Treatise* author, states that 'those who are continent have received continence from God', and without this gift from God, they could not be chaste.[34] He further extends this argument by locating the origins of this incontinence in the 'intemperance of the humour' (*intemperantia sue conspersionis*) or the 'weakness of their mind' (*animi infirmitate*). Both conditions lead a man to fulfil the desires of the flesh. These men, the Norman Anonymous asserts, would not do such things if they had received from God 'the grace and virtue of continence' (*continentiae gratiam et virtutem*). The writer explains that those who are not blessed by continence are driven by the 'law in their members' which holds them 'captive'; this 'law', essentially the combination of sin and carnal desire, provokes them either to marry or to fornicate. Such language on the 'law in their members' is also found in the *Treatise on Grace*, thereby suggesting that either they had consulted a common source (Romans 7:23) or that one of these writers had read the other's work. Regarding the 'law in their members', the Anonymous says that the Apostle is perfectly clear. He cites Paul, quoting his famous advice that it is 'better to marry than burn with passion' (1 Cor. 7:9).[35] Like those writers before him, the Norman Anonymous alludes to problems that may arise from clerical celibacy. While not specifically mentioning sodomy, incest or bestiality, the writer does distinguish between marriage and fornication, the former being the proper vehicle for the expression of sexuality. He suggests that celibacy may

---

[32] Translation in Barstow, *Married priests*, p. 119; Latin version in Frauenknecht, *Die Verteidigung*, p. 271.

[33] Frauenknecht, *Die Verteidigung*, pp. 274–5.

[34] Anonymous of York, p. 646.

[35] Anonymous of York, p. 646: 'Hac itaque eos lege captivante, et carnis concupiscentia stimulante, aut fornicari coguntur aut nubere. Quorum quid melius sit, apostolica docemur auctoritate, qua dicitur: *Melius nubere, quam uri.*'

be impossible for some men, and his argument implies that allowing sexual relations within marriage was the best way to restrain carnal desires.

The arguments produced by both authors have interesting implications for masculinity, and particularly for the discourse of clerical manhood produced by reformers. Reformers who advocated celibacy had offered that path as the pinnacle of manliness. They viewed conquering the flesh and fighting sexual desires as the ultimate challenge, and one that re-masculinised the celibate body; this repeated performance suggested that fighting carnal desires was a natural, attainable accomplishment of the male body. The argument of these two clerical authors, that celibacy could only be achieved as a gift from God, took the central component of ascetic masculinity, the fight against the flesh, and rendered it futile. How could there be a great struggle and great reward if what one earned (celibacy) was actually bestowed as a gift (from God)? At the very least, their arguments justified an alternative to manly celibacy in the form of marriage.

When Anglo-Norman ecclesiastical reformers honed their message on masculinity, the very one that dictated a code of proper manliness to elite men in an effort to prevent effeminacy, the message was clear: marriage, monogamous and indissoluble, was a necessary component of *lay* masculinity. The writer of the *Treatise on Grace*, perhaps aware of this agenda, focuses on the similarities between lay and clerical men. He adopts a very different polemic regarding the meaning of the male body, by emphasising the similarities between the male body, clerical and lay. 'Why are we', he asks, 'who are made from the same matter and assume the sin of the flesh from Adam's sin', not allowed wives?[36] By linking the physical nature of a priest with that of a layman, the author, intentionally or not, illustrates that both are men subjected to the same standards of manliness. Both groups of men suffer from sexual desires, and they both inherited sin from Adam. The author makes the case that Paul, in his most famous letter to the Corinthians, gave the same advice to the laity and the clergy, and that he made no distinction between the two groups. Reformers, our author maintains, try to enforce standards (celibacy) that they themselves do not abide by. This comparison completely disputes the reformist agenda to elevate clergy to a higher status over laymen.

The marital union was significant not only in terms of the relations between (conjugal) continence and conjugal sex, but also because it played an important part in defining masculine honour. A key emphasis of the *Tractatus* was the status of the woman in these unions. The *Tractatus*, in contrast to the other texts, particularly emphasised the difference between legitimate wives (*uxores*) and concubines (*mulieres subintroductae*).[37] No cleric was permitted to engage in concubinage, an essentially illegitimate union. The author referenced the decrees of Lisieux from 1064 that had prohibited canons from having *mulieres*

---

[36] Translation by Barstow, *Married priests*, p. 121.
[37] Kirsten A. Fenton has more recently found a similar connection in Henry of Huntingdon's *History of the English people*, in which the writer made an intentional distinction between lawful wives (*uxores*) and whores. See her essay in this volume.

subintroductae, while noting that this decree was focused on fornication, not legitimate marriage. It is clear that the author did not believe fornication to be appropriate, and he reaffirmed that clerics were allowed to marry or remain chaste, but they were not permitted to indulge in fornication. Fornication was a behaviour associated with concubines and whores, so this distinction was very relevant to his overall position on honour, status and legitimate clerical marriage. The author was concerned that legitimately married women were equated with the less honourable status of concubine, probably because this association had negative implications for the priest and devalued the status of his marriage. This emphasis on legitimate wives suggests that at the time of his composition, clerics' women were still seen as wives, and not concubines.

The issue of honour is approached again when the author alludes to the treatment of priests by the laity. He says married priests should not face censure by the laity, here referring to legislation that ordered parishioners to avoid the church services of married priests.[38] The author is quite incensed that the laity were encouraged to judge their priest, and states firmly that priests should only be judged by a formal ecclesiastical process, not by the 'madness of the laity' (*non laicorum insania*), who beat, insult and otherwise dishonour their priests. The laity are not qualified to judge their priests, and the author points out the consequences of this abuse and ostracism. Such treatment forces priests to abandon their churches. Instead, the author asserts that parishioners should respect their priest, and if judgment is due, then it should come from a legitimate ecclesiastical authority.[39] What is interesting here is that the clerical author of the *Tractatus* accepts the separate, elevated existence of the clergy, an idea preached by a reforming Church. The laity is a separate group, and they are not in a position of authority over the priest. By refusing the services of the priest, they usurp the higher status of his position. The author accepts the elevated social status that accompanies the clerical office; he does not, however, accept the forcible celibacy that accompanies this distinction between clerical and lay states.

The relationship between lawful marriage and masculine honour is best reflected in two letters from the archdiocese of Rheims, a region adjacent to Normandy. The *Tractatus* was likely read by the clergy who served the cathedrals of Cambrai and Noyon. These letters, clearly written after the *Tractatus* in the late 1070s, show a commonality in thinking, as the authors used similar concepts of honour, sexuality and masculinity in their polemical defence of clerical marriage. The letter from the Cambrai clergy to the Noyon clergy tells how they once 'enjoyed the highest honour and reverence, and the title of cleric, by God's own design, was considered more honourable than others and also enjoyed the highest consideration'. But the anti-marriage laws changed this revered status, and 'we have fallen into the contempt of our neighbours, and we have become a source of derision and mockery to those around us'.[40] The last statement likely

---

[38] Frauenknecht, *Die Verteidigung*, pp. 260–1.
[39] Ibid., p. 263.
[40] Letter of the clergy of Cambrai, trans. John S. Ott, available online at [http://www.web.pdx.edu/~ott/hst407Church/letter/index.html, accessed 13 November 2012]; *Cameracensium et*

refers to the bar on hearing mass from a married priest, and reflects the greater effort to involve the laity in disciplining unchaste clerics.

That these decrees were seen by the Cambrai clergy as an assault on their masculine honour is made clear in their letter:

> In all this, we consider the injury done to our name and above all the infamy in the eyes of the laity, for whom we have become an object of derision. Moreover, it is unheard of before our eyes and seems to us contrary to custom and honour. If you are men, you will want to act manfully (*viriliter*); you must set little store by these councils, which inflict so many and so great humiliations upon us . . . we in no way consent to these prescriptions, which are as unheard of as they are dangerous. You've heard our resolution and arguments, the dangers, the ignominy, which menaces us if we put up no resistance.[41]

Laden with echoes of masculine pride, status, and public persona, these clerics speak to their most pressing concerns of enforced celibacy. Defamed and denigrated by the laity, these clerics experienced public humiliation. They see enforced celibacy as 'contrary to custom and honour'. They also suggest an important, often overlooked, aspect of clerical marriage when they state 'we want to keep our previous customs, customs permitted by the wise moderation of our religious ancestors'. Custom resonates with them far more than the rogue decrees of celibate reformers. The response from the clergy of Noyon begins with a simple statement of solidarity: 'to hope for the best in adversity and in keeping faith to resist emerging adversaries manfully'. The letter from the Noyon clergy also suggests that the clergy viewed the movement against clerical marriage and clerical sons as a fleeting one, not likely to withstand time.[42]

These authors emphasised that continence is one path, while marriage is another, and the division between these two can be connected back to the traditional emphasis valued by the monastic and clerical life. For priests who performed manliness like laymen, honour was deeply embedded in lawful marriage. To assume that marriage was no longer lawful for these clerics was an assault on their masculine honour. The idea of celibacy as a gift from God, effectively took away the manliness of battling sexual temptations, a key component of clerical manhood. If one could only achieve chastity by the grace of God, then this meant that constant battle against the flesh was futile; thus, as the authors further explained, this could lead to greater transgressions particularly for clerics not blessed by the grace of God. There was an alternative clerical masculinity to the ascetic model, and it was a masculinity that incorporated procreative sexuality.[43]

Noviomensium clericorum epistolae, Monumenta Germaniae, vol. III, p. 574. I am indebted to John Ott for allowing me to cite his excellent translation.

[41] Ibid., p. 576.
[42] Ibid.
[43] Anonymous of York, p. 648.

Jennifer D. Thibodeaux

THE USES OF SODOMY AND THE 'NATURALNESS' OF CLERICAL MARRIAGE

Advocates of clerical marriage not only based their arguments for the necessity of marriage on lay models of manliness, they also employed an antithesis, an 'anti-norm', in the form of sodomy. These writers positioned marriage in opposition to sodomy, thereby highlighting the division between 'natural' and 'unnatural' sexuality. They also suggested, sometimes explicitly, that celibacy mandates originated with 'sodomite' reformers. By defending their arguments based on 'nature' the advocates of clerical marriage employed a technique well used by Christian reformers in their own definitions of manliness. Since 'nature' reflected the divine plan, the use of this idea played a central role in religious reform.[44]

The author of the *Treatise on Grace* used the discourse of the natural and the unnatural to underscore his point on clerical marriage and to cast sexual suspicion on the reformers who sought to eradicate it. He crafted an extensive argument by directly connecting the 'unnatural' to sodomy, juxtaposing it with the 'natural' act of marriage. He says that by prohibiting clerical marriage, 'the naturalness of marriage to one woman', clerics will go on to engage in 'unnatural' (*contra naturam*) practices, which may include 'cursed sodomitical fornication' (*execrabilis sodomitica fornicatio*). His insinuation, like that of other writers, is that denying priests what is natural, which is marriage, will result in the unnatural, in this case, sodomy. Interestingly, sodomy is the first offence mentioned in a list of other sexual transgressions, and one particularly focused on by this writer. The *Treatise* author then goes on to state that other offences, like adultery, the 'unspeakable pollution' of prostitution, and even incest, might also occur.[45] This line of thinking goes along with the presumption that uncontrolled sexuality will spill over into worse sexual sins; the author assumes that male sexuality, if uncontrolled, will create greater problems. By this logic, the author connects 'natural' sexuality to marital sexuality and the control of the male body.

The Norman Anonymous also employed the division between natural and unnatural sexuality, but with a more subtle approach. He based the majority of his argument in J25 on the natural order and the place of marriage therein, asserting that procreative sexuality was ordained by God; in contrast to the *Tractatus* author, the Norman Anonymous never specifically mentions sodomy as a consequence of celibacy in his advocacy of marriage.[46] This argument sustained the essentialist view of masculinity by its emphasis on the naturalness of procreative sexuality. The eternal law, which is the law of God, he argued, forbids the disruption of the 'natural order'. The mandate of celibacy, he concludes,

---

[44] See Pauline Stafford's argument in 'The meanings of hair in the Anglo-Norman world: masculinity, reform and national identity', in *Saints, scholars and politicians: gender as a tool in medieval studies*, ed. Mathilde van Dijk and Renee Nip, Medieval Church Studies 15 (Turnhout, 2005), p. 163; Giles Constable, *The reformation of the twelfth century* (Cambridge, 1996), p. 141.

[45] Frauenknecht, *Die Verteidigung*, p. 274.

[46] In fact, the Norman Anonymous argues in J3 that sodomy is not the most harmful transgression in the Bible, and that as such, it does not necessarily deserve capital punishment. See ENAP for this argument.

Defence of clerical marriage

blocks the 'natural order' from being conserved. It is therefore against the law of God.[47] The writer acknowledged that it was good for some to be continent and virgins, because God has preordained it. God also willed that some men reproduce. In short, God predestined the natural order of the world, so that men who were chaste and men who reproduced co-existed as part of the divine plan. Reproduction, after all, was necessary for the creation of saints, the Anonymous added. Without reproduction, the saintly would not have been born. Together with his argument on continence as a gift, the emphasis on divinely-mandated procreation further destroys the idea of manly celibacy. Not only did God bless certain men with continence, he ordered certain others to procreate. Those who marry 'desire to produce the fruit of marriage'.[48] By this statement, the author seems to suggest that procreation was the primary goal of marriage; this idea would imply that even chaste marriages do not serve the natural order. Thus, the implication follows, efforts to enforce celibacy interrupt God's divine plan.

The natural/unnatural binary can also be found in other pro-clerical marriage texts of the period. The *Tractatus* author implicitly suggests that the creators of these laws are sexually suspect themselves when he accuses them of hypocrisy (*ypocrisis*), even saying that legitimately married clerics are persecuted while fornicators escape discipline.[49] Other authors were more direct and even hostile towards the reformers. The Cambrai clergy noted that advocates of celibacy 'detest marriage because they practice with impiety and without respect a vice both abominable and without name', here referring to sodomy.[50] Both Serlo of Bayeux and the anonymous author of 'We married clergy' reveal this very perception that while reformers portrayed clerical marriage as an abomination, the same reformers turned a blind eye to sodomy, the 'unnatural' offence, and allowed it to run rampant without prosecution. Serlo wrote that the 'men who live the shameful, obscene lives of sodomites' created the laws against clerical marriage. He accused reformers of banning what was lawful (clerical marriage) and hiding what was 'a kind of sickness which might cause a grievous end to the human race'.[51] The author of 'We married clergy' uses similar language to express disgust at the acceptance of sodomy while married clerics were persecuted. Like other writers of the time, he defends his argument by recourse to a 'natural order', saying that 'this response rightly takes account of the laws of nature: if no one propagated, if no man procreated, everything would come to an end . . . you are driven by a lust which all of nature abhors'. He goes further than Serlo by directly positing procreative sex as oppositional to sodomy, the former marking manliness while the latter rendered one 'a half man, an effeminate (*semivir et mollis*)'.[52]

---

[47] Anonymous of York, p. 647.
[48] Ibid., p. 648: 'ipsi facere nuptiarum fructum appetunt'.
[49] Frauenknecht, *Die Verteidigung*, pp. 254, 258.
[50] *Letter of the clergy of Cambrai*, trans. Ott (see above, note 40);, *Cameracensium et Noviomensium clericorum epistolae*, pp. 573–8.
[51] Translated by Barstow, *Married priests*, p. 134.
[52] John Boswell, *Christianity, social tolerance and homosexuality* (Chicago, 1980), p. 400. I have changed Boswell's translation for *semivir et mollis* from 'half-man, debauchee', to 'half-man, an effeminate', which I think more closely expresses the sentiment of the passage.

At a time and in a region where marriage was prevalent among the secular clergy, the prohibition of this custom, seemingly by monastic reformers, resulted in hostility between the two groups. What may have increased the tensions even further was the perception by the secular clergy that their critics, those behind mandated celibacy, were sodomites, and that this behaviour was not being penalised and eradicated in the same manner as clerical marriage. Far more than an unjustified anxiety, secular clergy may have had valid reasons for believing that sodomy was an unpunished offence, at least in comparison to clerical marriage. A survey of Anglo-Norman regional ecclesiastical councils from 1072 to 1128 shows that there was no legislation created against sodomy, with the exception of Anselm's 1102 Westminster decree, which may have not been published. In contrast, many of these councils contained some measure against clerical marriage. The monastic William of Malmesbury, writing in 1125, made a rather curious statement that 'the rule about sodomites being excommunicated every Sunday Anselm himself later changed, for good reasons; but that only encouraged the evil to break the other rules more freely'.[53] William's remark is evidence that the decree of 1102 was published, but that the last section of it had been modified. Furthermore, Anselm's 1108 council, the very one that took severe legal measures against married clerics, did not include any prohibitions on sodomy. Thus, far more than being a baseless accusation, it seems that many secular clerics were justified in complaining that monastic reformers failed to persecute sodomites, while simultaneously prohibiting clerical marriage.

Undoubtedly, those writers who raised the question of sodomy in relation to mandated celibacy knew that suspicion of such behaviour could be associated with monastic life. Their attempt at creating an anti-norm, however, was not as successful as the advocates of clerical celibacy. While sodomy legislation increased over the course of the next two centuries, the promulgation of these laws had no bearing on the war against clerical marriage.

CONCLUSION

The four documents examined in this essay are crucial for understanding an elite perspective that saw clerical marriage as a component of clerical gender identity. This literature also shows a common consensus on the reasons for and value of clerical marriage. These writers defended a clear religious masculinity alternative to the ascetic ideology preached by reformers. By way of their arguments, they were able subtly to weaken the ideal of manly celibacy. The authors argued that priests might commit worse offences if they were not married – which seems to be a common polemical strategy, one even used by the author of the *Rescripta* – and they insisted that fornication, incest, sodomy and bestiality were all consequences of mandated celibacy. They discursively constructed the male body as sexually vulnerable, unable to retain its integrity without marital sex. They

---

[53] William of Malmesbury, *Gesta pontificum Anglorum. The history of the English bishops*, volume I, ed. and trans. Michael Winterbottom and Rodney Malcolm Thompson (Oxford, 2007), pp. 194–5.

Defence of clerical marriage

connected legitimate marriage to honour and public status. Finally, in hostile language, a few of these authors asserted that celibacy laws originated with sodomite reformers, monks who cared little for a wife but preferred sex with men. The accusation extends to even suggesting that church reformers turned a blind eye to sodomy but openly pursued the dissolution of legitimate, clerical marriages.

In the Anglo-Norman realm, the educated voices that spoke out in favour of clerical marriage were silenced at some point after the 1130s. By the mid twelfth century, it was uniformly recognised that celibacy was the rule for clerics in major orders, and clerical marriage was no longer legally permitted. Clerical unions continued to exist far into the later Middle Ages, but without the kind of vocal advocacy examined here. As the ideology of the manly celibate became the standard for male religious life, many secular clerics continued to live with their female partners and to create *de facto* marital unions, without any of the legitimacy their predecessors had once enjoyed.

WRITING MASCULINITY AND RELIGIOUS IDENTITY IN HENRY OF HUNTINGDON[1]

Kirsten A. Fenton

In 1125 the papal legate John of Crema arrived in England where he presided over an ecclesiastical council held at Westminster.[2] At this council, according to the twelfth-century chronicler Henry of Huntingdon, John

> dealt most severely with the matter of priests' wives, saying that it was the greatest sin to rise from the side of a whore and go to make the body of Christ. Yet, although on the very same day he had made the body of Christ, he was discovered after vespers with a whore. This affair was very well-known and could not be denied. The high honour which he had enjoyed everywhere was transformed into utter disgrace. So he retreated to his own land, confounded and discredited by the judgment of God.[3]

The apparent glee with which Henry tells this story adds new vitality to the idiom about the pot calling the kettle black. However this narrative episode does have more serious undertones. Right at its heart is the question of clerical celibacy and how far this was a marker of religious identity for men like the papal legate and the English chronicler. The public shaming of John after he was caught in bed with a woman despite his earlier denunciations suggests that sex and sexual behaviour was problematic and even a source of tension for religious men at this time. It

---

[1] My thanks to Professor Pauline Stafford for her comments on this essay.
[2] For details of the council see *The Anglo-Saxon Chronicle: a revised translation*, ed. Dorothy Whitelock with David C. Douglas and Susie I. Tucker (London, 1961), 1125 [references are given to date]; *The Chronicle of John of Worcester, iii: 1067–1140*, ed. and trans. P. McGurk (Oxford, 1998), 1125 [references are given to date]. For political context see Sandy Burton Hicks, 'The Anglo-Papal bargain of 1125: the legatine mission of John of Crema', *Albion* 8.4 (1976), pp. 301–10.
[3] 'Cum igitur in concilio severissime de uxoribus sacerdotum tractasset, dicens summum scelus esse a latere meretricis ad corpus Christi conficiendum surgere, cum eadem die corpus Christi confecisset, cum meretrice post vesperam interceptus est. Res apertissima negari non potuit. Summus honor ubique habitus in summum dedecus versum est. Repedavit igitur in sua Dei iudicio confusus et inglorius.' Henry, archdeacon of Huntingdon. *Historia Anglorum. The history of the English people*, ed. and trans. Diana Greenway (Oxford, 1996), book vii, chapter 36 (vii:36).

Henry of Huntingdon: masculinity and religious identity

also highlights that religious reform was a live issue in twelfth-century England given the legate's earlier criticism of those priests who were married. And indeed this fits into the wider trend of religious reform which was sweeping across Europe during this period under the auspices of the so-called Gregorian reform movement.[4] In this essay I want to explore some of these questions further and think about masculinity and religious identity in Henry of Huntingdon's work.

The recent surge in work dealing with the gender of the clergy has highlighted how profitable an area for research it is. Much of this scholarship builds on work concerning the issue of medieval masculinity more generally.[5] In particular the highly influential article by Jo Ann McNamara on *Herrenfrage* posed what remains a crucial question for scholars working in the field, namely 'Can one be a man without deploying the most obvious biological attributes of manhood?'.[6] This places the issue of sexuality and indeed celibacy at the forefront of definitions of religious masculine identity. The centrality of sexuality in definitions of masculinity more generally follows on from the work of scholars like Vern Bullough whose tripartite definition of masculinity defines men as those who 'impregnate women, protect dependents and serve as a provider to one's family'.[7] Of course, a celibate group of men like the clergy can never live up to such definitions by their very nature. This has often led scholars to view celibate clerics as an ungendered or even as a feminine group. For McNamara this expressed itself in a masculine crisis or *Herrenfrage* as both secular and religious men sought to redefine their identity within the context of church reform.[8] For others, like Robert Swanson, the gendered state of the clergy during this reforming period of the eleventh and twelfth centuries is best seen as a third gender or 'emasculinity'.[9] More recently still historians have begun to look at other areas

---

[4] A.L. Barstow, *Married priests and the reforming papacy: the eleventh-century debates*, Texts and Studies in Religion 12 (New York and Toronto, 1982); C.N.L. Brooke, 'Gregorian reform in action: clerical marriage in England, 1050–1200', *Cambridge Historical Journal* 12.1 (1956), pp. 1–21; K.G. Cushing, *Reform and the papacy in the eleventh century: spirituality and social change* (Manchester, 2005).

[5] The first monograph on medieval masculinity was Ruth Mazo Karras, *From boys to men: formations of masculinity in late medieval Europe* (Philadelphia, 2003). See also, *Becoming male in the Middle Ages*, ed. Jeffrey Cohen and Bonnie Wheeler (New York and London, 1997); *Masculinity in medieval Europe*, ed. D. M. Hadley (London, 1999); *Medieval masculinities: regarding men in the Middle Ages*, ed. Clare A. Lees, Thelma Fenster and Jo Ann McNamara (Minneapolis, 1994); *Conflicted identities and multiple masculinities: men in the medieval west*, ed. Jacqueline Murray (New York, 1999).

[6] Jo Ann McNamara, 'The *Herrenfrage*: the restructuring of the gender system, 1050–1150', in *Medieval masculinities*, ed. Lees, pp. 3–29, p. 5.

[7] Vern L. Bullough, 'On being a male in the Middle Ages', in *Medieval masculinities*, ed. Lees, pp. 31–45, p. 34.

[8] McNamara, '*Herrenfrage*', pp. 3–29.

[9] Robert N. Swanson, 'Angels incarnate: clergy and masculinity from Gregorian reform to Reformation', in *Masculinity*, ed. Hadley, pp. 160–77. 'Emasculinity' would be an example of an alternative masculinity, as suggested for nineteenth-century Britain by John Tosh, 'What should historians do with masculinity? Reflections on nineteenth-century Britain', in *Gender and history in western Europe*, ed. Robert Shoemaker and Mary Vincent (London, 1998), pp. 65–85 (esp. pp. 72–5).

besides sexuality in which religious men could define their masculinity.[10] By not making celibacy or sexuality the central thread of analysis historians can begin to weave a picture of masculine religious identity which takes into account other factors such as actions and behaviour and status.[11] This also allows an exploration of not only the different ways in which clerics could express masculinity but also how they were contested and negotiated within society at large.[12] One way to approach all this is to focus on a particular contemporary author and explore his work with a view to establishing what it can reveal about masculinity and religious identity.

Here I concentrate on Henry, archdeacon of Huntingdon (c. 1088–c. 1157), one of the most important English historians and poets of the twelfth century.[13] His chief work is the *Historia Anglorum* or *The History of the English People*. Bishop Alexander of Lincoln (d.1148) was patron of the text, which aimed to record the history of the kingdom and the origins of its people.[14] By 1130 Henry had completed a first version of his text, which comprised seven books and covered the period from the arrival of the Romans in Britain until 1129.[15] After this it seems that Henry continued to write, revise and add to his work until just before his death in around 1157. The final version of his text consists of ten books, which takes his historical narrative down to the coronation of King Henry II in 1154. The structure of the *Historia Anglorum* is strongly thematic since the five invasions of Britain – by the Romans, the Picts and Scots, the Angles and Saxons, the Danes, and the Normans – are seen as five punishments or plagues inflicted by God on a faithless people.[16] Indeed the highly didactic tone of the work permeates almost every page of it. Within the text we find numerous references to

[10] *Holiness and masculinity in the Middle Ages*, ed. P.H. Cullum and Katherine J. Lewis (Cardiff, 2004).

[11] Kirsten A. Fenton, 'The question of masculinity in William of Malmesbury's presentation of Wulfstan of Worcester', *Anglo-Norman Studies* 28 (2006), pp. 124–37; Kirsten A. Fenton, *Gender, nation and conquest in the works of William of Malmesbury* (Woodbridge, 2008); *Negotiating clerical identities: priests, monks and masculinity in the Middle Ages*, ed. Jennifer D. Thibodeaux (Basingstoke, 2010); Jennifer D. Thibodeaux, 'Man of the church, or man of the village: gender and the parish clergy in medieval Normandy', *Gender & History* 18.2 (2006), pp. 380–99.

[12] The essays in this volume by Jennifer D. Thibodeaux, Joanna Huntington and Matthew Mesley discuss the impact of reform and the negotiation of masculinity in other texts and contexts.

[13] John Gillingham, 'Henry of Huntingdon in his time (1135) and place (between Lincoln and the royal court)', in *The Gallus Anonymous and his chronicle in the context of twelfth-century historiography from the perspective of latest research* ed. K. Stopka (Krakow, 2010), pp. 157–72; John Gillingham, 'Henry of Huntingdon and the twelfth-century revival of the English nation', in his *The English in the twelfth century. Imperialism, national identity and political values* (Woodbridge, 2000), pp. 123–44; Diana Greenway, 'Authority, convention and observation in Henry of Huntingdon', *Anglo-Norman Studies* 18 (1995), pp. 105–21; Diana Greenway, 'Henry of Huntingdon and the manuscripts of his *Historia Anglorum*', *Anglo-Norman Studies* 9 (1986), pp. 103–26; Huntingdon, *Historia Anglorum*, pp. xxiii–clxxii; D.E. Greenway, 'Henry (Huntingdon, c.1088–c.1157),' *Oxford dictionary of national biography* (Oxford, 2004) [http://www.oxforddnb.com/view/article/12970 accessed 17 July 2012].

[14] Huntingdon, *Historia Anglorum*, prologue, pp. 4–9.

[15] For an overview of the chronology of composition see Huntingdon, *Historia Anglorum*, pp. lxvi–lxxvii.

[16] Huntingdon, *Historia Anglorum*, i:4.

Henry of Huntingdon: masculinity and religious identity

religious men from the whole spectrum of religious life and indeed book nine is devoted solely to miracles associated with English saints, all of which makes the work a good choice for a case study. Of even more interest is the fact that Henry himself was a married archdeacon whose father, Nicholas, had apparently occupied the same archdeaconry before him.[17] He is also known to have had at least one child, Adam, and two grandchildren, Simon and the superbly named Aristotle.[18] In the eyes of the twelfth-century reformers Henry was thus a sinner, not just in terms of procuring a hereditary archdeaconship but also through his marriage and children. It also makes his lively account of John of Crema's fall from grace due to his sexual antics, with which I started, all the more intriguing. For it places Henry at odds with the reforming tendencies of the twelfth century, and with the redefinition of clerical identity in sexual terms which was essential to it. In order to explore Henry's presentation of masculinity and religious identity I want to focus on his presentation of violence and its expression alongside the issue of sexuality.

RELIGIOUS SEXUALITY

The starting point in all this lies with the Gregorian reform movement of the eleventh and twelfth centuries. One of the key concerns of the reformers was the imposition of chastity and celibacy on the clergy in general.[19] For someone like Henry who was both married and a father this was naturally a matter of some importance as it had consequences for his identity as a religious man. In order to explore how Henry deals with the issue of religious sexuality in his work we can consider his presentation of the church councils and synods that occurred in his lifetime and which dealt with precisely these issues. The first reform council which Henry details took place at London in 1102.[20] He reports that,

---

[17] Huntingdon, *Historia Anglorum*, pp. xxiii-xxviii, xl-lii. See also C.N.L. Brooke, 'Married men among the English higher clergy, 1066-1200', *Cambridge Historical Journal* 12.2 (1956), pp. 187-8.

[18] Huntingdon, *Historia Anglorum*, pp. xxvii-xxviii. Compare Kathryn Ann Taglia, '"On account of scandal...": priests, their children, and the ecclesiastical demand for celibacy', *Florilegium* 14 (1995-1996), pp. 57-70.

[19] Of course the preoccupation with clerical celibacy was not new to this period and the idea of sexual control had been a feature of the western Church since before the fifth century. What was new to the eleventh and twelfth centuries was Gregory VII's stress on a sense of moral chastity and celibacy, which added a greater depth to these traditional notions of masculine self-control and which had particular significance for the clergy: H.E.J. Cowdrey, 'Pope Gregory VII and the chastity of the clergy', in *Medieval purity and piety: essays on medieval celibacy and religious reform*, ed. Michael Frassetto (London, 1998), pp. 269-302. See also Rachel Stone's essay in this volume.

[20] I am not the first to note the importance of Henry's record of these reforming councils: see Nancy Partner, 'Henry of Huntingdon: clerical celibacy and the writing of history', *Church History* 42.4 (1973), pp. 467-75. Partner, however, is interested in Henry's account as a reflection of the introduction of the reforming measures, whereas I am concerned with what they can tell us about his religious identity as a man.

In the same year [1102] Archbishop Anselm held a council in London at Michaelmas in which he forbade English priests to have wives which had not been prohibited before. This seemed to some to be the greatest purity, but to others there seemed a danger that if they sought a purity beyond their capacity, they might fall into horrible uncleanness, to the utter disgrace of the Christian name.[21]

There are two matters of note here. First, Henry's remark that wives 'had not been prohibited before'.[22] This is surprising. The issue of clerical celibacy appears in earlier councils and law codes such as those of King Aethelred in 1009 or the canons of Aelfric in 1049.[23] It may simply be the case that Henry was unaware of these earlier pieces of legislation for the *Historia Anglorum* contains no mention of them. At any rate it is certainly very telling about the ineffectual enforcement of such legislation on the English clergy and raises questions about the impact of the reform movement on England in general. Whilst Henry can perhaps be excused for his ignorance of earlier legislation, it is unlikely that he was not familiar with Lanfranc's decree of 1076.[24] The very first canon of this decree deals with clerical celibacy.[25] It allowed married priests to keep their wives but forbade marriage under any circumstances to canons. One of those who subscribed to this decree was Remigius, bishop of Lincoln, who made Henry's father, Nicholas, archdeacon of Huntingdon.[26] It therefore seems unlikely that Henry was not familiar with this particular piece of legislation and its consequences. Henry's assertion that wives 'had not been prohibited before' then is not strictly true. Rather this may be Henry's way of cautiously protesting against Anselm's efforts to prohibit marriage in 1102. As Nancy Partner argues, it was a way of saying that no one in the past had taken issue with the domestic arrangements of men like himself and his father and that there was no need to do so now either.[27] Moreover it is not the case that Henry was anti-reform *per se*. In his account of the 1102 council he states: 'In that council many abbots who had acquired their abbeys against God's will lost them, as God willed'.[28] This illustrates that Henry fully accepts the attack

---

[21] Huntingdon, *Historia Anglorum*, vii:24: 'Eodem anno ad festum sancti Michaelis, tenuit Anselmus archiepiscopus concilium apud Lundoniam, in quo prohibuit uxores sacerdotibus Anglorum antea non prohibitas. Quod quibusdam mundissimum visum est quibusdam periculosum, ne dum mundicias viribus maiores appeterent, in immundicias horribiles ad Christiani nominis summum dedecus inciderent.'

[22] Ibid.

[23] Concilium Aenhamense (1009), Canones Aelfrici (1049) in *Sacrorum conciliorum nova et amplissima collectio*, ed. Joannes Dominicus Mansi, vol. 19 (reprinted Graz, Austria, 1960).

[24] Primatial Council at Winchester, 1 April 1076, in *Councils and synods with other documents relating to the English Church AD 871-1204. Part II 1066-1204*, ed. D. Whitelock, M. Brett and C.N.L. Brooke (Oxford, 1981).

[25] Ibid.: 'Decretumque est ut nullus canonicus uxorem habeat. Sacerdotum vero in castellis vel in vicis habitantium habentes uxores non cogantur ut dimittant, non habentes interdicantur ut habeant. Et deinceps caveant episcopi ut sacerdotes vel diacones non presumant ordinare nisi prius profiteantur ut uxores non habeant.'

[26] Partner, 'Clerical celibacy', p. 468.

[27] Ibid., p. 469.

[28] Huntingdon, *Historia Anglorum*, vii:24: 'In illo autem concilio multi abbates qui adquisiverant abbatias suas, sicut Deus noluit, amiserunt eas, sicut Deus voluit'.

on simony put forward by the reformers and even views it as being God's will. The issue of clerical celibacy however is, for Henry, another matter. The reason for Henry's cautious protest over religious marriage is perhaps revealed in the second point of note in his account of the 1102 council. Anselm's prohibition of marriage represented for some 'the greatest purity' but for others it posed 'a danger that if they sought a purity beyond their capacity, they might fall into horrible uncleanness, to the utter disgrace of the Christian name'.[29] And here is the very crux of the matter. Henry recognises that for some celibacy is difficult and that marriage was a means of ensuring that they did not fall into 'horrible uncleanness'.[30] At the same time Henry is careful not to reveal himself as one of those who found celibacy impossibly difficult.[31] However Henry's concern with the issue, combined with his cautious protest about a married lifestyle, suggests that the negotiation and re-definition of a religious male identity as called for by the reformers was problematic and a source of tension for him.[32] Indeed the degree of his concern is signalled perhaps in his assertion that the danger is of lapses unworthy of the name of Christian itself. Henry is underlining the dangers and deliberately contrasting the purity some claimed for the new status with the 'horrible uncleanness' of those who could not or would not. In other words there is the sense here that Henry is hijacking the language of the reformers and using it back against them to make his point.

For Henry these matters and tensions seem to have reached something of a climax in relation to the reform council of 1108.[33] It was at this council that Anselm sought to vigorously enforce the canons that he had previously set out some six years earlier at the 1102 council. This implies that the earlier decrees had not been obeyed and indeed Eadmer's account of these events is marked by his outrage at the levels of mass disobedience experienced by the reformers.[34] Enforcement was clearly a central issue and within this the role of the archdeacon was especially acute. As the bishop's representative the office of archdeacon effectively involved the supervision of behaviour, both lay and clerical, at parish level.[35] Given the emphasis on reputation and discipline associated with this role archdeacons had a particular interest in the sexual morality of clerks.[36] The very nature of their office meant then that they could have a real effect on the extent to which reforming measures were adhered to within their own parishes. In 1108 the reformers were well aware of the potential power archdeacons could wield. As such they were keen to create legislation that could persuade archdeacons

---

[29] Huntingdon, *Historia Anglorum*, vii:24.
[30] Compare Paul in 1 Cor. 7:2.
[31] Partner, 'Clerical celibacy', p. 469.
[32] As it was for the Norman clerics discussed by Thibodeaux in this volume.
[33] For text of this council see Primatial Council at London, c. 28 May 1108, in *Councils and synods Part II*; *Eadmeri Historia novorum in Anglia, et opuscula duo de vita Sancti Anselmi et quibusdam miraculis ejus*, ed. Martin Rule, Rolls Series (London, 1884), pp. 193–5.
[34] *Eadmeri Historia novorum*, p. 193.
[35] Brian Kemp, 'Archdeacons and parish churches in England in the twelfth century', in *Law and government in medieval England and Normandy: essays in honour of Sir James Holt*, ed. George Garnett and John Hudson (Cambridge, 1994), pp. 341–64.
[36] Partner, 'Clerical celibacy', pp. 470–1.

to adhere to the canons themselves as well as putting these laws into practice on others.[37] For example, Partner identifies one of these pieces of legislation, which exacts an oath from all archdeacons that they were not to take bribes to overlook unlawful situations. If they refused to take such an oath they could lose their archdeaconry.[38] In 1108 then this negotiation of religious identity was a particularly complex issue for archdeacons who were expected to enforce such reforming measures and ensure that they themselves lived up to the standards outlined by the reforming councils. It is unknown whether Henry's father, Nicholas, took this oath in 1108 but in any case Nicholas did not lose his benefice and Henry succeeded to it some two years later, in 1110.[39] Of even greater significance however is the fact that the 1108 council is not mentioned in Henry's *Historia Anglorum* at all. It may be the case that Henry was embarrassed by his status and the fact that he had inherited it from his father made it an awkward subject to write about given current concerns. However, placed within the context of Henry's earlier quite outspoken protest about clerical marriage it seems that it was more than embarrassment that made him omit any mention of this council in his work. Following Partner, although it is dangerous to make an argument from silence it can be suggested here that Henry's protest about changes to his own way of life and identity reached a crescendo and that he deliberately excluded the 1108 council from his account as a mark of rebellion.[40]

Henry's silence in relation to the 1108 council is heightened even more by his ample account of the 1125 Council of London, which also dealt primarily with the issue of clerical celibacy.[41] Here Henry relates the story with which I began, with the papal legate, John of Crema, dealing strictly with the matter of priests' wives at the council before being later caught with a woman himself and as a result publicly humiliated. It is worth unpacking aspects of this narrative episode more fully given that we are now able to place Henry's remarks within the broader context of his views on the reforming councils of the time. For instance, Henry's choice of language within this passage is worth further comment.[42] He takes care to call the women who must separate from the clerks 'wives' (*uxores*). Yet when it comes to paraphrasing what the papal legate himself said on the matter Henry uses the word *meretrices* or 'whores'. And of course when John himself is caught with a woman she is described as a 'whore'. These distinctions are important. The term '*uxor*' or wife carries with it implications of social acceptability on a par with the secular status associated with husbands and fathers. By doing so Henry is defining clergy and their wives on comparable terms to their secular counterparts. The masculine identity of such men is therefore unquestionable given that marriage is a commonplace theme in definitions of masculinity. Thus when John describes such women as whores this is both an insult to the women and a

---

[37] Ibid., p. 471.
[38] Ibid.
[39] Huntingdon, *Historia Anglorum*, pp. xl-lii.
[40] Partner, 'Clerical celibacy', p. 470.
[41] '1125 Concilium Londoniense, seu Westmonasteriense', in *Sacrorum Conciliorum*, ed. Mansi, vol. 21.
[42] Contrast Partner, 'Clerical celibacy', p. 474.

critique of the status of their clerical husbands. The characterisation of married priests' wives as whores actually stripped married priests of their 'secular' status as husbands and instead marked them out as fornicators.[43] By doing so it called into question this key aspect of their identity as married religious men. Thus by calling the woman with whom John was found a 'whore' the insult is especially potent since it reduces John's identity to that of a fornicator. In this passage Henry is claiming legitimate social status for the married clergy by using the language of legitimate marriage. John undermines this by describing priests' wives as whores, using the language of fornication to make his point. Henry, for his part, turns that language back on John who is himself found with a whore. Given Henry's previous comments on church councils seeking to tackle the issue of clerical marriage this story becomes even more significant. As Partner suggests, it can no longer be explained as simply malicious gossip but instead reveals a personal, bitter attack on a cause which Henry felt he was losing.[44] This is perhaps compounded by the fact that Henry of Huntingdon remains our only source for John's actions and behaviour at the 1125 council.[45] It certainly reveals that Henry was upset by the redefinition of clerical status and clerical masculinity put forward by the reformers. It is also revealing for what Henry himself is feeling and thinking at this time. For underlying what Henry says here seems to be an acceptance that sexual activity was normal for men – both clerical and lay – and that to deny that was dangerous and certainly something which would be beyond most men, as it was beyond John in Henry's presentation of him.

The last council which Henry comments on with regards to clerical marriage is the 1129 Council of London. Here Henry tells us that King Henry I 'held a very great council on 1 August in London, concerning the prohibition of priests' wives'.[46] After listing those men present Henry continues,

> These were the pillars of the kingdom and the sunbeams of holiness at this time. But the king deceived them through Archbishop William's simplicity. For they granted the king jurisdiction on the matter of priests' wives, and showed a lack of foresight. This became obvious later, when the affair came to a most disgraceful conclusion. For the king took vast sums of money from the priests and released them. Then in vain did the bishops repent of their concession, when it became clear before the eyes of the whole world how the prelates had been deceived and the lower clergy humiliated.[47]

---

[43] Jacqueline Murray, 'Masculinizing religious life: sexual prowess, the battle for chastity and monastic identity', in *Holiness and masculinity*, ed. Cullum and Lewis, pp. 24–42 (p. 34).

[44] Partner, 'Clerical celibacy', p. 474.

[45] N. Partner, *Serious entertainments: the writing of history in twelfth-century England* (Chicago and London, 1977), p. 45.

[46] Huntingdon, *Historia Anglorum*, vii:40: 'Tenuit igitur concilium maximum ad kalendas Augusti apud Lundoniam, de uxoribus sacerdotum prohibendis'.

[47] Huntingdon, *Historia Anglorum*, vii:40: 'Hi columpne regni erant et radii sanctitatis hoc tempore. Verum rex decepit eos simplicitate Willemi archiepiscopi. Concesserunt namque regi iusticiam de uxoribus sacerdotum et inprovidi habiti sunt. Quod postea patuit, cum res summo dedecore terminata est. Accepit enim rex pecuniam infinitam de presbiteris, et redemit eos. Tunc sed

Here King Henry I seems to have adopted the cause of the reformers and taken it to new heights by essentially holding clerical wives to ransom. Henry of Huntingdon seems to despair not only of the money-grabbing opportunism exploited by the king but also of the inability of the higher clergy to have foreseen these events. Henry presents the king's actions in monetary terms not as idealism, which not only devalues them but also reveals, in his view, the naivety of the higher clergy who did not see it. The gloomy tone which pervades this particular passage suggests that Henry was beginning to accept that protests against the law of celibacy were no longer a realistic option.[48] Indeed by this time Pope Calixtus II at the Lateran Council of 1123 had declared that marriages contracted by clerks in higher orders were to be nullified.[49] Regardless of whether Henry knew Calixtus' decree, times were changing. Henry's endorsement of clerical marriage as an aspect of masculine behaviour which, for him, was entirely consistent with clerical identity was by this time a view that was increasingly outside the reforming mainstream. Henry's presentation of twelfth-century councils and synods in his work very much represents a personal journey as he seeks to make sense of the reforming principles' concern with celibacy. It underlines how debatable reforming measures could be. They were certainly not universally accepted and enforced in England during this period and for stalwarts like Henry it remained a source of tension even as he resigned himself to accepting that protesting against such matters was, in the end, pointless.

VIOLENCE AND ITS EXPRESSION

Henry thus seems to represent an older view of the clergy, one which did not separate them from the laity along this critical sexual line and one which therefore allows a common masculinity to be seen in this crucial area. It will be interesting therefore to look at what he has to say about the other great potential divide between lay and clerical masculinity – especially as defined by reform – namely violence and its expression. Violence and its expression are often seen as fundamental in explaining what it means to be a man because they involve the dominance of others, including social peers and women.[50] Yet it was generally agreed that the battlefield was no place for a religious man and indeed in accordance with the monastic rule they were supposed neither to fight nor to carry weapons. Could religious men therefore be male? Were there appropriate ways for them to express violence? In the *Historia Anglorum* there are a number of stories in which the theme of violence appears in connection with the actions and behaviour of religious men. Henry tells us of civil unrest and rebellion during the reign of William Rufus.[51] He reports how the chief men of Herefordshire

---

frustra concessionis sue penituit episcopos, cum pateret in oculis omnium gentium deceptio prelatorum, et depressio subiectorum.'
[48] Compare Partner, 'Clerical celibacy', pp. 474–5.
[49] Lateran Council of 1123 in *Sacrorum Conciliorum*, ed. Mansi, vol. 21.
[50] Karras, *From boys to men*, p. 21.
[51] Huntingdon, *Historia Anglorum*, vii:1.

and Shropshire, together with the Welsh, plundered the shire of Worcester, right up to the gates of the city itself. When however they prepared to attack the minster and castle they were not so fortunate. Bishop Wulfstan had been watching the on-coming attack and 'in his dire need, called on a certain familiar friend, namely the most high God, by whose help, as he lay in prayer before the altar, having sent out only a few soldiers, he either killed or captured 5,000 of the enemy. He miraculously put the rest to flight.'[52] Here we have a religious figure in the context of warfare successfully defending the minster and castle by fighting against a military threat. Henry is careful to ensure that Wulfstan is not on the battlefield itself but is instead lying in prayer before the minster's altar. Indeed Wulfstan's success in this matter lies in the prayers (*oratione*) he sends to God. It is prayer which can be seen as an appropriate 'weapon' for a religious man to wield and one which is exceedingly effective.

In a similar vein is Henry's account of St Germanus.[53] Henry tells how the Saxons and Picts joined forces to make war on the Britons. The Britons sought the assistance of St Germanus who offered himself 'as their leader in battle'.[54] Henry continues, 'And so, as military commander [Germanus] himself drew up the army in a valley surrounded by fairly high hills in the direction from which the enemy was expected to arrive.' As the enemy approached 'the saint, who was bearing the standard, suddenly ordered everyone to repeat his call loudly in unison ... the priests shouted "Alleluia" three times. A universal shout followed and the echo from the surrounding hills multiplied the rising sound.' As a result the enemy troops were afraid and fled. Henry concludes that 'the bishops rejoiced that the enemy had been scattered without bloodshed, in a victory obtained by faith and not by might.'[55] What is particularly striking about this narrative episode is the military and secular language and context in which Germanus appears. He is referred to as a 'military commander' or '*dux*', he organises the army, bears the standard, and even commands the army to shout 'Alleluia'. These are all arguably the actions of a strong and effective military leader. Yet in this context Germanus' success, like Wulfstan's, relies on his use of specifically religious language. It is from this religious language that such men gain their power, a point underlined in this story by the fact that it was recognised that victory had been obtained by faith rather than might. The military language and context used in each of these examples suggests that 'secular' masculine attributes were being applied to clerical men. This common language of masculinity is much wider and

---

[52] Ibid.: '... Wlstanus episcopus sanctus quendam amicum familiarem summis in necessitatibus compellavit, Deum videlicet excelsum, cuius ope coram altari iacens in oratione, paucis militibus emissis, quinque milia hostium vel occidit vel cepit. Ceteros vero mirabiliter fugavit'. For a fuller discussion of Wulfstan's masculinity see Fenton, 'The question of masculinity', pp. 124–37.
[53] Huntingdon, *Historia Anglorum*, ii:6.
[54] Ibid.: '... ducem se prelii profitetur. In valle igitur circumdata mediis montibus e regione qua sperabatur adventus hostium, componit exercitum ipse dux agminis ... Tunc subito sanctus signifer universos admonet ut voci sue uno clamore respondeant. Securisque hostibus, qui se insperatos adesse confiderent, "Alleluia" iam tercio repetitam sacerdotes exclamabant. Sequitur una vox omnium, et elatum clamorem repercusso aere montium conclusa multiplicant'.
[55] Ibid.: 'Triumphant pontifices hostibus fusis sine sanguine, victoria fide optenta non viribus'.

older than Henry alone. For instance, the Germanus story shows how far he is here continuing a very old pattern of thought since the story comes largely from Bede.[56] Thus Henry seems to be following well established ideas when it comes to the question of clerical masculinity and the expression of violence.

Yet whilst aware of a common language of masculinity there are instances where Henry may have been aware of the 'secularisation' of key religious figures. For example, in a critique of the powerful he describes Henry of Blois, bishop of Winchester, as 'a new kind of monster, composed part pure and part corrupt, I mean part monk and part knight'.[57] Given Henry of Blois' involvement in the civil war under Empress Matilda and Stephen this description of him as a 'monster' implies that he is being criticised for being too worldly and too involved in the secular world of the court and politics for a man of the cloth.[58] In other words religious men should reject violence in the secular sense and this is consistent with his views about how the clergy should fight as seen in the cases of both Wulfstan and Germanus. Similarly Henry provides a short account of St Wulfric, a priest and hermit from Haselbury in Somerset.[59] Wulfric 'always wore a hauberk next to his flesh to subdue his turbulent passions, and begged a new one from his earthly lord, since his own was almost worn out and torn in pieces by his sweat. He put on the new one, but was enraged at its length, because it might be seen below his garment. So he snatched up the shears and cut the soldered iron rings at the bottom and in the openings of the sleeves, as if it were linen cloth.'[60] Henry continues that Wulfric's lord was amazed at what he had seen but was told to keep it secret. However it could not be kept secret and many people rejoiced to have rings from the 'holy hauberk' (*lorice sanctissime*) in recognition of this miracle. This is a complex narrative episode although there are two key aspects which are worthy of immediate note. First, the fact that Wulfric is wearing a hauberk in order to 'subdue his turbulent passions'. This recalls Henry's comments in relation to the 1102 Council of London.[61] Here Henry revealed that he was aware how difficult a celibate life could be for some and again here we have a religious man taking efforts to ensure that he would be in control of his body at all times.[62] Secondly, Wulfric is wearing a hauberk (*lorica*), a central

---

[56] *Bede's Ecclesiastical History of the English People*, ed. Bertram Colgrave and R.A.B. Mynors (Oxford, 1969), book 1, chapter 20.

[57] Huntingdon, *Historia Anglorum*, c.15: '... quoddam monstrum ex integro et corrupto compositum, scilicet monachus et miles'.

[58] Edmund King, 'Blois, Henry de (c.1096–1171)', *Oxford dictionary of national biography* (Oxford, 2004) [http://www.oxforddnb.com/view/article/12968, accessed 17 July 2012].

[59] Huntingdon, *Historia Anglorum*, ix:54.

[60] Ibid.: 'Hic loricam carni proximam semper adhibens, ut eius motus intempestos cohiberet, a domino suo terreno novam poposcit, quia sua sudore suo iam pene demolita et dissarcita videbatur. Quam cum eo presente induisset longitudini eius infensus, ne sub veste quidem compareret, arrepta forcipe sub giris et in manicarum vestibulis ferrum compaginatum, quasi lineam texturam, dissecuit.'

[61] Above, pp. 67–69.

[62] There is a considerable body of work on ancient and late antique masculinity that indicates the significance of restraint and self-control in constructions of ideal masculine behaviour. See in particular, Peter Brown, *The body and society: men, women and sexual renunciation in early*

and visual symbol of a secular man. This suggests a common symbolic language of control and defence expressed not only in the military equipment but also in the control of passion and the body. Yet Wulfric is keen to ensure that no-one knows he is wearing a hauberk underneath his religious garb and indeed Henry notes that Wulfric in fact cuts the hauberk twice in order to ensure that it would not be seen. This again suggests that although secular and religious men might share many attributes and characteristics at the same time it was important that a distinction between them was maintained. This is perhaps why Wulfric rejects the view of his hauberk – it could be worn as a form of penance but he must not be seen as a man of violence.

In sum marriage and violence are generally seen as two of the great definers of masculinity. Modern historians have tended to view these as two key areas from which religious men were excluded, given their vocation. And yet they remain central to masculine religious identity in the work of Henry of Huntingdon. Henry's definition of clerical masculinity was arguably an old established one although we may only hear the sexual side of it clearly articulated now in the twelfth century vis-à-vis the more revolutionary attempts by reformers to generalise what had hitherto been the more restricted celibacy of monks and the few to all the clergy. Henry seemed to accept that sexual activity was normal for both lay and clerical men and that to deny this was dangerous. This is seen through Henry's presentation of marriage in relation to religious figures which can be seen through his account of various reforming councils and synods held in England during his lifetime. It is very much a personal journey and we can trace the trajectory of Henry's own response throughout the course of the councils he describes, from muted protest to downright rebellion to grudging acceptance of the reforming aims and principles. It demonstrates how fluid and contested clerical celibacy as a marker of religious identity was in the twelfth century. It was certainly a source of tension for Henry personally as a husband and father as he battled to maintain his traditional views of clerical masculinity in the context of Gregorian Reform. Henry's presentation of violence and its expression was similar in the emphasis it placed on an older, established language which here rejected violence for religious men. What was particularly striking in the examples of Bishop Wulfstan and St Germanus was the overtly military language and contexts in which they were portrayed as being involved. They acted as secular warriors should – defending their castles and rallying troops to victory. By doing so Henry is able to depict such religious men in a traditional masculine role that emphasises military prowess as a positive masculine attribute. Although

Christianity (London, 1988); Bullough, 'On being a male', pp. 31–45; Kate Cooper and Conrad Leyser, 'The gender of grace: impotence, servitude, and manliness in the fifth-century West', *Gender & History* 12 (2000), pp. 536–51; Kate Cooper, 'Insinuations of womanly influence: an aspect of the Christianisation of the Roman aristocracy', *Journal of Roman Studies* 82 (1992), pp. 150–64; Matthew Kuefler, *The manly eunuch: masculinity, gender ambiguity and Christian ideology in late Antiquity* (Chicago, 2001), *passim*; Conrad Leyser, 'Masculinity in flux: nocturnal emissions and the limits of celibacy in the early Middle Ages', in *Masculinities*, ed. Hadley, pp. 103–20; Aline Rousselle, *Porneia: on desire and the body in Antiquity*, trans. Felicia Pheasant (Oxford, 1988).

in both cases Henry is careful to present them using religious language and it is this which is an appropriate religious 'weapon' for them to wield. By doing so it suggests that Henry is drawing on a common language of masculinity that could be applied to both lay and clerical men. Certainly the question of religious masculine identity in the twelfth century is not an easy one to answer but one of the key benefits of a case study like Henry of Huntingdon is that it allows us to see the negotiation and re-definition of it 'in action' as Henry responded to the changing world around him in which he lived and wrote.

'THE QUALITY OF HIS *VIRTUS* PROVED HIM A PERFECT MAN': HEREWARD 'THE WAKE' AND THE REPRESENTATION OF LAY MASCULINITY[1]

Joanna Huntington

One Christmas, some years before the Battle of Hastings, Gilbert of Gent held his traditional festivities at his Northumbrian household. He held thrice-yearly contests, 'testing the strength and spirit of those young men who were hoping for the belt and arms of knighthood by letting wild beasts out from cages'.[2] This season's beast was a particularly ferocious bear: the 'offspring of a famous Norwegian bear which had the head and feet of a man and human intelligence, which understood the speech of men and was cunning in battle'.[3] Its father had allegedly raped a girl in the woods and fathered Beorn, king of Norway.

Gilbert's eighteen-year-old godson, Hereward, was visiting, having been banished from his homeland for being troublesome. Hereward was eager to have his strength and spirit tested, but Gilbert refused, 'because although ... [he]

---

[1] The research for this essay was undertaken during my Leverhulme Early Career Fellowship, held at Newcastle University, and research leave awarded by the University of Lincoln. I am grateful for the support of the Leverhulme Trust and of my colleagues. I am also grateful for the helpful comments and suggestions made by audiences at what my son dubbed the Hereward Tour, at the International Medieval Congress at Leeds, the International Congress on Medieval Studies at Kalamazoo, and the Religious Men in the Middle Ages conference at Huddersfield, and at research seminars at Harlaxton College and the Universities of Northampton and, in the very final stages of revision, St Andrews. I should also like to thank Philippa Hoskin and Krista Cowman for their unfailing encouragement, and the editors of this volume for their most welcome support and advice.

[2] Michael Swanton, trans., 'The deeds of Hereward the Wake', in *Medieval outlaws: ten tales in modern English*, ed. Thomas H. Ohlgren (Stroud, 1998), pp. 18–60, 294–9 [hereafter *Deeds*], p. 21. For the Latin original see 'Gesta Herwardi incliti exulis et militis', in *Lestorie des Engles solum la Translacion Maister Geffrei Gaimar*, ed. Thomas Duffus Hardy and Charles Trice Martin, 2 vols, Rolls Series 91 (London, 1888–89), vol. 2, pp. 339–404 [hereafter *Gesta*], p. 343: 'ex claustris eductis saevis feris juvenum vires et animos temptare, qui militare cingulum expectabant et arma'. Swanton's translation is cited here, unless otherwise noted, even when he has 'silently "improve[d]" the original' to render it readable to a modern audience, on which see his 'Introduction', in *Deeds*, pp. 12–18, at p. 18.

[3] *Deeds*, p. 21; *Gesta*, p. 343: 'inclyti ursi Norweyæ fuisse filium, ac formatum secundum pedes illius et caput ad fabulam Danorum affirmabant sensum humanum habentem, et loqualem hominis intelligentem ac doctum ad bellum'.

perceived the bravery of the young man, he feared for his youthfulness'.[4] The bear escaped, and went on a killing spree. Hereward leapt into action, heading the bear off as he was about to attack Gilbert's wife and her women. He drove 'his sword through its head as far as the shoulder-blades. Leaving the blade there, he lifted up the animal in his arms and held it out to those who followed, at which sight they were much amazed'.[5] Gilbert and his wife were understandably grateful, but the other young would-be knights were envious, and,

> because he increased daily as much in grace of body and of age as the virtues of magnanimity and of valour, leaving none to equal him in the chase and in hunting, nor in the sports of either the common people or of gentlemen, they looked for an opportue time and place to kill him.[6]

Hereward foiled their plot and told Gilbert's wife of his trials, and that he would leave the household. She begged him to stay, urging him to wait until her sick son should die, that she might make Hereward her adopted son and heir. Hereward declined her kind offer, and went on to forge a career as a young gun for hire, undertaking mercenary activity in Cornwall, Ireland, and Flanders. After an eventful life of romance, damsels in distress, rebellion, and manful resistance to the new Norman regime in England, Hereward finally made peace with William the Conqueror.[7]

Alternatively, he was treacherously murdered in Maine by Normans. Or he simply escaped away into the Fens and disappeared from historical record. Certainly, he was written and rewritten, eventually becoming a proto-Robin Hood figure, whose reputation was intrinsically bound up with ethnicity and Anglo-Saxon resistance against the dastardly usurping Norman oppressor: the darling of nineteenth-century national history and historical fiction.[8]

This opening snapshot features notions of youth, manliness, and *virtus* (i.e. manly virtue, strength, bravery), and therefore speaks directly to my present concerns with clerical constructions of masculinity. It appears in a remarkable

---

[4] *Deeds*, p. 21; *Gesta*, p. 343: 'domino illius magnanimitatem juvenis percipiente, et pubertatem ejus pertimescente'.

[5] *Deeds*, p. 21; *Gesta*, p. 344: 'gladium per caput et ad scapulas usque configens, atque ibi spatam relinquens, bestiam in ulnis accepit, et ad insequentes tetendit'.

[6] *Deeds*, p. 22; *Gesta*, p. 344: 'quia crescebat quotidie, ut corporis et aetatis gratia, ita in magnanimitatum virtutibus et fortitudinum, nullum parem sibi in captione et venatione nec in lusibus vulgaribus et liberalibus relinquens. Propterea tempus opportunum et locum illum perimendi inquirebant.' The translation here is slightly different to that of Swanton.

[7] *Deeds*, p. 60; *Gesta*, p. 404.

[8] Maurice Keen, *The outlaws of medieval legend*, rev. ed. (London, 1977), where 'Hereward is the lineal ancestor of the later English outlaws', pp. 11, 23–4. Charles Kingsley, *Hereward the Wake, 'last of the English'* (London, 1884); Edward A. Freeman, *The history of the Norman Conquest of England, its causes and its results*, 2nd edn, 5 vols (Oxford, 1870–1876), vol. 4. pp. 454–87; Andrew Wawn, 'Hereward, the Danelaw and the Victorians', in *Vikings and the Danelaw: papers from the proceedings of the Thirteenth Viking Congress, Nottingham and York, 21st–30th August 1997*, ed. James Graham-Campbell, Richard Hall and Judith Jesch (Oxford, 2001), pp. 357–68.

text, the *Gesta Herwardi*.[9] This is traditionally believed to have been written by Richard, a monk at Ely, between 1109 and 1131, but Paul Dalton has made a convincing case for a slightly later composition, placing it instead in the early years of the reign of King Stephen (1135-54).[10] It is allegedly based on a no-longer extant account written in Old English by Hereward's priest, who aimed 'to assemble all the doings of giants and warriors he could find in ancient stories as well as true reports for the edification of his audience; and for their remembrance to commit them to writing in English'.[11] It was further informed by material from local witnesses.[12] Hereward has many adventures, in which he excels in battle, one-to-one combat and harp-playing, goes incognito at every available opportunity, is a hit with the ladies, and generally does what we might now expect a medieval rebel to do. Elsewhere in the text, Hereward also encounters a witch, a mysterious wolf-guide, and magical fairylights.[13] Even this cursory outline should convey that the *Gesta* is a curious text, sitting at the intersection of fiction and history – a hybrid of historical writing and what would become common features of romance narratives.

The boundaries between fiction and history, however, were far less problematic to twelfth-century audiences and authors than they are to most people today.[14] Regardless of whether or not they are accurate, the stories which a society tells about its recent past – however fabulous they may seem – allow us to gauge which qualities and choices were deemed admirable when they were written. The *Gesta* is situated at the intersection of several traditional historiographical binaries in addition to history/fiction. It also sits in the grey areas between Anglo-Saxon/Norman, Scandinavian/English, vernacular/Latin, and, most importantly for my present purposes, clerical/lay and religious/secular. It has consequently been treated to various academic approaches, themselves often influenced (explicitly or otherwise) by modern academic disciplinary boundaries. Hereward and the *Gesta* have been considered in terms of landholding, of his socio-political networks, of rebels, of ethnic tension, of Ely's socio-political

---

[9] It is extant in one mid thirteenth-century manuscript, Cambridge University Library, Peterborough, Chapter Library 1, 320r-339r, on which see Elisabeth van Houts, 'Hereward and Flanders', *Anglo-Saxon England* 28 (1999), pp. 201-23, p. 202, n. 4.

[10] Paul Dalton, 'The outlaw Hereward "the Wake": his companions and enemies', in *Outlaws in medieval and early modern England: crime, government and society, c.1066-c.1600*, ed. John C. Appleby and Paul Dalton (Farnham, 2009), pp. 7-36, see especially pp. 31-2.

[11] *Deeds*, p. 19; *Gesta*, p. 339: 'omnes actus gigantum et bellatorum ex fabulis antiquorum, aut ex fideli relatione, ad edificationem audientium congregare, et ob memoriam Angliae literis commendare'.

[12] *Deeds*, p. 19; *Gesta*, p. 340.

[13] For an excellent précis of the plot, see Dalton, 'The outlaw Hereward', pp. 10-12.

[14] For further discussion of this issue in relation to the twelfth century see for example Nancy Partner, *Serious entertainments: the writing of history in twelfth-century England* (Chicago, 1977); Gabrielle M. Spiegel, 'History, historicism, and the social logic of the text in the Middle Ages', *Speculum* 65 (1990), pp. 59-86; Monika Otter, *Inventiones: fiction and referentiality in twelfth-century English historical writing* (Chapel Hill, NC, 1996); Robert M. Stein, *Reality fictions: romance, history, and governmental authority, 1025-1180* (Notre Dame, IN, 2006); Laura Ashe, *Fiction and history in England, 1066-1200* (Cambridge, 2007).

networks, and of literary influences.[15] Historians have not yet, however, fully explored the extent to which the narrative of the *Gesta* revolves around notions of youth, maturation, and *virtus*. It is therefore a very good source for helping us to understand clerical constructions of lay masculinity in a period of religious reform. By considering the *Gesta* as part of an efflorescence of historiographical activity in Ely in the twelfth century it can also be used to explore how narrative constructions of gender contributed to the negotiation of specific local tensions.

The broad interpretative context for this analysis is the consequences of the reform movements of the eleventh and twelfth centuries. Essentially, driven by collaboration and competition between *clerici* and *laici* for resources, status, and authority, and yet framed in religious rhetoric, these reform movements saw churchmen trying to limit what they perceived as lay interference in ecclesiastical concerns.[16] Across the sources of this period, we can see 'the general shaking down of authority, both secular and ecclesiastical'.[17] Effectively, the reform movements sought to divide Christendom into *laici* and *clerici* which entailed negotiation and renegotiation, definition and redefinition. We can clearly see this dynamic at play in the *Gesta*, which allows insight into the author's anxieties and aspirations. I have argued elsewhere that monastic chronicles of this period betray a concern with establishing different types of masculinity, with *clerici* firmly in control over *laici*.[18] This is a manifestation of a monastic anxiety about monastic masculinity, which was a byproduct of the 'bedding in' of reform, and can also be seen in the *Gesta Herwardi* at key points within the narrative.

Masculinity in the early twelfth century was in a state of flux. As Jo Ann McNamara influentially argued, 'broad social changes, complicated by the ideological struggle between celibate and married men for leadership of the Christian world, precipitated a masculine identity crisis'.[19] The standard markers of masculinity – 'impregnating women, protecting dependents, and serving as a provider to one's family' – were sites of contention.[20] Increasingly in this

---

[15] See the works cited *passim, infra*.

[16] The classic and rightly influential (though not uncontested) treatments of this interpretation of reform and its implications are those of R.I. Moore. See his *The formation of a persecuting society: power and deviance in Western Europe, 950–1250* (Oxford, 1987). See also the new edition (Oxford, 2007), for Moore's reflections on reactions to and developments of his thesis, at pp. vi–x, 172–96, and idem, *The first European revolution, c. 970–1215* (Oxford, 2000). For a useful overview of the historiography of the reform movements, see Maureen C. Miller, 'New religious movements and reform', in *A companion to the medieval world*, ed. Carol Lansing and Edward D. English (Oxford, 2009), pp. 211–30.

[17] R.I. Moore, 'Between sanctity and superstition: saints and their miracles in the age of revolution', in *The work of Jacques Le Goff, and the challenges of medieval history*, ed. Miri Rubin (Woodbridge, 1997), pp. 63–75, at pp. 69–70.

[18] Joanna Huntington, 'The taming of the laity: writing Waltheof and rebellion in the twelfth century', *Anglo-Norman Studies* 32 (2010), pp. 79–95.

[19] Jo Ann McNamara, 'The *Herrenfrage*: the restructuring of the gender system, 1050–1150', in *Medieval masculinities: regarding men in the Middle Ages*, ed. Clare A. Lees (London, 1994), pp. 3–29, at p. 3.

[20] Cited here from Vern L. Bullough, 'On being male in the Middle Ages', in *Medieval masculinities*, pp. 31–45, at p. 34, after David D. Gilmore, *Manhood in the making: cultural concepts of masculinity* (New Haven, CT, 1990), p. 34.

Hereward 'the Wake' and lay masculinity

period, however, the fundamental distinction between *clerici* and *laici* centred on whether or not they had sex; sexual activity and renunciation thereof thus became a key field of combat between competing masculinities.[21]

At one level, of course, every historical context has been or could theoretically be identified as one which saw a crisis of masculinity.[22] Recent scholarship on masculinities acknowledges that the hegemonic hierarchy of masculinities is always in a state of flux, continually being negotiated and renegotiated.[23] Similarly, the concern with clerical celibacy was by no means an exclusively eleventh- and twelfth-century phenomenon.[24] Nonetheless, the rhetoric of this period was particularly widespread, and particularly shrill, and the case for the High Middle Ages as a particular flashpoint stands.[25] This period saw a clerical and monastic redefinition of the relationship between celibacy and masculinity, whereby renunciation of sexual activity became a marker of a superior virility.[26] This superior virility was not, however, focussed solely on explicitly sexual conduct. Rather, its establishment allowed for rearticulation of other aspects of clerical masculinity, and situated *clerici*, as opposed to *laici*, as the rightful leaders

---

[21] See Jennifer D. Thibodeaux, Kirsten A. Fenton and Matthew Mesley's contributions to this volume for further discussion of the impact of the reform movement on perceptions and representations of masculinity.

[22] As also discussed by Ruth Mazo Karras, *From boys to men: formations of masculinity in late medieval Europe* (Philadelphia, 2003), p. 8.

[23] On this particular point, see, for example, Jennifer D. Thibodeaux, 'Odo Rigaldus, the Norman elite, and the conflict over masculine prerogatives in the diocese of Rouen', *Essays in medieval studies* 23 (2006), pp. 41–55, esp. 42; see also Rachel Stone, 'Masculinity without conflict: noblemen in eighth- and ninth-century Francia', in *What is masculinity? Historical dynamics from Antiquity to the contemporary world*, ed. John H. Arnold and Sean Brady (Basingstoke, 2011), pp. 76–93. See also Rachel Stone's essay in this volume.

[24] See, inter alia, C. Leyser, 'Masculinity in flux: nocturnal emission and the limits of celibacy in the Early Middle Ages', J.L. Nelson, 'Monks, secular men and masculinity, c.900', R. Balzaretti, 'Men and sex in tenth-century Italy', R.N. Swanson, 'Angels incarnate: clergy and masculinity from Gregorian reform to Reformation', and P.H. Cullum, 'Clergy, masculinity and transgression in late medieval England', all in *Masculinity in medieval Europe*, ed. D.M. Hadley (London, 1999), pp. 103–20, 121–42, 143–59, 160–77, 178–96.

[25] See, for example, Amy G. Remensnyder, 'Pollution, purity, and peace: An aspect of social reform between the late tenth century and 1076', in *The Peace of God: social violence and religious response in France around the year 1000*, ed. Thomas Head and Richard Landes (Ithaca, NY, 1992), pp. 280–307; Conrad Leyser, 'Custom, truth, and gender in eleventh-century reform', *Gender and Christian religion. Papers read at the 1996 Summer meeting and the 1997 Winter meeting of the Ecclesiastical History Society*. ed. R.N. Swanson. Studies in Church History 34 (Woodbridge, 1998), pp. 75–91; *Medieval purity and piety: essays on medieval celibacy and religious reform*, ed. Michael Frassetto (London, 1998); Jacqueline Murray, 'Masculinizing religious life: sexual prowess, the battle for chastity and monastic identity', in *Holiness and masculinity in the Middle Ages*, ed. P.H. Cullum and Katherine J. Lewis (Cardiff, 2004), pp. 24–42; Pauline Stafford, 'The meanings of hair in the Anglo-Norman world: masculinity, reform, and national identity', in *Saints, scholars, and politicians: gender as a tool in medieval studies*, ed. Mathilde van Dijk and Renée Nip, Medieval Church Studies 15 (Turnhout, 2005), pp. 153–71; Kathleen G. Cushing, *Reform and papacy in the eleventh century: spirituality and social change* (Manchester, 2005); Simon Yarrow, 'Masculinity as a world historical category', in *What is masculinity?*, ed. Arnold and Brady, pp. 114–38, at p. 130; Rachel Stone, *Morality and masculinity in the Carolingian empire* (Cambridge, 2012), esp. pp. 279–310.

[26] Murray, 'Masculinizing religious life', p. 37.

of the Christian community.²⁷ Hereward's masculinity can be seen as one of many instances of this renegotiation, redefinition and rearticulation.

Before considering the *Gesta's* representation of Hereward let us deal briefly with the historical Hereward, whose context is the Norman Conquest, and William's attempts to establish authority in the wake of the Battle of Hastings. A Hereward appears in the Domesday Book, holding estates in southern Lincolnshire, including one from Peterborough abbey.²⁸ Two entries mention that he had been outlawed, so this is presumably our Hereward. He also appears in two of the *Anglo-Saxon Chronicles*. The D Chronicle has a brief reference to Hereward, in the context of William the Bastard's siege of rebels at the Isle of Ely in 1071. The majority of the rebels have been brought to heel, 'except Hereward alone, and all who could flee away with him; and he courageously led them out'.²⁹ The *E Chronicle* also has this brief passage, but expands on the *D Chronicle*'s throwaway comment that Peterborough minster had been raided, allegedly as a protest because William had installed a French abbot. The rebels were generally disrespectful, burned the town to the ground and scurried back to Ely with booty.³⁰ The expansion of the account of Peterborough abbey's desecration is unsurprising, as this version of the *Chronicle* is the Peterborough chronicle. Dating these two versions of the Chronicle is notoriously problematic.³¹ Essentially, with some notable exceptions, most of the *D Chronicle* for this period was probably mostly written roughly contemporaneously. The *E Chronicle* is even more problematic, as it was copied in one fell swoop in 1121 from an older exemplar. It is unfortunately difficult, therefore, to establish the extent of twelfth-century interpolation or omission. Thus far, then, from the sources which may be roughly contemporaneous, the historical Hereward was a landholder, and was probably outlawed. He was probably somehow involved in resistance to the new Norman regime at Ely and thereabouts, in 1070–1, and possibly one of the thugs who ransacked Peterborough.

Much recent historiography on the Conquest has focussed on ethnicity – Anglo-Saxons *versus* Normans.³² Anglo-Saxon rebels fighting the Norman

---

²⁷ In addition to the works already cited see also Maureen C. Miller, 'Masculinity, reform, and clerical culture: narratives of episcopal holiness in the Gregorian era', *Church History* 72 (2003), pp. 25–52; Kirsten A. Fenton, 'The question of masculinity in William of Malmesbury's presentation of Wulfstan of Worcester', *Anglo-Norman Studies* 28 (2006), pp. 124–37; Scott Wells, 'The warrior habitus: masculinity and monasticism in the Henrician reform movement', in *Negotiating clerical identities: priests, monks and masculinity in the Middle Ages*, ed. Jennifer D. Thibodeaux (Basingstoke, 2010), pp. 57–85.

²⁸ Cyril Hart, 'Hereward "the Wake" and his companions', in his *The Danelaw* (London, 1992), pp. 625–51; David Roffe, 'Hereward "the Wake" and the barony of Bourne: A reassessment of a Fenland legend', *Lincolnshire History and Archaeology* 29 (1994), pp. 7–10; van Houts, 'Hereward', p. 201, n. 2.

²⁹ Michael Swanton, trans., *The Anglo-Saxon Chronicles*, new ed. (London, 2000), 1072 [r 1071] D, pp. 206–8, 208 cited.

³⁰ *Anglo-Saxon Chronicles*, E, 1070–1, pp. 205–8.

³¹ Recently, see Stephen Baxter, 'MS C of the *Anglo-Saxon Chronicle* and the politics of mid-eleventh-century England', *English Historical Review* 122 (2007), pp. 1189–1227.

³² See especially Hugh M. Thomas, *The English and the Normans: ethnic hostility, assimilation, and identity, 1066–c.1220* (Oxford, 2003).

oppressor have naturally figured quite prominently in the scholarship.[33] Unsurprisingly, Hereward has been considered in terms of Anglo-Saxon/English *versus* Norman – indeed the *Gesta Herwardi* has been called 'one of the most anti-Norman pieces of the period'.[34] Hereward's story does not, however, fit this neat antithesis. Hereward is not unequivocally Good, William is not unequivocally Bad, and Good *versus* Bad does not run along ethnic lines. Indeed, the happy ending provided by Hereward's submission to William as his lord in the *Gesta* would not be possible if William was a villain. This purported ethnic binary has been further undermined by Timothy S. Jones, who situates the *Gesta* in the context of Scandinavian literary tropes.[35]

Academic and popular historians have sought to unpick the historical facts in Hereward's legend. A recent work was lauded for 'rescu[ing] Hereward not only from historical obscurity, but from the myths associated with his life and career'.[36] The 'more fabulous elements' of the twelfth-century accounts of Hereward, are 'more suited to the study of literature in the Middle Ages than of history'.[37] But these fabulous elements are very revealing about the context in which they were written. If he is a hero in these texts, what might we glean?[38]

There are no extant sources from the next few decades concerning Hereward, but his story was clearly circulating, and re-emerges in extant evidence from the first half of the twelfth century. He appears in four important histories, which were written from the 1120s to the late 1140s, that is, at approximately the same time as the *Gesta Herwardi*. William of Malmesbury, John of Worcester and Henry of Huntingdon largely followed the *Anglo-Saxon Chronicles*' version of Hereward and his adventures. For Malmesbury, Hereward leads a gang of brigands (*latrunculi*), and is primarily a convenient means for William the Bastard to

---

[33] See, for example, Keen, *Outlaws*, pp. 23–38; Susan Reynolds, 'Eadric "Silvaticus" and the English resistance', *Bulletin of the Institute of Historical Research* 54 (1981); Stein, *Reality fictions*, pp. 90–103 on Waltheof.

[34] Thomas, *The English and the Normans*, p. 89; see also John Hayward, 'Hereward the outlaw', *Journal of Medieval History* 14 (1988), pp. 293–304; Hugh M. Thomas, 'The *Gesta Herwardi*, the English, and their conquerors', *Anglo-Norman Studies* 21 (1998), pp. 213–32; Rolf H. Bremmer Jr., 'The *Gesta Herewardi*: transforming an Anglo-Saxon into an Englishman', in *People and texts: relationships in medieval literature. Studies presented to Erik Kooper*, ed. Thea Summerfield and Keith Busby (Amsterdam, 2007), pp. 29–42.

[35] Timothy S. Jones, 'Fighting men, fighting monsters: outlawry, masculinity, and identity in the *Gesta Herewardi*', in *Marvels, monsters, and miracles: studies in the medieval and early modern imagination*, ed. Timothy S. Jones and David A. Sprunger (Kalamazoo, 2002), pp. 183–201. See also Keen, *Outlaws*, p. 11; Stephen Marritt, 'Drogo the Sheriff: a neglected lost romance tradition and Anglo-Norwegian relations in the twelfth century', *Historical Research* 80 (2007), pp. 157–84, at p. 181, which situates Hereward in a most useful discussion of twelfth-century connections between Lincolnshire and Norway, *passim*; Swanton's introduction to *Deeds*, p. 17; Timothy S. Jones, *Outlawry in medieval literature* (New York, 2010), pp. 74–87.

[36] Peter Rex, *Hereward: the last Englishman* (Stroud, 2005), back cover; See also Cyril Hart, 'Hereward'; Roffe, 'Hereward'; Keen, *Outlaws*, p. 13.

[37] Rex, *Hereward*, p. 8.

[38] On the historiographical value of depictions of heroes, see, for example, Laura Ashe, 'The hero and his realm in medieval romance', in *Boundaries in medieval romance*, ed. Neil Cartlidge (Cambridge, 2008), pp. 129–47; *Heroes and anti-heroes in medieval romance*, ed. Neil Cartlidge (Cambridge, 2012).

deal with a troublesome abbot, Turold. Turold was a monk of Fécamp who had inveigled himself into the abbacy at Malmesbury, where he was a tyrant. William, recognising his error, packed Turold off to Peterborough, where Hereward and his men were, declaring, 'By the splendour of God, ... he behaves more like a knight than an abbot; I'll find him someone who can stand up to his attacks on equal terms'.[39] Hereward here, then, plays a very minor bit-part, although by implication he is a redoubtable warrior. Similarly, John of Worcester has Hereward as superlatively vigorous (*vir strenuissimus*) twice, but again, he is but an extra.[40] For Henry of Huntingdon, too, he is a very minor character, albeit a superlatively vigorous one, who manfully led his men away after the siege at Ely.[41]

Hereward gets more development in Geffrei Gaimar's *Estoire des Engleis*, which gaily intersperses legends with what might be seen as more reliable history. Gaimar largely followed the *Anglo-Saxon Chronicles* up to the mid tenth century, and then occasionally deviated from their narrative. As others have noted, he was particularly concerned with the implications of treachery,[42] and Hereward provides one of his deviations.[43] He leaps, instantly virile, onto the folios of the *Estoire*.[44] From the outset, he is a *gentilz hom*,[45] he is valiant [*fors*][46] and leopard-like (something which is admirable elsewhere in the *Estoire*).[47] He fights like a lion,[48] has the strength of seven men,[49] wins his battles and attracts followers, 'a braver fighter than he was never seen'.[50] In short, he is a fully-formed and fully effective man. He is only vanquished by treachery, and is heroic to the last.[51]

As others have argued, Gaimar's *Estoire* provides a barometer of the mores and aspirations of French-speaking society in the 1130s/40s.[52] Like the *Estoire*,

---

[39] William of Malmesbury, *Gesta pontificum Anglorum. The history of the English bishops*, volume I, ed. and trans. Michael Winterbottom and Rodney Malcolm Thompson (Oxford, 2007), pp. 628–9: 'Per splendorem . . . Dei, quia magis se agit militem quam abbatem, inueniam ei comparem, qui assultus eius accipiat. Ibi uirtutem suam et militiam experiatur, ibi prelia proludat.'.

[40] John of Worcester, *The Chronicle of John of Worcester, Volume III. The annals from 1067 to 1140 with the Gloucester interpolations and the continuation to 1141*, ed. and trans. P. McGurk (Oxford, 1998), s.a. 1071, pp. 20–1.

[41] Henry, Archdeacon of Huntingdon, *Historia Anglorum, The history of the English people*, ed. and trans. Diana Greenway (Oxford, 1996), pp. 396–7:'qui suos uiriliter strenuissimus eduxit'.

[42] Jane Zatta, 'Gaimar's rebels: outlaw heroes and the creation of authority in twelfth-century England', in *Essays in medieval studies, 16: Out of bounds*, ed. W. Fahrenbach. Proceedings of the Illinois Medieval Association (Morgantown, WV, 1999), pp. 27–40, at p. 28.

[43] For a précis of Hereward's section, see Dalton, 'The outlaw Hereward', p. 12.

[44] Geffrei Gaimar, *Estoire des Engleis: History of the English*, trans. Ian Short (Oxford, 2009), lines 5467–5710, pp. 296–309.

[45] Ibid., line 5468, p. 296.

[46] Ibid., lines 5500, 5519, p. 298.

[47] Ibid., line 5520.

[48] Ibid., lines 5625, 5634, p. 304.

[49] Ibid., line 5589, p. 302.

[50] Ibid., 'unc plus hardi ne fu veü', line 5590, p. 302.

[51] Ibid., lines 5615–5700, pp. 304–9.

[52] Elizabeth Freeman, 'Geffrei Gaimar, vernacular historiography, and the assertion of authority', *Studies in Philology* 93 (1996), pp. 188–206; John Gillingham, 'Kingship, chivalry and love: political and cultural values in the earliest history written in French: Geoffrey Gaimar's Estoire des

the *Gesta* is a story of derring-do and very much in the romantic tradition, and also like the *Estoire*, its Hereward is a hero – he lived 'a distinguished life as a great warrior'; he is 'a notable warrior among the most notable'.[53] Hugh Thomas argues that the *Gesta* reveals more about the context in which it was written than about the events it describes. He focuses, however, on ethnicity, arguing that the text insists upon Anglo-Saxon valour and honour in battle.[54] Our understanding of the text is given still more nuance by Paul Dalton's analysis of Hereward's enemies, which writes local allegiances and enmities into the equation.[55] Whilst thinking about ethnicities has opened up the texts of this period fruitfully, I suggest that we need to go beyond approaching Hereward's representation purely in terms of an Anglo-Saxon/Norman binary, by approaching it in terms of its constructions of gender.

The most striking thing in the *Gesta* which is absent from the *Estoire* is a lengthy passage on Hereward's youth and pre-Ely career.[56] The development of his maturation is key to my reading of the text. As outlined above, how one could and should be a man was a contentious issue at this time. Thinking about how one should *become* a man is therefore instructive.[57] In some respects, the *Gesta*'s Hereward is immediately manly: 'From his childhood he exhibited such grace and vigour of body; . . . when a youth the quality of his *virtus* proved him a perfect man'.[58] He is generous, daring, and 'while still a youth excelled in manly deeds'.[59] Sadly, however, he is apparently too in thrall to his testosterone – he picks fights with anyone who could be a rival, and is over-generous, not just with his own possessions but also his father's. He antagonises everyone, and his parents get so fed up with having to resolve his quarrels and defending him against disgruntled neighbours, that they send him away. This does not, however, resolve the problem. Hereward skims the profits of his father's estates to give to his friends. Exasperated, his father asks King Edward to banish him, so at

---

Engleis', in *Anglo-Norman political culture and the twelfth-century Renaissance*, ed. C. Warren Hollister (Woodbridge, 1997), pp. 33–58; Zatta, 'Gaimar's rebels'; Paul Dalton, 'Geffrei Gaimar's *Estoire des Engleis*, peacemaking, and the "twelfth-century revival of the English nation"', *Studies in Philology* 104 (2007), pp. 427–54; *idem*, 'The date of Geoffrey Gaimar's *Estoire des Engleis*, the connections of his patrons, and the politics of Stephen's reign', *The Chaucer Review* 42 (2007), pp. 23–47. Henry Bainton has convincingly argued that we also need to write the local back into the *Estoire*, 'Translating the "English" past: cultural identity in the *Estoire des Engleis*', in *Language and culture in medieval Britain: the French of England c.1100–c.1500*, ed. Jocelyn Wogan-Browne et al. (York, 2009), pp. 179–87.

[53] *Deeds*, pp. 19–20; *Gesta*, p. 339, p. 341: 'insignis miles magnanimiter vivens', 'insignis miles cum insignioribus'.
[54] Thomas, 'The *Gesta Herwardi*', *passim*, see esp. p. 214.
[55] Dalton, 'The outlaw Hereward'.
[56] This is also noted by Jones, who draws comparisons with saga literature, 'Fighting men, fighting monsters'.
[57] For an extremely useful discussion of the lay nobility's shaping of male maturation in the German empire in this period, see Jonathan R. Lyon, 'Fathers and sons: preparing noble youths to be lords in twelfth-century Germany', *Journal of Medieval History* 34 (2008), pp. 291–310.
[58] *Deeds*, p. 20; *Gesta*, pp. 341–2: 'Inerat etiam illa a pueritia multa gratia et fortitudo corporis; et perfectum virum hujus rei ex facultate statim in adolescentia forma virtutis ejus eum demonstrabat'.
[59] *Deeds*, p. 20; *Gesta*, p. 342: 'juvenis supra modum in viriles actus transcenderet'.

eighteen, Hereward is outlawed, and exiled from his homeland. At this point, then, Hereward is manly, but not yet properly manly.

It is at this point in the narrative that Hereward performs his manly bear-wrangling.[60] As noted above, the contests were for young men to show that they were worthy of 'the belt and arms of knighthood' – a key life-stage transition.[61] Because of his success with the bear, 'he gained the status and rank of a knight, although at the time he put off being made a knight, saying that he ought to make a better trial of his *virtus* and spirit'.[62] Hereward thus conforms to Georges Duby's model of the 'youth', according to which knighthood is a rite of passage, but does not entail admission into adult masculinity, but rather into a period of 'a secular, heedless, and playboy style of life'.[63] Rejecting the lady's offer of waiting for her son to die, Hereward sets off for Cornwall, to join the court of Prince Alef. He encounters a 'very wicked and arrogant man' there,[64] who wants Alef's daughter. Hereward scoffs at the older man's wild bragging, which unsurprisingly results in a challenge. Hereward replies by stressing his youth – 'See that so tough a knight as you proclaim yourself to be doesn't employ trickery against a young man'.[65] After more mutual posturing, they fight – when Hereward is twice described as a *juvenis*, and once as *puer* –[66] and Hereward triumphs. Bear-wrangling notwithstanding, then, he is a young man. His victory entails a literal and metaphorical attack on the older man's masculinity, as he 'thrust his sword under the mailcoat into the groin/genitals' [*in inguine*]'.[67] The Cornish people are

---

[60] Jones points to parallels with this episode in Scandinavian literature, 'Fighting men, fighting monsters', p. 191, n. 15. See also *Deeds*, p. 294, n. 12.

[61] For a useful and succinct discussion, see Robert Bartlett, *England under the Norman and Angevin kings, 1075–1225* (Oxford, 2000), pp. 232–5. John Gillingham identifies the first appearance of dubbing [*dubbade to ... ridere*] in the Anglo-Saxon Chronicles' entry for 1086, 'Kingship, chivalry and love', p. 39. See also M. Bennett, 'Military masculinity in England and Northern France', in *Masculinity in medieval Europe*, ed. Hadley, pp. 71–88, at pp. 76–7; William M. Aird, 'Frustrated masculinity: The relationship between William the Conqueror and his eldest son', in ibid., pp. 39–55, at pp. 43–4; William M. Aird, *Robert Curthose: Duke of Normandy, c.1050–1134* (Woodbridge, 2008), pp. 54–5.

[62] *Deeds*, p. 21; *Gesta*, p. 344: 'locum et honorem cum militibus obtinuit; licet tunc militem fieri distulerit, dicens melius se virtutem et animum suum probare debere'.

[63] Georges Duby, 'Youth in aristocratic society', in *The chivalrous society*, trans. Cynthia Postan (London, 1977), pp. 112–22. Duby's model has been much modified since its original articulation but is still a useful approach to understanding the issue. The quoted characterisation of Duby's 'youths' as a life stage is David Crouch, *The birth of nobility: constructing aristocracy in England and France 900–1300* (Harlow, 2005), p. 18. See also Robert Bartlett, *The making of Europe: conquest, civilization and cultural change 950–1350* (Harmondsworth, 1994), pp. 24–59, esp. pp. 49–51. For a discussion of this in gendered terms see Karras, *From boys to men*. That dubbing was recognised at the time as a bestowal of manhood is demonstrated by Henry of Huntingdon's description of David of Scotland knighting the future Henry II of England: '[he] bestowed the arms of manhood [upon him]'; 'virilia tradidit arma', *Historia Anglorum*, pp. 754–5.

[64] *Deeds*, p.22; *Gesta*, pp. 344–5: 'nephandissimum virum et valde superbum'.

[65] *Deeds*, p. 22; *Gesta*, p. 345: 'vide ne miles robustissimus, ut jactatis, juvenem dolo praeveniat'.

[66] *Deeds*, p. 23; *Gesta*, p. 346.

[67] *Deeds*, p. 23; *Gesta*, p. 346: 'illi gladium in inguine subtus loricam infixit'.

disgruntled, but the prince and his daughter protect him – still a *juvenis*[68] – and send him with tokens to the prince of Ireland.

It is now that Hereward learns that his father has died and that he has come into his patrimony – again, a standard marker of becoming a man. But a local war detains him; he is pressed into service, and prepares for war *cum majoribus* ('with his seniors').[69] So he is still a *junior*, despite having proven himself in bear-battle, one-to-one combat, and having inherited his patrimony, all of which might reasonably be seen as key points of maturation. He fights so well in the battle that 'many tough men and the sons of leading families flocked to him to be instructed in arms and noble arts'.[70] He now, therefore, has a retinue – another sign of male adulthood. He gets a cry for help from a damsel – the Cornish princess is about to be married off against her will, so Hereward sets off to rescue her, disguising himself by dyeing his hair black and his 'youthful beard to a ruddy colour'.[71] After some astonishingly accomplished harp-playing and singing, he rescues the Irish prince's men who had been imprisoned and the damsel, who happily marries her prince, and Hereward sets off for home. He is blown off-course to Orkney, and then to St Bertin. He goes to the count of Flanders' court, incognito again, and wins the admiration of all in battle, including one Turfrida, a noble girl at St Omer. 'Having heard of Hereward's many achievements, she fell madly in love with him. . . . she displayed her manifold talents, and in this way secured the young man's affections'.[72] Note that he is still a *juvenis* here. He goes incognito again, desperate to meet his love, and despite his disguise she recognises him by his battle-scars, and they exchange pledges of faith.[73]

Immediately after this, there is a lengthy battle sequence – in which, naturally, Hereward does well. There is a shift in terms of his maturation at this point. When things look bleak, he rallies his troops, and as the attack starts, he 'asked for the central place in the vanguard, so that the young men and youths might test their mettle'.[74] Hereward is no longer the *juvenis*.

Job done, he sets off for England again, which is now 'subject to the rule of foreigners'.[75] Reaching his father's manor – again, incognito – he learns that his younger brother has been murdered by Normans, who cut off his head and placed it over the gate of the house. Hereward asks those present how this has come about. They reply, 'We shouldn't involve you in our misfortune, for we see that you're a great man ... Nevertheless, because you appear to be ... a great

---

[68] *Deeds*, p. 23; *Gesta*, p. 347.
[69] *Deeds*, p. 24; *Gesta*, p. 348.
[70] *Deeds*, p. 24; *Gesta*, p. 348: 'multi robustissimi ac filii potentum, comperto de eo, ad illum confluebant, cum eo armis et liberalitatibus instruendi'.
[71] *Deeds*, p. 25; *Gesta*, p. 349: 'barba juventutis in rubedinem'.
[72] *Deeds*, p. 29; *Gesta*, p. 356: 'Haec autem valde admavit Herwardum, comperta de eo multa magnalia, unde perplurimas ut fetur in amore illius exercuit artes, cum quibus tantumdem juvenis animum in se convertit'.
[73] *Deeds*, pp. 30–1; *Gesta*, p. 358.
[74] *Deeds*, pp. 31–2; *Gesta*, p. 359 'locum dimicandi contra fieri in medio postulavit, ut ephebi et pueri quasi suas vires probarent'.
[75] *Deeds*, p. 35; *Gesta*, p. 364: 'externorum ditioni nunc subjectam'.

and famous man, we might look to you for some remedy for our sorrow.'[76] The narrative now has Hereward as a man: he is no longer a *puer* or *juvenis*, but a *praeclarus vir*. It is significant that this is just before his first anti-Norman activity. He hears the Normans who killed his brother drunkenly mocking the English and himself personally, and slays all fourteen of them, as they are unarmed or too drunk to move.[77]

Immediately, he is feared by the Normans as 'such a man' [*tanto viro*],[78] and others flock to him for protection. It is now that he is protecting a large group of his people, that he suddenly remembers something he has yet to do: 'When Hereward realised that he was the leader and lord of such men, and day by day saw his force growing larger with fugitives, the condemned and disinherited, he remembered that he had never been girt with the belt and sword of knighthood'.[79] This is necessary, 'lest after becoming the chief and leader of so many men, the inhabitants of the country should disparage him for not being knighted'.[80]

To render himself worthy of respect, therefore, he sets off for Peterborough and asks Abbot Brand to do the honours.[81] Being knighted by a *clericus* is presented as an English custom, denigrated by the French as adulterous and abortive.[82] Hereward insists that all his men should be knighted by monks, frequently stating, 'I know from common experience that if anyone should receive the knightly sword from a servant of God, a knight of the kingdom of heaven [*a milite regis coelestis*], such a man will pursue *virtus* most excellently in every kind of military service'.[83]

We are given, to underline it still further, a description of what became customary at Ely:

> if anyone there wished to be made a knight, he ought always to offer his naked sword upon the altar at High Mass and the same day receive it back again after the gospel reading from the monk who was singing Mass, the sword being placed on

---

[76] *Deeds*, p. 35; *Gesta*, p. 365: 'te nostris calamitatibus inclytum virum ut videmus innectere, ... Sed tamen quia praeclarum virum in cunctis appares et inclytum, nostri vos aestimamus doloris aliquod remedium'.

[77] *Deeds*, p. 36; *Gesta*, pp. 366–7.

[78] *Deeds*, p. 36; *Gesta*, p. 367.

[79] *Deeds*, p. 37; *Gesta*, 368 'Herewardus dum se talium virorum praeceptorem conspiceret ac dominum, et quotidie ex effugatis et praejudicatis et ab exhereditatis manum suam non minime crescere cerneret in memoriam habuit morem suae gentis gladio nec baltheo militari praecinctum se non fuisse'.

[80] *Deeds*, p. 37; *Gesta*, p. 368: 'ne multorem princeps et ductor factus quasi non miles incolae patriae exprobrarent'.

[81] *Deeds*, p. 37; *Gesta*, p. 368: 'Ut eum militari gladio et baltheo Anglico more praecingeret'.

[82] *Deeds*, p. 37; *Gesta*, p. 368: 'si quis a monacho vel a clerico seu ab aliquo infra sacros ordines constituto militem fieret, non humilitatem inter milites haberi debere, sed quasi adulteratus eques et abortivus'.

[83] *Deeds*, p. 37; *Gesta*, p. 368: 'quoniam si quis a servo Dei et a milite regis coelestis gladium militarem acceperit, hunc servum suam virtutem excellenter in omni tirocinio agere scio, ut saepe expertus sum'.

his bare neck with a blessing; and by making over the sword to the recruit in that way, he was made a full knight.[84]

Presumably something like this did happen, as the Council of Westminster in 1102 states that it should not.[85]

Now that the narrative has made Hereward a *miles*, subjected to the abbot, and we have had, several times, the rationale for this, Hereward's resistance to the Normans commences. He is a man, and his exploits are those of a man with authority conferred by a monk. By contrast, William is later persuaded to use a different ally, namely a witch.[86] As the Normans besiege the Isle of Ely, she yells abuse at the enemy, casts spells, and then bares her behind at them. To no avail: the Normans are beaten, and the hag falls and breaks her neck.[87]

Hereward does not, however, always act in alliance with all monks. The *Gesta* does not gloss over the attack on Peterborough. Immediately after this, there are two supernatural interventions: one to set Hereward back on the right path morally, and another to do so literally. Having burned Peterborough and looted the church, Hereward has a vision in which St Peter warns him that if he wants to avoid dying horribly the next day, he should return the booty. Duly alarmed, he does as he is told. Leaving Peterborough, he and his men get lost in the dark of night, but are guided to where they need to be by an atypically friendly wolf, and their way is lit by some convenient floating lights. Both wolf and will-o'-the-wisps magically disappear when they have found their way – both literally and morally.[88] Now that Hereward has matured appropriately, is worthy of respect, and has been set on the right path, he is able, ultimately, to become reconciled with William the Conqueror and to have a happy ending.

Thus, in order to achieve adult masculinity, military *virtus* and spectacular deeds of derring-do are not enough. Training younger men is not enough. Marrying and getting a patrimony is not enough. Hereward stops being called *juvenis* when he marries, but he is only able to embark on the most famous part of his career when he has submitted himself to the lordship of an abbot. When he wavers from an appropriate respect for *clerici* – albeit exemplified by a dastardly Norman one – he is admonished, and when he makes amends, he is back on the right path. He is, in short, a layman who learns his place.

The *Gesta* is primarily concerned with the exploits of laymen, and is explicitly intended to give an exemplary model to them: 'to know who Hereward was and

---

[84] *Deeds*, p. 37; *Gesta*, pp. 368–9: 'Quod si quis ibi miles fieret, semper nudum ensem super altare inter magnam missam eodem die offere deberet, et a monacho qui missam cantaret post evangelium sic accipi imposito nudo collo gladio cum benedictione, isto modo tironi tradens ensem, eques sit factus emerite'.

[85] *Councils and synods with other documents relating to the English Church*, eds. D. Whitelock, M. Brett, and C.N.L. Brooke, 2 vols (Oxford, 1964–81), I.ii, pp. 676–7. According to Orderic Vitalis, *contra* the *Anglo-Saxon Chronicles* and William of Malmesbury, Archbishop Lanfranc knighted Prince Henry, later Henry I: *Historia Æcclesiastica, The Ecclesiastical History of Orderic Vitalis*, ed. and trans. Marjorie Chibnall, 6 vols (Oxford, 1969–1980), IV, pp. 120–1.

[86] *Deeds*, p. 47; *Gesta*, p. 384.

[87] *Deeds*, pp. 50–1; *Gesta*, pp. 389–90.

[88] *Deeds*, pp. 54–5; *Gesta*, pp. 395–6.

to hear about his magnanimity and his exploits, is conducive to magnanimous acts and generosity, especially in those wishing to undertake the warrior's life'.[89] At face value, there is little concern with religion. The few points at which God and divine intervention are explicitly mentioned, however, are telling.[90]

God features but five times in the narrative, mostly indirectly and with a light touch, but one might reasonably conclude that these are significant points in the narrative. Four of the five occasions are at key points in Hereward's development. When Hereward avenges his brother's death, he 'giv[es] thanks to the Bestower of all grace',[91] and proceeds to establish his reputation in his homeland. Soon after, God, *clerici*, and liturgy are central to being made a knight,[92] and thereafter God leaves men to their own devices for some time within the text. The vision of St Peter seizes Hereward with divine dread,[93] and Hereward and his men give thanks to God for the assistance of the mystical wolf and will-o'-the-wisps.[94] Finally, with the happy ending of Hereward's reconciliation with William, the *Gesta* concludes with a common formula: 'And thus in the end [he] rested in peace, upon whose soul may God have mercy'.[95] God's appearances in the narrative, therefore, are rare, but four of them are at key points of Hereward's becoming a good man.

The remaining mention of God brings me to the second context within which I wish to situate the *Gesta*, namely Ely's contemporaneous textual activity. William's advisors counsel him against making peace with the rebels at Ely, lest he should damage his regal reputation. William angrily replies that 'he could not take the Isle or any place so naturally fortified by the *virtus* of God'.[96] Thinking about the *Gesta* in the circumstances specific to twelfth-century Ely suggests broader conclusions about the functions of historical narratives, the permeability of the boundaries between medieval narrative genres, and the significance of the model of lay masculinity which it presents.

Ely's historiographical activity took various forms, and was itself part of a broader trend in twelfth-century England, which saw a remarkable increase in textual activity, as people tried to make sense of their present in the light of their past. As in all periods, the writing of history contributed to the establishment and consolidation of contemporary identities, status, and authority. Many

---

[89] *Deeds*, p. 19; *Gesta*, pp. 340–1: 'Propterea namque, ut estimamus, ad magnanimorum operum exempla et ad liberalitatem exercendam profectum erit Herwardum scire, quis fuerit, et magnanimitates illius audire et opera, maxime autem militiam exercere volentibus.'

[90] Bremmer also notes that mentions of God in the *Gesta* are rare. The instance which he cites is Hereward's dubbing, but he argues that the inclusion of God here is 'merely a red herring': 'Clearly, this sentiment belongs to the realm of popular religion: no mention is made of a personal bond with God, but the efficacy of the ceremony is attributed to its being conducted by clerics', 'The *Gesta Herewardi*', p. 39.

[91] *Deeds*, p. 36; *Gesta*, p. 367: 'gratias agens quidem universae gratiae largitori'.

[92] *Deeds*, pp. 37–8; *Gesta*, pp. 368–9.

[93] *Deeds*, p. 54; *Gesta*, p. 396: 'divino terrore corripitur'.

[94] *Deeds*, p. 55; *Gesta*, p. 396.

[95] *Deeds*, p. 60; *Gesta*, p. 404: 'ac sic demum quievit in pace, cujus animae propicietur Deus'.

[96] *Deeds*, p. 47; *Gesta* p. 384: 'non se posse expugnare insulam, nec locum ex virtute Dei naturaliter munitum'.

medieval narratives, like the *Gesta*, are explicitly exemplary.[97] The *Gesta* may be seen as a shot which is entirely commensurate with the concerns of the salvo of Ely's twelfth-century textual production. In 1109, Ely, unhappy with what was perceived as undue and uncustomary interference from Lincoln in Ely affairs, broke free of the bishop of Lincoln, and Hervey, bishop of Bangor, was appointed bishop of the new see of Ely, with the support of Henry I, Pope Paschal II, and Anselm, archbishop of Canterbury.[98] The institutional reorganisation did not, however, resolve Ely's problems overnight. The division of endowments and rights between monks and diocese was far from smooth, and the monks suffered from what they saw as episcopal as well as lay depredations.[99]

It is not in the least coincidental that there was a concomitant flurry of textual activity – the *Libellus Æthelwoldi episcopi* allegedly translated Old English charters of Ely's tenth-century land acquisitions into Latin, inventories and charters were drawn up, the hefty *Liber Eliensis* was compiled, and *vitae* of and *lectiones* for the Ely saints were copied.[100] The *Libellus Æthelwoldi* has harmony and concord between bishops and monks in the face of potentially hostile local laypeople as a central theme.[101] Jennifer Paxton has identified a historiographical programme of outreach to the local laity, centred on Ely, Peterborough and Ramsey, 'intended to serve as the basis for a sort of "textual community" that would draw the surrounding laypeople into the orbit of the monastic house'.[102] She has also convincingly argued that the *Liber Eliensis* specifically deploys 'very deliberate narrative strategies to emphasise the spiritual authority of the monastery's patroness and to undermine the legitimacy of the bishops' rule'.[103] Like many pre-Conquest saints, Æthelthryth was a fierce defender of the rights of her tomb custodians

---

[97] To give but one example, William of Malmesbury stated, in around 1126, that works of history, 'were written for kings or queens in order to provide them with a sort of pattern for their own lives, from which they could learn to follow some men's successes, while avoiding the misfortunes of others, to imitate the wisdom of some and to look down on the foolishness of others'. 'Solebant sane huiusmodi libri regibus siue reginis antiquitus scribi, ut quasi ad uitae suae exemplum eis instruerentur aliorum prosequi triumphos, aliorum uitare miserias, aliorum imitari sapientiam, aliorum contempnere stultitiam', *Gesta regum Anglorum: The history of the English kings*, ed. and trans. R.A.B. Mynors, completed by R.M. Thomson and M. Winterbottom, 2 vols. (Oxford, 1998–99), I, pp. 6–9.

[98] Edward Miller, *The abbey and bishopric of Ely* (Cambridge, 1951), esp. p. 75; Everett U. Crosby, *Bishop and chapter in twelfth-century England: a study of the mensa episcopalis* (Cambridge, 1994), pp. 151–74; Nicholas Karn, 'The twelfth century', in *Ely: Bishops and diocese, 1109-2009*, ed. Peter Meadows (Woodbridge, 2010), pp. 1–25, esp. pp. 1–4.

[99] Miller, *Abbey and bishopric*, pp. 75–7; Crosby, *Bishop and chapter*, pp. 159–74; Nigel Ramsay, 'The library and archives 1109–1541', in *A history of Ely cathedral*, ed. Peter Meadows and Nigel Ramsay (Woodbridge, 2003), pp. 157–68, 157; Karn, 'The twelfth century', pp. 13–24.

[100] For a useful overview, see Simon Keynes, 'Ely abbey 672–1109', in *A history of Ely cathedral*, pp. 3–58. See also Rosalind C. Love, 'Introduction', in *Goscelin of Saint-Bertin: the hagiography of the female saints of Ely*, ed. and trans. *eadem* (Oxford, 2004), pp. xiii–cxxviii, xlviii–liii.

[101] Catherine Clarke, *Writing power in Anglo-Saxon England* (Cambridge, 2012), pp. 145–70. See also Keynes, 'Ely abbey', p. 7.

[102] Jennifer Paxton, 'Textual communities in the English Fenlands: a lay audience of monastic chronicles?', *Anglo-Norman Studies* 26 (2004), pp. 123–37, p. 123 cited.

[103] Jennifer Paxton, 'Monks and bishops: the purpose of the *Liber Eliensis*', *Haskins Society Journal* 11 (2003 for 1998), pp. 17–30.

against would-be despoilers.[104] The burgeoning exuberance of Æthelthryth's cult boosted the authority and prestige of Ely itself. Support of the Anglo-Saxon saint did not wax or wane depending on whether the current abbot was Anglo-Saxon or Norman.[105] Instead, the Anglo-Saxon cult facilitated a post-Conquest corporate identity which transcended ethnicity. Perhaps counter-intuitively, it seems that an indigenous rebel performed the same function.

Even his staunchest supporter would not argue that Hereward was a saint. But the *Gesta* may be seen as doing the same work as that of many *vitae* and other texts of this period, namely establishing models of appropriate interrelationships between *clerici* and *laici*, and between *clerici* and other *clerici*. Given the period in which Hereward's exploits occurred, bishops of Ely naturally do not feature, but the *Gesta* establishes the monks of Ely as Hereward's spiritual, moral, and practical mentors. This is encapsulated in an episode associated with the Ely monks' potentially controversial capitulation to William, undertaken behind Hereward's back.[106] Having decided that he could not take Ely by force, William divides Ely's external estates amongst his followers. These lay depredations finally force Ely's monks to make peace. A furious Hereward storms back to Ely, intent on burning the church and town, but is headed off by one of the monks, Eadwine. The monk urges Hereward to withdraw:

> Eventually [Hereward] yielded to his words and arguments because he had been a friend to him and a good comrade in war and of practical help in many of his needs. Thus he was persuaded.[107]

Having submitted to the counsel of Eadwine, Hereward withdraws, spares Ely, ravages elsewhere, and lives to fight another day, soon turning his attentions instead to Peterborough. Here, as elsewhere at key points in the *Gesta*, despite Hereward's undeniable vigour, a monk is, as it were, wearing the trousers in lay-clerical interaction.

Hereward is constructed as a hero, and the way in which his heroism and his eventual achievement of adult masculinity are written allows us to think about what a good layman should be, and to whom he should defer. Eschewing the 'ethnicity lens' through which the narrative is often viewed, the *Gesta* has been considered here instead in terms of masculine clerical and lay interaction, in order to further illustrate the complex interplay between gender, religion, and

---

[104] S.J. Ridyard, 'Condigna Veneratio: post-Conquest attitudes to the saints of the Anglo-Saxons', *Anglo-Norman Studies* 9 (1987), pp. 179–206, esp. pp. 180–7; eadem, *The royal saints of Anglo-Saxon England: a study of West Saxon and East Anglian cults* (Cambridge, 2008), pp. 206–10. See also Virginia Blanton-Whetsell, 'Tota integra, tota incorrupta: the shrine of St. Æthelthryth as symbol of monastic autonomy', *Journal of Medieval and Early Modern Studies* 32 (2002), pp. 227–67; Virginia Blanton, 'Presenting the sister saints of Ely, or using kinship to increase a monastery's status as a cult center', *Literature Compass* 5 (2008), pp. 755–71.

[105] Ridyard, 'Condigna veneratio'.

[106] *Deeds*, p. 51–2; *Gesta*, pp. 390–2.

[107] *Deeds*, p. 52; *Gesta*, p. 391: 'Cujus tandem persuasionibus et verbis obtemperans, quia amicum eum et bonum consortem habuerat in militia et in multis necessitatibus illius effectus, propterea, sicut illi persuasit'.

the writing and functions of medieval history. At face value, the *Gesta* is primarily concerned with laymen. As it was written by a churchman and is primarily concerned with a layman's exploits, its explicit exemplarity allows us to see what is desirable, from the author's perspective, in laymen. At one level, this reveals a clerical ideal of lay masculinity, but it is also a revealing utterance within an ongoing textual conversation between *clerici* about the nature of *clerical* authority, which can be seen throughout the High Middle Ages. It was produced by discourses of religious authority but, significantly, repeatedly expressed in terms of gendered authority.[108]

---

[108] See further Joanna Huntington, *Heroes from histories: Shaping male virtue in post-Conquest England and Normandy* (forthcoming).

EPISCOPAL AUTHORITY AND GENDER IN THE NARRATIVES OF THE FIRST CRUSADE

Matthew Mesley

REFORM AND THE REPRESENTATION OF CRUSADERS

Analysis of medieval masculinities, and the various ways in which men were conceptualised and represented in different contexts, has often focussed on the rich evidence provided by the impact of the eleventh-century reform movements. One significant consequence of this movement was the unrelenting insistence by religious reformers that there should be a greater distinction made between the lives of the clergy and the laity. There were repeated calls for the improvement of clerical behaviour and education; celibacy was more strictly enforced upon the male clergy; and priests were restricted from taking up arms.[1] The behaviour of male professional religious discussed in explicitly gendered terms was thus a particular target, in part in order to establish the superiority of religious men over laymen. However, reform also left a wider mark on society as a whole.[2] There was an increasing tendency to position religious values and terminology within

---

[1] For introductions to this topic see the essays in *Medieval purity and piety: essays on medieval clerical celibacy and religious reform*, ed. M. Frassetto (New York and London, 1998); and K.G. Cushing, *Reform and the papacy in the eleventh century: spirituality and social change* (Manchester, 2005). Such changes to the clerical office brought about tensions in the way that priests were perceived and how they themselves saw their own identity: for the repercussions of this in the later medieval period see P. Cullum, 'Clergy, masculinity and trangression in late medieval England', in *Masculinity in medieval Europe*, ed. D.M. Hadley (London, 1999), pp. 178–96. See also the essays by Jennifer Thibodeaux, Kirsten A. Fenton and Joanna Huntington in this volume.

[2] There were also serious repercussions for perceptions of female behaviour and the treatment of women. For instance, see D. Elliot, *Fallen bodies: pollution, sexuality, and demonology in the Middle Ages* (Philadelphia, 1999). The classic analysis which situated reform in the context of changing definitions of gender is Jo Ann. McNamara, 'The *Herrenfrage*: the restructuring of the gender system, 1050–1150', in *Medieval masculinities: regarding men in the Middle Ages*, ed. C.A. Lees (Minneapolis, 1994), pp. 3–29. More recent approaches to clerical men include R.M. Karras, 'Thomas Aquinas's Chastity Belt: Clerical Masculinity in Medieval Europe', in ed. L.H. Bitel and F. Lifshitz, *Gender and Christianity in Medieval Europe* (Philadelphia, 2008), pp. 52–67 and J. Thibodeaux, 'Introduction: Rethinking the Medieval Clergy and Masculinity' in idem (ed) *Negotiating clerical identities: priests, monks and masculinity in the Middle Ages* (New York and London, 2010), pp. 1–15.

the secular sphere, as part of attempts to transform cultural attitudes concerning what was appropriate conduct for men and women. This was not a simple one-way process, as reform ideals encouraged a receptive and sometimes proactive laity to seek new spiritual outlets. Taking the crusading cross, for instance, was one way members of the laity could express their piety.[3] However, the texts which advocated these reform ideals were often written by the clergy and for the clergy; and, thus, as Katherine Cushing put it, these accounts 'may often be evidence merely of aspirations to effect change rather than real change'.[4] The success of the eleventh-century reform movements was neither guaranteed nor assured. Yet, investigating cultural aspirations or desires is a vital undertaking if we are to understand why certain texts or narratives were written or constructed in a particular way, and what ideas contemporaries sought to convey to their audiences. My contribution to this collection seeks to investigate the ways reform, and the changing ideas about gender that it occasioned, influenced how the authors of early twelfth-century narratives describing the First Crusade depicted religious men and their place within wider society.

These sources have been selected in part because they express so clearly the ways in which messages about reform could be moulded and adjusted to suit changing events and contexts.[5] Indeed, reform ideology would heavily influence how the expedition to Jerusalem came to be remembered and recorded. It would be combined with a triumphant narrative that described Pope Urban II's famous call for a crusade at the Council of Clermont on 27 November 1095 and the enthusiastic response this received in Western Europe from people at all levels of society, not simply the fighting men whom Urban had primarily sought to inspire. The narrative then related the progress of Christian armies through Western Europe and Byzantium, and their victories in a series of battles against Muslim forces – most famously at Nicea (1097), Antioch (1097–8) and Jerusalem (1099). The capture of Jerusalem had always been the main objective, yet the crusaders, perhaps surprised by their accomplishment, now had to understand and explain their feat, both to themselves and those that had remained at home, motivated in part by the need to secure support for the nascent kingdom of Jerusalem and ensure its defence. The job of interpreting this achievement was left mainly to the religious – the monastic or clerical classes, some of whom had taken part themselves, but others who had not witnessed these events firsthand. It was these writers who clarified and expanded upon the ideals, motives and goals of the participants and instigators of the Crusade.[6] They demonstrated how

---

[3] As an example of a much larger historiography see M. Bull, *Knightly piety and lay response to the First Crusade: the Limousin and Gascony, c. 970–c. 1130* (Oxford, 1993); see also J. Riley-Smith, *The First Crusade and the idea of crusading* (2nd paperback edition, London, 2009), pp. 26–7.

[4] Cushing, *Reform and the papacy*, p. 2.

[5] A useful survey of the sources can be found in S. Edgington, 'The First Crusade: reviewing the evidence', in *The First Crusade: origins and impact*, ed. J. Phillips (Manchester, 1997), pp. 55–77.

[6] The emphasis on how contemporaries sought to represent and remember the crusading past is highlighted in J.M. Powell, 'Myth, legend, propaganda, history: the First Crusade, 1140–ca. 1300', in *Autour de la première croisade: actes du colloque de la Society for the Study of the Crusades and the Latin East*, ed. M. Balard (Paris, 1997), pp. 127–41; and N. Paul and S. Yeager, 'Introduction:

the Church's careful supervision and management of the Crusade could mirror their success in reforming society and of making Christian practice central to it. Of course this meant that the expedition was often portrayed, to quote Giles Constable, 'as it should have been, rather than it actually was'.[7] Authors would draw upon a repertoire of hagiographical and biblical motifs in order to depict the crusaders, as Jonathan Riley-Smith puts it in an oft-quoted statement, 'like a military monastery on the move'.[8] This could not but affect the way that men and women would be represented within the texts.

In the last decade scholars have increasingly explored both the 'crusading experience' and its representation through a gendered lens, but largely with respect to the women who took part.[9] Less has been written on how chroniclers of the Crusade reflected or promoted specific expectations and ideals of the male sex.[10] Yet many examples litter the texts: a cowardly soldier might be described as lukewarm and effeminate; or Saracens as lacking reason or likened to beasts and demons.[11] It is not, of course, that gender is always explicit, nor the salient feature in all of these descriptions. Contemporary understandings of the roles that men and women were expected to have while on crusade also reflected understandings of social roles, race and religious affiliation.[12] That said, to put it another way, while societal hierarchies or classifications might not always be directly about gender, they were often not divorced from such considerations.

Neither was this simply about behaviour – it was about different cultural expectations of what it meant to be a man: for instance, the popular chronicler Robert

---

crusading and the work of memory, past and present', in *Remembering the Crusades: myth, image and identity*, ed. N. Paul and S. Yeager (Baltimore, 2012), pp. 1–25.

[7] G. Constable, 'The historiography of the Crusades', in *The Crusades from the perspective of Byzantium and the Muslim world*, ed. A.E. Laiou and R.P. Mottahedeh (Washington, DC, 2001), p. 5. For other works on Crusade historiography, see J. Riley-Smith, 'The crusading movement and historians', in *The Oxford illustrated history of the Crusades*, ed. J. Riley-Smith (Oxford, 1995), pp. 1–22; C. Tyerman, *The invention of the Crusades* (Toronto, 1998).

[8] Riley-Smith, *Idea of crusading*, esp. pp. 135–52. Discussed also by K.A. Smith, *War and the making of medieval monastic culture* (Woodbridge, 2001), esp. pp. 100–11.

[9] Natasha Hodgson provides perhaps the best analysis of how authors depicted medieval women in crusade narratives; N. Hodgson, *Women, crusading and the Holy Land in historical narrative* (Woodbridge, 2007). See also S. Lambert, 'Crusading or Spinning, pp. 1–15 and M. Bennett, 'Virile Latins, effeminate Greeks and strong women: gender definitions on crusade?' pp. 16–30 in *Gendering the Crusades*, ed. S.B. Edgington and S. Lambert (Cardiff, 2001); K.A. Fenton, 'Gendering the First Crusade in William of Malmesbury's *Gesta regum Anglorum*', in *Intersections of gender, religion and ethnicity in the Middle Ages*, ed. C. Beattie and K.A. Fenton (Basingstoke, 2010), pp. 1–11.

[10] As pointed out by P.H. Cullum, 'Introduction: holiness and masculinity in medieval Europe', in *Holiness and masculinity in the Middle Ages*, ed. P.H. Cullum and Katherine J. Lewis (Cardiff, 2004), p. 6.

[11] Race, although not discussed in this essay, also played an important component in crusade ideologies and interacted with ideas about gender. See the very useful article by D. Gerish, 'Men, women, and beasts at Clermont, 1095', *Rohatyn Center for International Affairs Working Paper Series* 20 (2005) [http://www.middlebury.edu/administration/rcfia/papers/papers.htm accessed 1 September 2012]. I would also like to thank Professor Gerish for providing me with another article in advance of publication.

[12] D. Gerish, 'Gender theory', in *Palgrave advances in the Crusades*, ed. H.J. Nicholson (Basingstoke and New York, 2005), pp. 130–47.

the Monk's description of Duke Godfrey of Bouillon, one of the leaders of the First Crusade, makes plain that contemporaries had certain beliefs about what was normal for particular kinds of men. Robert states that 'Godfrey was handsome, of lordly bearing, eloquent, of distinguished character, and so lenient with his soldiers as to give the impression of being a monk rather than a soldier.'[13] Presumably this was a compliment, but would secular men have thought so?[14] Perhaps this is an early example of what Andrew Holt has argued is the tendency for twelfth-century monastic authors, such as Bernard of Clairvaux, to develop a framework for crusaders in which a hybrid masculine identity was promoted.[15] This is particularly clear in Bernard's manifesto supporting the Knights Templar, *In praise of the new knighthood* (composed between 1128 and 1136). But is this simply to restate in a different way that men, even though they fought, were now more often associated with spiritual attributes? Holt argues that we need to perceive 'a new type of masculine identity specifically for crusaders', and that this was a 'newly constructed gendered identity'. There is clear validity to the idea that clerics helped to provide (or perhaps build upon) a theoretical framework which promoted the idea of a godly warrior. I am not, however, convinced these ideologies constitute a stable 'crusader masculinity', in part because such an analytical category obscures the reasons why clerical and monastic authors wrote about laymen in different contexts and genres, and for various audiences. As Holt notes, it is important to consider the possible consequences of such rhetoric. Yet it is also important to ask why Crusade authors depicted or articulated relationships between men in specific ways, and how these representations were often aimed not at a secular audience but those men who remained within the cloister. What utility did these illustrations of male behaviour serve? In part, they actually legitimised the religious life. Thus, writers of the Crusade incorporated the holy into the world of the warrior or knight without necessarily doing damage to claims concerning the superiority of the male religious way of life. Masculinities might seem to be in opposition, but they are not necessarily in conflict; co-operation between clerical and secular men (but guided by the former), rather than conflict, was often key. Cultural understandings of gender therefore are not simply about attributes, but also to do with how symbols work within texts to demarcate and normalise power hierarchies. To understand the representation of the clergy within Crusade narratives, we must then explore what roles clerical authors gave to different groups, and how authority and leadership was represented in these texts.[16]

---

[13] *Robert the Monk's History of the First Crusade: Historia Iherosolimitana*, trans C. Sweetenham (Aldershot, 2005), p. 84 (hereafter RM1); Robert the Monk, 'Historia Hierosolymitana', *Recueil des historiens des croisades: Historiens occidentaux*, 5 vols (Paris, 1872–1906), vol. 3, pp. 717–882, p. 731: 'Hic vultu elegans, statura procerus, dulcis eloquio, moribus egregius, et in tantum militibus lenis, ut magis in se monachum quam militem figuraret' (hereafter RM2).

[14] Robert made it clear in the next clause, however, that this did not affect his military capabilities. When he engaged an enemy, he became like a 'roaring lion'.

[15] A. Holt, 'Between warrior and priest: the creation of a new masculine identity during the crusades', in *Negotiating clerical identities*, ed. Thibodeaux, pp. 185–203.

[16] In part this essay seeks to respond to some of the questions Derek G. Neal raises concerning the interconnection between lay and clerical understandings of masculinity: idem, 'What can

Matthew Mesley

CRUSADE SOCIETY AND LEADERSHIP

In large part, authors of Crusade histories identified different classes of people by their function.[17] Secular men were described as Christian heroes and as soldiers of Christ, who readily accepted potential martyrdom. Clerical men were also part of Christ's army but usually appeared as non-combatants whose function was to motivate and inspire the soldiers, or as visionaries emphasising the moral purity required for victory. For example, describing a battle scene, Robert the Monk, writing circa 1106–7, pointed to the specific roles people had: he stated that 'the soldiers and those who could fight, fought; the priests and clergy wept and prayed; and the women, lamenting, dragged the bodies of the dead back to the tents'.[18] At first glance then, the behaviour of both lay and clerical men (and of women) rarely strayed from formulaic tropes, which were in part based on social classifications, but also reflective of gendered expectations. However, authors did not categorise different groups and leave it at that; they also sought to demonstrate the 'naturalness' of relationships founded upon clerical authority.

Social unity as derived from clerical supervision is a key theme within these crusade narratives, in part because this was how the expedition had originally been promoted. In his speech at the Council of Clermont in 1095, Urban II had emphasised a unified Christendom before calling for arms to recapture Jerusalem and to make safe Christian pilgrimage. The supposed content of this speech has been transmitted to us in large part through the early Crusade histories; authors offered their own version of Urban's sermon, often providing the spirit – rather than the letter – of his words.[19] It was, as Marcus Bull has explained, an event that contemporaries turned into 'a commemorative and explanatory device'; authors emphasised its position as the occasion that set the ball in motion, and which clarified to whom Urban was appealing.[20] Young able-bodied laymen were the principal targets of the Pope's speech; the bishops and clergy, instead, were expected to return to their dioceses and persuade their congregations to take up the cross. Robert renders Urban's words thus:

> We are not forcing or persuading the old, the simple-minded or those unsuited to battle to undertake this pilgrimage; neither should a woman set out under any

historians do with clerical masculinity? Lessons from medieval Europe', in *Negotiating clerical identities*, ed. Thibodeaux, pp. 16–38.

[17] A theme reiterated in C. Kostick, *The social structure of the First Crusade* (Leiden, 2008).

[18] RM1, p. 109; RM2, vol. 3, p. 761: 'Milites et ad bellum expediti pugnabant; sacerdotes et clerici plorabant et orabant; mulieres lamentantes mortuorum corpora in tentoria trahebant'.

[19] Contemporary accounts of Urban's speech are translated in E. Peters, *The First Crusade: the Chronicle of Fulcher of Chartres and other source materials*, 2nd edn (Philadelphia, 1998), pp. 25–37. For the speech see D.C. Munro, 'The speech of Pope Urban II at Clermont 1095', *American Historical Review* 11 (1906), pp. 231–42. For context, see R. Somerville, 'The Council of Clermont and the First Crusade', *Studia Gratiana*, 20 (1976), pp. 323–37; and H.E.J. Cowdrey, 'Pope Urban II and the idea of Crusade', in his *The Crusades and Latin monasticism in the eleventh and twelfth centuries* (Aldershot, 1999), pp. 721–42.

[20] M. Bull, 'Views of Muslims and of Jerusalem in miracle stories, c.1000–c.1200: reflections on the study of First Crusaders' motivations', in *The experience of crusading: western approaches*, ed. M. Bull and N. Housley (Cambridge, 2003), pp. 13–38.

circumstances without her husband, brother or other legitimate guarantor. That is because such pilgrims are more of a hinderance than a help, a burden rather than of any practical use ... No priest or cleric irrespective of his rank shall be allowed on pilgrimage without the permission of his bishop, since it would be of little use to them if they were to go without such permission.[21]

In terms of leadership, while secular direction over the military expedition was recognised, overall spiritual authority was deemed a necessity. Indeed, most authors did emphasise the combined efforts of the venture; as Orderic Vitalis would put it, 'spiritual and temporal, the clergy and the laity, join hands to lead the armies of God'.[22] Yet, it was also understood, even if only in theory, that overall leadership was to be given to the pope's representative, Adhémar, bishop of Le Puy, whom Urban designated as papal legate.

BISHOP ADHÉMAR AND WHY BISHOPS MATTER

Little is known about Adhémar's background. At some point between 1080 and 1087 he became bishop of Le Puy, and appears to have been an active and reform-minded prelate.[23] As the sources seem to imply, he was certainly also involved in the strategic and military practicalities of the expedition, even at one point ensuring that the soldiers trimmed their beards in order to avoid being mistaken for a Muslim and thus killed by friendly fire.[24] He was probably a figure of some significance, but it is difficult to unpick what his actual role involved.[25] Some have suggested that he was instrumental in maintaining a united front between the military leaders of the expedition. But in the 1950s, John and Laurita Hill, in an article that has been somewhat overlooked, convincingly argued that in many ways Adhémar's later reputation, as someone who brought 'unity and

---

[21] RM1, pp. 81–2; RM2, vol. 3, p. 729: 'Et non praecipimus aut suademus ut senes aut imbecilles et usui armorum minime idonei hoc iter arripiant: nec mulieres sine conjugibus suis, aut fratribus, aut legitimis testimoniis, ullatenus incedant. Tales enim magis sunt impedimento quam adjumento, plus oneri quam utilitari... Presbyteris sive clericis cujuscumque ordinis absque episcoporum suorum licentia non licet ire, quoniam inutilis fieret illis haec via, si irent sine illorum licentia.'

[22] Orderic Vitalis, *The Ecclesiastical History*, 6 vols, ed. and trans. Marjorie Chibnall (Oxford, 1968–1980), vol. 5, p. 19.

[23] For treatments of Adhémar see J. Brundage, 'Adhémar of Puy: the bishop and his critics,' *Speculum* 34 (1959), pp. 201–12, and more recently R. Somerville, 'Adhémar of Le Puy, papal legate on the First Crusade', in *Law as profession and practice in medieval Europe: essays in honor of James A. Brundage*, ed. K. Pennington (Aldershot, 2011), pp. 371–86. See also n. 26 and n. 27 below. Brundage provides an excellent overview of Adhémar's background and exploits, but he states at the beginning of his article, 'I have accepted as "facts" the credible accounts of the eye-witness narratives of the Crusade, especially when these are corroborated by other independent accounts' (p. 202, n. 10). For my purposes, regardless of whether or not these events are 'real', they are useful for what they tell us about how later authors sought to frame the bishop's actions.

[24] Guibert de Nogent, *The deeds of God through the Franks: Gesta Dei per Francos*, trans. R. Levine (Woodbridge, 1997) (hereafter GN), p. 93.

[25] Some chroniclers tied Adhémar with the secular lord Raymond of Toulouse. Raymond, however, was never given official (papal) endorsement to be in command of the venture.

order' to the Crusades, can be viewed as an elaboration of a narrative tradition. They stated that 'the answer lies in part in the very obscurity of his deeds and perhaps also in the human desire to find among the leaders of the crusade a man who could be praised by all. Adhémar was a non-controversial figure of good repute.'[26] Perhaps, however, it was not simply that he was uncontroversial. On one level his status as bishop associated a spiritual authority with the sometimes politicised and self-motivated actions of the various secular leaders. Even the post-mortem visions of Adhémar appear to be related in part to the power struggles that ensued in the vacuum his death left.[27] Yet, more broadly, authors, reflecting a spritualising tendency, also seem to have increasingly stressed the role that Adhémar had vis-à-vis the army and its governance; they thus described him in a way that reflected their ideas about how success was contingent upon the crusaders remaining both united and morally pure. This study approaches Adhémar from a different perspective; it uses him as a means by which to examine contemporary attitudes to the role of religious leadership in this period and what bearing such beliefs had on representations of religious men in a Crusade setting. Bishops are a fruitful group with which to think about medieval notions of gender and masculine identity. They held a religious vocation, but they also wielded both spiritual and temporal authority, and their position and status meant that they were often at the centre of government and power – involved in the affairs of kings or the nobility, but equally at home in the company of other clerical and monastic religious leaders. They were, as Sean Gilsdorf has put it, 'in the middle'.[28] Their office and role was also being redefined in the century in which the Crusade was called; indeed, the Council of Clermont promulgated canons which sought to reiterate the independence of the episcopal office from lay rulers, and legislated against simony and clerical illegitimacy.[29] Many bishops took an active part in these efforts to seek change – for instance, some promoted a reform rhetoric that included allusions to familial or gendered language that could be used to evaluate or critique relationships between clerical and secular men.[30] In part, this was about creating a space within the political world for

---

[26] See J.H. Hill and L.L. Hill, 'Contemporary accounts and the later reputation of Adhémar, bishop of Le Puy', *Medievalia et Humanistica* 9 (1955), pp. 30–8.

[27] C. Kostick, 'The afterlife of bishop Adhémar of Le Puy', in *The Church, the afterlife and the fate of the soul. Papers read at the 2007 Summer meeting and the 2008 Winter meeting of the Ecclesiastical History Society*, ed. P. Clarke and T. Clayton. Studies in Church History 45 (Woodbridge, 2009), pp. 120–30.

[28] S. Gilsdorf, 'Bishops in the middle: mediatory politics and the episcopacy', in *The Bishop: Power and piety at the first millennium*, ed. S. Gilsdorf (Munster, 2004), pp. 51–73. The literature on the changing nature of the episcopal office is extensive, but two works provide a number of insightful case studies of the period between the tenth and twelfth centuries: *The Bishop reformed: studies of episcopal power and culture in the central Middle Ages*, ed. J.S. Ott and A.T. Jones (Aldershot, 2007); and *Patterns of episcopal power: bishops in 10th and 11th century western Europe*, ed. L. Körntgen and D. Wassenhoren (Berlin, 2011).

[29] See as an example Orderic Vitalis, *The Ecclesiastical History*, vol. 5, pp. 12–3. The canons do not survive complete – this is discussed by Marjorie Chibnall at ibid., n. 5.

[30] M. McLaughlin, *Sex, gender, and episcopal authority in the Age of Reform, 1000–1122* (Cambridge, 2010), esp. pp. 1–15.

bishops to retain a separate or distinct kind of authority.[31] Later narratives written by those influenced by reform, such as works of hagiography, might distinguish the behaviour of bishops from the secular nobles with whom these men were required by their vocation and status to interact, in order to show how little political struggles or warfare caused them to alter their behaviour.[32] We can, perhaps, see something similar when we examine how Crusade authors represented Adhémar; later monastic writers thought it was important to point to the bishop's military experience, but also to his pastoral and penitential functions – to show that while he was comparable to other men, he also held a special position. This was not without purpose; such representations, like the literary genres in which they appear, were a way to explain events and any potential concerns that they might elicit from their audience.

ADHÉMAR WITHIN THE CRUSADE NARRATIVES

If we are to assess Adhémar's representation, we must recognise first the degree to which much previous research on Crusade narratives has focussed upon the relationship later texts had with the *Gesta Francorum* (hereafter *GF*). This was the first (likely eyewitness) account of the First Crusade, written before 1105, perhaps in stages, by either a cleric or a knight with clerical training.[33] Most later writers drew upon the *GF*, but they also believed it to be insufficient both in style and content.[34] Therefore, they edited, updated, and in their minds improved upon the narrative. In particular, writers sought to make clear the theological framework in which the Crusade should be viewed.[35] As we shall see, this

[31] See for instance their role as counsellors: B. Weiler, 'Bishops and kings in England, c. 1066– c. 1215', in *Religion and politics in the Middle Ages: Germany and England in comparison*, ed. D. Wassenhoven and L Körntgen (Berlin and New York, 2013), pp. 87–134

[32] See for instance the study by M.C. Miller, 'Masculinity, reform, and clerical culture: narratives of episcopal holiness in the Gregorian era', *Church History* 72 (2003), pp. 25–52.

[33] Much about this text still seems subject to debate; see E. Albu, 'Probing the passions of a Norman on Crusade: the *Gesta Francorum et aliorum Hierosolimitanorum*', *Anglo-Norman Studies*, 27 (2005), pp. 1–15, and J. Rubenstein, 'What is the *Gesta Francorum*, and who is Peter Tudebode?' *Revue Mabillon*, 16 (2005), pp. 179–204. See also Nirmal Dass's discussion in his new translation of the *Gesta*. *The Deeds of the Franks and other Jerusalem-bound pilgrims: the earliest chronicle of the First Crusades*, ed. and trans. N. Dass (Plymouth, 2011).

[34] A. Krey's comment is perhaps classic in this respect: 'It [should] be regarded as a tribute to the widespread extent of Culture in northern France that so many persons should have been so deeply affected by the literary crudeness of the *Gesta*': idem, 'A neglected passage in the *Gesta* and its bearing on the literature of the First Crusade', in *The Crusades and other historical essays presented to Dana C. Munro*, ed. L.J. Paetow (New York, 1928), pp. 57–76, at p. 74. More recent scholars have defended the *Gesta* from charges that it is somehow second-rate or crudely written. Colin Morris has pointed to the wealth of spiritual terminology that lies within the text, and argues that we should view the text as part of a Latin tradition (different from that of later scholars) which had a close affinity with the vernacular culture of its day: idem, 'The *Gesta Francorum* as narrative history', *Reading Medieval Studies* 19 (1993), pp. 55–71.

[35] See J. France, 'The use of the anonymous *Gesta Francorum* in the early twelfth-century sources for the First Crusade', in *From Clermont to Jerusalem; the Crusades and crusader societies 1095-1500*, ed. A.V. Murray (Turnhout, 1998), pp. 29–42.

certainly had an influence on the depiction of Adhémar's character, or at least the contexts in which he appears within the texts. Focussing on the relationship between texts is clearly worthwhile, but we must also view these works as literary creations whereby authors sought to explain and clarify how God had worked his hands upon these momentous historical events.

It is no exaggeration to say that in the *GF* Adhémar is somewhat of a background figure; prominence instead is given to the secular lord Bohemond of Taranto, who was one of the most important nobles leading the Crusade, and became the first prince of Antioch after the city surrendered to him in June 1098.[36] Bohemond is provided with a number of heroic speeches within the text. Nonetheless, the bishop is still listed as one of the main Crusade leaders, and the author provides Adhémar with a brief obituary. The anonymous author's non-monastic background (or his possible Southern Italian background) might explain why Adhémar is shown, rather matter of factly, to be involved in strategic preparations and military battles throughout the text. For instance, at the siege of Nicea (May-June 1097), we are told that:

> After this the count of St Gilles and the bishop of Le Puy took counsel together how they could undermine a tower which stood over against their camp, so they set men to sap it, with arbalists and archers to protect them.[37]

After Nicea had been captured there was a counteroffensive against the Christian troops. In the text, Adhémar is presented as coming to the army's rescue, by leading his section of the army around a mountain and attacking the Turkish army from the rear. The author presents the bishop in the thick of battle; he might be without any ornamentation, but it is clear that he is a leader.[38]

By contrast, an eyewitness account by Raymond d'Aguilers (writing before 1101) seems to begin to show the first signs of portraying Adhémar as a different kind of leader, of having a more spiritualising influence, of being more trustworthy than the secular lords, and as being central to the Crusade's success. In an episode in which Raymond describes how Adhémar was kicked off his mule and severely beaten over the head, his recovery is interpreted as necessary to God's plan. His belief in the Holy Lance, a view which is contested by other chronicles, is used by Raymond to provide the relic with a veil of episcopal acceptability. Even Adhémar's ghost was useful – appearing as it did on the battlements of Jerusalem.[39] Another eyewitness account was written by the French chaplain

---

[36] For discussion of the attention paid to Bohemond in the *GF* see K.B. Wolf, 'Crusade and narrative: Bohemond and the *Gesta Francorum*', *Journal of Medieval History* 17 (1991), pp. 207–16.

[37] *GF*, p. 15: 'Denique comes sancti Egidii et episcopus Podiensis consiliati sunt in unum qualiter facerent subfodi quamdam turrim, quae erat ante tentoria eorum. Ordinati sunt homines qui hanc suffodiant, et arbalistae et sagittarii qui eos undique defendant'. And also found in GN, p. 62.

[38] *GF*, pp. 19–20.

[39] For Raymond's text see *Le 'Liber' de Raymond d'Aguilers*, ed. J. Hugh and L.L. Hill (Paris, 1969). The attack on Adhémar is related on page 39 and his apparition, which was viewed and testified by many, appears on page 151. See also Kostick, 'The afterlife of Bishop Adhémar', and idem, *The social structure*, pp. 27–39.

Fulcher of Chartres after both the *GF* and Raymond's *Liber* and drawing upon both.[40] Fulcher's description, at least of the early battles, omits Adhémar's military role (that is to say he is not shown to be commanding soldiers or leading troops into battle), but his leadership capabilities are never questioned. Indeed Fulcher described the bishop as 'acting as vicar apostolic (who) prudently and wisely governed the entire army of God and vigorously inspired it to carry out the undertaking'.[41] Unlike the episode related in the *GF*, in which the bishop participated in the attack against the Turkish army, here he is isolated from the battle and placed with the other clerics. Alongside four bishops and a great many priests, Adhémar is depicted, in a penitential style, as humbly beseeching God to destroy their enemies.[42] Of course violence and its expression could be used metaphorically by members of the clergy, who could call down the wrath of God upon their enemies.[43] Yet if spiritual violence was here considered acceptable, a line seems to have been drawn about actions that were acceptable for a man like Adhémar. Proponents of reform ideology frowned upon the existence of the warrior-cleric, although for bishops it was recognised that as a consequence of their office and social status involvement in military action was often required.[44] While Fulcher does not ignore Adhémar's status as leader, then, his decisions are associated with his religious and episcopal status. Before the battle of Antioch in 1098, for instance, we are told that he 'himself commanded by herald that each knight in the army of God give his steed as much as possible of his dole of grain, however precious, lest the horse should collapse the next day in the hour of battle, weak with hunger'.[45] Clearly, this could have been depicted as the practical decision of an experienced military leader; horses had indeed been dying in great numbers in the period before Antioch.[46] But Fulcher placed the bishop's action within a pastoral and intercessory context; not only is there an initial

---

[40] *A history of the expedition to Jerusalem, 1095–1127*, ed. H.S. Fink and trans. F.R. Ryan (Toronto, 1969). As many scholars have noted, Fulcher did not write his narrative in one piece; but an initial history of the early battles at which he was an eyewitness was written by at least 1106, possibly around 1101. He may have finished his work in 1106, but then decided to continue it in about 1109. Ibid., pp. 18–24.

[41] Ibid., p. 67; Fulcher of Chartres, *Historia Hierosolymitana*, ed. H. Hagenmeyer (Heidelberg, 1913) (hereafter FC), pp. 138–9: '[qui postea vice] fungens apostolica cunctum Dei exercitum prudenter et consulte rexit ed ad negotia peragenda vivaciter animavit'.

[42] *History of the expedition to Jerusalem*, pp. 85–6. I have provided the Latin here to show how this event is portrayed as a penitential ritual, FC, pp. 196–7: 'aderat ibi episcopus Podiensis, patronus noster, et IV alii, aderantque sacerdotes quamplurimi, albis induti vestimentis, qui Dominum humillime deposcebant, ut virtutem hostium nostrorum prosterneret et dona misericordiae suae nobis infunderet. Plorando cantabant, cantando plorabant'.

[43] See Fenton's contribution in this collection for further discussion of this.

[44] Particularly useful for background is T. Reuter, '*Episcopi cum sua militia*: the prelate as warrior in the early Staufer era', in *Warriors and churchmen in the high Middle Ages: essays presented to Karl Leyser*, ed. T. Reuter (London, 1992), pp. 79–93.

[45] *History of the expedition to Jerusalem*, p. 104; FC, p. 252: 'vespere praecedente iusserat ipse cunctae militiae Dei exercitus sub edicto praeconario, ut unusquisque pro posse suo quasi caritative de annona praebendam equo suo impenderet, ne in crastino subter equitantes, hora bellica, debiles fame deficerent'.

[46] Riley-Smith, *Idea of crusading*, pp. 64–5.

clause, 'Oh pious precaution' [*O pia res*!], but the line proceeding Adhémar's decision describes him as 'a truly apostolic man ... [who] always kindly comforted the people and strengthened them in the Lord'.[47] The one place in the text where Adhémar is shown to be part of the army, is when a Turkish leader views the standard of the bishop of Le Puy and warns his own lord that he sees the banner of the mighty pope advancing. The Saracen 'perspective' therefore made clear the extent to which the Franks were fighting a holy war that was led by the pope's representative.[48] How the bishop participates and what he signifies is key; Fulcher minimalised any characteristic that Adhémar might have shared with the other secular military leaders, yet still made clear that he was a significant authority.

Fulcher appears to have been an exception in this respect: in the texts that were written in the aftermath of Bohemond's tour through France in 1105–06 (during which he married Constance, daughter of the French king Philip I), Adhémar's military status and experience was not necessarily deemed to be problematic.[49] Authors often referred to Adhémar's military credentials, because it drove home their central message – that the Crusade was a religious conflict in which clerical leaders were a necessity. Indeed, Adhémar was often represented in military garb. This did not detract from his spiritual role, in fact it often validated this function. Thus, even while warfare (and the use of weapons) might be thought of as a lay male prerogative, clerics were not rendered powerless within the sphere of war and combat. An emphasis on episcopal participation in warfare might not have been new – there were certainly earlier precedents, but authors could strengthen or innovate upon those traditions that provided clerical approval of conflicts aimed at enemies of Christianity.[50]

One could argue that there was perhaps cross-over appeal too. In later texts Adhémar could be presented to both the clergy and the laity as an ideal 'masculine exemplar'. One text, *The Song of Antioch* (probably composed in the later twelfth century) describes Adhémar as wearing a gold helmet, set with gems, and spurs of gold on his feet, carrying a bow, shield and stole, and also holding the Holy Lance in his arms.[51] The duke of Bouillon is even shown mistaking him for a knight!

> When he had completed Mass, he came back from the church
> and made his way as fast as possible to his quarters. He took

---

[47] *History of the expedition to Jerusalem*, p. 104; FC, p. 252: 'vir apostolicus ... benigne semper populum confortabat et in Domino robarabat'.
[48] *History of the expedition to Jerusalem*, p. 105.
[49] See Krey, 'A neglected passage'.
[50] For the earlier traditions see R. Stone, *Morality and masculinity in the Carolingian empire* (Cambridge, 2012), pp. 69–115.
[51] *The Chanson d'Antioche: an Old French account of the First Crusade*, trans C. Sweetenham and S. Edgington (Farnham, 2011), p. 282. The text as extant comes from the early thirteenth century, but was probably composed in the third quarter of the twelfth century. However, much of the material may be derived from earlier oral and written traditions disseminated soon after the First Crusade.

off the flowing robes he was wearing and was supplied with
superb battle equipment. He put on a hauberk with gilded
panels and laced on a gold bejewelled helmet; some golden
spurs were fastened to his feet, then he buckled a sword at his
left side. His swift warhorse was led up to him, worth more
than a thousand pounds in penny coins. He put his foot in
the stirrup and swung into the saddle, his shield round his
neck and his stole next to it. Two dragons were riveted to
his firm spear haft. He spurred the horse on both sides and
leapt a good 30 feet forwards ... The good duke of Bouillon
rode to meet him and shouted loudly: 'Sir knight, where are
you from? I do not recognise you with those dragons. I have
never seen you before in the army, which is why I am confused.'[52]

As a *chanson de geste* the literary form of the text is obviously quite different from the Latin chronicles, but we should not treat them as genres which had no influence upon each other.[53] Clearly the above image of Adhémar would have been attractive to a man of high status, whether a member of the laity or a courtier cleric. If the text was aimed more at a secular audience, it demonstrates that the author appreciated a need for clerical heroes. This did not mean that they could not reflect upon Adhémar's spiritual qualities; the author of the *chanson* describes how the bishop performed Mass before equipping himself in armour, and made it clear that Adhémar's main responsibility within the camp was as a preacher.[54] At the same time, the bishop could sometimes be an object of humour as in the occasion where a messenger tells Adhémar that the last thing they need is a sermon.[55] For a secular audience Adhémar could be portrayed both as a religious hero, yet still where it mattered 'one of the men'.

Of course, for different reasons, the earlier Latin Chronicles had also sought to highlight the bishop's relationship with the soldiers in the camp; in particular, they included his sermons or speeches within the narrative. In Albert of Aachen's chronicle *History of the journey to Jerusalem*, written before 1119, there are

---

[52] *The Chanson d'Antioche*, p. 282. See also S.B. Edgington, 'Holy Land, holy lance: religious ideas in the Chanson d'Antioche', *Studies in Church History* 36 (2000), pp. 142–53.

[53] *The Chanson d'Antioche*, p. 9: 'the Latin chronicles written in the years immediately following the Crusade contain material that reflects closely the conventions of the *chanson de geste*'. And similarly the Song of Antioch drew upon material found in the Latin chronicles (ibid., p. 10). See also J. Beer, 'Heroic language and the eyewitness: the *Gesta Francorum* and the *Chanson d'Antioche*', in *Echoes of the epic: studies in honor of Gerard J. Brault*, ed. D.P. Schenck and M.J. Schenck (Birmingham AL, 1998), pp. 1–16 and S.B. Edgington, 'Albert of Aachen and the *chansons de geste*', in *The Crusades and their sources: essays presented to Bernard Hamilton*, ed. J. France and W.G. Zajac (Aldershot, 1998), pp. 23–37.

[54] Another text, the *Gesta Tancredi*, portrays a rather more bloodthirsty Adhémar, who is positively overjoyed at a gift of seventy decapitated heads. Yet even this author represented the decaptitated heads as a tithe: *The 'Gesta Tancredi' of Ralph of Caen: a history of the Normans on the First Crusade*, ed. and trans. B.S. Bachrach and D.S. Bachrach (Aldershot, 2005) (hereafter GT), p. 77.

[55] *The Chanson d'Antioche*, p. 191.

three occasions before a battle in which the bishop addresses the troops.[56] Here Adhémar reiterated the degree to which God fought on their side, and sought to calm any fears that they may have had. In other texts he provided the army with moral support before battles and reiterated the spiritual unity which held them all in common.[57] For example, in *The deeds of God through the Franks* (written c. 1106–9), Guibert of Nogent states in verse that the bishop 'strengthened the army not only with his shining arms, but with his counsel and sacred prayers: if they had been hesitant, he ignited the army'.[58] Speeches also allowed writers to reflect upon the rewards of martyrdom. In the *Song of Antioch*, before the battle of Antioch, Adhémar says to the assembled forces: 'Anyone who loses his life here will have his soul saved. The first one to go out onto the field will, if he suffers martyrdom or death from a weapon, find his garlanded soul rising to Almighty God.'[59] The move towards providing Adhémar with direct speech within the early Latin narratives reflects how authors were often presenting and interpreting the Crusades for a monastic and clerical audience, and were writing from within a religious milieu that was profoundly influenced by monastic ideology.[60] This is certainly different to the *GF* where, as has been mentioned, the author instead focussed primarily on Bohemond and his speeches to the troops.[61] Later Adhémar is given more attention; and importantly he is seen addressing the laity, rather than the laity speaking to their own.

Why might this relationship between the clergy and laity have been increasingly stressed? By describing the bishop as speaking to the army before each of their encounters with their enemies, it reframed each battle as a spiritual confrontation, which importantly had been approved and encouraged by the clerical hierarchy. This is made expressly clear in Robert's description of the battle

[56] Albert of Aachen, *Historia Ierosolimitana: history of the journey to Jerusalem*, ed. and trans. S.B. Edgington (Oxford, 2007), at pp. 191, 233 and 313–15. For the dating of the text see pp. xxiv-xxv.

[57] David Bachrach suggests that authors employed a greater level of rhetorical devices and *exempla* in their depiction of clerics orating sermons. See D.S. Bachrach, 'Conforming with the rhetorical tradition of plausibility: clerical representation of battlefield orations against Muslims, 1080–1170', *International History Review* 26 (2010), pp. 1–19; discusses Adhémar on pp. 5–7.

[58] GN, p. 66; *Dei gesta per Francos*, ed. R.B.C. Huygens (CCCM 127A, Turnholt, 1996), p. 155: 'multis quibus emicat armis, sed monitis precibusque sacris communiit ipsum, sique foret tepidum fervescere compulit, agmen'. For the insertion of verse into Guibert's prose, see A. Leclercq 'Vers et prose, le jeu de la forme mêlèe dans *les Dei gesta per Francos* de Guibert de Nogent (XIIe siècle)', in *The medieval chronicle III: proceedings of the third international conference on the medieval chronicle Doorn/Utrecht 12–17 July 2002*, ed. E. Kooper (Amsterdam, 2004), pp. 101–15. Leclercq argues that Guibert uses verse to strengthen those passages which convey more of an ideological message to his readers. Of this passage he writes: 'La description de l'évêque du Puy, présenté comme un guide spirituel qui insuffle de l'ardeur aux troupes est constituée d'une phrase en prose qui s'achève par un tercet formant une note plus solennelle' (p. 107).

[59] *The Chanson d'Antioche*, p. 287. For the theme of martyrdom see H.E.J. Cowdrey, 'Martyrdom and the First Crusade', in *Crusade and settlement: papers read at the first conference for the Society for the Study of the Crusades and the Latin East and presented to R.C. Smail*, ed. P.W. Edbury (Cardiff, 1985), pp. 46–56.

[60] The spiritual themes within the Crusade narratives and their relationship to monastic ideology is addressed in detail by W.J. Purkiss, *Crusading spirituality in the Holy Land and Iberia, c.1095-c.1187* (Woodbridge, 2007), esp. pp. 30–58.

[61] *GF*, in particular p. 30 and p. 35. On both occasions he stresses that the knights are *prudentissimus*.

of Antioch. Not only does Adhémar deliver a sermon 'wearing a breastplate' and holding the relic of the Holy Lance, but in the ensuing conflict a celestial army of saints add their strength to the Christian knights, and it is this and the encouragement Adhémar gives, the author claims, that provides them with the will to fight. Robert completes the scene with the bishop exhorting them to thank God for their victory.[62] One could say that Adhémar here is depicted almost in the costume of a warrior, or as the figurehead of God's army. Indeed, Carol Sweetenham states that in Robert's text Adhémar becomes 'the personification of the Church Militant'.[63] But it is not only in Robert's text that this happened. Another author, Gilo of Paris, writing before 1120, depicted the same battle, and stated, 'Here the bishop of Le Puy did the duty of a general, and duly governed the men of Raymond, who was ill; the holy lance of God, carried before him, gave heart to the men, and a glittering breastplate weighed heavily on his priestly fame'.[64] Wearing the symbols of the lay military class might highlight similarities, but it was not done in order to suggest there was no difference between the laity and the clergy. Ultimately these accounts showed that the clergy could participate and even outdo laymen in their conventional roles, and it reiterated how indispensable their presence was.

This is why the French monks, Guibert and Robert, as well as Baldric of Dol (writing around 1107), also reiterated Adhémar's pastoral duties, particularly concerning his attitude towards the moral behaviour of the men in the camp. According to one chronicler, the bishop's mere presence was enough to ensure that nobody made stupid comments.[65] At his initiative, the troops were shown to participate in penitential fasting for their sins, and chastity was also imposed upon them. This is indicative of a particular concern about the sexual behaviour of the crusade armies observable in a number of sources.[66] Guibert of Nogent states that sexual crimes specifically were punished with severity; for example, 'if any of the unmarried women were found to be pregnant, she and her pimp were

---

[62] Ibid., p. 69, 169–73. This legend appeared in the *GF* also, yet in this text Adhémar is not mentioned. The imagery would influence later texts such as the *Song of Antioch* which drew in part upon Robert the Monk's *Chronicle*.

[63] RM1, p. 57.

[64] *The Historia vie Hierosolimitane of Gilo of Paris and a second, anonymous author*, ed. and trans. C.W. Grocock and J.E. Siberry (Oxford, 1997), pp. 184–85: 'His ducis officium presul Podiensis habebat/Et populos egri Raimundi rite regebat;/Lancea sancta Dei preuecta uiros animabat,/ Membraque pontificis lucens lorica grauabat.' The editors of this text suggest Gilo's part of the poem was composed 'probably in the first decade of the century', and should be placed in the same category as the histories of the First Crusade written 1100–1120, ibid., p. xxiv.

[65] RM1, p. 173. Adhémar apparently also prohibited laughter and telling lies; *Song of Antioch*, p. 318.

[66] Such themes were first explored by J. Brundage, 'Prostitution, miscegenation and sexual purity in the First Crusade', in *Crusade and settlement*, ed. Edbury, pp. 57–64. For a more recent appraisal see A. Holt, 'Feminine sexuality and the Crusades: clerical opposition to women as a strategy for crusading success', in *Sexuality in the Middle Ages and Early Modern times*, ed. A. Classen (Berlin, 2008), pp. 449–70. More broadly see also, E. Silberry, *Criticism of crusading 1095–1274* (Oxford, 1985), esp. pp. 69–108; and P.J. Cole, '"O God, the heathen have come into your inheritance" (Ps. 78.I): the theme of religious pollution in crusade documents, 1095–1188', in *Crusaders and muslims in twelfth-century Syria*, ed. M. Shatzmiller (Leiden and New York, 1993), pp. 84–111.

submitted to hideous punishments'.[67] Guibert also includes the story of a monk who had left his monastery, moved 'not by piety but by whim' (*non pietate sed levitate*), who, having been caught with a woman, was made by Adhémar to be led, along with his lover, naked around the camp and whipped.[68] The punishment here was perhaps all the more severe because male religious were held to a higher standard than lay soldiers. Perhaps a similar moral was echoed in Albert of Aachen's chronicle where an archdeacon and 'a certain woman of great birth and beauty' who were playing dice in a pleasure garden, were found by Turkish men and killed horribly.[69] Such *exempla* also reiterated the extent to which the crusaders themselves and later writers equated moral purity with victory, and sexual deviancy with the loss of God's favour and defeat.[70] In these narratives, Adhémar, rather than the secular leaders of the camp, is the one described as enforcing celibacy upon the camp; why was this the case? Pilgrimage was an act of penance, and therefore pilgrims were expected to abstain from sex; thus monastic writers showed how Adhémar and the clergy were responsible for policing the sexual behaviour of the crusaders.[71] Here societal expectations of women also helped to construct this relationship between laymen and clergy. Evidently, the sexual behaviour of clerical and laymen in the context of these Crusade narratives was an indicator of both situational and broader concerns of male and female sexuality. The crusaders were shown to submit to clerical oversight; and this mirrored the philosophy of the 'Gregorian' reforms.

A final area where discussion of Adhémar is included is in the eulogies of his death; Adhémar died of plague on 1 August 1098 following the Christian victory at Antioch. While authors employed *topoi*, they nonetheless drew attention to more specific ideas about religious leadership within the Crusade. In the *GF*, the author comments upon the bishop's previous duties: 'for the bishop was a helper of the poor, and a counsellor of the rich, and used to keep the clergy in order and preach to the knights'.[72] The army is here conceived to be a microcosm of medieval society, and Adhémar's responsibilities bridge both class and status. Many Crusade authors followed the *GF* with similar epitaphs. Baldric of Dol, in a more flowery passage, tells us that that: 'he had been counsellor of the nobles, the hope of the orphans, [and] the prop of the weak'. Nonetheless the emphasis is also upon what kind of man he was and whom he represented. Baldric states that both rich and poor had wept for his death, 'to knights a knightly man, he led and instructed the clergy as a priest should. Distinguished by remarkable foresight, he was persuasive and cheerful and all things to all men.'[73] What Baldric

---

[67] GN, p. 78; *Dei gesta per Francos*, p. 196: 'Quod si gravidam inveniri constitisset aliquam earum mulierum, quae probabantur carere maritis, atrocibus tradebatur cum suo lenone suppliciis'.

[68] GN, p. 88; *Dei gesta per Francos*, p. 196.

[69] Albert of Aachen, *Historia Ierosolimitana*, pp. 209–11.

[70] For example, see Hodgson, *Women, crusading and the Holy Land*, pp. 3–4.

[71] See n. 66.

[72] *GF*, p. 74: 'quia ille erat sustentamentum pauperum, consilium diuitum, ipseque ordinabat clericos, predicabat et summonebat milites'.

[73] 'Factus est itaque luctus immoderatus in tota Christi militia, quoniam ipse fuerat consilium nobilium, spes orphanorum, imbecillium sustentamentum, militibus homo militaris, clericos

highlights – Adhémar's ability to promote social cohesion and unity – is shown to have repercussions by Guibert of Nogent, who suggests that the bishop's death was a catalyst for disunity and disharmony amongst the secular leaders:

> After the death of the noble Bishop of Le Puy, who had managed, by a combination of love for his flock and discipline, to bind them together in harmony and unity, arguments and rude, arrogant behaviour began to arise among the leaders; in particular, the middle and lower ranks began to behave badly so that one might have thought that the Old Testament statement, 'There was no longer a king in Israel, but each man did what seemed right in his own eyes,' was being fulfilled. [74]

Some writers, however, used different language to reinforce how essential the bishop's presence had been. In a deathbed speech that is related in the *Gesta Tancredi* (written before 1118)[75] the author offers a maternal image with which to represent Adhémar's relationship with the crusaders: the bishop states, 'I have cultivated, taught, warned and urged you on like a mother with her nursling. I have torn away what was fatal and spread the seeds of life. I have taken care and performed the tasks assigned to me.'[76] Such an image reinforced the idea that the bishop was essential for the crusaders' spiritual nourishment, but it also reflects a broader tendency within the narratives to conceive of Adhémar's relationship with those undertaking the Crusade, in familial terms. Reflecting on the bishop, Guibert in fact equated his fatherly office with his leadership role.[77] Similarly Gilo of Paris stated that 'he [Adhémar] strove to bring them comfort as a father to his son'.[78] Such a role placed the crusaders in either a subordinate or dependent category and could be understood in relation to society's own attitudes to parent-child relationships.[79] Gender, to use Joan Scott's well-known definition, is about 'signposting relationships of power'.[80] Adhémar is shown, on one level, to be

---

clericaliter educebat et educabat, prudentia singulari praecluebat eloquens et jocundus, omnibus omnis erat': Baldric of Dol, *Historia Ierosolimitana* in *Recueil des historiens des croisades: Historiens occidentaux* (Paris), vol. 4, pp. 3–111, at p. 82. Copied verbatim by Orderic Vitalis: I have used Marjorie Chibnall's translation of the Latin here.

[74] GN, p. 121: *Dei gesta per Francos*, p. 262: 'Post mortem plane viri admirabilis Podiensis episcopi, qui amore pastorali ac rigore omnium sibi invicem animos concordiae ac unanimitatis visco devinxerat, cepere inter principes simultates aliquotiens ac insolentiae oboriri, apud mediocres preterea et vulgares licentiae quas non omnino deceret haberi, ut Veteris Historiae dictum, quia videlicet rex non esset in Israel, sed quod cuique in oculis suis bonum videretur agebat, aliquando putaretur impleri'.

[75] GT, pp. 1–5 for background relating to the composition of the history.

[76] GT, p. 113; Ralph of Caen, *Gesta Tancredi in expeditione Hierosolymitana* in *Recueil des historiens des croisades: Historiens occidentaux* (Paris), vol. 3, p. 673: 'Sollicitus fovi, docui, monui, stimulavi; / Lethifera avulsi, vitalia semina sparsi; / Pervigili cura solvi mihi tradita jura / Jam nunc delibor, jam vitae terminus instat'.

[77] GN, p. 121.

[78] *Gilo*, p. 18–19: 'Vt pater in natos curam conferre sategit'.

[79] The way familial language is used to designate clerical-lay relationships is discussed in McLaughlin, *Sex, gender, and episcopal authority*, passim.

[80] J.W. Scott, 'Gender: a useful category of historical analysis', *American Historical Review* 91 (1986), pp. 1053–75.

able to relate to and represent all people in society, but authors still placed him in a familial position of authority. Both ways of depicting his character, however, signalled his unique and distinctive position within crusader society.

The writers of the early Crusade narratives emphasised Adhémar's role before battle as a preacher and as a moral guardian. As the former he channelled their fears and interpreted the crusaders' violence as spiritual warfare; as the latter he emphasised their pilgrim status and made clear their behaviour was subject to clerical oversight. The process whereby later monastic authors adapted Adhémar's character, which has been explored here, needs to be placed alongside efforts by the professional religious to use reforming ideology in their explanations of events. In explaining the Crusade, authors associated secular with religious ideals, but in so doing they seem to have felt it necesary to reiterate once again how spiritual authority was derived from the clergy, who were required to guide laymen in appropriate conduct. Thus, even if the actions of secular men were placed within a spiritual framework, religious men were positioned above them in order that their authority was maintained and legitimised. The implication of the positioning of the two groups of men within these texts is that clerical men are shown to be able to exert influence and power through paternalism and persuasion. In practice, this might set one ideal of masculine behaviour over another, but then such texts were expressing the sentiments of their audiences. In other words, the kind of message which on the one hand reassured, but also equated spiritual authority with superiority over laymen, would have been readily accepted.

Indeed, the early Crusade narratives were used in part to encourage or promote Urban II's crusading efforts, and thus in a sense their message might reach a wide audience. Nevertheless, most of these early chroniclers of the Crusade, writing in Latin, aimed their texts at a literate clerical audience which included high-status patrons such as bishops. These texts also reflected a didactic approach to history, in which events were retold in ways that provided moral instruction and reiterated spiritual truth over the literal. This also affected how relationships between secular and clerical men were depicted; thus, we see Adhémar enforcing a standard of behaviour within the camps in which self-control and resistance to sexual relations with women were key. And, what is more, writers of the Crusade used the bishop's military experience as a narrative tool. The spiritual dimensions of the text were heightened, and in so doing, authors demonstrated that clerical men wielded a useful kind of power within a military setting, even acting as a figurehead of values which laymen strove to imitate. In order therefore to reflect upon medieval male religious identity, it is important to think of contemporary understandings of gender as not simply related to particular attributes associated with different kinds of men or women. Neither do we need always to see conflict between the clergy and the laity, as prescriptive codes of behaviour could reinforce the assumptions and identity of both groups. What we do need to ask is to whom these representations or depictions of clerical men speak, and what they seek to achieve. Often such texts did not challenge the assumptions of their readers, so much as reflect what was, or what was not, being considered to be an ideal. 'Masculine exemplars' were directed to particular audiences in order to edify and entertain, but at the same time they undoubtedly provided comfort and assurance to those who lived according to clerical or monastic precepts. These texts also played a part in a broader cultural dialogue in which tensions and compromises were made between sections of lay and clerical society, over what was acceptable for different kinds of men. Clerical ideals about masculine behaviour clearly influenced ideas circulating within society as a whole, but in many texts written for a religious audience the clergy were addressing their own concerns and needs, while validating their way of life.

'WHAT MAN ARE YOU?'[1] PIETY AND MASCULINITY IN THE *VITAE* OF A SIENESE CRAFTSMAN AND A PROVENÇAL NOBLEMAN

Marita von Weissenberg

As the historian Jacques Dalarun has written: 'The saint is abnormal because he is a being of exception, but also because he places himself against the norms, separate from the world.'[2] The norm for laymen in the Middle Ages was to marry and raise a family. They secured their livelihoods through landholding and farming, or mercantile enterprise and other worldly activities. As is well known, the majority of saints rejected this secular world – they became monks, tertiaries, hermits, and so on.[3] However, several male saints married, and fathered and raised children. Many bought, sold, or manufactured goods. Saints from among the royalty and nobility had to uphold the law, even if it meant sentencing people to death; and men-at-arms had to participate in warfare. Several married saints were wealthy in money and chattels. Of course, some abandoned such secular lives to join religious orders, but others remained in the world as laymen, performing the duties associated with their stations in life as husbands, lords, merchants, artisans, or pursuing other means of livelihood. They lived 'ordinary' lives of laymen in their secular circumstances.[4] However, they were hardly ordinary: they came to be viewed as saints. As such, their lives, motives, actions, thoughts, words and, above all, faith were understood to be exceptional and exemplary. Some biographies, *vitae*, of husband-saints who remained in the world, performing their duties as secular men while at the same time pursuing a religious calling, show that this paradox could have implications both for the

---

[1] 'Vida de sanh Alziari, compte d'Aria', in *Vies occitaines de Saint Auzias et de Sainte Dauphine*, ed. Jacques Cambell, O.F.M. (Rome, 1963), p. 92, 'qual home hies tu' (hereafter VOE).

[2] Jacques Dalarun, *L'impossible sainteté. La vie retrouvée du Robert d'Arbrissel (v. 1045–1116), fondateur de Fontevraud* (Paris, 1985), p. 237, 'Le saint est anormal parce qu'il est un être d'exception, mais aussi parce qu'il se place à l'encontre des norms, à l'écart du monde.'

[3] By the term 'saint' I mean those who gained reputations of sanctity, regardless of official canonization. For an elaboration of this, see the essay by Katherine J. Lewis in this collection.

[4] For further discussion of this type of saint and specific examples see André Vauchez, *La sainteté en occident aux derniers siècles du Moyen Âge (1198–1431)* (Rome, 1981); *Les laïcs au moyen age: pratiques et expériences religieuses* (Paris, 1987). Donald Weinstein and Rudolf M. Bell, *Saints and society. The two worlds of Western Christendom, 1000–1700* (Chicago, 1982).

individual's reputation of sanctity and for his performance as a secular man. My argument is twofold. First, by being exceptionally pious, these lay saints were also shown to excel in their secular roles. Second, spiritual and secular concepts of masculinity were intrinsic to making this seeming contradiction function in the didactic narratives of sacred biography. The clerical and secular views of what it meant to be male, and how maleness manifested in actions and appearance, differed but ultimately they complemented each other in these texts.[5]

Studies of medieval masculinity often identify two spheres: the clerical and the secular.[6] While there are many forms of masculinity, most medieval manifestations of manliness fall into these two general spheres. Within both of these groupings multiplicities of manliness and their expressions coexisted. This plurality of gendered maleness is evident in one of the most fundamental aspects of masculinity: relationships between men. As Ruth Mazo Karras has shown, it is important to look at men's interactions with other men because masculinity was defined primarily in relation to men, not women. Women could be instruments in this process of male gendering, but they were not central to it. Maleness was defined in relation to masculinity, not femininity.[7] 'Secular masculinity' centers on the worldly positions of men, physical prowess, fatherhood, violence, power, etc. 'Clerical masculinity' has typically been used to denote a form of manliness centered on self-mastery. This was of primary concern for intellectual, non-physical, concepts of masculinity during the Middle Ages. Of course, clerics embraced this latter form and it could also be applied to devout laymen to denote a form of gender identity which marked them out as different from their peers. However, I prefer the term 'spiritual masculinity' to avoid confusion, precisely because these latter men were not necessarily clerics, albeit many lay saints adopted a 'religious' (i.e. quasi regular) style of life while living in the world. Others embraced forms of masculinity that were centred on the mind and spirit, not the physical and secular, before they became clerics, when they were still laity, and, in some cases, still married. Thus 'spiritual masculinity' is a more appropriate term for the religiously centred manliness of my two case studies here, especially as neither ever became clerics.

Saints' *vitae* offer ample evidence of relationships between men and their role in creating and maintaining particular forms of gender identity. The texts I study originated in the twelfth century, after the official recognition of sanctity came to be controlled by the Church, and so all investigations into sanctity had to adhere to the juridical forms set by the papacy. This was reflected in the genre of sacred biography. The authors depict the laudable aspects of an individual who has gained a reputation of sanctity, yet the narrative conforms to tropes that

---

[5] Andrew Romig, 'The common bond of aristocratic masculinity: monks, secular men and St. Gerald of Aurillac', in *Negotiating clerical identities: priests, monks and masculinity in the Middle Ages*, ed. Jennifer D. Thibodeaux (Basingstoke, 2010), pp. 39–56, p. 50.

[6] See for example Jennifer Thibodeaux, 'Introduction', in *Negotiating clerical identities*, pp. 1–15. For the plurality of masculinity, see R.W. Connell, *Masculinities* (Berkeley and Los Angeles, 1995, reprint 2005). For medieval masculine plurality, see Ruth Mazo Karras, *From boys to men: formations of masculinity in late medieval Europe* (Philadelphia, 2003).

[7] Karras, *From boys to men*, especially pp. 151–62.

make holiness easy to identify for the audience, allowing us access to the social ideals and assumptions of the time.[8] These texts were also part of an intertextual tradition. Individuals learned religious expression and behaviour from texts like these, and modeled their lives on those of the protagonists. In turn, some of those who modeled their behaviour on models learned from texts became themselves the object of both a cult and a biography. This process enforced tropes of piety.[9]

The significance of saints' *vitae* as a didactic tool for learning religious practices accepted and even promoted by the Church was especially important for the education of the laity. The late twelfth and early thirteenth centuries saw a dramatic rise in lay sanctity, as André Vauchez as well as Donald Weinstein and Rudolph Bell have shown.[10] Vauchez in particular points out the concurrence of the Church gaining control over marriage legislation, the sacralisation of marriage, and the dramatic increase of married, lay saints during the twelfth century. The *vitae* that I examine are part of this rise in lay sanctity.

The holiness of an individual needed to be set within a framework of the daily life and social setting of the protagonist. It is one of the foundational points of the hagiographic method of source analysis that a putative saint's secular circumstances must be described in a salient manner in order to make the text didactically valid, to teach the audience how to incorporate piety into their daily lives.[11] This was especially important for the laity whose daily routines were not regulated by religious orders and vows. These quotidian episodes of daily life, rather than miracles or mystical experiences, are the focus of my work. There are several illuminating examples of saints whose *vitae* show the same themes, but I have chosen to focus on a few episodes from two biographies. The first case study is from the *vita* of a thirteenth-century urban craftsman from Siena, the second from that of a count loyal to the king of Naples from the early fourteenth century: Pietro Pettinajo († 1289) and Elzéar de Sabran († 1323). The problems posed by wealth and social prestige figure in both worlds.

The defining responsibilities of urban citizens would seem to conflict with an exceptionally deep religious calling. City life required participation in civic affairs and the dependency on a cash economy. Cities were fundamentally anchored to the secular world.[12] The question many individuals grappled with was how to reconcile personal piety with dependency on hard cash that had not resulted from one's own labour. Charity provided an outlet for religiosity in the urban setting, yet it had its limitations, both financially and spiritually. After all,

---

[8] This is a contention which also informs the essays by Sanok and Lewis in this collection.

[9] For a concise description of the intertextuality of *vitae* see, for example, Maiju Lehmijoki-Gardner, *Worldly saints; social interaction of Dominican penitent women in Italy, 1200-1500* (Helsinki, 1999), pp. 20-5.

[10] See the works cited in note 4 above.

[11] See, for example, the very clear explanation in Lehmijoki-Gardner, *Worldly saints*, pp. 20-5. For how the juridical development of the canonisation process changed the formation of hagiographic sources, see Felice Lifschitz, 'Beyond positivism and genre: hagiographical texts as historical narrative', *Viator* 25 (1994), pp. 96-113.

[12] As pointed out by Karras, only masters could be full civic participants, *From boys to men*, pp. 109-29.

alms alone were unlikely to alleviate the perceived burden of wealth: 'It is easier for a camel to pass through the eye of a needle, than for a rich man to enter into the kingdom of heaven.'[13] Likewise, the world of the nobility, based on oaths, family ties, military prowess, and lordship, pivoted around secular concerns. Countless saints turned their backs on the urban and noble worlds, even while living within them as mendicants or beguines, or becoming monks, martyrs, hermits, or clerics. Thus, it is not unproductive to ask how somebody ensnared in matters of the world could gain religious perfection. The following case studies offer examples of how it was possible to excel at both spiritual calling and secular duty and to do so while embodying and maintaining an idealized form of masculinity.

Pietro Pettinajo was a comb-maker from Siena. Elzéar de Sabran was a count in fealty to the king of Sicily. The latter was born in Provence, and was later a baron there as well as a count of Ariano in Italy. Both men are portrayed in their *vitae* as pious and humble Christians prone to mystical ecstasies, great charity, and humility. Elzéar lived for twenty-three years in a virginal marriage with his wife, St Dauphine de Puimichel.[14] Pietro ceased all sexual relations with his wife once they concluded that they were sterile. Both saints followed traditional tropes of piety, enough to gain reputations of sanctity. Yet the authors of the *vitae* describe their secular duties with great care. Both men remained in the world largely because of their spouses.[15] They maintained their social and emotive roles as husbands, although not as fathers. In addition to remaining in the world, they embraced their duties as members of their social strata, performing their secular, social duties with care and commitment. An example of this is professional comportment, as we will see in the case of Pietro Pettinajo.

---

[13] Cf. Matthew 19:23-24, Mark 10:24-25, and Luke 18:24-25. For issues of religion and rising urbanization, see Lester K. Little, *Religious poverty and the profit economy in medieval Europe* (Ithaca, NY, 1978). This anxiety and its alleviation have often been cited as one of the successes of the mendicant orders. The Franciscans and the Dominicans in particular lived in urban areas, not sequestered in monasteries, and shared the same space as the townsmen. The mendicants' presence in preaching and care for the poor and sick was comforting, but also gave the faithful an outlet for their piety through charity, a significant Christian virtue. Friars were the ultimate manifestation of worthy, even saintly, poverty, and so ideal recipients of pious alms.

[14] Dauphine gained a reputation of sanctity in her own right and her cult was officially recognized in the seventeenth century – Elzéar was canonized in the fourteenth. A significant dossier of primary sources was compiled around the couple. They have been studied most prominently by André Vauchez for his monumental *La sainteté en Occident*, and he dedicates a chapter to the couple in *Les laïcs au moyen age*; see also Florian Mazel, 'Affaire de foi et affaire de famille en haute Provence au XIVe siècle. Autour de saint Elzéar († 1323) et de sainte Dauphine (†1360)', in *Provence historique; de Provence et d'ailleurs. Mélanges offerts à Noël Coulet*, ed. Jean-Paul Poyer and Francois-Xavier Emmanuelli (Gémenos, 1999), pp. 248–57; and Dyan Elliott, *Spiritual marriage. Sexual abstinence in medieval wedlock*, (Princeton, 1993). More attention has been paid to Dauphine and the couple's joint cult in existing scholarship than to Elzéar himself.

[15] Pietro remained in the world to fulfil a deathbed promise to his wife to care for her godson and his mother; Elzéar's marriage protected him from having been married by his family to someone else who would perhaps not have lived with him in celibacy. This is not made explicit in his *vita*, but is made clear in his wife's.

Marita von Weissenberg

THE SAINT AS URBAN PROFESSIONAL

Pietro Pettinajo was an artisan, a comb-maker in Siena, fastidious with both the raw materials and the quality of work for his combs. His hagiographer tells us 'he practiced his craft with such justice and purity, that he did not seem a craftsman or a merchant but a god-fearing and devout monk.'[16] Pietro's products were superior in quality, and their popularity made his fellow comb-makers less successful. Realising this, he would wait to until after vespers to set up his stall on the market place. He had no shortage of customers even with this restriction. More importantly, he did not incite hostility from his fellow artisans, but was respected and admired by them.[17] Pietro's piety made his work a manifestation of devotion, but as a Christian he strove to ensure that his colleagues' business was diminished as little as possible. The hagiographer gives a further concrete example of Pietro's desire to maintain peace in the marketplace: one day as a fellow citizen rushed past, he tipped over Pietro's stall. When the man saw the mess he had caused, as well as the comb-maker patiently retrieving his goods from the ground, he begged Pietro's forgiveness. Pietro said it would be bad for his soul not to have pardoned the man already.[18] This showcases Pietro's virtues of forgiveness and patience, as well as his civic mindedness and neighbourliness. These examples are piety in action, and something that is used by the author to highlight Pietro's civic qualities: dedication to profession, quality of his products, and collegiality at the marketplace.[19]

These incidents are indicative of mature urban masculinity. Karras discusses how young men, especially apprentices, journeymen, and wageworkers, would participate in unruly and even violent behaviour because they were not able to obtain the mature masculinity of master craftsmen. The mature masculinity of a master was characterized by independence, dominance over others, respect, and the social status of master. It was also not until becoming a master that a craftsman could feasibly marry. Thus, marriage in itself was one marker of maturity in the urban setting of craftsmen.[20] Pietro possessed all the markers of a mature male in this setting. He was a master craftsman in his own right. The quality of his combs 'dominated' those of his colleagues. Pietro was respected by his customers and fellow citizens. Lastly, the comb-maker was married. As a master craftsman he was in a relationship of power, over both others and himself.

The most consistent medieval ideas of mature masculinity refer to self-mastery: to restrain personal desires, be they related to food, sex, violence, or use

---

[16] Pietro da Monterone, *Vita del B. Pietro Pettinajo, sanese, del terz'ordine di San Francesco volgarizzata da una leggenda latina del 1333*. 'L'arte ... con tanta giustizia e purita esercitava, che non artifice o mercatante mondano, ma timorato e devotissimo religiose pareva.' In other words, 'ora et labora' (work and pray), but also 'orare est laborare' (to pray is to work). This is a new edition of a translation by Iot. Di S. Ferri L., (Siena, 1529, reprinted 1802) (hereafter VPP).

[17] Ibid., pp. 6–8.

[18] Ibid., p. 114.

[19] Augustine Thompson comments: 'Moderns would have called the saint a good union man', in his *Cities of God: the religion of the Italian communes 1125–1325* (University Park, PA, 2005), p. 194.

[20] Karras, *From boys to men*, p. 128, pp. 148–50.

of harsh words.²¹ Self-mastery and discipline were indicative of all mature masculinities, and necessary to become a successful artisan, whose combs were durable, smooth, and aesthetically pleasing. Pietro spent years dedicated to learning his craft, and was a master in more than one sense. The hagiographer took care to portray Pietro as skilled, holding a respected position in society as well as the title of master. Other examples of self-mastery include squires becoming knights through mastering arms and the self-discipline of practice; monks mastering themselves in fasting and prayer, or apprentices mastering their craft to become independent from their teachers, just as Pietro must have done.²² Pietro's work was part of his spiritual masculinity: religiously significant and motivated, yet set in the secular world.

As long as Pietro the comb-maker remained a layman practicing his profession, he had the responsibilities that fell to all adult men of property in Siena, as in all the Italian city-states. In addition to mercantile life and civic mindedness noted above, the hagiographer describes several references to citizenship. One episode in the text tells of how, to ensure peace, nobody was allowed to wander about the city at night. Regardless, Pietro would habitually go to church in order to pray at an image of the Virgin Mary. On one such night, the city's nightwatch came across him on one of Siena's streets, but recognizing that the figure on the streets was Pietro, 'the man of God' they did not stop him but let him pass unhindered. Instead of returning home, Pietro called the guards over in order for them to do their duty and fine him. Nevertheless, the men waved him on without demanding a fine. The next day the comb-maker went at his own initiative to the governor (*podestà*) of the city to pay his fine. The *podestà*, impressed by the craftsman's sense of justice, told him the law had not been made for the likes of Pietro. In fact, the comb-maker was not subject to the statute, or required to pay other dues to the city.²³

Another similar incident told by the hagiographer centres around the Sienese commune's efforts to protect itself from bandits ravaging the Sienese hinterlands. In order to cover the costs of hiring mercenaries to keep the city's resources safe, all citizens were obliged to pay a fee, each according to their means. Pietro did not know of the levy immediately, but hearing his neighbours complain about the costs, he went straight to deliver his share. He humbly presented the money to the men assigned to collect it:

> Gentlemen, bad news for me, that through ignorance [that has lasted] for many days, I have withheld the money which I ought to have paid to my Commune.

---

²¹ See for example Karras, *From boys to men*, pp. 1–19, pp. 151–68.

²² It is notable that in the rapidly expanding fields of masculinity studies, cultural studies and urban history, the connections between masculinity and civic rectitude have not yet been studied systematically. For an exception see Shannon McSheffrey, 'Men and masculinity in late medieval London. Civic culture: governance, patriarchy and reputation', in *Conflicted identities and multiple masculinities: men in the medieval West*, ed. Jacqueline Murray (New York, 1999), pp. 243–78. The essay examines sexual misbehaviour and reputation in London, arguing that men's sexual misconduct undermined their authority and position through the perception that it indicated a lack of self-governance. See also Karras, *From boys to men*, pp. 109–50.

²³ VPP, pp. 81–2.

And today, having understood the levy, I have brought you my share: so, take it, and pardon me for my ignorance.[24]

The officials were astounded at his sense of justice (*giustizia*), and exclaimed that the collectors had done well not to tell Pietro about the levy: everyone knew this man of God was not 'rich in worldly things'. They would only ask him to pray for protection of the city from all evil. They pressed him to take his money back. Pietro responded that the money belonged to the commune and he declined these privileges.[25] Here the comb-maker was acting in contributing to the common good in accordance with Scripture, which admonishes 'every man according to his ability'.[26] Pietro was a citizen above and beyond the expectations of his co-citizens and city, performing his worldly duties so fastidiously because he was devout. He completed his secular obligations as carefully as if they were religious ones. Although his neighbours and the *podestà* expected Pietro to withdraw from the affairs of the world due to his piety, it was precisely this piety that drove him to engage with the city.

Pietro's piety and civic actions undoubtedly resonated with many in the audience of the text: the merchants, artisans, and Franciscans who made up Pietro's cult, just as they had been his neighbours. The laymen would have had to pay taxes, participate in extra levies, and obey the city laws! The friars lived and prayed for citizens and many originated from among the urban citizenry. If a man known to be so holy as to be exhorted not to pay taxes still insisted on doing so, what could lesser men do but follow his example? Pietro was an example of Christian civic mindedness in action for other citizens. The instances of Pietro's dedication described above not only depict an exemplary saint, but also how a citizen and artisan ought, according to the hagiographer, to view his role in the commune. By extension, the examples show how a citizen could incorporate Christian values into his lay life.

Pietro was known as an exceptionally holy man, perhaps even as a living saint.[27] Dante mentions his prayers as being particularly effective.[28] Why would the hagiographer have chosen to portray his lay life and engagement in the commune so carefully? As a biography of a saint, would it not have been enough to prove his sanctity that Pietro's fellow citizens and the *podestà* of Siena himself are told to view him as a saint? The hagiographer was, however, not only portraying a saint, but an exemplary citizen. Intrinsically connected to his identity

---

[24] VPP, p. 83. 'Signori miei mala novella per me, che più giorni per ignoranza ho ritenuto quei denari, quali dovevo pagare alla mia Comunità, e oggi avendo inteso l'imposta, vi ho portata la mia parte: sicchè pigliatela e pardonatemi questa ignoranza.' I thank Siobhan Quinlan for invaluable advice on the Italian translations – all errors or unclarities are, of course, my own.

[25] VPP, pp. 82–3.

[26] Acts 11:29. For further discussion of this biblical passage in relation to Pietro, see the interesting note by father Luigi de Angelis, editor, VPP, p. 80, note 1. Note also the axiom 'render unto Caesar', Matthew 22:21, Mark 12:17, Luke 20:25.

[27] For the notion of living saints, see Gabriella Zarri, *Le sante vive: cultura e religiosità femminile nella prima età moderna* (Torino, 1990).

[28] Dante, 'Il purgatorio', *Commedia divina*, canto XIII, line 128.

Vitae of a Sienese craftsman and a Provençal nobleman

and roles as artisan and master, Pietro was a citizen of Siena. Citizenship was acquired primarily through baptism. The conferral of citizenship on worthy individuals who moved to a commune was also not uncommon. Legal studies of medieval citizenship emphasize that citizenship was defined not in terms of birth, but according to civic qualifications such as reputation, wealth, and property. Above all, citizenship was granted through election by a council of citizens and the subsequent oath taken when citizenship was conferred.[29] Thus citizenship was defined both proscriptively (citizenship could be revoked for misbehavior) and hortatively (citizens should behave a certain way). Legal citizenship was based on oaths. The oath formally placed the individual under obligation to uphold the statutes of the commune, imposed on all its citizens. Thus, the oath 'guaranteed the fulfillment of the duties assumed with the community and symbolized the mandatory presence of the individual within the city walls.'[30] These oaths included obedience to the official representatives of the city, such as councils, guilds, or guards. In addition, they prohibited any threatening actions against the material goods of the city, or, significantly, the 'peace and honor of the city'.[31] The citizen was bound by his honour, verbalised in the oath, to perform military service, as well as to own real estate within the parameters of the city. This property was to be maintained by the citizen.[32] A citizen had to possess a certain amount of wealth and live within the city walls.[33] Of course, a citizen had to pay taxes. Of craftsmen only masters, typically married and proprietors of their own workshops, could fully participate in a city's political and ritual life as citizens.[34]

Pietro Pettinajo was not born in Siena, where he came to be viewed as a saint, but rather seven miles outside the city, in a village in the surrounding Chianti region.[35] Thus, he must have been elected to join the citizens of the city by his peers-to-be. Bartolus of Sassoferrato (1313–1357) concisely phrased the creation of citizenship: 'Civitas sibi faciat civem': the city makes the citizen for itself.[36] Pietro's financial and social circumstances were such that his citizenship was welcome: he was a master artisan, married, and financially solid, as well as having an independent workshop. Elected citizenship was a form of

---

[29] Augustine Thompson, *Cities of God*, pp. 193, 311. On legal citizenship see Peter Riesenberg, 'Citizenship at law in late medieval Italy', *Viator* 5 (1974), pp. 333–46; Julius Kirshner, 'Civitas sibi faciat civem: Bartolus of Sassoferrato's doctrine on the making of a citizen', *Speculum* 48 (1973), pp. 694–713; Diego Quaglioni states that citizenship could be conveyed through *iure sanguinis*, i.e. by blood inheritance, or *iure loci*, by place of birth, 'The legal definition of citizenship in the late Middle Ages', in *City states in classical antiquity and medieval Italy*, ed. Anthony Molho, Kurt Raaflaub, and Julia Emlen (Stuttgart, 1991), pp. 155–67, esp. p. 161

[30] Quaglioni, 'The legal definition of citizenship in the late Middle Ages', pp. 155–67, p. 161.

[31] Ibid.

[32] Ibid.

[33] William M. Bowsky, 'Medieval citizenship: the individual and the state in the commune of Siena, 1287–1355', in *Studies in medieval and Renaissance history*, vol. IV (Lincoln, NE, 1967), pp. 193–243, especially p. 205. These requirements were typical for cities, especially in Northern Italy.

[34] Karras, *From boys to men*, p. 112

[35] VPP, p. 118.

[36] Bartolus of Sassoferrato quoted in Kirshner, 'Civitas sibi faciat civem', p. 698.

self-perpetuation of the mercantile and civic values of the urban community. Legal citizenship was essential for an individual's ability to participate in the affairs of his city, profession, and neighbourhood. Cultural citizenship, based on shared values and participation in civic life, was central for a sense of community and to urban life itself. The material aspects of citizenship – property, income, taxes, and other levies – were complemented by shared expectations of behaviour and values that can be grouped under the caption 'civic-mindedness'.[37] Civic rectitude manifest in service, neighbourliness, shared responsibility, in short citizenship, in many ways formed the ties that bound urban men together beyond their oaths and legal enforcement. An individual's reputation – be it of holiness, upstanding social position, or manliness – was tied to how he met the expectations of his neighbours, peers, and other inhabitants of the city. Pietro's *vita* clearly shows his membership in the commune. His neighbours' efforts to prevent him from paying taxes were based on their argument that he was doing his share for the city in prayer. He was already participating in the group effort.

Civic duties defined Pietro Pettinajo as a man.[38] He combined ideals of manliness both in pursuing his personal religious calling and by fastidiously upholding civic rectitude. If he had given away all he owned and become a pauper, that would have fitted into a different kind of model of holiness, and one where secular performances of masculinity were not necessary. Beggars were not perceived to be part of the power structures that defined medieval society and manliness. His piety and humility, charity and obedience, were moral strengths that underlined his spiritual masculinity based on self-restraint, control, and, above all, status among his male peers. His commitment to the city and to the quality of his products, as well as his social standing among other men, were the strengths of a secular man. It was this braiding together of complementary masculinities in one person that made the example of Pietro so salient in both the secular and the spiritual spheres of medieval urban life. It is also significant that the hagiographer describes Pietro's secular performance as heightened by his spiritual fortitude. The author brings the two spheres of life together most compellingly the moment the saint's manliness manifests itself in his profession and citizenship. The same trend is present in texts on the nobility, as we will see in the following example.

---

[37] I borrow this useful term from Thompson, who shows that civic rectitude was an important part of their cults and *vitae*: 'communal holiness flourished in community; it was social', Thompson, *City of God*, p. 194.

[38] Cf. 'The nature and quality of his citizenship defined a man and largely determined his responsibilities and range of action. His tie to *patria* called upon a man to fight, to father, and to sacrifice his property, certainly to surrender some time, and possibly his life. Citizenship gave the individual one of his few essential characteristics. Only his family conferred more; and only family commitment grew in like capacity and degree of involvement as one advanced in age.' Riesenberg, 'Citizenship at law in late medieval Italy', p. 334.

Vitae of a Sienese craftsman and a Provençal nobleman

THE SAINT AS SECULAR LORD

Elzéar de Sabran was a Provençal baron and an Italian count, in addition to being a confessor-saint.[39] After his father's death in 1309, Elzéar inherited his father's domains, and moved to Italy to take over the county of Ariano. Here he became an intimate of his liege, the king of Naples, Robert the Wise (1277-1343). Elzéar died on a diplomatic mission to France where he was negotiating the marriage contract of Robert's heir.[40] Elzéar was a man of considerable power and influence. His hagiographer pays great attention to the young count's financial ability, rule, and relationship with his vassals and liege – all-important parts of a nobleman's secular world.

When Elzéar inherited his father's fiefdoms, he found the patrimony deeply in debt and on the brink of revolt.[41] As count and baron, Elzéar managed to pay his father's and grandfather's debts, stabilize the economies of his fiefs, and win over reluctant vassals. According to the anonymous hagiographer, this was no mean feat. The impact these actions had on the young heir's control of his fiefdom is significant. His ability to solve the economic problems and gain the respect of his vassals and peers solidified his, and his family's, position. Inheriting his father's lands did not mean that Elzéar automatically inherited the loyalty of his father's vassals. In fact, the young count discovered letters sent to his father in which vassals had counseled the old count to disinherit his heir. This indicated not only disloyalty, but also active resistance from Elzéar's future men even prior to his succession. They considered him unfit to rule. Whether the reason for the vassals' lack of confidence was his extraordinary piety or lack of an heir – both decidedly undesirable traits in a lord, as well as unmasculine – or some other reason, is not disclosed. The importance of the incident for the hagiographer is in how Elzéar is said to have dealt with this opposition and disloyalty: he negotiated his relationship with his vassals not as an expression of lordship and masculinity, but as an expression of his piety. When the young count discovered the letters mentioned above, he did not confront his new vassals, but treated them with Christian kindness and generosity – against the advice of his closest councilors who recommended punitive measures. The latter would have quickly established Elzéar as a decisive and active lord not afraid of crushing those who opposed him. This would have guaranteed control of his vassals, his lordship as well his masculinity. However, the count bore criticism and opposition with marvelous patience. Instead of forcing his position on his vassals and peers, he won their loyalty over time with the excellence of his performance as a secular

---

[39] 'Confessor' designates men who, due to their outstanding virtue and piety, came to be venerated as saints. By living lives marked by heroic virtue, they confessed their faith in Christ – hence the term.

[40] VOE, pp. 88-97. I have relied on the vernacular, Provençal, *vita* for this essay, not the Latin version. Based on internal evidence as well as linguistic, I believe the vernacular text's audience to have been conceived as lay, and the Latin text to be directed to a clerical audience, most likely the Franciscan communities to whom the saint's cult is attached. For more on Elzéar's cult, see Mazel, 'Affaire de foi et affaire de famille en haute Provence au XIVe siècle'.

[41] The following summary is taken from VOE, pp. 90-5.

lord, for example by embracing his duties and social status. He led by example, not by force.

The practical manifestations of Elzéar's lordship are an important part of the *vita*'s narrative and for the hagiographer's social positioning of his protagonist. As a count and baron, it was Elzéar's duty to hold court and judge misdemeanors in his fiefdoms. According to the *vita*, he had great respect for law, and in his own judgments he combined the rule of law with Christian mercy. He treated those accused of crimes with patience, fairness, and grace, criticising his officers when they failed to mete out justice fairly.[42] He is portrayed as a great judge and gaoler, just and merciful. These actions gained Elzéar respect and admiration from all, peers and vassals alike. His performance as count secured his status among his peers. His vassals came not only to obey him, but also to respect and love their lord. Elzéar was both a liege lord over his own subjects and vassal to the king of Naples. He is described as devoted and obedient to his sovereign as a courtier and knight. In fact, he is the exemplary courtier, even acting as foster-father for the royal heir, which also allowed him to exhibit exemplary paternal qualities despite not having fathered a child himself.[43] The count's *vita* reminds us that lordship in the Middle Ages was reciprocal.

As in the case of Pietro Pettinajo, we see how the hagiographer elaborates on Elzéar's actions in a secular forum, although this time that of lords and vassals. Here again the saint excelled at his secular duties as a man. The lay circumstances and actions in Elzéar's *vitae* play a prominent role – conspicuously so. Positioning the count's holiness in his social situation is important, but the hagiographer is doing more than that. He portrays Elzéar as an admirable peer for the noble male audience of the *vita*. For readers or hearers of lower social strata, Elzéar is an idealised lord in his performance of lordship – especially as a fair and just lord. Elzéar is described as setting out to bolster his fiefdom, at the same time gaining the respect of his men through highly successful conduct in the secular sphere. He embraced his secular position as a Christian of exceptional self-possession. Elzéar's character as a Christian confessor-saint as well as an active lord was posited as unusual by the hagiographer. This is best seen in his wife's amazement at his patience: 'Elzéar, what man are you who never loses your temper because of the injuries against you, and that you seem insensible to them? I believe you do not know how to become angry!'[44] With these words, Dauphine not only marvels at her husband, but she also describes the expected behavior of powerful men: lords – and men in general – were expected to show vexation or even anger when provoked or injured. To completely lose one's temper was viewed as unmanly because it involved loss of self-control, but measured anger was understood as masculine and appropriately lordly behavior, especially when justified, as the passage indicates. In his response to his wife, Elzéar explains:

---

[42] In addition, he would routinely help pay fines, ordering that this should not be revealed to the culpable individuals. VOE, pp. 39–127, pp. 94–7.

[43] VOE, pp. 88–97.

[44] VOE, p. 92, 'Alzeas, qual home hies tu, que nulhtemps no te yrasses contra os enjurias a tu, e hiest vist ensencible. Crey que tu no te sapias yrasser!'

Dauphine, there are things that rouse frustration and indignation in me; but such emotions never rule over me because I immediately begin to contemplate the reproaches that Jesus Christ endured; and I tell myself: Elzéar, Jesus Christ, your master, was bound by his subjects . . . all these things were inflicted on him by his evil and ungrateful subjects whose innocent and good lord he was. If your subjects do to you one of these injuries and you do not bear them with patience, you are not a true disciple of Jesus Christ, or his true son, or faithful servant.[45]

This patience and rejection of all, even temperate, anger is self-control beyond secular masculinity. Even as a model Christian, he would have had the cultural right as lord to punish those who vexed him. Elzéar's response refutes any questioning of his masculinity with the example of Christ, *imitatio Christi*, and self-control. However, rejecting flaring tempers was not what made the count exceptional; after all, monks were to be calm and restrained, turning the other cheek.[46] Elzéar was exceptional because he was a secular lord who was as committed to the example of Christ as a monk would be; to the extent that anger was not an option for him, even in his duties as a lord – a most secular pursuit. Elzéar acknowledged anger and frustration, rejecting them from his own life: the count's adherence to a spiritual model of manly *imitatio Christi*, much like fasting or prayer, demonstrated exceptional self-control, humility, and perhaps even mortification. Elzéar's devotion is highly present in a most secular situation: holding court. Spiritual masculinity enables him to tap into *imitatio Christi* as well as his obligations as a secular lord.

If Elzéar had not been so pious, his experiences and performances of masculinity, and by extension lordship, would have been different. Dauphine's ventriloquism of secular expectations and Elzéar's response make it clear that the hagiographer depicts a man who sees and carries himself in a certain way: as a man in control of his emotions and actions because of his deep (and exemplary) commitment to Christ. As the author narrates it, this was in no way contradictory to Elzéar's social position as a lord or his practices of lordship in the situations that demanded that role of him. Instead, Elzéar brought spiritual masculinity into the forum of secular manly action, and excelled at both. The paradox of a lord-saint was possible, and beneficial to both secular and spiritual realms.

The count of Ariano may not have had children, been a renowned warrior, or won tournaments – the most prominent secular markers of masculinity – to prove aspects of his manliness, but as baron and count he actively and successfully administered his fiefdoms and held court.[47] Thus, he manifested his masculinity

---

[45] VOE, pp. 92–5, 'Dalphina, ieu lacunas vagadas per aytals cauzas me comensi a muore e endignaren mon coratge; mas aytal movemen nustemps no senhoreia en mi, quar al dese me meti a cogitar los oprobris que Jhesu Crist sufertec; e parli ayssi a mi mezeis en mon coratge: Alzeas, Jhesu Crist, to mestre, per sos sosmes fo pres e lhat, . . . Totas aquestas cauzas sufertec per sos sosmes mals e ungratos aquel que era lor senhor innocen e bo. E si tos sosmes fazien a tu alqunas d'aquestas cauzas, sino que pascienmen o portesses, tu no heist veray discipol de Jhesu Crist, no son bo filh, ni serz fizel . . .'.
[46] Matthew 5:38–42; Luke 6:27–31.
[47] See Joanna Huntington's essay in this volume for further discussion of contemporary benchmarks of maturation and manhood among high-status laymen.

in his secular duties. This was enhanced by the admiration and respect of other men, including his own liege-lord. Women have only marginal roles in Elzéar's *vita,* appearing largely as admirers (most prominently his own wife), household servants, or, incidentally, as the wives of the condemned receiving his alms. This supports Karras' theory of women being tools in the formation of masculinity, not as those against which masculinity is formed – masculinity is defined both against and with other men, not women.[48] This evidence of manliness also served to draw his exceptional piety into the secular sphere. Indeed, the hagiographer's portrayal of Elzéar makes him more successful than a thoroughly worldly man due to his embrace of the spiritual masculinity of a saintly Christian. I posit this as a significant reason why the *vita* describes so many of the count's worldly roles.

CONCLUSIONS

These texts show that men could remain in the secular world and perform their duties while at the same time living lives that set the stage for reputations of holiness. Both Elzéar and Pietro were exceptional. As saints, they were hardly emblematic of ordinary laymen, but the texts show how the hagiographers conceived their lay lives and their role as men in them. As didactic narratives providing examples of lived religion, they validate the duties of artisans and nobility, respectively. While most saints rejected the norms for laymen, *vitae* of men like Pietro Pettinajo and Elzéar de Sabran showed that being a comb-maker or a count was not an impediment to religious calling, even sanctity.

The circumstances of these men's lives and roles as nobleman and artisan needed to be rendered recognizably in the texts in order to provide the secular framework for their sanctity. However, the texts contain more than proof of the saints' heroic virtues – they also tell the reader how a good, Christian lord or artisan ought to behave and give practical examples of how a man of the world could bring his faith into the secular spheres of his life. It is clear in the way the hagiographers present Pietro and Elzéar's success that their holiness is not a burden impeding their worldly actions and roles. It is beneficial for their secular performances. Secular duties in the texts are influenced by the religious motives. In addition, the duties and the saint's performance of them are characterised by manifest notions of manliness: relationships of influence with other men, self-control, and worldly agency in acts culturally gendered as male, such as sitting as judge. The lives of Pietro and Elzéar were defined by their secular social status as men, but they acted and reacted as Christians. Their masculinity was spiritually defined, even Christocentric, hence the appropriateness of the term 'spiritual masculinity' to describe them.

The protagonists of late medieval biographies of lay, male, married saints navigated social positioning between men, establishing and maintaining their masculinity in male dominated society. In fact, at the moments in the texts where

---

[48] Karras, *From boys to men,* pp. 151–62.

the men were most dragged into matters of their secular, social position, they excelled by implementing spiritual guidelines for behaviour: obedience, patience, mercy, generosity, self-control. This not only resolved any possible tensions, but also helped the men excel as laymen. Elzéar de Sabran and Pietro Pettinajo are shown as men highly aware of their social positions and obligations. Their place as men in their respective societies is unambiguously portrayed as one of success, respect, and influence. These saints embody spiritual masculinity as powerful examples of how to incorporate spiritual values into secular lives. Thus, the hagiographers were aware both of more strictly secular and of spiritual manliness, describing them not as contradictory, but complementary. The ideal male saint who remained in the world could bolster either personal piety or social positioning, or both. By performing his secular duties according to the models of spiritual masculinity he could excel as a saint and also as a layman.

'IMITATE, TOO, THIS KING IN VIRTUE, WHO COULD HAVE DONE ILL, AND DID IT NOT': LAY SANCTITY AND THE REWRITING OF HENRY VI'S MANLINESS[1]

Katherine J. Lewis

Henry VI was murdered in the Tower of London during the night of 21–22 May 1471. Earlier on 21 May Edward IV had entered London in triumph, following his victory at the Battle of Tewkesbury on 4 May. Henry's only son, Prince Edward of Westminster, had been killed at or shortly after the battle, and his death evidently sealed the fate of his father. Edward IV had Henry buried out of the way at Chertsey abbey, doubtless in part to forestall veneration of his body. Nonetheless, rumours of miracles performed at Henry's tomb began to spread and he became the focus of an extremely popular cult. This cult provides abundant evidence for the great value which medieval people continued to find in saints on the eve of the Reformation. However, initial academic approaches to it emphasised its political dimensions, exploring the ways in which devotion to Henry (in common with devotion to men such as Simon de Montfort, Thomas of Lancaster and Richard Scrope) formed an expression of opposition to the crown.[2] Tudor interest in the cult was clearly political, involving the systematic recording of Henry's miracles as part of an attempt to have him canonised.[3] But

---

[1] I am grateful to audiences at the Universities of Huddersfield, York and Edinburgh, and at the International Medieval Congress at Leeds and the International Congress on Medieval Studies at Kalamazoo for comments on early versions of this essay; to P.H. Cullum, David Green, Joanna Huntington, W. Mark Ormrod and Victoria Whitworth for advice and suggestions; and to Craig Taylor for first suggesting to me that I should read John Blacman's life of Henry VI.

[2] John W. McKenna, 'Piety and propaganda: the cult of Henry VI', in *Chaucer and Middle English studies in honour of R.H. Robbins*, ed. B. Rowland (London, 1974), pp. 72–88; John M. Theilmann, 'Political canonization and political symbolism in medieval England', *Journal of British Studies* 29 (1990), pp. 241–66; Simon Walker, 'Political saints in later medieval England', in *The McFarlane legacy: studies in late medieval politics and society*, ed. R.H. Britnell and A.J. Pollard (Stroud, 1995), pp. 77–106; Danna Piroyanski, *Martyrs in the making: political martyrdom in late medieval England* (Basingstoke, 2008) provides a thorough discussion of this phenomenon.

[3] Sydney Anglo, *Images of Tudor kingship* (Guildford, 1992), pp. 61–73; P. Grosjean, *Henrici VI Angliae regis miracula postuma* (Brussels, 1935) collates a range of sources relating to the attempted canonisation and the cult more widely.

it is far from certain that political motives lay behind the increasing regularity with which people sought Henry VI's intercession, particularly once Richard III moved his body to a prestigious location, St George's chapel, Windsor, in August 1484. More recent studies of the cult have given greater consideration to its devotional aspects; the evidence of his miracles, taken in concert with testamentary bequests and surviving visual representations of Henry, indicate that he was venerated in most parts of England, by people drawn from across the social spectrum.[4] There was widespread belief in Henry's thaumaturgical powers, the majority of his 174 recorded miracles recounting cures of physical injury or infirmity, or mental incapacity, and the restoration of life to those who appeared to be dead (many of these children).[5] There is evidence that Henry was sometimes seen as the particular protector of those facing sudden death, or as a plague saint, like St Roche, but the essence of his appeal seems to have been the multifunctional nature of his power.[6]

Thus, the fact that Henry did not achieve canonisation does not mean that his cult had 'failed', or that he was not a 'real' saint, for by this period canonisation was essentially a matter of politics and patronage rather than any sort of straightforward recognition of the 'genuine' saintliness of the proposed candidate.[7] Henry was perceived and frequently addressed as a saint by his devotees even without the papal imprimatur; he was arguably the most successful saint in late medieval England. It adds nothing to our understanding of his creation as a saint or of the dynamics of his cult to question whether he really deserved this veneration.[8] Indeed, modern scholarship on medieval saints has moved away from debating the veracity of sanctity in individual cases and generally proceeds with the assumption that sanctity is never simply innate, but has to be observed and

---

[4] Diana Webb, *Pilgrimage in medieval England* (London and New York, 2000), especially pp. 175-9; Richard Marks, 'Images of Henry VI', in *The Lancastrian court: proceedings of the 2001 Harlaxton Symposium*, Harlaxton Medieval Studies 13, ed. Jenny Stratford (Donington, 2003), pp. 111-214; Leigh Ann Craig, 'Royalty, virtue and adversity: the cult of Henry VI', *Albion* 35 (2003), pp. 187-209; Piroyanski, *Martyrs in the making*, pp. 74-98 is the most recent discussion.

[5] The text of the miracles was edited by Grosjean; *The miracles of King Henry VI*, ed. and trans. Ronald Knox and Shane Leslie (Cambridge, 1923), provides a translated selection; for further discussion see Alison Hanham, 'Henry VI and his miracles', *Ricardian* 12 (2000), pp. 638-52. More miracles performed at Windsor were recorded in English, but 174 is the total number of those which were translated into Latin, probably in the early 1490s. The English depositions do not survive, see Hanham, 'Henry VI and his miracles', pp. 640-1.

[6] Craig, 'Royalty, virtue and adversity', pp. 205-9; Piroyanski, *Martyrs in the making*, pp. 85-6.

[7] For the best account of the development of canonisation in this period, see André Vauchez, *Sainthood in the later Middle Ages*, trans. Jean Birrell (Cambridge, 1997; orig. pub. 1988).

[8] For a more detailed discussion of the nature and evaluation of holiness, see John H. Arnold, *Belief and unbelief in medieval Europe* (London, 2005), pp. 69-104 (especially p. 90.) Webb also notes, 'To ask whether ... Henry VI deserved to attract pilgrims is less important than to ask why', *Pilgrimage in medieval England*, p. 175. Similarly W.M. Ormrod focuses on 'the cultural messages provided by the legends of the pious Henry VI' rather than their accuracy, 'Monarchy, martyrdom and masculinity', in *Holiness and masculinity in the Middle Ages*, eds P.H. Cullum and Katherine J. Lewis (Cardiff and Toronto, 2004), pp. 174-91, p. 183.

identified in order to exist.⁹ Thus it is always more or less constructed, to serve a range of devotional, political and social functions.¹⁰ In the case of the most popular and long-lived cults this became an ongoing process of reinvention, to meet changing needs and priorities, a phenomenon that renders saints' cults an invaluable means of understanding the societies in which they flourished.¹¹ The value of examining Henry's cult lies in accounting for the nature and significance of his representation as a saint, both in general terms (for what this tells us about contemporary trends in saint-making) and those more specific: Henry's sanctity served as an explanation for his character flaws (as they were perceived at the time) and even as an antidote for his disastrous kingship. Henry's piety (if not his actual sanctity) has often been seen as a crucial dimension of his many shortcomings as king, a tradition which found influential articulation in Polydore Vergil's early-sixteenth-century account of him as:

> a man of a mild and simple nature, who preferred peace to war, tranquility to care, the honorable to the advantageous, and leisure to troubles. Nothing was more chaste than he, nothing more upright, nothing more pious. In him existed bashfulness, modesty, integrity, and supreme patience, and he bore human calamities, cares, and afflictions as calmly as if they were the result of his own sins. He controlled himself as readily as he controlled those he ruled, he was not greedy for wealth, nor thirsty for honors, being only concerned with his soul's salvation, reckoning as good only those things that promoted this, and as bad only those things which tended to his soul's loss.¹²

The prevalent stereotype of Henry depicts him as more interested in praying than ruling, a man of meek and rather feeble character easily dominated by others; too weak to wield justice effectively or to punish wrong-doers, and profligate with his favours.¹³ This was compounded by his failure to exhibit the qualities

---

⁹ Anneke B. Mulder-Bakker, 'The invention of saintliness: texts and contexts', in *The invention of saintliness*, ed. Anneke B. Mulder-Bakker (London and New York, 2002), pp. 3–23, p. 16.

¹⁰ Pierre Delooz, 'Towards a sociological study of canonized sainthood in the Catholic Church', in *Saints and their cults: studies in religious sociology, folklore and history*, ed. Stephen Wilson (Cambridge, 1983), pp. 189–216, has been very influential on approaches to the constructed nature of sanctity. See also Donald Weinstein and Rudolph M. Bell, *Saints and society: the two worlds of western Christendom, 1100–1700* (Chicago and London, 1982).

¹¹ For some of the most recent work in this area see *Saints and sanctity*, ed. Peter Clarke and Tony Claydon, Studies in Church History 47 (Woodbridge, 2011).

¹² This comes from Vergil's *Anglica Historia* written between about 1507 and 1531, first published 1534. This translation, by Dana F. Sutton, comes from her hypertext critical edition and translation of the 1555 version available online [http://www.philological.bham.ac.uk/polverg/, chapter 23, accessed 31 October 2012].

¹³ The most substantial assessments of Henry VI's rule are provided by R.A. Griffiths, *The reign of King Henry VI* (originally published 1981, this edition Stroud, 1998); Bertram Wolffe, *Henry VI* (originally published 1981, this edition New Haven and London, 2001); John Watts, *Henry VI and the politics of kingship* (Cambridge, 1996). They draw differing conclusions about the extent of Henry's limitations as king, and the explanations for these. Any assessment of Henry's character has to recognise the propagandist influence of the Wars of the Roses on many contemporary accounts, as well as the impact of his mental breakdown in 1453 both on his conduct, and on perceptions of it.

of a warrior leader, which played a crucial role in establishing standards of good kingship at the time. The problems of Henry's rule have thus often been seen (more or less explicitly) as stemming from deficient manliness, his gender identity being characterised by notions of childishness and/or effeminacy, picking up on the judgements of a range of his contemporaries.[14] In the light of these understandings of Henry this essay builds on the work of scholars who have traced the socio-cultural as well as religious significance of Henry's sanctity, by adding the dimension of gender to an analysis of his cult. It will argue that the representation of Henry as saint deals with his equivocal manliness by re-writing him as the embodiment of holy masculinity, and placing him in the same register as other later medieval lay saints of high social status.

The most important factor in the popular attribution of sainthood to Henry was not so much the conviction that he had led a saintly life, but rather his sudden, brutal death, and the belief that his fate was unmerited and unjust.[15] This allowed his murder to be understood as martyrdom. The cult thus belongs within a wider phenomenon of popular saint-making described by André Vauchez as characteristic of England and Germanic countries: the high status male who died violently, and was subsequently reported to be a miracle-working martyr.[16] The papacy evidently became increasingly uncomfortable with this development and Vauchez's study shows that between 1254 and 1481 no-one who had died a violent death was canonised, yet the veneration of murdered individuals continued unabated on a popular level.[17] He links this to the Church's attempts to promote the idea of the *rex justus* or *rex bonus* over the king who simply came to a sticky end, and, more widely, to place the emphasis on a saint's exemplary life, and the imitable aspects of their conduct, rather than his/her death.[18] This was indeed the emphasis in Alexander VI's commission inquiring into the life, death and

---

[14] For a useful survey of the historiography see R.A. Griffiths, 'Henry VI (1421–1471)', *Oxford dictionary of national biography* (Oxford, 2004); online edn, September 2010 [http://www.oxforddnb.com/view/article/12953, accessed 31 October 2012]. The importance of gender to the ideology and practice of medieval kingship has received little scholarly attention, although important studies have appeared: Ormrod, 'Monarchy, martyrdom and masculinity'; Cynthia Herrup, 'The king's two genders', *Journal of British Studies* 45 (2006), pp. 493–510; Christopher Fletcher, *Richard II: manhood, youth and politics, 1377–99* (Oxford, 2008). Jonathan Hughes, *Arthurian myths and alchemy: the kingship of Edward IV* (Stroud, 2002), discusses the gendered implications of Henry VI's health and breakdown. Helen E. Maurer, *Margaret of Anjou: queenship and power in late medieval England* (Woodbridge, 2003), includes some consideration of Henry's gender as part of her analysis of Margaret. See also my *Kingship and masculinity in late medieval England* (London and New York, 2013), pp. 141–252.

[15] For more detailed accounts of the development of the cult see the works cited in notes 2, 3 and 4 above.

[16] Vauchez, *Sainthood*, pp. 146–56; Piroyanski, *Martyrs in the making*, for discussion of English examples of high status male martyrs. Webb notes examples of more localised cults focused on men of lower status who had died violently, *Pilgrimage in medieval England*, pp. 154–8.

[17] Vauchez, *Sainthood*, pp. 414–20.

[18] Ibid., pp. 357–69, 420, 531, 536–7. For a more focused account of the increasing tendency for royal sanctity to be seen as the product of an exemplary life, see also Gábor Klaniczay, *Holy rulers and blessed princesses: dynastic cults in medieval central Europe*, trans. Éva Pálmai (Cambridge, 2002; orig. pub. 2000).

miracles of Henry VI.[19] Such considerations also governed the only detailed narrative account of Henry's sanctity which survives: John Blacman's *Collectarium mansuetudinum et bonorum morum regis Henrici VI*.[20] This text does not survive in manuscript form and the earliest extant version of it is an edition printed by Robert Copland in about 1523.[21] Blacman was part of a spiritual circle around Henry VI, whose members were connected with the king's foundations: Eton College and King's College, Cambridge. Blacman perhaps acted as an unofficial confessor or spiritual advisor to Henry VI. Roger Lovatt's work has established the extent to which this text constitutes the account of someone who had enjoyed personal contact with Henry and also drew on the reminiscences of others who had been close to the king.[22] Blacman was a fellow at Eton from 1443 to 1454 and in the late 1450s underwent a year's probation as a Carthusian at the London Charterhouse. For reasons unknown he never took the final vow, but remained within the order nonetheless, recorded as a *clericus redditus* in 1474.[23] In about the mid 1460s he moved to the Witham Charterhouse in Somerset, where he stayed until his death in the mid 1480s. Internal evidence suggests that Blacman wrote this account towards the end of his life, probably before Henry's body was translated in 1484.[24]

Blacman's text has been cited in support of the contention that Henry VI was 'genuinely' saintly during his lifetime and that this was the inspiration for his cult.[25] But there has been sizeable disagreement over the status of Blacman's text as a reliable source for Henry's character and conduct. Bertram Wolffe argued that Blacman's presentation of Henry as a saint, which involved deliberate mis-

[19] Grosjean, *Henrici VI*, 167*-169*.
[20] John Blacman, *Collectarium mansuetudinum et bonorum morum regis Henrici VI*, published by Robert Copland c. 1523. The most accessible edition is John Blacman, *Henry the Sixth: a reprint of John Blacman's memoir*, ed. and trans. M.R. James (Cambridge, 1919).
[21] I have consulted a facsimile copy of the original publication in the Bodleian Library, available via Early English Books Online [http://eebo.chadwyck.com, accessed 31 October 2012].
[22] The biographical information about Blacman given here is taken from Roger Lovatt, 'John Blacman: biographer of Henry VI', in *The writing of history in the Middle Ages: essays presented to Richard William Southern*, ed. R.H.C. Davis and J.M. Wallace-Hadrill (Oxford, 1981), pp. 415-44, pp. 417-29. See also Roger Lovatt, 'The library of John Blacman and contemporary Carthusian spirituality', *Journal of Ecclesiastical History* 43 (1992), pp. 195-230, pp. 196-200. William Aiscough, bishop of Salisbury and Henry's confessor in the 1440s, has been identified as a possible major source for Blacman. He and Blacman were both closely involved with Eton and King's College; see Margaret Lucille Kekewich, 'Aiscough, William (c. 1395-1450)', *Oxford dictionary of national biography* (Oxford 2004) [http://www.oxforddnb.com/view/article/954, accessed 31 October 2012].
[23] Lovatt explains that in this period two or three *clerici redditi* were permitted to live in every Charterhouse; they were professed and tonsured, and followed the same routine as the monks, but could own property and leave the order if they wished, 'John Blacman', p. 428.
[24] The precise dating remains a matter for debate, but Wolffe's assertion (*Henry VI*, p. 6) that the text was written as part of the Tudor canonisation project, and therefore not by Blacman, was countered at some length by Roger Lovatt, 'A collector of apocryphal anecdotes: John Blacman revisited', in *Property and politics: essays in later medieval English history*, ed. A.J. Pollard (Gloucester, 1984), pp. 172-97, pp. 173-6.
[25] The most fervent promoter of this view was F.A. Gasquet, see his *The religious life of King Henry VI* (London, 1923).

representation of some verifiable aspects of his conduct and court, meant that it should be dismissed as evidence for the 'real' Henry VI because it said nothing about his failings as a king.[26] Roger Lovatt answered this charge by emphasising the spiritual nature and purpose of the text. He contended that Blacman implicitly supports the evidence from elsewhere of Henry's well-established failings as a king, which derived fundamentally from his overly pious demeanour and conduct, rendering him (in Blacman's eyes) a bad king, but a good man.[27] In so doing, Lovatt argued, Blacman presented Henry as a model of lay piety and his conclusions have been influential upon subsequent understandings of the text.[28] More recently Thomas S. Freeman, while agreeing that Blacman presented Henry VI as a model, took a different approach to the relationship that this model bore to the real Henry, asserting that 'the *Collectarium* is a carefully constructed work and not merely artless reportage. Blacman carefully massaged and moulded details of the real Henry to create an ideal Henry.'[29] Like Wolffe he focuses on the parts of the text which are 'demonstrably inaccurate' and states that, while it 'does not contribute much to our understanding of ... [the] historical Henry', it can further our understanding of a particular brand of late medieval piety.[30]

Like Freeman I understand this text as evidence, primarily, for Blacman's perception of Henry's holiness, based to some extent on his knowledge of the man. It is, of course, impossible to say whether this opinion was originally formed during the time he actually spent with Henry, or later in Henry's lifetime, or only after Henry's death and the development of the cult. Besides which, Blacman also drew on the opinions of others, which further complicates the issue.[31] It is perhaps most useful to think of the text as a story based on Henry's life, told in order to explain Henry's sanctity, drawing on established modes of high status lay male holiness to provide corroboration.[32] Blacman was writing at a time when Henry's status as a miracle-working martyr was well known, but his account has a different focus. As he explains in the prologue:

---

[26] Wolffe, *Henry VI*, pp. 7–12.

[27] Lovatt, 'John Blacman', especially p. 435; and 'A collector of apocryphal anecdotes', pp. 182–3.

[28] Lovatt, 'John Blacman', p. 440; 'A collector of apocryphal anecdotes', p. 174. For Lovatt's influence see Jonathan Hughes, 'Blacman, John (1407/8–1485?)', *Oxford dictionary of national biography* (Oxford, 2004) [http://www.oxforddnb.com/view/article/2599, accessed 31 Oct 2012]; Karen A. Winstead, *John Capgrave's fifteenth century* (Philadelphia, 2007), pp. 151–3.

[29] Thomas S. Freeman, '"*Ut verus Christi sequester*": John Blacman and the cult of Henry VI', in *Of mice and men: image, belief and regulation in late medieval England. The fifteenth century V*, ed. Linda Clark (Woodbridge, 2005), pp. 127–55, p. 140.

[30] Freeman, '"*Ut verus Christi sequester*"', pp. 139, 141.

[31] For example, if Bishop Aiscough was an important source, Blacman was writing over thirty years after the last possible date at which Aiscough could have passed information on (having been murdered by a mob on 29 June 1450).

[32] My wording at the beginning of this sentence is taken from Albrecht Diem, 'Monks, kings and the transformation of sanctity: Jonas of Bobbio and the end of the holy man', *Speculum* 82 (2007), pp. 521–59, p. 524.

I have therefore thought fit to treat of some matters to the praise of God and of the serene prince King Henry VI now deceased . . . this especially because to praise the saints of God, (in the register of whom I take that excellent king to be rightly included on account of the holy virtues by him exercised all his life long) is to praise and glorify Almighty God, of whose heavenly gift it cometh that they are saints.[33]

Blacman gives only one passing mention to Henry's posthumous miracles in the text, and does not give an account of Henry's martyrdom, noting simply that he 'suffered a violent death of the body that others might, as was then the expectation, peaceably possess the kingdom'.[34] Blacman, apparently working within the papal-driven definition of sanctity noted above, set out to explain that Henry's status as a saint was predicated on his way of life, which may well have been a deliberate attempt to counter the emphasis which the popular cult had inevitably placed on Henry's miracles. Rather than presenting a comprehensive account of Henry's life, Blacman presents a series of interlinked vignettes of his holy conduct, asserting that these derived from his own knowledge of the king, and 'from the relation of men worthy of credit who were formerly attendant on him'.[35] However, Blacman explicitly eschews a biographical approach, stating at the outset that he has deliberately avoided discussion of Henry's family background and events relating to his status as king of both England and France, partly as these are 'a matter plainly known to all'.[36] Instead the text is divided up into eleven non-chronological sections, titled, for example: 'He was a diligent worshipper of God', 'His devout habit in Church', 'Against avarice' and 'The humility of the king'.[37] Henry's holiness is seen to reside in the predication of his conduct on a strong faith and particular emphasis is placed on Henry's scrupulous personal morality. As the following analysis shows, Blacman's depiction of Henry was not only informed by developments in lay piety but also presents him in terms which highlight his similarity to many other lay male saints, such as Homobonus of Cremona (d. 1197), a draper-tailor who was the first layman to be canonised (in 1199), Louis IX of France (1214–70, canonised 1297), Elzéar of Sabran, count of Ariano (1285–1323, canonised 1371) and Charles of Blois, duke of Brittany (1319–64, subject of an unsuccessful canonisation bid in 1376).[38]

---

[33] Blacman, *Henry the Sixth*, p. 25 (3): 'idcirco in laudem Dei & serenissimi principis regis Henrici VI corpora jam defuncti . . . Maxime quia sanctos Dei laudare, quorum in cathologo istum puto regem eximium, ob sancta sua merita quoad visit per eum exercitata, merito computari, omnipotentis Dei laus est & Gloria, ex cujus coelesti dono est, ut sancti sint.' All quotations are taken from James' edition. In all subsequent references to this source the first page number gives the English translation, the second page number the Latin original.

[34] Ibid., p. 41 (19): 'mortis ibi corporis violentiam sustinuit propter regnum, ut tunc sperabatur, ab aliis pacifice possidendum'.

[35] Ibid., p. 26 (4): '. . . ex relate fidedignorum, quondam ei assistencium, didicerim, propalabo'.

[36] Ibid., p. 25 (3): '. . . quasi manifestum & notum'.

[37] Ibid. 'Cultor Dei sedulous erat', p. 27 (5); 'Devota habitudo ejus in ecclesia', p. 28 (6); 'Contra avaritiam', p. 31 (9); 'Humilitatis regis', p. 35 (13).

[38] For further discussion of this class of saint see Vauchez, *Sainthood*, pp. 158–67, 263–7, 356–69; for specific discussion of Italian urban lay saints, of whom Homobonus was just one example,

Particularly relevant in this context is William Caxton's unique Middle English life of Louis IX, contained in his 1483 translation of the *Golden Legend*.[39] Caxton cannot have been unaware of the popularity of the cult of Henry VI, although before the 1484 reburial it would not have been politic to include direct reference to it in his collection. But, as the issue of kingly sanctity was extremely current and Henry's cult was growing in popularity at exactly the time Caxton was putting his collection together, this may have given Louis' appearance in the *Golden Legend* additional significance. In common with all these saints Henry is shown by Blacman to embody a fundamental element of lay sanctity: the strength of will to live in the world and combat the temptations of worldly glory and self-gratification.[40] As Marita von Weissenberg argues elsewhere in this volume, this understanding of lay sanctity derived from contemporary standards of masculinity, and these standards have not previously been applied to Blacman's text. Examination of its contents reveals that while it is possible to read this account of Henry as evidence that the king was actually weak and effeminate, Blacman's intention was to establish quite the reverse.

One obvious indication of the influence of the hagiographic framework within which Blacman was writing is provided by his description of Henry's appearance. Despite Henry's great wealth and power Blacman shows him to have been humble in his bearing and in his clothing:

> Further of his humility in his bearing, in his clothes and other apparel of his body, in his speech and many other parts of his outward behaviour; – it is well known that from his youth up he always wore round-toed boots. He also customarily wore a long gown with a rolled hood like a townsman, and a full cloak reaching below his knees, with shoes, boots and foot-gear wholly black, rejecting expressly all curious fashion of clothing.[41]

---

see André Vauchez, 'A twelfth-century novelty: the lay saints of urban Italy', in his *The laity in the Middle Ages: religious beliefs and devotional practices*, ed. with an introduction by Daniel E. Bornstein, trans. Margery J. Schneider (Notre Dame, IN, and London, 1993; orig. pub. 1987), pp. 51–72. See also von Weissenberg in the present volume. For the construction of Louis IX as a saint see Jacques Le Goff, *Saint Louis*, trans. Gareth Evan Gollrad (Notre Dame, IN, 2009; orig. pub. 1996) and M. Cecilia Gaposchkin, *The making of Saint Louis: kingship, sanctity and crusade in the later Middle Ages* (Ithaca, NY, 2008).

[39] William Caxton, *Golden Legend*. I have consulted a facsimile of the 1483 edition available via Early English Books Online [http://eebo.chadwyck.com, accessed 31 October 2012]. The pages are numbered only on the recto. Caxton's source was a liturgical version of Louis' life contained in a French version of the *Golden Legend* known as the *Légende Dorée*, see Gaposchkin, *The making of Saint Louis*, p. 115

[40] Weinstein and Bell, *Saints and society*, pp. 73–80.

[41] Blacman, *Henry the Sixth*, p. 36 (14): 'De ipsius etiam humilitate in incessu, in vestibus et aliis corporalibus indumentis, in verbis et ceteris corporis gestibus compluribus, constat, quam obtusis sotularibus et ocreis a juventute uti consueverat adinstar coloni. Togam etiam longam cum capucio rotulato ad modum burgensis, et talarem tunicam ultra genua demissam, caligas, ocreas, calceos omnino pulli coloris &c. Omnimoda curiositate per eum prohibita in consuetudine habuit.' See p. 35 (13), p. 37 (15) for further evidence of Henry's humility. For Louis' comparable sobriety of dress see Caxton, *Golden Legend*, p. ccccxxx recto and verso.

Blacman's representation of Henry as habitually dressing in rather a shabby fashion has been identified as an instance where his narrative is demonstrably contradicted by other evidence which shows that Henry paid for plenty of fine clothes.[42] Rather than being an indication that Blacman was mistaken or confused in his recollection of Henry, this is clearly a 'deliberate mistake', demonstrating the ways in which Blacman rewrote aspects of Henry's conduct in order to make it fit more neatly into a saintly paradigm of austerity and generosity. Henry's humility is enforced by physical self-mortification: Blacman tells us that on ceremonial occasions, when Henry implicitly did dress finely, he 'would always have put on his body a rough hair shirt, that by its roughness his body might be restrained from excesses, or more truly that all pride and vain glory, such as is apt to be engendered by pomp, might be repressed'.[43] Wearing hair shirts and practising self-mortification was commonplace among high status lay saints, both male and female. Caxton tells us that Louis IX 'forced hym self to serue his spyryte by dyuers castygacion or chastysyng/ he vsed the hayre many tymes nexte hys flesshe' and if 'feblenesse of his body' led him to remove it he instructed his confessor to give 40 shillings to the poor for every day that he did not wear it.[44] Henry and Louis' practices were relatively restrained compared with Charles of Blois, who not only wore simple dress with a hair shirt underneath, but also tied knotted cords so tightly around his chest that they broke the flesh and the resultant sores became infested with vermin, while on Fridays he beat himself so severely that he bled profusely.[45]

Blacman highlights the significance not merely of Henry's own behaviour, but also of his endeavours to change and improve the morality of the court, especially with respect to the conduct of the men. In common with Louis, Henry is shown to have a marked hatred of blasphemy, Blacman says: 'a swearer was his abomination', Henry using only the oath 'Forsothe and forsothe' himself and correcting those who swore 'either by a mild admonition or harsh reproof'.[46] Henry's concern here is not just with the swearing per se:

> When he heard a great lord who was his chamberlain suddenly break out and swear bitterly, he sternly rebuked him, saying: 'Alas! You, that are lord of a great household, when you utter oaths like this contrary to God's commandment, give a

---

[42] Wolffe, *Henry VI*, pp. 9–11; Freeman, "'*Ut verus Christi sequester*'", p. 137.

[43] Blacman, *Henry the Sixth*, p. 36 (14): '... indui ad nudum corpus suum aspero cilito, ut per asperitatem talem corpus ejus arctaretur a lascivia, potius vero ut omnis arrogantia vel inanis gloria, quae hujusmodi oriri solet, reprimeretur'.

[44] Caxton, *Golden Legend*, p. ccccxxx recto.

[45] Vauchez, *Sainthood*, p. 365. Anthony Woodville, Earl Rivers, wore a hairshirt at his execution in 1483 which subsequently became a relic, exhibited at Doncaster and attracting pilgrims, see Michael Hicks, 'Woodville, Anthony, second Earl Rivers (c.1440–1483)', *Oxford dictionary of national biography* (Oxford, 2004); online edn, September 2011 [http://www.oxforddnb.com/view/article/29937, accessed 16 September 2012].

[46] Blacman, *Henry the Sixth*, p. 38 (16): '... abhominabilis erat eis quisque jurans' and '... tum blande consulendo, tum dure corripiendo'. For Louis and swearing see Caxton, *Golden Legend*, p. ccccxxxi verso.

Lay sanctity and Henry VI's manliness

most evil example to your servants and those that are under you, for you provoke them to do the like.'[47]

Henry is aware that people imitate the conduct of great men and is very concerned that his court should be setting the right example. Thus 'he would never suffer hawks, swords or daggers to be brought into church, or business agreements or conferences to be carried on there'.[48] This is similar to the measures which we know Louis took against his aristocrats, and he may actually have prohibited the carrying of arms.[49] Henry attended church on Sundays and feast days and 'was earnest in trying to induce others to do the like'.[50] On lesser feast days he wasted no time in sloth, with gossip, or overindulging in food or drink 'but such days he passed not less diligently either in treating of the business of the realm with his council, as need might require, or in reading of the scriptures or of authors and chronicles'.[51]

Thus Henry is shown to be seriously at odds with courtly culture and the version of masculinity embodied by those around him. Similarly, Charles of Blois did 'little honour to the values of his estate', as Vauchez puts it, drawing on the witness statements collected to support his canonisation, which reveal just how uncomfortable many of those at his court were with his rigorous devotional regime.[52]

Blacman's depiction of Henry in these terms establishes the king's status as a guardian of morals, a version of masculinity that Derek Neal terms husbandry, which entails '[t]he prudent and honourable management of property and household dependents' but also 'the rule and limitation of the self'.[53] This particularly manifested itself in Henry's concern for the young. Henry VI's son, Prince Edward, is mentioned only in passing by Blacman.[54] But Henry is shown to be an attentive surrogate father to the boys of Eton: '... he would advise them concerning the following of the path of virtue ... and if he discovered that any of them visited his court, he sometimes restrained them with a rebuke, bidding them not to do so again, lest his young lambs should come to relish the corrupt deeds

---

[47] Ibid.: 'Audiens autem rex quondam magnum dominum, sibi camerarium, ex abrupt et improvise graviter jurare, graviter increpavit eum, dicens: Prohdolor! Vos dominus familiae multae dum juramenta sic editis contra Dei mandatum, pessimum exhibitis exemplum servis et subditis vestries. Ipsos enim similia facere provocatis'.

[48] Ibid. pp. 28–9 (7): '... in ecclesia nullatenus accipites, gladios, basillardos, contractus, confabulations ve fiery sinebat'.

[49] William Chester Jordan, *Louis IX and the challenge of the crusade: a study in rulership* (Princeton, 1979), p. 204. Louis issued a raft of bans in an attempt to circumscribe the military activities of his nobility, part of his wider endeavour to prevent in-fighting between Christians, that they might all unite to go crusading, Jordan, *Louis IX*, pp. 196–204.

[50] Blacman, *Henry the Sixth*, p. 37 (15): '... ad similiter agendum etiam alios inducer diligenter studuit'.

[51] Ibid.: 'Sed dies illos aut in regni negotiis cum consilio suo tractandis, prout rei exposcerat necessitas, aut in scripturarum lectionibus, vel in scriptis aut cronicis legendis non minus diligenter expendit'.

[52] Vauchez, *Sainthood*, p. 365.

[53] Derek G. Neal, *The masculine self in late medieval England* (Chicago and London, 2008), p. 58.

[54] Blacman, *Henry the Sixth*, p. 29 (7).

and habits of his courtiers, or lose partly or altogether their good characters'.[55] Henry was also at pains to ensure the welfare of his two half-brothers Jasper and Edmund Tudor, 'providing for them most strict and safe guardianship, putting them under the care of virtuous and worthy priests, both for teaching and for right living and conversation, lest the untamed practices of youth should grow rank if they lacked any to prune them'.[56] Nor did Henry restrict his advice to the young, 'So to every sort and condition and age of men he was a diligent exhorter and adviser, counselling the young to leave vice and follow the path of virtue; and admonishing men of mature age and elders (*or* priests) to attain the perfection of virtue and lay hold on the prize of eternal life.'[57] Henry is show to practise what he preaches and never himself gives in to the temptations of the court.

Perhaps the best example of this is provided by Blacman's description of Henry's chastity. As opposed to issues of dress and appearance there is better evidence to suggest that this element of the text does reflect something of Henry's actual behaviour and/or anxieties surrounding it. There is certainly evidence of contemporary concern revolving around Henry's sex life. It took him and Margaret of Anjou eight years to produce Prince Edward, which led to public speculation and rumour.[58] Louis IX actually had a similar experience, being married to Margaret of Provence for six years before their first child was born, which also worried their contemporaries.[59] It is impossible to say for sure whether this reflected a genuine unwillingness to have sex on Henry's part. Piero da Monte's report that the sixteen-year-old Henry was intensely religious, that he 'chastises his body through abstinence and continence, he flees the sight and speech of women' and detests 'the indecorous gestures of mimes and plays' could support such a contention.[60] But Henry did not necessarily remain sexually reticent subsequently; indeed in 1442 he sent instructions to those negotiating a possible marriage with one of the three daughters of the count of Armagnac requesting portraits of the daughters be painted so that he could choose the one whom he liked best.[61] Moreover, one rumour about Henry, dating from January 1448, claimed that when he 'wold have hys dysporte wyth our sovrayn lady the

---

[55] Ibid., pp. 34–5 (12): '... admouit eos de virtutis via prosequenda ... Et si aliquos eorum curiam suam visitare deprehenderit, aliquando cohibuit corripiendo eos, ne hoc amodo iterarent, ne agnelli sui perditos suorum curialium actus vel mores saperent: vel proprios bonos mores in parte vel in toto amitterent'.

[56] Ibid., p. 30–1 (9): '... quibus pro tunc actissimam & securissimam providebat custodiam, eos ponens sub tutela virtuosorum et honestissimorum sacerdotum, tum ad erudiendum, tum ad virtuose vivendum, et conversandum, ne scilicet indomitae adolescentulationes sucrescerent, si omnino suppressore carerent'.

[57] Ibid., p. 27 (5): 'Unde omni statui, omnique conditioni hominum et aetati sedulous hortatory & consultor extiterat, juvenibus consulens, ut a vitiis declinarent, et virtutis viam affequerentur. Provectaeque aetatis viros et presbiteros, ut virtutis complementum, braviumque aeternae vitae prosequendo attengerent, ammonuit'.

[58] Joanna Laynesmith, *The last medieval queens: English queenship 1445–1503* (Oxford, 2004), pp. 131–9.

[59] Le Goff, *Saint Louis*, p. 600.

[60] Translated and quoted by Karen A. Winstead, *John Capgrave's Fifteenth Century* (Philadelphia, 2007), *volume 4: 1327–1485*, p. 135

[61] *English historical documents*, ed. A.R. Myers (London and New York, 1969), pp. 256–7.

quene' William Aiscough, bishop of Salisbury, and William de la Pole, duke of Suffolk, 'counselyd hym that he schuld not come nye her' and that this is why England did not have a prince.[62] This allegation is about Henry being too biddable, not about him being averse to sex *per se*. But, arguably, the explanation for Henry's childlessness is less important than the implications of it. According to some medieval definitions masculinity entailed being sexually virile and potent, Henry's childlessness and suspected unwillingness to have sex would, by these standards, have shed a negative light on his manhood.[63] But for Blacman it was evidence of Henry's holy superiority to those around him. Blacman describes Henry as 'chaste and pure from the beginning of his days' and wholly faithful to his wife.[64] Henry guarded his chastity carefully and was particularly concerned to avoid displays of nakedness 'lest like David he should be snared by unlawful desire'.[65] Blacman describes Henry's abhorrence for the naked bathing which he witnesses at Bath, and his use of secret windows to ensure that members of his household did not behave licentiously.[66] A more palpable example of Henry's reaction to nakedness is provided by this episode, often seen as evidence of his prudishness:

> Hence it happened once, that at Christmas time a certain great lord brought before him a dance or show of young ladies with bared bosoms who were to dance in that guise before the king, perhaps to prove him, or to entice his youthful mind. But the king was not blind to it, nor unaware of the devilish wile, and spurned the delusion, and very angrily averted his eyes, turned his back upon them, and went out to his chamber, saying: 'Fy, fy, for shame, forsothe ye be to blame'.[67]

---

[62] Laynesmith, *The last medieval queens*, p. 133. Aiscough had performed Henry's marriage to Margaret and there is no reason to believe that he would actually have advised Henry not to have sex with her. The naming of him and Suffolk here is largely testament to their great unpopularity and the extent to which they were generally held to be responsible for the poor state of Henry's kingship and government. See Griffiths, *Henry VI*, p. 256.

[63] Jacqueline Murray, 'Hiding behind the universal man: male sexuality in the Middle Ages', in *Handbook of Medieval Sexuality*, ed. Vern L. Bullough and James A. Brundage (New York and London, 1996), pp. 123–52; Derek Neal, *The masculine self*, pp. 123–86. Henry's childlessness was also political dynamite, given his lack of close, legitimate male relatives. This is discussed at greater length in my *Kingship and masculinity*, pp. 193–213.

[64] Blacman, *Henry the Sixth*, p. 29 (7): 'Pudicus enim & purus suerat ... ab ineunte aetate sua'.

[65] Ibid.: '... ne, ut David, amore illicit caperetur'. Guillaume de Saint-Pathus, who composed an influential life of Louis, describes the lengths he went to ensure that no-one saw his unclothed body, except for his feet and hands, and occasionally part of his arms and legs, Le Goff, *Saint Louis*, p. 707.

[66] Blacman, *Henry the Sixth*, p. 30 (8).

[67] Ibid.: 'Unde semel contigit, quod tempore natalis Domini choreas, vel spectaculum quoddam generosarum juvencularum, resolutis finibus suis nudatas mamillas propenentium, quidam aduuceret magnus dominus coram eo, ut ante regis aspectum juvenes illae mulierculae sic denudatae tripudiarent, ad probandum forsan eum, vel alliciendum regis juvenilem animum. Sed rex iste non improvidus, nec diabolicae fraudis ignarus, his spretis praestigiis, nimium indignatus, oculos avertens, dorsum ejus citius posuit, et ad cameram suam exivit dicens, "Fy, fy, for shame, forsothe ye be to blame"'. Griffiths mentions Henry's 'prudish sensitivity', *The reign of King Henry VI*, p. 249; Lovatt says that Blacman emphasises Henry's 'extreme prudishness', 'A collector of apocryphal anecdotes', p. 186.

M.R. James' translation here actually downplays the meaning of the original Latin, which uses the word 'mulierculae' to describe the women, a term which implies that they were prostitutes rather than 'young ladies'.[68] Moreover Blacman says that the women 'stripped off their clothes as they danced'.[69] The depiction of this episode fits into a longstanding tradition of the sexual trials and temptation of monastic heroes such as St Benedict and St Bernard of Clairvaux, right down to Henry's ability to discern that this is devilish in origin, even a delusion.[70] The life of St Benedict contains an almost identical episode in which an evil priest attempts (unsuccessfully) to corrupt the monks. As related by Caxton the priest 'toke seuen maydens all naked / & sente them in to the gardyn to daunse & to carolle for to meue the monkes to temptacion'.[71] Henry's virtue allows him to turn his back on a spectacle which a lesser man would not have been able to resist. Moreover, he has the strength to do so simply by averting his eyes, turning away, and leaving, without having to resort to rolling in nettles, or submersing himself up to the neck in freezing water (standard remedies or self-inflicted punishments for lust in monastic hagiography).[72] This hagiographic trope derived from monastic constructions of a manly religious identity, which used martial imagery to establish the superiority of monks (and subsequently clerics) to secular men.[73] Chastity forms a significant element in the representation of other king saints and high status lay male saints too; for example Charles of Blois rarely shared his wife's bed and Caxton explains that Louis was only persuaded to marry in order to safeguard the kingdom by providing an heir, and therefore implicitly not to satisfy his lust.[74] A king saint's chastity is therefore partly about purity, and partly about his 'virilitas': his strength as a leader.[75] It is telling that contemporary didactic texts belonging to the Mirrors for Princes

---

[68] J.N. Adams, 'Words for 'prostitute' in Latin', *Rheinisches Museum für Philologie* 126 (1983), pp. 321–58 (354).

[69] Blacman, *Henry the Sixth*, p. 30: 'illae mulierculae sic denudatae tripudiarent'.

[70] For other examples of male saints, including Thomas Aquinas, resisting lust and temptation see Weinstein and Bell, *Saints and society*, pp. 81–7.

[71] Caxton, *Golden Legend*, p. clxvi verso. Le Goff discusses an episode in which Louis is tempted by beautiful woman and its relationship to monastic traditions, *Saint Louis*, p. 705. This stands in opposition to Freeman's contention that 'Such stories are hardly a normal feature of hagiography', '"Ut verus Christi sequester"', p. 139.

[72] Benedict overcame the temptation of a woman shown to him by the Devil and then 'walowed' among thorns and nettles to punish himself, Caxton, *Golden Legend*, p. clxvi recto.

[73] Jacqueline Murray, 'Masculinizing religious life: sexual prowess, the battle for chastity and monastic identity', in *Holiness and masculinity*, ed. Cullum and Lewis, pp. 24–42; Katherine Allen Smith, 'Saints in shining armor: martial asceticism and masculine models of sanctity, ca. 1050–1250', *Speculum* 83 (2008), pp. 572–602.

[74] Vauchez, *Sainthood*, p. 365; Caxton, *Golden Legend*, p. ccccxxx recto. See also the life of St Magnus, Maria-Claudia Tomany, 'Sacred non-violence, cowardice profaned: St Magnus of Orkney in Nordic historiography and hagiography', in *Sanctity in the north: saints, lives and cults in medieval Scandinavia*, ed. Thomas A. DuBois (Toronto, Buffalo and London, 2008), pp. 128–53, p. 147.

[75] My argument here has been influenced by P.H. Cullum, '*Virginitas* and *virilitas*: Richard Scrope and his fellow bishops', in *Richard Scrope: archbishop, rebel, martyr*, ed. P.J.P. Goldberg (Donington, 2007), pp. 87–100.

genre make explicit a point which is largely implied in saints' lives, namely that the truly masculine man is the one who resists the flesh; the man who gives in renders himself unmanly: '... bowe not to þe vse of women, ffor swylk a vse ys a properte to swine ... lychery ys distruccioun of body, shortynge of lyf, corypcioun of virtue3 trespass of þe lawe, And hit engendrys women maners.'[76] Such invective, which appears frequently in the Mirrors, was at pains to establish that the sexually dissolute man could not be king, for he was unable to rule himself, let alone anyone else. Thus kingly chastity, in these contexts, was seen as desirable and admirable rather than anomalous and problematic.[77] The implication of Blacman's account may be that the 'great lord' was trying to turn Henry into his own definition of a 'real man', but Blacman seeks to show that Henry's self-mastery is truly manly.[78] The idea of Henry's chastity was also part of his popular cult, as liturgical evidence demonstrates.[79]

Blacman's Henry, then, is seen to be wise, sober, generous, pious and conscientious; moreover, self-governance is identified as the key to successfully governing others, and this clearly informed Henry's status as an exemplar. We know from the spiritual commonplace book that Blacman wrote at about the time he entered the London Charterhouse that he was very concerned with mortality and proper preparations for death, which clarifies part of his purpose in presenting Henry VI as a spiritual role model.[80] It may be that, in the first instance, Blacman's portrait of Henry was aimed at his fellow Carthusians, the same austere, conservative group to whom he left his library. This would explain his references to Henry being like 'a young monk', and a 'professed religious'.[81] Just as Blacman presents Henry's moral strength as the means by which he attained sanctity, so the monks could use him as a pattern for their own lives. In this way they would not be found wanting should they face death suddenly, just as Henry himself had. Indeed, by the later medieval period the holy essence of lay male sanctity was no longer seen to reside in the exemplary exercise of worldly roles and responsibilities, as it had been in earlier centuries.[82] Instead by the fifteenth century, the very idea of 'lay' sanctity had become ambiguous, for saints like Louis IX, Charles of Blois and Henry VI gave the appearance of being laymen, but were in fact following an essentially monastic lifestyle. The comments of many of Charles of Blois'

---

[76] *Three prose versions of the* secreta secretorum, ed. Robert Steele, Early English Text Society, Extra Series, 74 (London, 1898), p. 58. Such rhetoric and gendered imagery is common in these texts, see also pp. 10–11, 14, 139, 190.

[77] Chastity and self-control played a central role in the presentation of Henry V's ideal kingship, as discussed in my *Kingship and masculinity*, pp. 84–102.

[78] For discussion of the importance of heterosexual relationships to knighthood see Ruth Mazo Karras, *From boys to men: formations of masculinity in late medieval Europe* (Philadelphia, 2003), pp. 47–57.

[79] Craig, 'Royalty, virtue and adversity', p. 199.

[80] Lovatt, 'Library of John Blacman', pp. 204–5.

[81] Blacman, *Henry the Sixth*, p. 26 (4): 'juvenis ... religiosus', p. 35 (13) 'quasi religiosus'. Vauchez, *Sainthood*, p. 365, for Charles of Blois being likened to professional religious men by his contemporaries.

[82] As discussed by von Weissenberg in this volume, see also Vauchez, *Sainthood*, pp. 362–3.

contemporaries testify to this, one of whom judged that 'he would be a better bishop, abbot, or man of the church than prince'.[83]

Monastic models were deemed to have wider devotional applicability in this period, and Freeman and Lovatt both argue that Blacman's Henry is an ideal model for the educated layman.[84] Certainly, Blacman offers Henry as a model to a wide range of people, both professional religious and lay, men and women:

> O what great watchfulness, O what care to please God was found in this creature so high-placed and so young! Consider it, all ye kings and princes, young men and maidens, and all peoples, and praise the Lord in His saints. Imitate, too, this king in virtue, who could have done ill, and did it not, but utterly eschewed, to his power, while he lived, in view of the displeasure of God, all evil and injury of this sort.[85]

The fact that this text was written in Latin restricts its actual audience in the first instance, but the trope is significant nonetheless. Blacman shows that Henry was subject to temptation yet could resist it, and not because of any defect in his complexion, but because he had the strength of will to fight and surmount illicit urges. This exhortation is informed by the sense that a holy king's example was not simply relevant to kings, or high status men, but could provide a much more widely applicable example of ideal religious and moral conduct. Essentially the virtues which Henry embodied were relevant not just to rule of a kingdom, but to rule of oneself. The appropriateness of king saints as models to the laity is underlined by the use of the four cardinal virtues (the mainstay of Mirrors for Princes) as a template for moral and devotional conduct in works of vernacular instruction.[86] Thus, Henry's rendering as a saint became, ironically, a celebratory rewriting of his ambivalent manhood. What may have appeared to some to be a failing was in fact a triumph, according to Blacman's account.

To conclude: Blacman's portrait of Henry owes much of its structure and substance to hagiography, and to ideals of holy masculinity. But that does not mean that the version of Henry he presents is therefore a complete invention. The precise nature of the correlation between the 'real' Henry and Blacman's

---

[83] Vauchez, *Sainthood*, p. 365, see also Vauchez, *A twelfth-century novelty*, pp. 70–2, for the argument that the mendicant orders were responsible for this development, which he terms 'monasticization of the laity' (p. 72). This also relates to Catherine Sanok's contention in this volume that strictly lay and monastic categories of male religious identity had become blurred by the later medieval period.

[84] Freeman, '"*Ut verus Christi sequester*"', pp. 139, 141. Lovatt, 'John Blacman', p. 151. For male monastic saints' lives as models of holy masculinity for lay readers (both male and female), see Katherine J. Lewis, 'Male saints and devotional masculinity in late medieval England', *Gender & History* 24 (2012), pp. 112–33.

[85] Blacman, *Henry the Sixth*, p. 27 (5): 'O! quanta diligentia placendi Deo in tam sublimi et juvenili persona reperta est! Attendite reges & principes universi, juvenes et virgines & populi quique, & laudate Dominum in sanctis ejus. Hunc quoque regem virtute imitamini, qui malum fecisse poterat & non fecit: sed omnino dum vixit refugit, in quantum potuit, propter Dei displicentiam, hujuscemodi malum vel noxam'.

[86] E.g. *A myrour to lewde men and wymen: a prose version of the speculum vitae*, ed. Venetia Nelson, Middle English Texts 14 (Heidelburg, 1981), p. 89.

St Henry is unknowable, and will remain a matter of debate. But, as has already been indicated, there is apparently some resonance between Henry's interests and conduct (as recorded in a variety of sources) and Blacman's representation of them. Moreover the notion of a saintly king would have been very familiar to Henry himself. John Lydgate wrote a lengthy life of St Edmund of East Anglia which portrays the saint as a kingly paradigm for Henry, in terms that draw explicitly from Mirrors for Princes. This text was presented to Henry in a lavishly illustrated manuscript to commemorate his stay at the abbey of Bury in 1443.[87] Louis IX was presented as a model to Henry VI by John Capgrave and also by Lydgate.[88] In addition Henry's psalter contains an illumination showing Henry being presented to the Virgin and child by St Louis, which would encourage Henry to perceive Louis as his spiritual patron.[89] At the end of his *De illustribus Henricis*, dedicated to Henry VI in the late 1440s John Capgrave invokes the protection of the Anglo-Saxon king saints Oswald, Edmund, Edward the Martyr, Kenelm, Æthelbert, Oswine, Æthelstan and Edward the Confessor on behalf of Henry VI, and expresses the wish that Henry should share their manifold virtues.[90] Elsewhere in the volume Capgrave offers other holy Henries as a model for the young king, such as the sainted Emperor Henry II, whose childless marriage to Cunegund was universally presented, after their deaths, as the result of a mutual vow of virginity, and Henry VI's own great-great-grandfather Henry of Grosmont, the first duke of Lancaster, who composed a sort of devotional autobiography, the *Livre de seyntz medicines*.[91] Henry attempted to have another

---

[87] John Lydgate, *The lives of Ss Edmund and Fremund and the extra miracles of St Edmund*, edited from British Library MS Harley 2278 and Bodleian MS Ashmole 46, ed. Anthony Bale and A.S.G. Edwards (Heidelberg, 2009). Katherine J. Lewis, 'Edmund of East Anglia, Henry VI and ideals of kingly sanctity', in *Holiness and masculinity*, ed. Cullum and Lewis, pp. 158–74. The entire manuscript is available online via the British Library website http://www.bl.uk.

[88] John Capgrave, *The book of illustrious Henries*, trans. Francis Charles Hingeston (London, 1858), p. 150. Lydgate, *The lives of Ss Edmund and Fremund*, p. 38, line 105. Extensive political use was made of Louis during this period to support English claims to the French crown during the Hundred Years War, John W. McKenna, 'Henry VI of England and the dual monarchy: aspects of royal political propaganda, 1422–1432', *Journal of the Warburg and Courtauld Institutes* 28 (1965), pp. 145–62.

[89] The psalter is now London, British Library, Cotton MS Domitian A. xvii. It is available on the British Library website. The illumination showing Henry and Louis is on f. 50 recto. The manuscript was probably originally made at the beginning of the fifteenth century for the Dauphin Louis, Duke of Guyenne, and the royal youth on f. 50 (and f. 75 recto) originally wore the arms of France alone, but at a later date these were quartered with those of England, reflecting the identity of the book's new owner. It may have come to England with Louis' sister Catherine, mother of Henry VI. See Scott McKendrick, John Lowden and Kathleen Doyle, *Royal Manuscripts: The Genius of Illumination* (London, 2011), p. 396.

[90] Capgrave, *The book of illustrious Henries*, pp. 217–18. As well as the texts already mentioned, an anonymous Latin verse life of Edward the Confessor (*Vita beati Edvardi regis et confessoris*) was also dedicated to Henry VI around 1440–50, *Lives of Edward the Confessor*, ed. and trans. H.R. Luard, Rolls Series 3 (London, 1858), pp. 361–77. Henry is addressed at the opening and closing of the text (p. 361, lines 13–16, p. 377, lines 529–32). Whether Henry actually read this life, or any of the didactic texts dedicated to him, can only be a matter of speculation of course.

[91] W.M. Ormrod, 'Henry of Lancaster, first duke of Lancaster (c.1310–1361)', *Oxford dictionary of national biography* (Oxford, 2004); online edn, 2008 [http://www.oxforddnb.com/view/article/12960, accessed 31 October 2012].

king, Alfred, canonised in 1442, an interest generally explained by their shared patronage of educational establishments.[92] But another reason for Henry's interest may have been Asser's account of Alfred's illnesses and the ways in which these constituted physical manifestations of Alfred's struggle against the flesh. The young Alfred 'realised that he was unable to abstain from carnal desire' and asked God to visit upon him 'some illness which he would be able to tolerate' in order that he could still carry out his worldly responsibilities properly.[93] Alfred was subsequently struck by 'a sudden severe pain' after his wedding feast.[94] This link between illness and sexual desire is not just a matter of Asser's interpretation of events; David Pratt demonstrates the extent of Alfred's preoccupation with sexual sin in an analysis of the king's own writings and notes the 'close parallel that Asser . . . emphasises between Alfred's bodily sufferings and the many other difficulties that he is facing as king'.[95] In the late 1450s and very early 1460s the account of a king attempting to rule a country threatened by war while seriously ill would have been particularly pertinent to Henry. He may even, like Alfred, have interpreted his own afflictions as part of some divine trial; both Blacman and Vergil certainly perceived Henry as Job-like in his patient suffering, which, for them, was part of his sanctity.[96] That being the case it is worth considering that hagiographic tropes may have influenced not just the author, but also the subject.[97] When scholars discuss the 'holy' or 'saintly' aspects of Henry's character these generally go hand in hand with the idea of him as simple, well meaning, naïve and artless, which gives the impression that these qualities were somehow 'natural' to him. But perhaps there was something more 'knowing' than this at work. It is possible that the image of Henry as saint was, to some extent at least, an act of self-fashioning, influenced by the depiction of the holy men who had so frequently been held up to him as exemplars.

---

[92] Nicholas Rogers, 'Henry VI and the proposed canonization of King Alfred', in *The Lancastrian court: proceedings of the 2001 Harlaxton Symposium*, ed. Jenny Stratford (Donington, 2003), pp. 211–20.

[93] Asser, *Life of King Alfred*, in *Alfred the Great: Asser's life of King Alfred and other contemporary sources*, trans. Simon Keynes and Michael Lapidge (London, 1983), pp. 89–90. For analysis of Asser's description of Alfred's illness and its meanings see Janet L. Nelson, 'Monks, secular men and masculinity', in *Masculinity in medieval Europe*, ed. D.M. Hadley (Harlow, 1999), pp. 121–42; David Pratt, 'The illnesses of King Alfred the Great', *Anglo-Saxon England* 30 (2001), pp. 39–90 (p. 73 for the suggestion that Alfred suffered from Crohn's disease). Piroyanski also notes that Alfred's suffering would have been of relevance to Henry, *Martyrdom in the making*, p. 78.

[94] Asser, *Life of King Alfred*, p. 88.

[95] Pratt, 'Illnesses of Alfred', pp. 74–90, p. 84.

[96] Blacman, *Henry the Sixth*, p. 26 (4); Vergil, *Anglica Historia*, ed. and trans. Sutton, chapter 24. Maurer also suggests that Henry's piety may have become more marked in this period as a way of making sense of his illness and the challenges to his crown, *Margaret of Anjou*, p. 40.

[97] A point also made by von Weissenberg in her contribution to this volume. As an example Bernhard Gallistl argues that Bernward, bishop of Hildesheim (d. 20 November 1020), 'was clearly aiming for his own veneration as a saint', 'Bernward of Hildesheim: a case of self-planned sainthood?', in *Invention of saintliness*, ed. Mulder-Bakke, pp. 145–62, p. 159, and it is often assumed that Margery Kempe's conduct was self-consciously modelled on hagiographic motifs.

JOHN OF BRIDLINGTON, MITRED PRIOR AND MODEL OF THE MIXED LIFE

Catherine Sanok

John of Bridlington, the last English person to be canonized before the Reformation, enjoyed a vigorous, if short-lived, cult. His tomb in the church of the Augustinian house where he had been prior became a site of pilgrimage soon after his death in 1379: it was the site, Thomas Walsingham records, of 'miracles so great and so manifest that astonishment fell upon almost the whole of England'.[1] Alexander Neville, archbishop of York, lost no time in amassing evidence of his sanctity, and the official canonization proceedings went forward with notable speed. The papal inquiry began in 1391, and John was canonized just ten years later.[2] In 1404, he was translated to a shrine near the high altar of the priory church, lending even greater spiritual authority to one of England's largest and most venerable Augustinian houses.[3] The saint quickly became a favorite of English kings and nobles: Henry V included Bridlington in his thanksgiving pilgrimage after Agincourt, and royal promotion of the cult was enthusiastically continued by his son and later by Edward IV.[4] Thomas Beaufort,

---

[1] *Chronica maiora of Thomas Walsingham*, trans. David Preest (Woodbridge, 2005), p. 273.

[2] The pope's attentive response may have been inspired by his interest in showing support for Archbishop Neville, recently accused of treason by Richard II for his affiliation with the Lords Appellant.

[3] 'Houses of Austin canons: Priory of Bridlington', ed. William Page, *Victoria County History: A history of the county of York*, vol. 3 (1974), pp. 199–205. British History Online [http://www.british-history.ac.uk/report.aspx?compid=36261, accessed 14 November 2012].

[4] Jonathan Hughes suggests that Lancastrian support of the cult was calculated to draw off some of the enthusiasm for the nascent popular cult of Richard le Scrope, the archbishop of York who was executed for treason in the years just before St John's canonization: Hughes, *Pastors and visionaries: religion and secular life in late medieval Yorkshire* (Woodbridge, 1988). J.S. Purvis details royal devotion to the saint: in 1413, four years after the saint's canonization, Henry V cited his devotion to John of Bridlington when he excused Bridlington priory from its financial obligation toward defending the coast. The priory was exempt from the Alien Priories Act in 1421, and in the 1440s from all tithes and clerical subsidies, on the same ground. Henry VI claims 'great affection and singular devotion' to the 'glorious Confessor St John of Brydlyngton' in a 1450 exemption from an Act of Parliament requiring support for the king's debts. Royal patronage continues under the Yorkists: in 1468 Edward IV also exempted the priory, citing his devotion to the saint in language very similar to that of Henry V and Henry VI: Purvis, *St. John of Bridlington* (Bridlington, 1924), p. 49.

duke of Exeter, was on pilgrimage to the shrine in 1417 when he heard news that the Scots were besieging Roxburgh.[5] Richard Beauchamp's extraordinary chapel at Warwick castle features St John in a window, and he also appears in the Book of Hours made for Sir William Porter, who campaigned with Henry V in France and served as an executor of his will.[6] But devotion to St John, whose claim to sanctity, Walsingham says, 'rested on his humility and his pity for the afflicted', was not confined to the elite: traces of the cult surface in local wills and parish churches across England until the very eve of the Dissolution.[7] Despite this popularity, little survives of the cult, no doubt partly because of its late date and partly because of the special zeal with which the house was destroyed by government agents in the wake of the role that the last prior, William Wode, played in the Northern rebellion of 1537.[8]

Representations of the saint in vernacular literature and visual culture that do remain are remarkably eclectic. My primary interest in this essay is the Middle English verse Life of John of Bridlington preserved in Yale University Beinecke MS 331, the only extant vernacular legend, aside from a brief entry in the *Kalendre of the New Legend of England*.[9] The Beinecke legend is not only unique in subject, but eccentric in form. It is in tail-rhyme stanzas, not in the narrative-driven couplets of so many Middle English saints' lives, nor in the rhyme royal stanzas used in the conspicuously literary saints' lives by John Lydgate and other Benedictine poets in this period, especially for their lives of English saints.[10]

---

[5] *Chronica maiora*, p. 426.

[6] The Hours of William Porter, Pierpont Morgan Library MS M. 105, fol. 52r. A digital facsimile of the image can be found at utu.morganlibrary.org/medren/single_image2.cfm?imagename=m105.052r.jpg&page=ICA000143372.

[7] E.g. Ralph Taylor, a carpenter, left money for Masses at an altar of St John of Bridlington in the parish church of St Peter in Sandwich in 1475: Purvis, *St John of Bridlington*, p. 43. For further testamentary evidence of devotion to St John, see ibid., pp. 43–4; John Burton, *Monasticon Eboracense*, 1758, p. 250; and Marmaduke Prickett, *History of the priory church of Bridlington* (1836), pp. 113–14, see also pp. 25–6.

[8] Wode was executed for treason; Prickett, *History of the priory church of Bridlington*, pp. 32–3. Cromwell's agent, Richard Bellycys, wrote from York in November 1538 to apologize that winter weather would delay the destruction of the priory until the following March: Burton, *Monasticon Eboracense*, p. 372.

[9] Yale University, Beinecke Rare Book and Manuscript Library, Beinecke MS 33, written sometime after 1435, comprises Rolle's *Incendium amoris* and *Form of living*, both in Robert Misyn's English translation – books that were extremely popular among lay readers – as well as a short poem added by a sixteenth-century reader, Richard Hutton, on the value of the book and the verse life of John of Bridlington, which is incomplete: online catalogue of Yale University, Beinecke Rare Book and Manuscript Library, medieval and Renaissance manuscripts [brbl-net.library.yale.edu/pre1600ms/docs/pre1600.ms331.htm accessed 14 November 2012]. The manuscript provides a rough date *ante quem* for the legend. Amassian's argument that the poem was composed in the late fourteenth century, on the grounds of the narrator's claim to have seen Prior John with his own eyes, cannot stand: Margaret Amassian (ed.), 'A verse Life of John of Bridlington', *Neuphilologische Mitteilungen* 71 (1970), pp. 136–45 at p. 137.

[10] The use of tail-rhyme for the John of Bridlington legend is rare but not unique: there are Middle English tail-rhyme legends of Ss Eustace, Alexius, and Anne. In these examples, the form points to French sources and affiliations, as it is a common verse form in Anglo-Norman saints' lives, See Rhiannon Purdie, *Anglicising romance: tail-rhyme and genre in Middle English literature*

John of Bridlington

Tail-rhyme is a form familiar enough from romance, but so unusual for Middle English saints' lives that the legend's modern editor mistook the offset lines for 'marginal annotations' and printed them alongside the main text of the poem, rather than as part of it.[11] As we will see, the use of tail-rhyme is an index of the saint's accessibility as a model and of the general applicability of the ethics he embodies: the form links the saint to the ethics of popular romance, which are of course lay ethics. Borrowing from tail-rhyme romance the translation of an elite identity to a popular audience, the legend makes the holy prior a generic model of good behavior, appropriate to all.

This representation stands in diametric opposition to the depiction of the saint in a window in the parish church of St Lawrence in Ludlow, Shropshire (figure 1). There is a mistake of sorts here, as well, in this case by a medieval glazier rather than a modern scholar. The saint – an Augustian canon and prior revered for his humble piety – is pictured with pontificalia: the cope, stole, crozier, and even the mitre of a bishop.[12] The error is not misidentification, as it may at first appear, but historical elision: the prior of Bridlington was granted the privilege of the mitre in 1409 by Pope Alexander V.[13] John of Bridlington never wore a mitre, but those who followed him in office did. In contrast to the simple model of everyday piety in the tail-rhyme legend, the Ludlow window exalts the saint through the prestige granted his office.

These seemingly antithetical representations of John of Bridlington point to the correspondence of two late medieval phenomena that are usually addressed separately, though they are both important to the status of religious men and the protocols of masculinity in the period: on the one hand, the development in late medieval England of discourses of the 'mixed life', and related forms of devotional identity and practice that blurred the line between professed religious and the laity, associated above all with Walter Hilton's *Epistle on the mixed life*, and on the other, the competition among religious orders and houses for symbols of power and prestige, which reached a fever pitch in the fifteenth century. Together these phenomena contributed to a partial erasure of the social and vocational

---

(Cambridge, 2008). Purdie makes the interesting suggestion that Beneit's tail-rhyme *Vie de Thomas Becket* inspired the use of tail-rhyme for romances with English heroes. If so, the Yale John of Bridlington is a very interesting return and extension of this tradition. Nevertheless, the use of tail-rhyme in the John of Bridlington legend above all signals formal, social, and thematic affiliation with popular romance.

[11] Amassian, 'A verse Life of John of Bridlington'. Amassian's error was noted by C.F. Sleeth, 'Textual observations on a verse Life of John of Bridlington', *Neuphilologische Mitteilungen* 74 (1973), pp. 128–30. All quotations of the poem referenced in the text are from Amassian, as corrected by Sleeth. See also Jessica Brantley, 'Reading the forms of *Sir Thopas*', in *Medieval English literature and its manuscript forms: aesthetics and codicology*, a special issue of *Chaucer Review*, ed. Alexandra Gillespie and Arthur Bahr 97/4 (2013) pp. 416–38, which discusses the relationship between the poem's form and its presentation in the manuscript.

[12] Purvis, *St John of Bridlington*, p. 8.

[13] *Calendar of entries in the papal registers relating to Great Britain and Ireland: Papal letters*, ed. W.H. Bliss, 15 vols (London, 1893–1960), vol. 6, p. 161; Martin Heale, 'Mitres and arms: aspects of the self-representation of the monastic superiors in late medieval England', in *Self representation of medieval religious communities: British Isles*, ed. Anne Müller and Karen Stöber (Berlin, 2009), pp. 99–122, at p. 101.

Figure 1 St John of Bridlington, parish church of St Laurence, Ludlow.

differentiation that had traditionally defined medieval men.[14] In the cult of John of Bridlington we can see how these two challenges to the categories of masculine identity converge, and we may also be able to see in some of the saint's afterlife how this convergence, blurring the boundaries that had once distinguished lay men from religious men and religious men from one another, helped to produce the kind of unmarked masculine identity that theorists have associated with the emergence of a 'public' culture in the Early Modern period.

More immediately, the cult of John of Bridlington can help us extend our analysis of masculinity in the late Middle Ages from recent work that has drawn our attention to its several varieties – that is, the existence of medieval *masculinities* – to a consideration of that variousness itself.[15] Jennifer D. Thibodeaux has recently called for greater attention to the varieties of clerical masculinities, pointing to the very different norms and practices that distinguished monks, friars, priests, hermits, bishops, and other kinds of religious men. It is a central assumption of this essay that this variety was definitional for medieval gender paradigms: that is, in late medieval England masculinity was defined less by a set of practices, styles of body or gesture, emotional or intellectual capacities, or modes of desire or sexual activity, than by its vocational specificity and hence its variety.

Although it is beyond the scope of this essay to theorize or historicize this variousness, it may be helpful to remark that the plural modes of masculinity described in recent scholarship – including in essays in this volume – are consonant with important recent work on the history of sexuality, in particular arguments against the existence of a normative sexuality in the premodern period. Karma Lochrie dates the advent of scientific and sociological models of the 'normative' to the nineteenth century, while Valerie Traub traces its emergence in sixteenth- and seventeenth-century representational technologies and metrics of analysis.[16] If in later periods gender is an effect of heteronormativity, as Judith Butler has so influentially argued, in the premodern era it had yet to be pressed into the binary paradigm produced by heteronormativity. Clerical masculinity in particular, as the growing body of scholarship on the topic has already demonstrated, far from an effect of a normative heterosexuality, is correlative to a host of social, vocational, and institutional categories.[17]

---

[14] A differentiation that underpinned the Gregorian reform movement in particular, see Jennifer D. Thibodeaux, Kirsten A. Fenton, Joanna Huntington and Matthew Mesley's essays in this volume.

[15] Important contributions to our understanding of medieval masculinities include *Medieval masculinities: regarding men in the Middle Ages*, ed. Clare A. Lees (Minneapolis, 1994); Ruth Mazo Karras, *From boys to men: formations of masculinity in later medieval Europe* (Philadelphia, 2003); *Negotiating clerical identities: priests, monks and masculinity in the Middle Ages*, ed. Jennifer D. Thibodeaux (Basingstoke and New York, 2010).

[16] Karma Lochrie, *Heterosyncrasies: female sexuality when normal wasn't* (Minneapolis, 2005); Valerie Traub, 'The nature of norms in Early Modern England: anatomy, cartography, *King Lear*', *South Central Review* 26 (2009), pp. 42–81.

[17] Although it is beyond the scope of this essay to address the status of femininity/femininities in this period, very generally speaking, we may note that medieval discourses more often represent women as a single ethical and social category, defined by shared practices and dispositions regardless of economic or vocational status. It may be that in late medieval England men are

Late medieval England witnessed a notable diminution of such variety, however, not through the establishment of a norm, but through the confusion of marks of particular institutional, vocational, and social identities that had differentiated men in earlier periods. Thus, while the narrative and visual representations of John of Bridlington – as humble canon or mitred prelate – reflect some of this variety, they also index an increasing fluidity between categories or inattention to them. This essay tracks the way in which the cult of John of Bridlington seems to index a shift toward a generic notion of a 'good man' at the end of the Middle Ages, in contrast to the paradigm of vocationally-specific masculinities scholars have explored in recent scholarship. As we will see, visual depictions of the saint, in particular, are remarkably inconsistent. We might be tempted to attribute this to the absence of an established iconographic tradition for a new saint, or to the expectations of different patrons and communities. But we might also expect that historical proximity would lead to depictions of the saint that are relatively faithful to his institutional affiliation and vocational status. Instead, the representations of John of Bridlington reveal a confusion of late medieval vocational categories and a corollary development of a relatively uninflected masculine identity.[18]

According to the Latin *vita* written by a fellow Augustinian named Hugh, John of Bridlington was born to worthy parents, probably in the village of Thwing.[19] He showed exceptional piety even as a child and took a vow of chastity at the age of twelve. He spent some time at Oxford and was professed as a canon at fourteen, having refused an opportunity to serve as tutor to a wealthy patron. Hugh represents John as an exemplary religious man, competent and virtuous in the various roles he occupies, from master of novices, to cellarer, sub-prior and finally, despite John's humble demurrals, prior.[20] As prior, John remained as devout as ever, following the rule just as he had in earlier years, 'bearing himself like a brother' among the canons in his charge, and avoiding the 'worldly pomp' that comes with higher office. John even slept in the dormitory with the other canons, rather than in the more luxurious accommodations afforded to a prior. He wore simple clothing, ate simple food, avoided idleness, fed the poor, supported students, and instructed his charges in monastic discipline. He died, too, in exemplary fashion, forgiving and begging forgiveness. In his final moments, he had visions of the 'citizens of heaven' and other blessed spirits coming to greet him, to whom John politely doffed his cap in response.

---

distinguished from women less by any particular practice or disposition than by the variegation of masculine identities, in sharp contrast to the limited identities available to women.

[18] John Blacman's later fifteenth-century representation of Henry VI, discussed by Katherine J. Lewis in this volume, also involves a blending of vocational categories in order to portray the king as a saint.

[19] The primary source is the life by Hugh, an Augustinian canon (Purvis, *St John of Bridlington*, p. 12); another legend is found in *Nova Legenda Anglie* (which Purvis refers to as Capgrave's). My account of John of Bridlington's life is indebted to Purvis, which remains the best overview of the cult. See also Michael Curley, 'John of Bridlington (c. 1320–1379)' *Oxford dictionary of national biography* (Oxford, 2004); online edn, September 2010 [http://www.oxforddnb.com/view/article/14856, accessed 20 September 2012].

[20] Purvis, *St John of Bridlington*, p. 14.

John of Bridlington

The Middle English legend adds nothing to this account; indeed, it waters down the specificity of Hugh's contemporary account into very weak tea. Although several of the details of John's career are mentioned, they are overwhelmed by vague praise of generic virtues. Thin on narrative and long on commonplaces about the saint's good morals and manners, John of Bridlington in the vernacular legend represents not a special vocation, much less the special authority of Bridlington priory, but a general Christian identity, stripped of detail and available to a very broad social spectrum. The poem makes this point repeatedly: 'In his lifyng who wilde behald,/ It was ensaumple to all men' (fol. 171, lines 9–10); 'Of his lifyng he was meroure/ Bothe unto lerned and lewed' (fol. 171, line 28–29). Hence the poem defines its audience as anyone with an interest in the lives of 'good men', whether that interest is passionate or merely passing:

> Who þat lufes or likes to here,
> Of gude mens lifes þat are has bene,
> Be thame ensample may þai lere,
> Here for to life bothe wele and clene.
> Bot now be on þat had no pere,
> Whils þat he lifed is þat I mene,
> His name is knawen bothe fer & nere,
> And I myself I haue hym sene,
>   Be right
> The gude prior of Bridlyngtonne,
> A hale man of religion,
> And als of gude perfeccion.
> Sir John off Thiveng
>   he hight (fol. 168, lines 1–10).

The vernacular poem understands John of Bridlington as an ideal – he has no peer – but he is a peerless model of a bland goodness, the kind of person that anyone, lay or religious, who loves, or even just likes, to hear about 'good men' might strive to imitate. His ethical proximity to the broad audience of vernacular tail-rhyme poetry is figured as familiarity, in the narrator's claim to have seen the saint himself. Although the sextet of the tail-rhyme stanza recalls John of Bridlington's office and his excellence (as 'good prior of Bridlington, a hearty man of religion, and also of good perfection'), this is by way of establishing the credentials of a saint who has already been offered as a paradigm of generic masculine virtue.

The legend's unusual use of tail-rhyme is part of this argument: it is a formal cue that this legend, like tail-rhyme romance, translates elite ethics for a broad audience. This translation often produces a general and conventional account of those ethics, a quality that is satirized in the most famous Middle English tail-rhyme romance, Chaucer's *Tale of Sir Topas*. In the case of the John of Bridlington legend, the generic representation of the saint is also an effect of translating the religious ethics embodied by John of Bridlington as depicted in Hugh's *vita* into secular terms. Thus while the legend recounts the extraordinary childhood piety that led John to his profession at Bridlington priory, the account of his behavior there corresponds to the broad moral value of the tale advertised in its opening lines:

> And þus fra þat he was profest,
> He kepte hym oute of syn & shame,
> And to gude company hym kest,
> And did so þat he hd no blame.
> Comune lifyng þoght him þe best,
> Sauand ay wele here his gude fame,
> He serued God in ese and rest,
> And þus began his nobil name.
>   And raise.
> He was wel taght and manerly,
> And couth hymself ful felawly,
> In worde and dede meke and esy,
>   To all men ay curtase.
> Stedfast, true, witty, war, and wise,
> Of fair maners honest and hende,
> To tham at wele did at dyuyse,
> He couth be both felaw & frende (fol. 170, lines 8–22).

At just the moment that the legend might extol the special authority of John's office, it celebrates instead his own ethical proximity to ordinary people – fellow and friend 'to them at wele did at devise', that is, to anyone who intends to, or even anyone who seems to, behave reasonably well.

The lukewarm account of John's virtue, deleterious as it may be to the literary quality of the poem, is a part of the striking representation of the saint as a generic 'good man'. It is not only that his virtues are banal, but that they are not specific to his identity as canon or prior. The only exceptional status claimed for him is an absolute form of sociability, one that observes no hierarchies of rank or distinctions of office: in his life he was courteous to 'all men', just as he is a model to them all as a saint. The legend develops, that is, a paradigm of masculinity as an uninflected category, lacking even the basic subdivision into lay and clerical masculinity.

This is especially clear if we compare the vernacular legend to Hugh's *vita*, which is preoccupied with the difference between clerical and lay ethics. The miracles that conclude the *vita*, in particular, work to distinguish the role of the prior from that of a secular lord, despite the very great similarity between them. It is worth noting that the prior of Bridlington, like the head of many prominent religious houses, had considerable secular obligations: Bridlington priory owned and administered considerable lands, and it had jurisdiction over the entire township, with its own prison at the foot of the priory gate.[21] It is no wonder that the miracles seek to differentiate the prior from the kind of wealthy secular

---

[21] Prickett, *History of the priory church of Bridlington*, pp. 17–20.

lord he so resembled and with whom he was obligated to work. In one miracle, for example, when John, as prior, hosts a visiting nobleman his miraculous transformation of water into wine works precisely to distinguish him from his lay guest, despite homologies in their responsibilities and social status. One day 'a certain nobleman' visited the priory, inspired by – but also eager to test – the stories he had heard of the prior's piety. Preparations are made so that the prior can entertain this guest appropriately: 'for such a man,' remarks Hugh, 'certain of the finer foods were prepared': the prior knows his institutional role and observes it. But he also knows his spiritual obligations, so he covertly drinks plain water instead of wine. His little silver cup has a top, which John carefully replaces every time he takes a drink to hide his pious abstinence. The cup, interestingly, is the point of intersection between religious and lay identity in the anecdote, the material center of a venn diagram of the social practices of lay and religious men: as Hugh explains, 'It is the custom in that province for men, as well religious as worldly, to drink from silver cups, and Prelates, like other nobles, have always by them on the boards covered cups, and the server always sets the cover on the cup before he sets it down.'[22] The nobleman is terribly curious to know what is in the cup and asks for a sip. John politely refuses, noting that his guest has his own cup of wine, but the nobleman smiles and reaches for it anyway. In a narrative detail that threatens to turn the miracle into slapstick, the prior is forced to hold the cup just out of the reach of his importunate guest. When the nobleman snatches it away, John hastily prays that the water taste like wine. The prayer is almost too successful: the nobleman believes that John's wine is better than his own. The priority of the holy man's spiritual virtues – over his guest's social status and his own – is, in a neat inversion, manifest in very worldly form as the superior taste of his wine-flavored water.

The miracle emphasizes some shared aspects of elite masculine identity, which take material form in the silver cup that they share: the prior and his guest alike perform their elite status through what and how they eat and drink and through the objects they use. They are alike obligated to uphold the institutions they represent through modes of consumption. But these similarities also serve to mark the difference between religious and laymen, in particular, the higher value placed on asceticism and humility in the portrait of an ideal religious man. The miracle represents religious masculinity as more complicated than lay masculinity, because of the profound incompatibility of personal spirituality and public function. John of Bridlington cannot act at once as an ideal canon and an ideal prior without subterfuge, or indeed miracle. This is in fact how Hugh's *vita* distinguishes lay and religious men: by suggesting that apparent similarities linking them are in fact the source of doubleness, a miraculous difference between appearance and reality which trumps the material trappings they have in common.

Within the discourse of the 'mixed life' the prior's spiritual commitments, defined in Hugh's *vita* against both the noble man's worldly status and his own, shift in significance. In that framework, spiritual and worldly concerns are fully

---

[22] Purvis, *St John of Bridlington*, p. 22.

complementary, and they characterize the lives of lay as well as religious men. Hilton addressed his *Epistle on the mixed life* to a wealthy landowner and he presents the mixed life as characteristic especially of secular men of substance and authority: 'temporall men which haue souereynte with moch fauer of worldlye goodes/ & haue also as it were lordshyp ouer other men for to gouerne & susteyne them as a fader hath ouer his chyldren & a mayster ouer his seruantis & a Lorde ouer his tenauntys'.[23] Such men, Hilton argues, have spiritual as well as material obligations which affiliate them with the heads of religious houses. Indeed, Hilton acknowledges that the complication or division within the role of prior, as wealthy lord with secular obligations and as religious paragon with spiritual ones, differs only in degree, not in kind, from the dual charges of secular men. What are presented in Hugh's *vita* as the special ethical demands placed on a religious man, that is, are shared by lay men too in the discourses of the mixed life.

Moreover, the *Epistle* defines the mixed life – the vast gap between the two poles of contemplative and active life – in such a way that most readers, not just those who enjoy the privilege and authority of Hilton's first addressee, can recognize it as their own form of life. Lay readers were, of course, excluded from the kind of absolute removal from the world that defines the contemplative life in its pure form, a category Hilton reserves to those who leave behind 'all busynes/ changes & gouernaunce of worldly goodes & make them selfe poore & nakyd to the bare nede of the bodyly kynde & flee fro souereynte of all other men to the seruyce of god'. Indeed, this definition excludes even the most pious and ascetic prior: it resets the line demarcating lay and religious to one separating a life of abject piety from the many ways in which lay and secular men were alike preoccupied with what the tail-rhyme legend of John of Bridlington calls the 'two gret charge': 'thing warldly,/ With odir spiritual thingis' (fol. 173, lines 6–8). Hilton's account of the strictly active life – defined by a total lack of devotional feeling – might have seemed just as alien to late medieval lay readers as the strictly contemplative one. Entirely ignorant of 'ghostlye occupacyon', they 'ne fele sauour ne deuocion by feruoure of loue as other men doo/ ne they canne no skylle of it'. Given the abundant instruction in feeling such 'savor' available to English audiences – in works such as Rolle's *Incendium amoris*, which accompanies the John of Bridlington legend in the Beinecke manuscript, as well as in the many dramatic, lyric and other narrative traditions that encouraged affective identification with Christ – very few late medieval readers can have readily placed themselves in this category.[24]

The 'mixed life' thus quickly became an omnibus category, embracing anyone who recognized in their own lives the two great charges of an active life in works of mercy and the 'ghostly occupacyons' of devotion. It is this idea of mixed life that John of Bridlington represents in the tail-rhyme legend: not, as in Hugh's *vita*, the difference between religious and lay men, and between religious ethics

---

[23] S.J. Ogilvie-Thomson, *Walter Hilton's Mixed Life edited from Lambeth Palace MS 472* (Salzburg, 1986). All citations are to this edition.

[24] Jennifer Bryan calls the *Incendium amoris* 'a Passion meditation for the mixed life', and notes that it frequently circulated with Hilton's *Epistle on the Mixed Life*: Bryan, *Looking inward: devotional reading and the private self in late medieval England* (Philadelphia, 2008), p. 128.

John of Bridlington

and secular ethics, but their complementary relation and significant overlap. John of Bridlington is a kind of patron saint of the mixed life in the *Kalendre of the New Legende of England* as well, where he is praised for performing works of mercy by day and keeping vigils at night, 'so usyng actif lyfe that he forget nat contemplatyfe'.[25] Although the head of a wealthy priory may be especially burdened by the dual charges of the mixed life, they are shared by the broad audience addressed by the poem. They account not only for the saint's ethical proximity to good men of any station, but for the very idea of 'good men' developed in the poem, in which differences of vocation or social status have no particular consequence.

We can see in the poem, that is, potential implications of the discourse of the mixed life for medieval conceptualizations of men and masculinity, which are traditionally defined by social or institutional position. The variegation of masculine identities is precisely what is emphasized in the story of St John's cup of water, which offers miraculous evidence of the ontological difference between religious and lay men despite the notable similarities between them. In the discourses of the mixed life, in contrast, that difference is muted and generalized. The tail-rhyme legend is so generic precisely because it is modeling an ethics unmarked by the social differentiation that had long defined masculinity.

The image of the saint in the window at St Lawrence's, Ludlow, is interested in such differentiation: hence its careful attention to the regalia of elite clerical office. But it also attests to challenges to discrete categories of vocational identity from another quarter.[26] In the Ludlow window, the ahistorical elevation of the saint through the accoutrement of elevated religious office distances him from the laity and it posits the prestige of the office as more consequential than the simple piety of the man. The mitre is the most conspicuous aspect of this, but other elements of episcopal regalia are important as well, and John of Bridlington is figured with them in many images, as we will see. The only other image which may represent a mitred John of Bridlington is bound into a copy of William Staunton's vision of St Patrick's purgatory, which is dated to 1409, the year in which the privilege of the mitre was granted to Bridlington priory.[27] A mitred saint, holding a cross-staff in his left hand and raising his right in a blessing, stands amid horned demons who torment the poor souls in Purgatory, some

---

[25] *Kalendre of the Newe Legende of England*, ed. Manfred Görlach (Heidelberg, 1994), p. 118. Interestingly, Pynson prints Hilton's *Mixed life* with the *Kalendre*, encouraging his audience to 'take it charytably' even though it already exists in print because 'the more a good thynge is knowen the better it is, and parcase by this occasion it may come to the knowlege of some men that otherwise shulde neuer haue harde speke of it': ibid., p. 46.

[26] The window was commissioned by the clothiers' guild of Ludlow (Purvis, *St John of Bridlington*, p. 11), and is thus evidence for the cult's appeal to mercantile elites.

[27] London, British Library, MS Royal 17 B XLIII, fol. 132 v. A digital facsimile of the page is available in the online British Library Catalogue of Illuminated Manuscripts at www.bl.uk/catalogues/illuminatedmanuscripts/record.asp?MSID=6856, where the figure is identified as St Patrick. Staunton's vision is edited by Robert Easting, *St. Patrick's Purgatory*, EETS o.s. 298 (1991), pp. 78–117. Easting identifies the Royal manuscript image as John of Bridlington, though he also suggests that it could represent the bishop that Staunton encounters in the Earthly Paradise, pp. xxxiii–xxxiv. For the date of Staunton's vision, see ibid., pp. lxxiv–lxxv.

boiled together in a pot, others beaten with sticks. It is possible that the saint is, or was assumed by some readers to be, St Patrick, the Irish bishop whose portal to Purgatory is the location of Staunton's vision. But John of Bridlington is a central character in the vision: he is one of two saintly guides who lead Staunton through the moral topography of Purgatory, amid the devils and the fires that torment those who have transgressed – precisely the landscape depicted in the drawing inserted in the book.[28] Although the vision never refers to John of Bridlington as wearing a mitre – indeed when Staunton first sees the saint, he is said to be dressed in white 'in a chanons is abite' (78) – it is at the very least a possibility that a later reader of this book added an image of the saint wearing the pontificalia granted to the prior of Bridlington in the very year that Staunton is said to have experienced his vision.

The representation of John of Bridlington graced by the mitre is evidence of the increasing prestige of Bridlington priory, already a wealthy and venerable institution when John served as prior. It is an example of a wider trend in which prominent (as well as some less prominent) religious houses were granted the right to symbols that had been reserved for bishops and a few important monasteries. The rapidly growing number of prelates entitled to such displays of authority in the late Middle Ages provoked increasingly vocal opposition. The topic was taken up at the Council of Constance and it resurfaced as a concern across the fifteenth century. The way in which such privileges confused differences in status – not only in relation to other religious men but also secular lords – was a central concern: as early as the 1360s, John Bokyngham, bishop elect of Lincoln, objected to the extension of the mitre to the prior of Sempringham on the ground that 'other prelates without comparison greater than the prior, and peers of the realm would disdain to take a lower place'.[29] In 1439, Pope Eugenius IV promised the archbishop of Canterbury that he would cease new grants of the mitre and staff to abbots and priors.[30] In retrospectively granting pontificalia to Bridlington's most famous prior, the Ludlow window provides saintly authority for the privilege granted to his successors in the face of such criticism. In the context of the Middle English legend of John of Bridlington, the Ludlow window is also a reminder that in spite of, or in response to, the discourses of the mixed life, there were countervailing efforts to confirm and even increase the difference between religious and lay identities, through elaborate symbols of the special status of religious men of authority. Decked out in cope, stole, and mitre in the uppermost register of the light, the Ludlow St John is well beyond the reach of his lay devotees.

---

[28] The other guide is identified as St Ive of 'Quitike' in the Royal manuscript and as St Hild of Whitby in the only other extant manuscript of the text, London, British Library, MS Additional 34,193.

[29] Alfred Sweet, 'The Apostolic See and the heads of English religious houses', *Speculum* 28 (1953), pp. 468–84, at p. 482. See also Heale, 'Mitres and arms'. The currency of debates over the status of the mitre at Bridlington is suggested by the commonplace book of Thomas Ashby, a Bridlington canon, Durham University, Cosin MS V.V.19, which includes accounts of the saint's miracles, including one from 1406, as well as a discussion of the symbolic meaning of the mitre: see A.G. Dickens, 'The writers of Tudor Yorkshire', *Transactions of the Royal Historical Society* 13 (1963), 5th ser., pp. 49–76.

[30] Sweet, 'The Apostolic See', p. 481.

John of Bridlington

We might be tempted to read the Ludlow window and the tail-rhyme legend as evidence of a contest over John of Bridlington as an exalted prelate of an elite institution or a humble model of the mixed life – or indeed of a contest between different modes of medieval masculinity, one rooted in access to institutional authority and the other in practices of 'fellowship'. But I want to understand them together as indices of parallel and compounding phenomena, that is, of two ways that the status of religious men shifted in this period that I have discussed: in the first place, through the discourses and practices of the mixed life and, second, through competition for institutional and personal prestige among religious men that blurred once clear distinctions between them. In the same period in which discourses of the mixed life blurred the distinction between lay and religious devotional practices, the rapid expansion of the privileges and symbols of elite religious authority blurred the differences between bishops, abbots, and other prelates. Both of these phenomena elided, or threatened to elide, some of the variegated forms of identity that had differentiated religious men not only from the laity but also from one another. John of Bridlington's cult witnesses the surprising range of representations that these elisions made possible: the increasing convergence of religious and lay ethics leads to his association with ordinary lay people in the tail-rhyme legend, and his representation as mitred prior in the Ludlow window testifies to the erasure of differences between religious men through the granting of once rare and specific symbols of elite office.

Extant images of John of Bridlington provide abundant evidence for crossing between different categories of identity in the remarkable instability of the visual tradition. In a window of the splendid Beauchamp chapel in St Mary's parish church, Warwick, built by the earl of Warwick in the mid fifteenth century, the saint is shown tonsured, his head bare, but he wears the cope and stole, and he carries a pastoral staff.[31] This is a visual analogue to the Latin *vita*, insisting on both the saint's humility and the prestige of his office. We may contrast this image and that of the Ludlow window with the depiction of the saint in the Beaufort Hours where he is dressed, as we might expect, in the black habit of an English Augustinian canon (figure 2).[32] But this careful identification of his institutional identity is the exception. Thus while he is also dressed in a canon's habit, of sorts, in a window in St Matthew's parish church, in Morley, Derby, it is a rich blue and brown, colors set off by the brilliant green of the saint's shoes, a far cry from the order's austere black and white.[33] Perhaps this was simply meant to take advantage of the beauty of the glass, but it mutes and muddles the saint's identification as an Augustinian canon. It is, in any case, careless of a more accurate, which is to say more specific, index of John's particular institutional affiliation.

---

[31] Purvis, *St John of Bridlington*, p. 9.

[32] Pace Curley, there is no image of John of Bridlington in the Bolton Hours; see Kathleen Scott, *Later gothic manuscripts, 1390–1490* (London, 1996), ii, p. 119. The image of the saint in William Porter's Book of Hours (see note 6 above) represents the saint in the habit worn by Augustinian canons in France, where the book was produced.

[33] Purvis, *St John of Bridlington*, p. 4. Purvis notes the saint's 'ascetic and rather plaintive countenance', perhaps a hedge against his expensive clothing.

Figure 2 St John of Bridlington, Beaufort Hours: London, British Library, MS Royal 2 A XVIII, fo. 7v.

John of Bridlington

The image of the saint on a rood screen, unfortunately damaged, in St Andrew's, Hempstead, on the Norfolk coast, shows him not only in a canon's dress, but evidently holding a fish.[34] Purvis suggests that the fish is a symbol of humility, recalling a moment in the Latin *vita* in which John is compared to Tobias, who is sometimes represented with the fish central to his story.[35] While it is true that St John is lauded especially for this virtue, I think that the fish more likely registers the role of St John – who hails from the seaside town of Bridlington, with its busy harbour – as a patron of fishermen. One of his most celebrated miracles was to guide five sailors to safety during a storm.[36] On this roodscreen in a small parish church in Norfolk we see the saint represented either with a symbol of his own humility or as himself an object of humble devotion, linked to some of his devotees by a token of their own vocation and basic needs. The various ways in which the holy prior is represented witness the appeal of his cult across a broad social and economic spectrum. They allow us, moreover, to account for that breadth in terms of the increasing porousness of once-fast categories of social, vocational, and institutional identity.

The best evidence that John of Bridlington served as the patron saint of mixed, mobile, and ultimately unmoored categories of social identity is the life story of his most famous follower, Margery Kempe.[37] She imitates St John most conspicuously in adopting his confessor, William Sleightholme, as her own. When Henry Bowet, the archbishop of York – and the very man who presided over the translation of John of Bridlington's body[38] – demands that Margery leave his diocese, she insists that she first be permitted to go to Bridlington to speak with her confessor: 'I must, ser, wyth yowr leve, gon to Brydlyngton and spekyn wyth my confessor, a good man, the whech was the good priowrys confessor that is now canonysed.'[39] This affiliation with the saint is surely meant to advertise her own (potential) sanctity, as well as to point to a spiritual authority that exceeds even that of the archbishop himself. Margery models herself on John of Bridlington in more subtle ways, as well. He is very likely an important, if overlooked, model for her gift of tears: the *Kalendre of the New Legende of England* remarks that during

---

[34] A photograph of the screen can be found at http://www.norfolkchurches.co.uk/hempstead/hempstead.htm.

[35] Purvis also notes that this is a humble parish church, and he thus takes it as evidence of the saint's popularity among the 'middle class ... cloth-traders, weavers, and farmers of fifteenth-century Norfolk'.

[36] Purvis provides evidence of devotion to St John in the seaport towns of Sandwich and Dover (*St John of Bridlington*, pp. 43–4).

[37] The *Book of Margery Kempe* refers to two specific occasions on which Margery traveled to Bridlington: in addition to the encounter with Henry Bowet discussed below, Margery and her husband are headed 'Brydlyngtonward' when they discuss Margery's desire for a chaste marriage in Chapter 11. *Book of Margery Kempe*, ed. Lynn Staley (Kalamazoo, MI, 1996), line 541. Anthony Goodman notes Margery's 'modish' devotion to the saint; few other scholars have commented on her interest in him: *Margery Kempe and her world* (Harlow, 2002), p. 136.

[38] The translation was performed by the archbishop of York, with the bishops of Ely, Lincoln, Durham, and Carlisle in attendance: Purvis, *St John of Bridlington*, p. 18; Prickett, *History of the priory church of Bridlington*, p. 25; *Chronica maiora*, p. 331.

[39] *Book of Margery Kempe*, ed. Staley, lines 2961–63.

prayer St John experienced 'so hyghe deuocyon that he coulde nat absteyne fro wepynge'.[40] Even some of Margery's specific miracles seem to be borrowed from the saint: in particular the stone and beam that fall from the church roof and strike Margery is very like a miracle included in Hugh's *vita* of John.[41]

Although Margery's imitation of a male saint is not in itself remarkable, it does help us to see that the virtues exemplified by John of Bridlington in the tail-rhyme legend and offered as paradigmatic of 'good men' – charity, piety, patience – are also fully appropriate to women, just as they are appropriate to both religious and lay men. Indeed, the non-gendered quality of the virtues emphasized in the legend may be seen as an effect of their 'mixed' nature. Precisely because traditionally masculinity was not a single homogenous category – that is, because there were many kinds of medieval men whose ethical, sexual, and social practice was defined by varying social and institutional roles – the elision of some of those roles can seem to elide the ostensibly more basic difference between masculinity and femininity, too.

But the real interest of Margery's identification with St John, especially in her bravado response to Henry Bowet, lies in the possible implications of this elision for the emergence of the public role that she takes up. As we have seen, the fluidity of social and vocational categories that defined medieval men – a fluidity especially visible in the cult of St John, variously represented as patron of the mixed life and as mitred prior – produces an omnibus paradigm of the 'good man', as Margery herself calls him, a notably unmarked or non-particular identity. Such an unmarked masculine social identity has often been seen as the product of a later humanism, and it is posited as the *sine qua non* for horizontal forms of affiliation and for the formation of a public sphere.[42] But the Bridlington legend reminds us that religious culture could also be an important forum for imagining identities that were not defined by vocation, institutional or regional affiliation, social class, or even by gender. I think it may possible to link what I am calling, for want of a better term, 'non-particular identity' in representations of John of Bridlington to the attribution to him of a set of enigmatic political 'prophecies', some obscure verses on the nature of the state and the monarchy. The attribution – readily debunked in modern scholarship – has been difficult to explain other than as an attempt to authorize the prophecies through their affiliation with the saint.[43] But I wonder if it is also evidence for something like a medieval public sphere, that is, for an emerging sense of a shared public that depends on the very sort of non-particular identity represented by England's last

---

[40] *Kalendre of the New Legende of England*, ed. Görlach, p. 118.

[41] Cf. *Book of Margery Kempe*, chapter 9, and Purvis, *St John of Bridlington*, p. 22 (Miracle of the Stone).

[42] It is also associated with the advent of a 'national' community, which makes Pynson's decision to append Hilton's *Mixed life* to the *Kalendre of the Newe Legende of Englande* especially interesting (see note 25 above). I take up this topic in a longer study of English saints lives, currently underway.

[43] See Michael Curley, 'The cloak of anonymity and the *Prophecy of John of Bridlington*', *Modern Philology* 77 (1980), pp. 361–9, and A.G. Rigg, 'John of Bridlington's *Prophecy*: a new look', *Speculum* 63 (1988), pp. 596–613.

medieval saint, who occupied and eluded many particular categories of identity, appearing sometimes as humble canon, sometimes as mitred prelate, and, in the rhythms of tail-rhyme romance, as an exemplar to just about anyone who participates in the active life of late medieval England with basically good intentions. It is perhaps no coincidence that Margery Kempe, during the period of her most robust interventions in the public life of late medieval England, identifies herself with him.[44]

---

[44] On Kempe's engagement with contemporary social, political, and ecclesiastical concerns, see Lynn Staley, *Margery Kempe's Dissenting Fictions* (Philadelphia, 1994).

WHY MEN BECAME MONKS IN LATE MEDIEVAL ENGLAND

James G. Clark

The monastic life held a powerful attraction for men in late medieval England. Such an assertion sits uneasily with the usual associations of later monastic history, the rising tide of public complaint and popular conflict which even inundated the precincts in 1327 and 1381, and the receding waterline of patronal support. Yet the customary focus on trouble at the frontier between convent and community tends to obscure the simple fact that throughout the period between the Black Death and the Break with Rome, successive generations of men continued to cross the battle-lines, pass into the precincts, enter the enclosure and make their solemn profession. In an age whose outlook is often characterised as increasingly secular and which certainly came to question the value of religious vows, in fact, the forms of clerical living in all their variety, the resilience of the monastic vocation is remarkable indeed.

A precise measure of recruitment to the principal monastic orders (Benedictines, Cluniacs, Cistercians and the Regular Canons), even to their largest, leading abbeys and priories, remains elusive. Where patterns of recruitment to the secular clergy can be focused with some clarity from episcopal records of ordination, which are well preserved (though far from complete) from the close of the thirteenth century, there is no corresponding class of document that can be counted upon to capture the passage of more-or-less every postulant into the monastic life.[1] There is a variety of proximate sources: the appearance of a

---

[1] There is now a rich literature on the ordination records of pre-Reformation England and the insights they offer into recruitment to the secular clergy. The starting-point remains David Smith's *Guide to the Episcopal Registers of England and Wales. A survey from the Middle Ages to the abolition of Episcopacy in 1646*, Royal Historical Society, Guides and Handbooks, 3 (London, 1981). From there see H.S. Bennett, 'Medieval ordination lists in English episcopal registers', in *Studies presented to Sir Hilary Jenkinson*, ed. J. Conway Davies (London, 1957), pp. 20–34; J.A.H. Moran, 'Clerical recruitment in the diocese of York, 1340–1530', *Journal of Ecclesiastical History* 34:1 (1983), pp. 19–54; W.J. Dohar, 'Medieval ordination lists: the origins of a record', *Archives* 20:87 (1992), pp. 17–35; V. Davis, 'Episcopal ordination lists as a source for clerical mobility in England in the fourteenth century', in *England in the fourteenth century. Proceedings of the 1991 Harlaxton Symposium*, ed. N. Rogers, Harlaxton Medieval Studies, 3 (Stamford, 1993), pp.

monk in the surviving lists of ordinations before the bishop does not mark the beginning of his monastic life but is likely, especially in the later period, to show him in the earliest years of his claustral career, even at the close of his noviciate; electoral rolls, visitation *comperta*, obituary notices, burial registers, the short-lived poll-tax records, and a passing reference in domestic accounts – for example, expenditure for the clothing of a novice – offer an irregular witness to the number, and duration, of monastic careers; together they allow at least an informed estimate of the turnover in each generation.[2] Between the final quarter of the fourteenth century and the first quarter of the sixteenth century, the trend is striking for its continuity. Monasteries were not as crowded as they had been in the expansive, high medieval era of new orders and new foundations, but they held to the number they had come to consider their capacity – 60–80 at the upper end, 12–15 at the lower – until advancing reforms and receding resources constrained admissions, in the majority of cases only after 1534.[3] Their stability is set in relief by the well documented fall in the numbers of secular clergy, precipitated by the first pestilence of 1348–50 but sustained to the end of the following century.[4] In fact, with the necessary caveat of approximate data, the case may be made for an expansion of the monastic population in the decades either side of 1500: the total number living under vows in early Tudor England may have been 53 per cent greater than its nadir at the time of the pestilence, and at least 5 per cent greater than at the succession of Henry VI; certainly, a number of houses can be shown to have exceeded their customary capacity in these years.[5]

152–70; M.C. Cross, 'Ordinations in the diocese of York, 1500–1630', in *Patronage and recruitment in the early Tudor and Stuart Church*, ed. M.C. Cross, Borthwick Studies (York, 1996), pp. 1–19.

[2] There are now a number of case-studies founded on these categories of source but the most detailed analyses are those by Barbara Harvey for Westminster abbey and Joan Greatrex for the Benedictine cathedral priories of the southern province: see B. Harvey, *Living and dying in England: the monastic experience, 1100–1540* (Oxford, 1993), pp. 73–7 at p. 73; J. Greatrex, *A biographical register of the English cathedral priories* (Oxford, 1996), where the variety of sources used are listed at the head of the register for each house (e.g. Canterbury, pp. 58–65). See also eadem, *English Benedictine cathedral priories, c. 1270–c. 1470* (Oxford, 2011), pp. 35–42 at p. 36.

[3] For an assessment of patterns of recruitment across monastic England as a whole see the outline in Knowles, *Religious orders*, ii, pp. 255–63 at p. 257, and the numerical data collected in D. Knowles and R.N. Hadcock, *Medieval religious houses of England and Wales*, 2nd edn (London, 1971), pp. 58–177 (Monastic orders and Regular Canons). Some data have been revised in recent case-studies for which see J.G. Clark, *A monastic renaissance at St Albans. Thomas Walsingham and his circle, c.1350–c.1440* (Oxford, 2004), pp. 15–17; R.B. Dobson, *Durham priory* (Cambridge, 1973), pp. 55–8; Harvey, *Living and dying*, pp. 73–7; J. Greatrex, 'Who were the monks of Rochester?', in *Medieval art, architecture and archaeology at Rochester*, ed. T. Ayers and T. Tatton-Brown, British Archaeological Association Conference Transactions, xxviii (Leeds, 2006), pp. 205–17 at p. 205.

[4] For the trend among the secular clergy see Moran, 'Clerical recruitment in the diocese of York', pp. 21–4; Cross, 'Ordinations in the diocese of York', p. 2; V. Davis, 'Rivals for ministry', pp. 99–109 at p. 99; A.K. McHardy, 'Careers and disappointments in the medieval Church', pp. 111–30 at p. 114; D.M. Robinson, 'Clerical recruitment in England, 1282–1348', *Fourteenth Century England*, V (2008), pp. 52–77.

[5] For the recovery, and rise in the population of regular religious see S.H. Rigby, *English society in the later Middle Ages. Class, gender, status* (London, 1995), p. 215. For examples of growth among

Perhaps the most telling measure of the vigour of monastic recruitment, however, is the pattern apparent at moments of greatest pressure. For the damaging effects of the Black Death (and subsequent outbreaks) upon monastic communities, historians have often drawn attention to the papal dispensations sought to priest men below the canonical age (24 years) to ensure their (especially extra-liturgical) obligations could be fulfilled. These are indeed evidence of the decimation of their numbers but they might also be taken as a sign of the ready supply of postulants, perhaps more robust than anticipated, to replenish them.[6] There is contemporary witness to the general trend: from the Augustinian abbey of St Mary-in-the-Meadows, Leicester, Henry Knighton believed he was observing a renewal of religious vocations in response to the spectre of plague.[7] Episcopal records of ordinations show a marked increase in monastic candidates presented from 1348 until the mid 1350s in a number of dioceses, north and south; the pattern in York suggests there was a surge before the plague reached the North Country, although to the end of the decade numbers remained higher than they had been pre-plague.[8] The surge may have been arrested by the second pestilence, to which the younger were said to be especially vulnerable, although there were evidently regional variations and a number of houses show a sustained recovery from 1375 to 1425.[9] By the same token, there is a common assumption that the monastic population dwindled to the point of extinction under the interventions of the crown after 1534. Yet recent re-examinations have revealed that there was no sudden exodus: youths and the elderly offered a release from their obligations chose to remain; there is also evidence of new professions, even after the first wave of suppressions of 1536–7, a trend that runs counter to the widely attested decline in new entrants to the secular clergy in the decade after 1529.[10] Given

the monastic and canons' orders between the early fifteenth and early sixteenth centuries, see Knowles and Hadcock, *Religious houses*, pp. 61, 65, 114, 152 (Bury, Evesham, St Osyth, Rievaulx).

[6] For these post-plague requests for dispensation see Knowles, *Religious orders*, ii, pp. 11–12. See also *Calendar of entries in the papal registers relating to Great Britain and Ireland: Papal letters*, ed. W.H. Bliss, 15 vols (London, 1893–1960) (hereafter *CPL*) 3: *1342–1362*, p. 383 (Bury, Suffolk); *CPL, 3:1362–1404*, pp. 37, 47, 91, 366 (Coventry, Nostell, Lincs., Rochester, Worcester); *CPL, 5: 1396–1404*, p. 429 (Newbo, Lincs.).

[7] '... confluebant ad ordines maxima multitudo...': *Knighton's Chronicle*, ed. G.H. Martin, Oxford Medieval Texts (Oxford, 1995), pp. 102–3.

[8] Moran, 'Clerical recruitment in the diocese of York', pp. 19–20.

[9] Knowles and Hadcock, *Religious houses*, pp. 58–82 at, e.g., pp. 61 (Bury, St Augustine's, Canterbury), 62–3 (Colchester, Crowland), 72 (Norwich), and 75 (St Benet Hulme): Greatrex, *Biographical register*, p. 466 (Norwich); eadem, *English Benedictine cathedral priories*, p. 36.

[10] The (albeit partial) notes of the visitors' investigations show that the desire to abandon the precincts was patchy at best in the autumn and winter of 1535 and the spring and summer of 1536: *Letters and papers, foreign and domestic, of the reign of Henry VIII*, ed. J.S. Brewer et al., 21 vols (1862–1932) (hereafter *LP*), x, p. 364. See also the reports of the commissioners effecting the surrender, which note the presence of novices: Kingswood, 1538 (British Library, Cotton MS Cleopatra E IV, fo. 325r-v (*LP*, 13/1, p. 433)); Burton-upon-Trent, 1539 (*LP*, 14/2, p. 521) and the presence of 'younge lustie men' (John London, July 1539: ibid., fo. 284r (*LP*, 14/1, p. 1321)). For a further examination see F.D. Logan, *Runaway religious in medieval England, c.1240–1540* (Cambridge, 1996), pp. 156–67 at pp. 160–7; idem, 'Departure from the religious life at the Dissolution', in *The religious orders in pre-Reformation England*, ed. J.G. Clark, Studies in the History of Medieval Religion, 30 (Woodbridge, 2002), pp. 211–26 at pp. 219–21. For case-studies

Why men became monks in late medieval England

the place of priesting in the formation of a pre-Reformation monk, the men that offered themselves as candidates for the priesthood shortly after the closure of their house were likely also to have been novices as late as 1538 or 1539.[11] The last monks of medieval England, it might be said, were a rising generation of the recently professed.[12]

The attraction of the monastic profession in this period may also be measured in a constituency whose connection to the monastic enclosure is often overlooked. Just as in early centuries, the monasteries of the later Middle Ages drew into their precincts a variety of men who sought affiliation with monastic religion but whose attachment fell short of solemn profession. Each of the monastic orders (monks and regular canons) continued to permit the entry of men to live as lay brothers of the monastery; although their presence was vestigial and sporadic, they were to be found even at the Dissolution.[13] Occasionally admitted in this period, even into their private spaces, were men of status in secular life who sought the end-of-life seclusion of the monastery in a manner not unlike the *ad succurrendum* professions of earlier times.[14] Most significant were a diverse group of secular clerks – academics, lawyers, perhaps independent pluralists holding papal chaplaincies and suffragan titles *in partibus* – who chose the monastery, and often its inner spaces rather than its outer precincts, as a place of settled residence.[15] This extra-claustral community of men was not strictly parallel to the community of professed religious. Often, and perhaps increasingly in the pre-Reformation period, their domestic, social and spiritual lives were interwoven; there were even purpose-built passages to convey them from their chambers to the monastic church.[16] Men might enter into an experience of the monastic

---

see also Greatrex, *English Benedictine cathedral priories*, p. 36. For the Augustinian chapter at Carlisle, see H. Summerson, 'Medieval Carlisle: cathedral and city from foundation to dissolution', pp. 29-38 at p. 36. For the contrary trend among the secular clergy see R.N. Swanson, *Church and society in late medieval England* (Oxford, 1989), p. 32; P. Marshall, *The Catholic priesthood and the English Reformation* (Oxford, 1994), p. 81; Cross, 'Ordinations in the diocese of York', pp. 7-8.

[11] Cross, 'Ordinations in the diocese of York', pp. 10, 14: the instances being of Mount Grace and Roche (Carthusian and Cistercian respectively, both in Yorkshire).

[12] The youth of the men presenting themselves for profession may have been matched in the mendicant orders, at least at those (comparatively) few houses continuing to make professions: it was perhaps intended as a pointed swipe at his age that a notorious friar of the Gloucester Blackfriars was dubbed by reformist townspeople as 'the two year-old': The National Archives (hereafter TNA), SP1/104/157: B. Lowe, *Commonwealth and English Reformation. Protestantism and the politics of religious change in the Gloucester Vale, 1483-1560* (Aldershot, 2010), p. 100.

[13] For example at Kingswood (Cistercian, Gloucestershire), in January 1538: British Library, Cotton MS Cleopatra E IV, fo. 325r-v (*LP*, 13/1, 433).

[14] For example, Edmund Walker, gentleman, who occupied rooms on the south side of the cloister at Cleeve abbey, for which he paid a sum of £27: Bettey, *Suppression*, p. 17.

[15] For such a presence see Greatrex, *English Benedictine cathedral priories*, pp. 27-8. For an evidence of their involvement in conventual business see the record of an abbatial election: R.M. Haines, *Ecclesia Anglicana. Studies in the English Church of the later Middle Ages* (Toronto, 1989), pp. 15-25 at pp. 16, 21.

[16] It was the appeal of the monastery's daily service to the unprofessed that led the monks of Burton in 1459 to seek a dispensation to celebrate mass before daybreak: *CPL*, 11: 1455-1464, pp. 544-5. For the fabric traces of such arrangements see B. Sloane, 'Tenements in London's monasteries,

life in this period, in particular its homo-sociability, without the commitment of a profession.[17]

*

The cultural climate of England, shifting and changing in the wake of the Black Death, in the recessionary conditions of the fifteenth century, and on the brink of the Break with Rome, was very different from the circumstances which had shaped the foundation and expansion of the monastic establishment, but it would be wrong to conclude that later generations looked upon the prospect of monastic profession in wholly different terms. The view prevailed of the monastic life, at least in its purest form, as first in the hierarchy of forms of regulated religious living, and the end to which any instinctive spiritual vocation naturally would tend, from Clergie's notion of heaven on earth (*Piers Plowman*, C.v. 152–3) to the popular woodblock image of the *Orcherd of Syon* (1519), representing those 'called & chosen besyly to labour . . . in the vyneyerde of oure holy sauyoure . . . to kepe continuallye . . . [a] seruyce onely to rede and singe'.[18] In spite of the currency of tales of misconduct in the cloister, there was still an underlying identification of the monastic vocation with the highest forms of asceticism and sanctity.[19] The monastic heroes of the past (especially England's past) were widely popular, and the tales of their personal rigour and masculine vigour which had inspired early converts – Dunstan's commitment to physical labour, in construction and craft, for example – still bore repetition.[20] Perhaps their well worn narrative portraits carried a renewed appeal for generations – from the second half of the fourteenth century onward – whose conception of human virtue were also informed by the popular tradition of the Nine Worthies and by the models of Roman antiquity now enjoying wider circulation.[21] At Norwich cathedral

---

c. 1450–1540', in *Archaeology of Reformation*, ed. Gaimster, pp. 290–8 at p. 295; R. Gilchrist, *Norwich Cathedral Close. The evolution of the English cathedral landscape*, Studies in the History of Medieval Religion, 26 (Woodbridge, 2005), pp. 131–2.

[17] For the appeal of the homosocial capacity of the clerical life see M.J. Ailes, 'The medieval male couple and the language of homosociality', in *Masculinity in Medieval Europe*, ed. D.M. Hadley (London, 1999), pp. 214–37.

[18] C.A. Grisé, '"Moche profitable unto religious persones, gathered by a brother of Syon": Syon Abbey and its English books' in *Syon Abbey and its books. Reading, writing and religion, c.1400–c.1600*, ed. E.A. Jones and A. Walsham (Woodbridge, 2010), pp. 129–54 at p. 146.

[19] Even in satire, it seems there was an underlying recognition of the special rigours of the monastic vocation: 'Quis nescit quam sit speciosa cohors monachorum / lacrima leccio parca refeccio luxus eorum' ('Monastic glory's known to one and all. Their treats are reading, tears and dinners small.') runs a verse in an English manuscript: A.G. Rigg, *A history of Anglo-Latin literature, 1066–1422* (Cambridge, 1992), p. 231.

[20] See, for instance, John of Glastonbury's attention in his mid fourteenth-century chronicle to this dimension of Dunstan's character, as exemplified by his repulsion of a diabolical apparition using the burning tongs from his own forge, 'and the tongs are preserved to this day as a witness': *The Chronicle of John of Glastonbury. An edition, translation and study of John of Glastonbury's Cronica, siue antiquitates Glastoniensis Ecclesie*, ed. J.P. Carley (Woodbridge, 1985), p. 117.

[21] The place of these monastic pioneers in the later medieval imagination is especially apparent in the decorative schemes of abbey and cathedral churches. Figures such as Anthony, Augustine, Basil, and Benedict and Bede, Cuthbert and Dunstan were the subject of narrative cycles and of

priory the connection was tangible, the carved capitals of the cloister carrying representations of classical gods and heroes, among them Odysseus.[22] For those contemplating profession in their teens, having passed through at least some of the common experiences of male formation, the grammar schoolroom, the pages' service passage, perhaps, for some, at the targets (for practice with bow and sword), the inference of monastic prowess was powerfully affirmative.[23]

From the middle years of the fourteenth century it appears there was a special interest in the person of the progenitor of the monastic order itself, Benedict of Nursia. The appeal of the person of Benedict as model for the professed man had always been apparent in monastic discourse but remains somewhat latent in England until the later period.[24] Edward III presented the monks of Westminster with a relic of Benedict's head, a gift that appears to have attracted, indeed resonated, with a rising interest in the *pater monachorum*, at least among the monastic establishment and its affiliates.[25] The naming of Benedict among the confessors in the Ashley Psalter may signal his growing presence in the landscape of lay devotion.[26] He was among the fathers of monasticism featured in the *South English Legendary*, which enjoyed a wide reception in late medieval England; such a renewed and rising profile ensured his selection as an exemplum in popular (vernacular) homiletics.[27] It was the order itself which may have focused public interest: the capitular authorities of the Benedictines prescribed elaborations for the observance of the saint's festival, while a number of prominent

---

reliquaries: D. Park and S. Cather, 'Late medieval paintings at Carlisle', in *Carlisle and Cumbria. Roman and medieval architecture, art and archaeology* (Leeds, 2002), pp. 214–31 at pp. 214–22; B.J. Nilson, *Cathedral shrines of medieval England* (Woodbridge, 1998), p. 32. For the Worthies see P. Boitani, *Chaucer and the imaginary world of fame* (Cambridge, 1984), pp. 127–9.

[22] Gilchrist, *Norwich Cathedral close*, p. 80.

[23] For the role of such figures, represented verbally or visually, in shaping the masculine identity of secular and regular clerks see J. Murray, 'Masculinizing religious life: sexual prowess, the battle for chastity and monastic identity', in *Holiness and masculinity in the Middle Ages*, ed. Katherine J. Lewis and P.H. Cullum, *Religion and culture in the Middle Ages* (Toronto, 2005), pp. 24–42 at pp. 29–30. For the patterns of pre-adult male formation see N. Orme, *From childhood to chivalry. The education of the English kings and aristocracy* (London, 1989), pp. 188, 202–5; idem, *Medieval children* (New Haven and London, 2003), esp. pp. 237–72, 313–15.

[24] For the role of Benedict's life in moulding view of monastic manhood see R.M. Karras, 'Thomas Aquinas' chastity belt: clerical masculinity in Medieval Europe', in *Gender and christianity in medieval Europe: new perspectives*, ed. L.M. Bitel and F. Lifshitz, The Middle Ages Series (Philadelphia, 2008), pp. 52–67 at p. 57. It has been suggested that a certain diffidence in monastic culture towards the professed saint, reflected, and reinforced, by a dearth of new candidates, lifted in the later period, as not only new models (such as John of Bridlington, discussed by Catherine Sanok in this collection), but also some of the earliest, were brought into sharper focus. See André Vauchez, *Sainthood in the Middle Ages*, trans. Jean Birrel (Cambridge, 1997), pp. 123, 328, 368–9.

[25] *Chronica Johannis de Reading et Anonymi Cantuariensis*, ed. J. Tait (Manchester, 1914), p. 120. See also W. M. Ormrod, 'The personal religion of Edward III', *Speculum* 64 (1989), pp. 849–77 at p. 873.

[26] The Ashley psalter survives as British Library, Additional MS 63593. An early fourteenth-century manuscript, it passed into the possession of the Ashley family, connected with the Northamptonshire village of that name, although certain prayers suggest a monastic origin.

[27] For the role of Benedict and other monastic saints in the later literature of lay formation see Katherine J. Lewis, 'Male saints and devotional masculinity in late medieval England', *Gender & History*, 24/1 (2012), pp. 112–33 at pp. 115, 118.

abbeys and priories installed new schemes of images, on tablets and in stained glass, featuring Benedict and scenes from his life, a subject which in earlier times had been markedly less popular than in continental monastic settings.[28]

The identification of the monastic settlement as *locus sacri*, a source of spiritual energy, which propelled the early pioneers, also persisted, inflected but not entirely altered in the later period. In fact the sacred significance of the oldest monasteries in England was reaffirmed for audiences after the Black Death in a succession of new or newly collated accounts of the coming of Christianity, the conversion of the Anglo-Saxon kingdoms, the ecclesiastical patronage of Edgar, and the achievements of the earliest English saints. Even the old legend of King Lucius was retold, impressing on a new readership the claim to the foundation of monasteries some four centuries before the mission of Augustine.[29] This literature was largely for clerical consumption, but the monasteries themselves sought to retail it for lay society by means of the pulpit (where they were increasingly active), and the decorative schemes of the public spaces of their churches and shrines. It might be suggested that they were assisted in this enterprise by a new historicism apparent in the public, and popular, imagination. The expanding coteries of extra-clerical, and lay, readers evinced a taste for history in general, and the history of England in particular, and their reading of it returned them repeatedly to the country's monastic heritage. As John Stretch, Augustinian canon of Kenilworth, reminded readers of his prosimetrical history, which traced the islands' story from the expulsion of the Britons to the battle of Agincourt, the

---

[28] For prescriptions for the commemoration of St Benedict see *Documents illustrating the activities of the General and Provincial Chapters of the English Black Monks, 1215–1540*, 3 vols., ed. W.A. Pantin, Camden Society, Third Series, 45, 47, 53 (1931–7), i. pp. 68, 98; ii. p. 83. For visual representations see, for example, at Durham priory the scheme of portraits painted on panels surrounding the altar of St Benedict and St Jerome, which was the second altar in the north alley of the lanthorne, showing, in the words of a sixteenth-century memoir, 'St Bennett in a blew habit, with a crozier in his hand': *Rites of Durham*, pp. 91–102 at p. 94. For witness to possible frescoes and stained glass depicting Benedict in the infirmary chapel at the abbey of Bury see: *On the Abbey of St Edmund at Bury, II. The church*, ed. M.R. James, Cambridge Antiquarian Society, 28 (1895), pp. 148, 186. These later medieval representations of the founder of the order contrast with the comparatively few depictions found in the early and high medieval fabric of English houses; see, for example, the fresco of an unidentified monk with the Virgin and Child in the nave of St Albans Abbey, which may be identified with Benedict. Abbot Thomas de la Mare of St Albans (d. 1396) provided a new image of St Benedict costing 5 marks: *Gesta abbatum monasterii sancti Albani*, ed. H.T. Riley, 3 vols., Roll Series, 28 (1867–9), iii. p. 386. It is worth noting in parallel the renewed attention in the early sixteenth century to the relics of Dunstan and Oswald: the saint's head was removed from its resting-place in 1508 and re-set in silver: Nilson, *Cathedral shrines*, pp. 32, 55.

[29] For the legend of King Lucius see Geoffrey of Monmouth, *The history of the kings of Britain. An edition and translation of the De gestis Britonum*, ed. and trans. M.D. Reeve and N. Wright (Woodbridge, 2007), pp. 215–48 (IX. 158–XI. 176). For its reprise in later narratives see, for example, the opening chapters of the Winchester monk Thomas Rudbourne's *Historia maior* in *Anglia Sacra I*, ed. Henry Wharton (London, 1691), pp. 179–286, at pp. 180–2. For further annals of monastic fathers and foundations compiled by Andrew Aston, monk of Bury St Edmunds: *Memorials of St Edmund's Abbey*, ed. T. Arnold, 3 vols., Rolls Series 96 (1890–6), iii, pp. 145–51 at p. 150; John of Glastonbury's chronicle: *Chronicle of John of Glastonbury*, ed. James Carley (Woodbridge, 1985), p. 39; a Durham priory annal, BL, Add. 6162, fos. 26r–31v and a (?Glastonbury) history among Worcester material in Oxford, Bodl., Bodley MS 832, beginning at fo. 180r.

record of many of England's monarchs, and their mortal remains, are held in the custody of her monastic churches.[30] The persistent pressure of the Anglo-French war, and the political instability that attended it, heightened this historical sensibility and sharpened a sense of English identity.[31] And it might be suggested that among other effects these patterns of thought returned the monasteries to public attention as a conspicuous proof of England's claim to primacy, past, present and into an uncertain future, as the very embodiment of antiquity and continuity.

The monastic movement of the High Middle Ages had been fuelled by a mass religious fervour. The popular religion of the post-Black Death period was propagated in large part in the new (or at least newly elaborated) context of the parish and its surrounding social community but it would be wrong to represent it as channelling religious sensibility away from monastic religion. The lively parishes of late medieval England were, in many instances, in the custody of monastic institutions and some even under the pastoral care of their professed brethren.[32] The devotional vigour of lay worshippers was derived from associations, cults, liturgical ceremonies and dramas which were in many cases directed by their neighbouring monasteries.[33] It was perhaps as natural for this generation, as for their forebears of two or three centuries past, to regard the presiding monastery as the fount of the spirituality with which they themselves were charged.

The pragmatic attraction of the settled, secure and (generally) well supported existence of the monastic enclosure which undoubtedly acted upon early generations perhaps also continued to have some bearing in the later period. There may be a case to be made that rural depopulation, urban dilapidation and the general dislocation of labour encouraged a gravitation towards institutions whose shoulders were sufficiently broad to withstand the short-term shocks and long-term instability of the 'long fifteenth century'.[34] Here it is unhelpful that much of the available data on patterns of recruitment relates to prestige houses, whose

---

[30] John Stretch's prosimetrical history is preserved uniquely in British Library, Additional MS 35295, fos. 228v-279v; his notes on John and Edward II, buried respectively at Worcester and Gloucester are at fos. 251v, 255r. See also F.M. Taylor, 'The chronicle of John Stretch for the reign of Henry V', *Bulletin of the John Rylands Library* 16 (1932), pp. 137-87.

[31] There is an extensive critical literature on the cultural consequences of the century of Anglo-French conflict. See especially, A. Butterfield, *The familiar enemy: Chaucer, language and nation in the Hundred Years War* (Oxford, 2009), also K. Dockray, 'Patriotism, pride and paranoia: England and the English in the fifteenth century', *The Ricardian* 8 (1990), 430-42, and for a longer chronological perspective E. Caldwell, 'The Hundred Years War and national identity', in *Inscribing the Hundred Years War in French and English cultures*, ed. D. Baker, SUNY Series in Medieval Studies (Albany, NY, 2000), pp. 237-66.

[32] For the interdependence of monastic and neighbouring parish communities see M. Heale, 'Monastic parish churches in late medieval England', in *The parish in late medieval England*, ed. C. Burgess and E. Duffy, Harlaxton Medieval Studies 14 (Donington, 2006), pp. 54-77. For a full study of an, albeit singular, case see M. Harvey, *Lay religious life in late medieval Durham*, Regions and Regionalism in History (Woodbridge, 2006).

[33] For example, see G. McMurray Gibson, *The Theater of Devotion. East Anglian drama and society in the later Middle Ages* (Chicago, 1994), esp. pp. 107-17; Harvey, *Lay religious life*, pp. 36, 157.

[34] It is worth noting that comparative study of secular clerical recruitment in this challenging climate has found contrasting trends which do not follow local economic conditions: Robinson, 'Clerical recruitment', p. 73.

admissions were always highly selective. The smaller, poorer foundations may have presented a different prospect to the social community in their own regions. Pragmatism might explain the passage of successive generations of men from the same gentry and mercantile families into a regional network of monasteries from the turn of the fourteenth century to the brink of the Reformation. It may well be the reason for the persistence of an (albeit small) lay brotherhood at the greater abbeys and priories in spite of the fact that their contribution to conventual life was increasingly unclear.[35]

Yet it is also possible to identify a definite shift in approaches to the monastic profession in this period, one which gave a number of other impulses particular force. Even at the beginning of the period, the profile of the monastic postulant had narrowed considerably. There had been no child oblates since the close of the twelfth century (and in England in fact few of them even before) and the incidence of middle-aged professions – men past their youth, in the middle, or indeed the end of life – which had been the mainstay of monastic leadership in the early centuries now dwindled.[36] Increasingly, the postulant was a youth aged between mid-teens and early twenties, between, say, 15 and 21, that is, some years short of the canonical age for priesthood. While profession and ordination of those under age was not a general and widespread irregularity, it does seem entry was bound very tightly to the required minima: Canon Raynold Colyer of Smithfield may well stand not only for his own but for all generations of religious in the century and a half before 1540: born in February 1391, he was 'schorne canon' just under three weeks shy of his eighteenth birthday and priested only two months after he turned 24 in 1414.[37] At his mid-teens, a youth in late medieval England might expect (if the opportunity had been open to him) to be at the close of his years of elementary schooling: the expanding network of endowed grammar schools accepted boys from as young as seven for a period of between five and seven years; at 21, or thereabouts, if he had been in a position to pursue academic study he could expect to be at an advanced stage of the university arts course.[38] In other words, it came to be understood that the point-of-entry into the (male) monastic life should follow a period of formal education at an age appropriate for a youth to begin his progress through the orders of clergy to the priesthood. Candidates were subject to examination, one more consistently applied, and perhaps more rigorous than those undertaken for entrants to the secular priesthood.[39] Thus the monastic profession was marked out as the

[35] For evidence of lay brethren see Knowles, *Religious orders*, i. p. 287. For examples, a list of the community at St Albans abbey in 1380 preserved in the *Liber benefactorum*, now British Library, Cotton MS Nero D VII, fos. 81v-83v; a reference in a fifteenth-century compotus roll from St Augustine's abbey, Bristol: *Two compotus rolls of St Augustine's Abbey, Bristol, for 1491-2 and 1511-12*, ed. G. Beechcroft and A. Sabin, Bristol Record Society (Bristol, 1938), pp. 56, 190, 193.

[36] For the decline of child oblation in England see Knowles, *Religious orders*, ii, p. 294.

[37] Raynold's biography is recorded on the final, rear flyleaf of British Library, Royal MS 17 D XXI, fo. 187v.

[38] For the age of study at school and university see N. Orme, *Medieval schools. Roman Britain to Renaissance England* (New Haven and London, 2005), p. 129.

[39] For example, see selection criteria codified in the Canterbury registers, and the record there of a candidate rejected for 'usum et artem cantandi et legendi nondum habet': *Literae Cantuarienses*.

occupation of a lifetime, no longer an expression of a contingent ascetic impulse but a career, secured as much (if not more) by education as spiritual formation. Of course, it would be true to say that men had entered the cloister for the course of their life in earlier times – although for many it was a lifetime commitment made by others on their behalf – but it was only in the later period, and perhaps only, fully, in England, that entry came to be managed with such a degree of uniformity, with specified academic pre-requisites and a prescribed progression from the clothed novice to solemn profession, priesting and, finally, the fully observant performance of the monk and the prospect of office. Recast from vocation to learned occupation, the monastic life lost nothing, indeed perhaps gained somewhat in its social esteem, but its separation, its reputed 'e-masculinity', from other male roles, many of which were now also managed by their own pre-requisites and paths of progression, surely narrowed.[40]

The emergence of such a career structure can be connected with changes both within and outside the monastic orders. The growing liturgical and extra-liturgical obligations of any observant community of at least middling size from the turn of the thirteenth century placed an ever greater imperative on the clerical capacities – linguistic, musical, ceremonial – of the brethren.[41] Also, the corporate ambitions of their leadership, first in the face of conflict with mendicants in their old spheres of influence, and later in response to public alarm over heterodoxy, brought a search for something of their old magisterial authority.[42] There were parallel developments in the orders of clergy, conferral of the lowest of the minor orders being elided to regularise progression and candidacy for the priesthood being subject, at least in principle, to satisfactory examination.[43]

The letter books of the monastery of Christ Church, Canterbury, ed. J.B. Sheppard, 3 vols., Rolls Series 85 (1887–9), I, pp. 398–99. See also Greatrex, *English Benedictine cathedral priories*, pp. 52–5. For examination of seculars, apparently 'perfunctory' by contrast with the scrutiny applied to would-be regulars, see P. Heath, *The English parish clergy on the eve of the Reformation* (London, 1969), p. 15.

[40] Studies of monastic masculinity have at any rate misunderstood the degree to which regular discipline *unmanned* the professed even in the formative centuries of the religious orders, and the emergence of a common career path served to give professional attributes still greater purchase over the personal aesthetic in the making of claustral identity. For a recent, more nuanced approach to monastic men which shows some awareness of the changing climate in the later Middle Ages see Derek G. Neal, *The masculine self in late Medieval England* (Chicago, 2008), pp. 89–90, and re-iterated in idem, 'What can historians do with clerical masculinity?', in *Negotiating clerical identities: priests, monks and masculinity in the Middle Ages*, ed. J.D. Thibodeaux, Genders and Sexualities in History (Basingstoke, 2010), pp. 16–36 at pp. 25–6. For the conflation of male roles on either side of clerical or monastic profession in the later period see also Sanok's study of John of Bridlington in this collection.

[41] For the experience of these pressures, and the new imperatives that followed from them, see for example, Greatrex, *English Benedictine cathedral priories*, esp. pp. 270–81.

[42] For the background to these developments see W.A. Pantin, 'General and provincial chapters of the English Black Monks, 1215–1540', *Transactions of the Royal Historical Society*, 4th series, 10 (1927), pp. 195–263; Knowles, *Religious Orders*, I, pp. 9–27; ii, pp. 5–7, 14–15.

[43] For the elision of orders, which began early in England, see J. Barrow, 'Grades of ordination and clerical careers, c.900–c.1200', *Anglo-Norman Studies* 30 (2008), pp. 41–61 at p. 48; Moran, 'Clerical recruitment', pp. 29–30; Cross, 'Ordinations in the diocese of York', p. 4. For the examination of prospective secular priests, and the suggestion of greater rigour from the end of the

The cycles of visitation, internally from the capitular authorities of the respective orders and externally from the diocesan, more frequent in the later period than before, placed the competence of the professed community under regular scrutiny for the first time.[44]

The (new) terms of the monastic profession re-focused its appeal to the men of late medieval England and in propelling them to the point of entry arguably it reinforced the role of their social and occupational contexts. Perhaps above all the determination to satisfy the pre-requisites and commit to a structured and increasingly professional progression from youth was drawn from the dynamics of the family. It should be said that the available biographical data suggests that the social catchment of the male houses (of all orders) in England had contracted in the later Middle Ages.[45] Scions of aristocracy were rare – a marked contrast to female monasteries – as were men 'raised from out of the filth (de stercore elevasti)' as one exceptional convert described it.[46] Most of the men making their profession in this period were of middle rank whose families might be identified among the minor gentry, merchants or yeomen of the region.[47] To such families monastic profession represented a compelling source of social capital. Ecclesiastical office had always held out to the ambitious, or indeed, needy family of modest status the possibility of social advancement, but in the diverse clerical environment of the later Middle Ages it was perhaps the changing character of claustral careers that again set the prospect of a profession into sharp relief. The growing selectivity of the greater monasteries only enhanced its *éclat*: the admission of a candidate was itself a conspicuous measure of his calibre and the quality of his preparation at school and (perhaps) university, as well as in the household(s) of his kinfolk. Moreover, the narrow opportunities for entry extended the promise of office to almost any able postulant that lived beyond the years of probation: such were the corporate responsibilities of monasteries of even middling income in this period that as many as two-thirds of the professed community occupied managerial positions either at the parent community or at one of its dependent institutions; indeed it was a feature of monastic England that although estates, properties and rights were let out to farm, the responsibilities

---

fifteenth century, see Moran, 'Clerical recruitment', p. 28; T. Cooper, *The last generation of English Catholic clergy: parish priests in the diocese of Coventry and Lichfield in the early sixteenth century*, Studies in the History of Medieval Religion, 15 (Woodbridge, 1999), pp. 15–18.

[44] For a general account of the cycles of monastic visitation in the later period and their witness to the quality of regular discipline see Knowles, *Religious Orders*, ii, pp. 214–17; iii, pp. 62–86.

[45] For the evidence of particular monasteries see, for example, Dobson, *Durham priory*, pp. 58–60; Harvey, *Living and dying*, pp. 75–77 at 76; Greatrex, *English Benedictine cathedral priories*, pp. 42–9.

[46] The phrase is found in one of the prayers said to have been composed by Richard of Wallingford, monk, and later abbot of St Albans, and references his own exceptional entry into the monastic life: 'recolo utcumque quomodo cum essem obscurus genere elevasti me de stercore et sic honorasti me ut sederem cum principibus': *Gesta abbatum monasterii sancti Albani*, ed. H.T. Riley, Rolls Series 28 (London, 1867–9), ii, pp. 295–7 at p. 296.

[47] Of course, detailed documentary evidence of parents and kinfolk is scarce indeed and judgements remain at the level of inferences from the variety of names recorded correlated with other regional sources. For impressions of this kind for particular houses see Greatrex, *Biographical register*, pp. 6 (Bath), 380 (Ely), 581 (Rochester), 656 (Winchester).

of administration were never secularised. The scope of the obedientiary offices at the apex of the monastery hierarchy was wide, with properties, rights and jurisdictions equal to or even exceeding those of many secular foundations.[48] Their status, at least in terms of provincial society, was at least equivalent to that of the secular hierarchy of the liberty (i.e., burgess), although there was no formal designation of armigerous rank as there was for the secular cathedral chapters.[49] For families whose horizons were firmly regional, there were obvious, substantive benefits that accrued from a kinsman holding office under the presiding monastic lordship. At the upper end of the middling constituency, among gentry whose status and sources of income were well established, the monastic career of a kinsman carried the potential to form an affinity that reached across the temporal and spiritual jurisdictions of the region. It was not that it provided any scope to unsettle the prevailing authority of the monastery; on the contrary, it was an opportunity to tie the fortunes of the family to a lordship whose material condition was secure indeed. Such was the promise of monastic office that the family network might seek to manage elections as closely as the process of admission and profession. Unnamed laymen were responsible for the suspect election of Nicholas Ascheby to the priorate of Westminster abbey.[50] Of course, these impulses were no less apparent among the monastic officers themselves: the expectations of the family affinity shaped appointments to lay offices, leases and grants, particularly in the shadow of the Dissolution: it was perhaps with an eye to his brother's uncertain future that in 1538 Roger Reve, burgess of Bury St Edmunds, bequeathed Abbot John four-score wethers 'going in westey flock either to see or to keep'.[51] In no way did monastic profession emasculate, or infantilise, men of this class, as has been suggested. They carried the expectations of family with them throughout their claustral career.[52]

For those at the lower end of this social band, the promise of a monastic career and office carried a different emphasis. Those families that found the scope for

---

[48] Harvey, *Living and dying*, pp. 100–2. See also B.F. Harvey, *The obedientiaries of Westminster abbey and their financial records* (Woodbridge, 2002). For the system in the cathedral priories see Greatrex, *Biographical register*, pp. 337 (Coventry), 377–80 (Ey), 755–6 (Worcester); idem, *English Benedictine cathedral priories*, pp. 165–215.

[49] D. Lepine, 'Origins and careers of the canons of Exeter, 1300–1455', in *Religious belief and ecclesiastical careers in pre-Reformation England*, ed. C. Harper-Bill, Studies in the History of Medieval Religion 3 (Woodbridge, 1989), pp. 87–120 at p. 97.

[50] *CPL*, 8: *1427–1447*, pp. 587–8. For contentious appointments to obedientiary office, albeit where the chief source of tensions was episcopal authority, see also Greatrex, *Biographical register*, pp. 53–4 (Canterbury).

[51] For example, A. Savine, *English monasteries on the eve of the suppression*, Oxford Studies in Social and Legal History, ed. P. Vinogradoff (Oxford, 1909), pp. 256–8. This was not the preserve of male monasteries. For family affinity in a female monastic context see the appointments and grants of the final abbess of Lacock, Joan Temmse: *Victoria Count History* (hereafter VCH). *Wiltshire*, iii, pp. 303–16 at p. 314. For the bequest of Roger Reve see TNA, PCC, Prob. 11/27, fos. 194v-195r.

[52] For example, R. M. Karras has suggested 'such men [priests, monks, canons, friars] were never fully adult or fully masculine ... In some ways monks never achieved full masculinity', and 'monks had no families to provide for': *From boys to men: formations of masculinity in later medieval Europe* (Philadelphia, 2003), pp. 17, 164.

social mobility in spite of the prevailing climate – for example, the burgess clan that benefitted from a modicum of self-governance in an old monastic town, the city merchants extending their sphere into the provinces – a monastic profession that prospered in prominent office was an important, perhaps a necessary milestone.[53] For the less fortunate in these troubled times a presence within the monastic corporation was surely an anchor-hold, a security for the status of the family. The profession of William Benett of Reading in or around 1533, perhaps an instance, rare in this period, of mid-life entry, suggests that the cloister could still be regarded as a positive refuge from the material pressures of the secular world. It appears William carried debts with him into the cloister from where a kinsman (possibly a brother) sought to recover them.[54]

The considerations of social capital are readily apparent in the records of admission. Although there was no customary expectation of a dowry for a male postulant, there were occasional suspicions of simony.[55] Certain families made licit arrangements to secure their claim over monastic admissions: by the turn of the thirteenth century the Wiltshire Percies had purchased the right to nominate a novice at the Cluniac house of Monkton Fairleigh.[56] The continuing weight of these concerns in the years after the profession of the monk is conspicuous in the conflict over progression and promotion, recurrent in the later period, even at smaller, poorer monasteries of limited prestige. Elizabeth Sayghor (Sagar) made provision in her will for her (?younger) son, Stephen (?recently) professed at Whalley abbey, to ensure that he arrayed appropriate to the dignity of the family with £3 for 'six gowns and six doublets', 6s. 4d. 'to be sole his', 10s. towards the expenses of ordination and 3s. 4d. 'to buy him a book'; her post-profession investment won rich return, since Stephen ended his monastic career as an abbot.[57] It was surely the hope of securing a hold over the monastic hierarchy that led some families to endow an exhibition for the maintenance of a monk in academic study, as did the Bolton Scropes as early as 1356.[58] Such impulses were still apparent after 1500: John Pulton of Lydd (Kent) left £30 to provide

---

[53] For possible examples of such behaviour see John Re(e)ve, monk, and ultimately abbot of Bury St Edmunds, member of a propertied family whose holdings were evidently extended under his influence: R.M. Thomson, *The archives of the abbey of Bury St Edmunds*, Suffolk Records Society 21 (Woodbridge, 1980), pp. 58–9; Hubert Bosse of Colchester seeking at least secular office at the abbey: R.H. Britnell, *Growth and decline in Colchester, 1300–1525* (Cambridge, 1986), p. 113; John Bodley, monk of St Albans, and son of Thomas, London tailor: A.F. Sutton, 'Lady Joan Bradbury (d. 1530)', in *Medieval London widows*, ed. C.M. Barron and A.F. Sutton (London, 1994), pp. 209–38 at p. 219.

[54] TNA, C 1/991/1: Robert Benett seeks to recover a debt arising from repairs to Whistley fulling mill, Hurst, he having been possessed of goods and of messuages in Newbury and Reading.

[55] William, prior of Cartmel, was deprived in 1391 for simony, among other offences, although the subject of his illicit profit is not specified: *CPL, 4: 1362–1404*, p. 382.

[56] *VCH Wiltshire*, iii, pp. 262–68 at p. 268.

[57] Lancashire Record Office, DDTO K 5/81, dated 1505.

[58] Northumberland Record Office, ZSW/4/31: indenture dated 4 August, recording Henry Scrope's grant of 10 marks per annum for three years for the support of Roger de Castello to study at Oxford and 40s. per annum for another monk of the community to be selected by the abbot and convent. It is possible that Roger, bearing the name 'de Castello', was kin to the Scropes of Castle Bolton.

an exhibition for one or two monks of Battle abbey to study at either Oxford or Cambridge.[59] It was perhaps the undertow of family affinity that so frequently unsettled the authority of superiors, inviting the intervention of the diocesan and later, the legate and his agents. Family imperatives also acted to inflect monastic identity: while there was a general shift from toponyms to family names, monks of these later generations made overt reference to their social status, adopting the armorial bearings that was their heredity, and the punning personal rebus that was now the currency of their class, and even employing the courtesy titles that were the currency of the social community from which they had come: John Stone, observer of conventual life at Christ Church priory, Canterbury, for much of the fifteenth century, recorded among the dinner guests at the prior's table one Thomas Ballard, monk of St Mary's abbey, York, and 'armiger'.[60] Informed, too narrowly perhaps, by the paradigms of preceptive literature, the monastic profession has been understood as a mode of manhood that was not 'socially adult'.[61] In England after the Black Death – and arguably for much of the high and later Middle Ages – it was quite the opposite: a role in which the obligations, responsibilities, and status, of secular adulthood could be retained and, crucially, in an uncertain economic and social climate, secured.

The compulsion to secure or recover the social capital of the family by means of monastic profession raises the question of routine provision in this period for the second son or younger sibling. In the constituency of secular clergy perhaps best suited to comparison, the chapters of the secular cathedrals, a trend of ordination of second or younger sons has been found continuing in the fifteenth century.[62] The biographical information for the monks of the period is too sparse for a secure judgement on the general pattern. There may have been regional differences, and in particular different approaches adopted in those parts of the country with a high density (and diversity) of ecclesiastical foundations, as well as a greater variety of economic and social opportunities. Certainly, among London merchants of the fourteenth and fifteenth centuries, it seems there was no predictable pattern as to the family member(s) entering the religious life, or indeed whether they made their profession at an urban, suburban, or distant monastery.[63] By contrast, among the dispersed monasteries of mid- and

---

[59] The provisions are recorded in East Sussex Record Office, DYK 569, 22 June 1520, an indenture between the executor of Pulton's will, Thomas Sewell, monk of Battle, and Thomas Pulton, John's cousin and heir.

[60] For the use of arms by the professed men of this period see, for example, the surviving books of Abbot Robert Steward of Ely, e.g. Cambridge, St John's College, B. 1 [James 23], last leaf; London, Lambeth Palace Library, MS 448, fo. 107v. The personal rebus was widely adopted by the monastic superiors of these later generations. Among the most arresting examples, are the eye-and-slip symbol employed by Abbot John Islip of Westminster. See his so-called prayerbook, Manchester, John Rylands Library, MS Lat. 165. For Thomas Ballard see *Chronicle of John Stone*, ed. Searle, p. 44. For the changing form of names-in-religion see also Harvey, *Living and dying*, p. 75.

[61] For example: P.H. Cullum, 'Clergy, masculinity and transgression in late medieval England', in *Masculinity in medieval Europe*, ed. D.M. Hadley (London, 1999), pp. 178–96 at p. 194.

[62] Lepine, 'Origins and careers of the canons of Exeter', p. 96.

[63] For example, the progeny of Henry de Sudbury, skinner (d. 1375): Agnes, a nun at the Minories, John a monk of Battle and William a monk of Westminster; Walter Coleman, a monk of Bury St

West Wales, the admission of the second and younger sons of gentry families appears commonplace down to the Dissolution. The 'gentleman clerk' Robert ap Rhys positioned no fewer than four younger sons across the Cistercian network, while his eldest retained the secular status of armiger acquired by his father.[64] Positioned between the two in terms of regional social and clerical prospects were the boys of the Barlow family established in Essex at the beginning of the sixteenth century: Roger, the eldest, went into trade, while William, the second son, was professed as a canon of St Osyth; his two younger brothers entered the secular clergy.[65]

The admission and profession of monks was contested largely by a middling constituency of English society whose material position and seigniorial status was already apparent, if not always secure, but it appears that it also continued to promise the possibility of upward mobility for those lacking these advantages. The entry of men of no background was rare but not unknown. Men of illegitimate birth can be identified occasionally, when dispensed from the prohibitions connected with their status, although it seems they were notably fewer in number than those among the seculars. The tale of Sir John Stanley, bastard son of Bishop Stanley of Ely (d. 1515), taking the cowl for shame of his origin, suggests a lingering sense of the cleansing property of monastic profession scarcely a decade before the Break with Rome.[66] Men born legitimately to parents of the lowest sort did sometimes benefit from monastic patronage. The celebrated scholar-monk of St Albans abbey, Richard of Wallingford, the son of a husbandman, was schooled by the monks Wallingford priory and supported through the arts course at Oxford before he returned to make his solemn profession.[67] The spread of grammar and song schools as a part of the provisions of the monastic almonry from the turn of the thirteenth century may have extended the opportunities for youths of limited means to aim at monastic profession. These were not narrowly charity schools, and those that took on a fully-formed institutional structure

---

Edmunds, nephew of Reginald Coleman (d. 1383) of the city parish of St Margaret's, Lothebury; Simon, the (?younger) son of William Grantham, goldsmith (d. 1416), a monk of Hythe, brother to John, who inherited his father's city property: R.R. Sharpe, *Calendar of wills proved and enrolled in the Court of Husting, London: Part 2: 1358–1688* (1890), pp. 225, 246, 410. See also S. Thrupp, *The merchant class of medieval London* (Chicago, 1948), pp. 188–90, 231, 235.

[64] *Heads of religious houses*, ed. Smith, iii, pp. 323–7. See also G. Williams, *The Welsh Church from Conquest to Reformation* (Cardiff, 1976), pp. 323–6.

[65] Barlow progressed through patronage to the priorate and successively the sees of St Asaph, St David's, Bath and Wells, and Chichester: for his family background see G. Williams, 'Barlow [Finch] William (d. 1568)', *Oxford dictionary of national biography* (Oxford, 2004); online edn, September 2010 [http://www.oxforddnb.com/view/article/1442, accessed 14 November 2012].

[66] For examples of the profession of men of illegitimate birth see Thomas Arnewood, Augustinian canon, and Simon London, Benedictine, both dispensed from the prohibition on holding a benefice because of illegitimacy: *CPL, 7: 1417–1431*, p. 182; John Brenthingham, prior of Tywardreath, Cornwall: Cornwall Record Office, ART/5/4, 26 November 1433. For the Stanley story see A. Taylor, *The songs and travels of the Tudor minstrel. Richard Sheale of Tamworth* (York, 2012), p. 36.

[67] *Gesta abbatum*, ed. Riley, iii, pp. 181–2. For a summary of Richard's life and career see J.D. North, 'Wallingford, Richard (c.1292–1336)', *Oxford dictionary of national biography* (Oxford, 2004); online edn September 2010 [http://www.oxforddnb.com/view/article/23525, accessed 14 November 2012].

held a proportion of fee-paying pupils, but it would appear that there were also pupils supported on the foundation.[68] For the house itself, the purpose of these provisions may have been to provide a cohort with the prerequisites for monastic profession. By no means every almonry scholar followed this course, however, and at any rate a restriction on the number of new admissions at any one time, which appears to have been applied throughout the later period, even at the best endowed houses, acted as a constraint.[69]

The possibility of social mobility was perhaps a particular compulsion in this period for certain minorities. Internal migrants were drawn to clerical status in general not only as a source of material security but also as a means of conveyance to the stable and better resourced centres of settlement, and the comparatively sparse opportunities for clerical progression on the outer reaches of the realm propelled them to prospect in midland, western and north-western England. Recent studies have traced their passage into the ranks of the secular clergy but their place among entrants to the monastic life remains to be fully explored. Particular houses at points-of-entry into England evidently received a succession of migrant professions: men bearing names of an Irish cast – e.g. Moyne – are to be found at Dore in the Welsh March; there was a Welsh minority apparent among the canons of St Augustine's Abbey, Bristol, at intervals in the fifteenth century and at the Dissolution.[70] If toponyms can serve as a signal of origin, then it would appear migrant professions reached further into the network of English houses, to the Midlands, and the Wiltshire Downs.[71]

The scope of the monastic profession was likewise a focus for families of aliens. There was perhaps a greater degree of stability for incomers in this period, notwithstanding the obvious threats at moments of popular unrest, but still the challenges of a complex and restrictive commercial environment, a recessionary economy and the political disturbance and social dislocation of intermittent war. The opportunities within the monastic network were perhaps enhanced as much as they were for their native counterparts. Although it may be no more than the distortion of an unrepresentative sample, it is worth noting the men from families of alien origin numbered among the monastic superiors in the century before

---

[68] For the development of this form of provision see R. Bowers, 'The almonry schools of the English monasteries, c. 1265–1540', in *Monasteries and society in medieval Britain. Proceedings of the 1994 Harlaxton Symposium*, ed. B.J. Thompson, Harlaxton Medieval Studies, 6 (Stamford, 1999), pp. 177–222; Orme, *Medieval schools*, esp. pp. 279–83.

[69] For the variable evidence of the role of these schools as a source of recruitment to monasteries see Dobson, *Durham priory*, pp. 60–1; Harvey, *Living and dying*, pp. 74, 77; Greatrex, *English Benedictine cathedral priories*, pp. 188–90 at p. 188.

[70] Richard Moyne is recorded as abbot of Dore in c.1427: *Heads of religious houses, III, 1377–1540*, ed. D.M. Smith (Cambridge, 2008), p. 297. For Welsh family names (e.g. Gryffyth, Ap Guilliam, Ap Rhys) associated with the canon community of St Augustine's Abbey, Bristol, see *Two compotus rolls of St Augustine's abbey, Bristol, for 1491–2 and 1511–12*, ed. Beechcroft and Sabin, pp. 136, 164, 264. For a recent survey of such internal migration see V. Davis, 'Irish clergy in late medieval England', *Irish Historical Studies* 32 (2000), 145–60.

[71] For example, William Griffith, prior of St Katherine's, Lincoln, -1538; Thomas Wallashe [Walsh], prior of Bradenstoke (Wiltshire), *fl.* 1484–1521: *Heads of Religious Houses*, ed. Smith, iii, pp. 386, 599.

the Dissolution: Pascal Gylot, who ended his career as abbot of St Mary Graces; Stephen Sagar, who progressed from Furness to hold the abbacy at Hailes, and Robert Peterson, prior of Lewes.[72] It may not be coincidental that these aliens had held high office in houses of the Cistercians and Cluniacs, orders of continental heritage whose congregational ties remained in place in the early sixteenth century. Aliens are to be found among admissions to other orders but rarely so in the hierarchy. The experience of John Musard, monk of Worcester Priory, exemplifies that the promise of monastic profession to an alien was not always fulfilled. Accused of conspiracy against his prior during the Royal Visitation of 1535, Musard was placed in custody, from where he appealed directly to the king, recounting that his father and his three brothers had come into England in the service of the first Henry Tudor, and 'for their true service your father made two of them yeomen of the Crown, and gave the other two honest men's livings'; the family was ready to reaffirm their loyalty, 'My brethren and my uncle's sons and their children, to the number of 16, are ready to set upon 24 of your Grace's evil willers'.[73]

It was not only the material imperatives of the family that propelled men towards a monastic profession but also the underlying matter of its identity. The choice of the regular as opposed to the secular clergy, and the inclination to one order, or indeed, convent over another, was moulded by family dynamics. It was common among families of the middle rank, indeed in the later Middle Ages perhaps more so than among the aristocracy, to have cultivated ties to a particular convent over several generations.[74] Where it is possible to trace professions over more than one generation, it may be a manifestation of such family ties. The succession of male (and indeed, female) professions was so prodigious for certain families that there was surely a palpable awareness of a monastic lineage, one that offered up a variety of models, both of vocation and career, to the rising generation. In this context men encountered not only the prospects of clerical office but also the possibilities of male occupation beyond the secular roles of their rank and region; they were also presented with a counterpoint to the customary, paternal mode of male formation, since it was (necessarily) their uncles, brothers and cousins that were to induct them into a monastic life.[75] These filial

---

[72] *Heads of religious houses*, ed. Smith, iii, pp. 242, 299, 307–8.

[73] The letter is dated 8 August 1535: TNA, SP1/95, fo. 48r (*LP*, ix, p. 52). See also Greatrex, *Biographical Register*, pp. 853–4.

[74] For such ties, most clearly evidenced in patterns of burial, see K. Stöber, *Late medieval monasteries and their patrons. England and Wales, c. 1300–1540*, Studies in the History of Medieval Religion 29 (Woodbridge, 2007), pp. 122–33.

[75] For examples of such patterns evident in (especially) testamentary evidence see: the kinsmen of Thomas Palmer, fishmonger in the city of London, whose son, Roger, was a canon of Christ Church, London, and whose kinsman (? nephew, cousin), Henry, was a canon of Leeds (Kent): *Calendar of wills proved and enrolled in the Court of Husting, London: Part 2: 1358–1688* (London, 1890), pp. 356; the network of male and female kinfolk in secular and regular orders apparent in the will of John Lovelich (d. 1438), rector of St Aelphege, Canterbury: *The Register of Henry Chichele, archbishop of Canterbury*, 4 vols., ed. E.F. Jacob and H.C. Johnson, Canterbury and York Society, i, pp. 42, 45–6 (1937–47), ii, pp. 560–2; the variety of kinfolk living under monastic profession referenced in the will of Sir Thomas Cumberworth: *Lincoln diocese documents, 1450–1544*, ed. A. Clark, Early English Text Society, 149 (London, 1914), pp. 45–57. For examples found in

patterns of entry are not unique to the regular clergy in this period,[76] but it does appear they were more frequent and forceful in shaping the character of particular houses and networks of houses. In the early sixteenth century, the Ap Rhys clan commanded almost a monopoly over a chain of Cistercian houses between the Marches and West Wales.[77] And at the heart of the old monastic establishment, the Wheathampsteads held sway at St Albans abbey and its northernmost dependency at Tynemouth for almost a century until the death of Abbot John in 1465. He reflected in verse on the senior uncle who had generated a succession of nephew religious.[78] Here, a distinction should perhaps be drawn between lineage and parentage. In the shadow of the Dissolution there were a handful of instances of men following their fathers into a monastic profession: Abbot Thomas Buttler alias Pennant of Basingwerk (Cistercian) was succeeded in the abbacy by his natural son, Nicholas; between them they governed the abbey for six decades, down to its dissolution.[79]

The re-focusing of the monastic profession as a lifetime occupation for those with school learning, which carried with it the almost certain prospect of magisterial, sacerdotal and temporal authority, also arguably raised its profile among the constituency of young men with a general inclination towards the clerical life. The sharp decline in entrants to the secular clergy after the first pestilence and the long depression in their numbers thereafter was compounded by a narrowing of opportunity: every candidate was required to demonstrate his title to a benefice before ordination, ideally by having a living already in hand but otherwise (the position for the majority) by offering a surety in lieu of one. The supply of livings had proved insecure even before the turbulence of the post-Black Death decades, which also limited other forms of patronage. The purchase of a putative title to a benefice from a monastic patron for the purpose of ordination became widespread as a contingency of mutual benefit – as an additional source of income even the best endowed houses saw profit in it – but here too the demand outstripped the opportunities.[80] At the same time, the

---

recent case-studies see Clark, *Monastic renaissance*, pp. 15–16; Greatrex, 'Who were the monks of Rochester', p. 209, and in respect of women religious, M. Oliva, 'All in the family: monastic and clerical careers among family members in the late Middle Ages', *Medieval Prosopography*, 20 (1999), pp. 161–80.

[76] For genealogies among the secular clergy see Lepine, 'Origins and Careers of the canons of Exeter', pp. 112–13 (Exeter); McHardy, 'Careers and disappointments', pp. 126–7 at p. 127 (Hereford, Lincoln, Worcester).

[77] *Heads of Religious Houses*, ed. Smith, iii, pp. 323–7. See also Williams, *The Welsh Church.*, pp. 323–6.

[78] The verse on William Wheathampstead, 'et de suis avunculis nominis eiusdem: tres lactabantur ibidem', is preserved in the abbot's commonplace book, now Cambridge, Gonville & Caius College, MS 230, fo. 57r. For a further recollection in correspondence with the subprior of Tynemouth see *Registrum abbatiae*, i. pp. 311–26 at pp. 315–16: 'sumpsisti uitque in te laborem, nedum scribendi vitam et conversationem carissimi nostri avunculi, quinimmo etim miracula varia quae tam post mortem quam etiam in vita altissimo per ipsum placuit operari'.

[79] *Heads of religious houses*, ed. Smith, iii, pp. 264–5.

[80] For these developments see R.N. Swanson, 'Titles to orders in episcopal registers', in *Studies in Medieval History presented to R.H.C. Davis*, ed. H.M.R.E. Mayr-Harting and R.I. Moore (London, 1985), pp. 233–45. See also Cooper, *Last generation of English Catholic clergy*, pp. 19–29 at

practice of conflating minor orders to expedite progression to the priesthood, already apparent in the first quarter of the fourteenth century, created a new and narrower career structure that required candidates to satisfy the qualification for priesthood more-or-less from the outset.[81] Such an environment can scarcely have failed to invigorate interest in the monastic profession as a point-of-entry to the ranks of the clergy. At a time, perhaps the century after 1350 in particular, when it was readily apparent that men of monastic profession might hold the highest offices of the prelacy, the metropolitan see, even the cardinalate, there may have been a renewed recognition – for the first time in England for more than a century – of the monastic profession as a source of preferment, spiritual and even temporal influence.[82] It would appear that the more judicious, indeed strategic, saw the opportunity of a point-of-entry from which progression in the ecclesiastical hierarchy could be possible. William Wellys (d. 1443/4), closed his career occupying the see of Rochester; his will represents him as the consummate prelate, giving only a backward glance to his 'young days in monk's orders', at the Benedictine abbey of St Mary, York.[83]

The narrowing of entry-points to clerical office allowed for a greater importance to be attached to the learning of the candidate. There was at any rate an ongoing anxiety over the presence, and preferment, of candidates lacking even elementary schooling and, under the conditions prevailing from the mid fourteenth century, patrons were in a position to be strictly selective. At the same time, prospective clerks required patronage or resources of their own to pursue the higher studies – e.g. at least a taste of the university arts course – which might win them preferment: an episcopal licence *ad studendum* was a viable route to the schools only if the clerk had first secured a living.[84] In this respect, the monastery may have been recognised as rich in opportunities for learning. As the network of provincial schools narrowed in the first quarter of the fifteenth century, the burgeoning schoolrooms of the monastic almonry or precinct presented the best, perhaps the only, regional opportunity for schooling to the level of undergraduate study.[85] The colleges of the Benedictines rising in the centre of Oxford

pp. 19–20; Moran, 'Clerical recruitment', pp. 30–1; Cross, 'Ordinations in the diocese of York', pp. 6–7.

[81] Moran, 'Clerical recruitment', pp. 28–30, where in the late fifteenth century there is archiepiscopal intervention to scrutinise those who had rapidly progressed; Robinson, 'Clerical recruitment', pp. 52–3; Swanson, 'Titles to orders', pp. 239–40.

[82] For a summary of this trend see Knowles, *Religious orders*, ii, pp. 369–75: 'Appendix III, Regulars as bishops'.

[83] Wellys's will is dated 7 February 1443/4: Lambeth Palace Library, Reg. Stafford, fo. 122v–123r. See also Emden, *BRUO*, iii. 20212. M. Jurkowski, 'Wells, William (d. 1444), ODNB, 95173.' Despite a decade dedicated to the higher clergy, and the past tense inference to 'monk's orders', it appears he was never dispensed from his monastic vows.

[84] For a case study of clerks seeking study opportunities by such means see N. Bennett, 'Pastors and masters: the beneficed clergy of north-east Lincolnshire, 1290–1340', in *The foundations of medieval English ecclesiastical history: studies presented to David Smith*, ed. P.M. Hoskin, C.N.L. Brooke, and R.B. Dobson, Studies in the History of Medieval Religion 27 (Woodbridge, 2005), pp. 40–62 at pp. 49–52.

[85] For the case that provincial opportunities for education were contracting in the early fifteenth century see Moran, 'Education, economy and clerical mobility', pp. 194–5.

even before the Black Death demonstrated the scope for a secure academic career promised by a monastic profession.[86] Moreover, just as the monastery was recognised as a portal to the priesthood, there was also perhaps recognition that a temporary sojourn under vows might secure the academic status to propel a clerical career far beyond the precincts. Such was the route for James Berkeley, who began his clerical life at Kingswood abbey (Gloucestershire) but proceeded into the ranks of the secular clergy and entered the chapter at Exeter cathedral.[87] In fact the monastic authorities appear to have accepted, indeed encouraged the prospect, entering into collaborations with secular patrons, institutions and individuals, to make provision for students both at grammar school and at university. Both Christ Church cathedral priory and Worcester cathedral priory assisted Merton College, Oxford, in its early years.[88] The abbot and convent of Bruton (Somerset) entered into a conjoint endowment for a grammar school with Richard Fitzjames, bishop of London, who was also warden of Merton.[89] The co-patrons' expectation was surely that their endowments would generate parallel cohorts of clerks destined for the secular church and novices for their own convents.

The re-casting of the monastery in this period as a portal to a clerical career that might not be confined to the cloister brought a community of clerks, young men, unprofessed, unpriested into the precincts which itself may have served to stimulate interest in the monastic environment. Nobles and gentry now preferred to place their sons in the monastic *studia* at Oxford.[90] Certainly, a wide variety of clerks in this period chose the monastery as a place of settled residence, and it is possible it was not only its material benefits but the professional, clerical and learned society – and, it might be said the homosocial bonds that, at best, it afforded – that brought them there. Most did not make a monastic profession, although their close integration with the domestic life of the community is suggestive of a mode of living mid-way between lay brotherhood and an *ad succurrendum* conversion. Simon Bredon, a former fellow of Merton College, Oxford, died at Battle abbey in 1368 as a secular clerk, but the bequests of his will reflect final years lived alongside the professed men of the monastery.[91] Yet the scope to

---

[86] For a survey of this development see R.B. Dobson, 'The religious orders, 1270–1540', in *The history of the University of Oxford, II. Late medieval Oxford*, ed. J.I. Catto and T.A.R. Evans (Oxford, 1992), pp. 539–79.

[87] For Berkeley's career see *BRUO*, pp. 174–5. See also Lepine, 'Origins and careers of the canons of Exeter', p. 99.

[88] For Christ Church and Merton College see *Literae Cantuarienses*, ed. Sheppard, I, pp. 258, 287. For Worcester Priory see *Documents illustrating early education at Worcester, 685–1700*, ed. A.F. Leach, Worcestershire Historical Society (1913), pp. 42–4. See also *Liber ecclesiae Wigorniensis. A Letter Book of the Priors of Worcester*, ed. J.H. Bloom, Worcester Historical Society (1912), pp. 39–40.

[89] *VCH Somerset*, ii, pp. 134–8 at p. 136.

[90] J.I. Catto, 'Masters, patrons and the careers of graduates in fifteenth-century England', in *Concepts and patterns of service in the later Middle Ages*, ed. A. Curry and E. Matthew (Woodbridge, 2000), pp. 52–63 at p. 56.

[91] For Bredon and his will see F.M. Powicke, *The medieval books of Merton College* (Oxford, 1928), pp. 82–6.

practice their professional arts did lead a number of clerks as far as profession: it was the (presumably) scale and certainly the skill in music (for which it was renowned) that brought several clerical musicians to take the cowl at Canterbury in the fifteenth century.[92]

It should not be forgotten, of course, that, just as in any earlier period, these men chose to adopt a mode of life regulated – to a greater or lesser extent – by a set of spiritual precepts. Quite apart from the social pushes and occupational pulls that surely worked upon them in this period, it would be wrong to overlook the spiritual dimension. It is a truism that the personal spirituality of the professed is rarely revealed in the surviving records. The very essence of the monastic *ascèse* is to suppress the individual will, and its dominant idiom is one which consciously conceals any hint of personality. Where professed men have left spiritual reflections, letters, meditations and prayers, the verbal reminiscence of scriptural, patristic and monastic *formulae* tends to crowd out personal expression. One possible measure of their spiritual impulses is the requests, made at regular intervals throughout the period, to migrate to a different house of the same order, or to a different (regular) order.[93] The customary formula presents such requests as a search of a mode of life of greater (or lesser) rigour – 'vitam ducere arciorem' – in its personal and conventual regulation; when a greater or lesser house of the same order is sought, there is perhaps also the implication that it is not only a matter of the rigour of the rule but also the weight of the observant regime: monks from a provincial priory seeking to join the community of Christ Church, Canterbury, perhaps had in view the grand ceremonial of the premier Benedictine monastery.[94]

Among these requests are a number from established secular clerks seeking a monastic profession. The monks of Canterbury encountered schoolmen at Oxford whom it would appear were persuaded of the benefits of the monastic life while studying alongside them.[95] This might suggest there remained at least a trace of the conception of the monastic life as progression from the clerical office, articulated by the commentators who first confronted the proliferation of orders.[96] Another echo of the great era of monastic expansion which can be

---

[92] Their entry was recorded among the observations of John Stone: *Chronicle of John Stone*, ed. Searle, p. 12.

[93] For examples of such requests that required the grant of a papal dispensation, see *Calendar of papal registers relating to Great Britain and Ireland*, 5, *1398–1404* (London, 1904), pp. 346–7, 350 (John Abirford, monk of Pontefract (Cluniac) to transfer to any house of the order of St Benedict or St Augustine, 1400); Ralph de Byker, monk of St Mary Graces, to regularise his unlicensed transfer from Swineshead, 1401). For correspondence concerning such requests, dating from the fourteenth century, recorded in the registers of Canterbury cathedral priory, see *Literae Cantuarienses*, ed. Sheppard, ii, pp. 136–7, 326, 432, 485, 497.

[94] *Literae Cantuarienses*, ed. Sheppard, ii, p. 432. For the formulaic phrase see ibid., pp. 326, 497.

[95] Ibid., p. 136.

[96] See, for example, the view of the anonymous, secular, clerical author of the *Libellus de diversis ordinibus*, who perceived a spectrum, plotted by proximity to the world, and moving from the eremitical life to the threefold orders of monks and canons, closing with those canons that live among men ('qui inter homines habitant': *Libellus de diversis ordinibus qui sunt in aecclesia*, ed. G. Constable and B. Smith, Oxford Medieval Texts (Oxford, 1972), p. 117); also the conception

found in the later period are instances of profession *ad succurrendum*.⁹⁷ There is a suggestion that a Devon landowner ended his life under vows at Dunkeswell in the fourteenth century, albeit on the slender claim that later the abbey laid claim to his estates.⁹⁸ Famously, Henry IV's valued envoy ('erat in seculo vir magnus et potens, magneque fame et officii in curia domus regis'), John Kynton, lived his last six years as a professed monk at Canterbury.⁹⁹ References to a youth professed in the infirmary chapel, and to a mother seeking to retrieve the bed that belonged to her dead son, professed at Stratford, may be the remains of *ad succurrendum* story that is not so well preserved.¹⁰⁰

These requests also testify to the number of professed men whose spiritual impulses remained unfocused and who were resigned to an unstable life in search of a clerical occupation to which they were suited. For example, Ralph de Byker, a monk of Swineshead (Cistercian: Lincolnshire) absconded after a searching visitation in which he had been cited for irregularity and made for the abbey of St Mary Graces, where he renewed his profession and sought to start his regular life afresh; eighteen-year-old Thomas Twyning, a monk of Winchcombe (Benedictine: Gloucester) who had 'laudably lived for some time as a professed monk' left the abbey and 'wandered about for about four months', during which time he acted irregularly as a celebrant of holy offices, that is as a secular clerk, but then determined to re-enter the monastery; William Everton, a professed Carthusian, migrated from house to house in the English congregation, and counted the cost at the close of his career, deprived of the conventual vote in his final community at Hull.¹⁰¹ Such cases were not confined to the later period of monastic history: at the height of the monastic expansion of the twelfth century, the Cistercian Walter Daniel lamented the 'rolling stones' who wandered the monastic landscape in search of spiritual fulfilment.¹⁰² It may be that such a tendency had returned in a period which had witnessed a diversification and invigoration of the devotional scene and (though there was no proliferation of

---

of the schoolman turned regular canon, Alexander Nequam from his commentary on the Song of Songs: 'vita claustralium media est inter vita scolarium sors ultima est delitiosa iocunditas vite triumphantium, media tranquillitas claustralium': R.W. Hunt, *The schools and the cloister. The life and writings of Alexander Nequam* (Oxford, 1984), p. 9, n. 43.

97 For the concept of profession *ad succurrendum* see G. Constable, *The reformation of the twelfth century* (Cambridge, 1998), p. 82. See also J.H. Lynch, *Simoniacal entry into religious life from 1000 to 1260. A social, economic and legal study* (Columbus, OH, 1976), pp. 27–36.

98 J.A. Sparks, *In the shadow of the Blackdowns. Life at the Cistercian abbey of Dunkeswell and on its manors and estates, 1201–1539* (Bradford on Avon, 1978), pp. 46–7.

99 *Chronicle of John Stone*, ed. Searle, p. 7. See also Greatrex, BRECP, 216.

100 *Chronicle of John Stone*, ed. Searle, p. 12. See also a man in the first year of his profession dying in the sacrist's chamber: p. 114; TNA, C1/874/21: Elizabeth Parys pursues Abbot William Huddilston of Stratford, 1533x1538.

101 *CPL, 5: 1398–1404*, pp. 346–7; *CPL, 12: 1458–1471*, pp. 510–11. For Everton see J. Hogg, 'Everyday life in a contemplative order in the fifteenth century', in *Medieval mystical tradition: England, Ireland and Wales: Exeter Symposium VI: papers read at Charney Manor, July 1999*, ed. M. Glasscoe (Cambridge, 1999), pp. 62–76 at p. 67.

102 *The Life of Ailred of Rievaulx by Walter Daniel*, ed. F.M. Powicke, Nelson's Medieval Classics (London, 1950), c. 29 (p. 37): 'et utique illi qui vagantes in seculo quibus nullus locus religionis prestabat ingressum'.

foundations) a widening distinction between the monastic orders, the oldest and the self-consciously reformed.

*

At the last moment before making his profession, the postulant monk was required to affirm his desire to enter the monastic life. As he knelt on the chancel step the presiding superior demanded, 'What desyr ye?', 'To be mad broder'. 'Ys it your wyl and your hertey desire to be parte takr of all . . . dedes don yn thys holy plas?'. 'Ye', was the expected response.[103] While it is likely the ceremony had changed little from earlier times (other than the language in which it was spoken, or recorded), the postulant of later medieval England may have been propelled to this point by forces that carried something of a different emphasis to those that acted on his forebears. The monastery could no longer be seen as part of a new and expanding movement. Now it was a symbol of antiquity and continuity, and, particularly at a time of internal conflict and external threat, of national identity, a point-of-contact with the country's social and spiritual heritage, but it was no less powerful for that. Where men had 'swarmed' (as Orderic Vitalis had observed) to the new foundations of the twelfth century to eschew the burdens of the secular world, on the contrary, it would appear the postulants of late medieval England saw in their profession the possibility of securing, perhaps extending, their social enterprise. Those converts of the 'monastic century' were seeking to place themselves among a self-conscious spiritual *avant garde* but for the generations after the Black Death it was the promise of a conventional clerical progression (and its rewards) that drew men towards the precincts. It has been suggested that clerical identity proved ever less compelling in the later Middle Ages as the special capacities of clerk (whether secular or regular) could now be realised without recourse either to orders or vows.[104] Such a view overlooks the constraints on academic, professional and family opportunities which were palpable for the generations that followed the Black Death. The prospect of monastic profession was now that of an assured route to the rewards of elite male adulthood. This is not to suggest that men who made their profession in the years before the Reformation lacked the fervour of their forebears. Although the traces of what they thought are faint, and what they read and wrote only fragmentary, there is circumstantial evidence of spiritual impulses that were sincere and sustained, if sometimes also misapplied and unfulfilled even after a lifetime in religion. In fact these generations were distinguished from their forebears by the course of their careers. They were, with few exceptions, lifetime religious. They entered the cloister as youths when they completed their schooling, they became monks before they advanced far in clerical orders and certainly before they became priests; they were monks at an age when they could scarcely claim their

---

[103] These instructions are preserved in 'collation book' of the Benedictine priory of Tywardreath (Cornwall), now Cornwall Record Office, RS/60, fos. 37r-38r. For a discussion and partial transcript see also G. Oliver, *Monasticon Dioecesis Exoniensis* (Exeter, 1846), pp. 33-47 at p. 36.

[104] R.N. Swanson, 'Angels incarnate: clergy and masculinity from the Gregorian reform to the Reformation', in *Masculinity in medieval Europe*, ed. D.M. Hadley (London, 1999), pp. 160-77 at p. 195.

majority in the secular world. As such it might be said that these men assumed a monastic identity with a completeness unmatched in earlier eras except by the minority (in an English context) whose formation began as infant oblates. While their monastic estate enabled them to exercise forms of clerical, social, even seigniorial authority, it did not necessarily erode their identity as professed religious: even the last generation of English monks, some of whom had entered only months before the suppression, still identified themselves by their name in religion or their original monastic office to the very end of their lives.[105]

---

[105] For example, John Bromsgrove alias Barret, former prior of Deerhurst (Gloucestershire) who identifies himself by his monastic toponym in his will of 1545: TNA, PCC, Prob. 11/30, fo. 335r-v; Richard Page, former Augustinian prior of Ivychurch (Wiltshire), who retained his title four years later in the will he made as prebend of Upavon in 1540: TNA, PCC, Prob. 11/28, fo. 11v; John Stoneywell, former abbot of Pershore, who remembered in 1551 the suffragan title *in partibus* he had claimed during his abbacy: TNA, PCC, Prob. 11/37, fo. 218r.

FEASTING NOT FASTING: MEN'S DEVOTION TO THE EUCHARIST IN THE LATER MIDDLE AGES[1]

P.H. Cullum

At the time of writing it is twenty-five years since Caroline Walker Bynum published *Holy feast, holy fast: the religious significance of food to medieval women*; it has remained highly influential in the field of lay piety, and a major landmark in the historiography that argues for a distinctive feminine piety in the Middle Ages.[2] But in the absence of an exploration of male devotion, and particularly eucharistic devotion or devotion to the person of Christ, the extent to which that can be defined as a distinctively feminine form of piety, as opposed to a form of piety which was distinctively medieval, will remain unclear. This essay will explore both the historiographical significance of the book and also address evidence of men's (both lay and clerical) devotion to the Eucharist and the body of Christ. One of the areas of medieval masculinity which has received relatively little attention is the nature or extent of specifically masculine forms of piety.[3] While female and feminine piety has received extensive attention over the last thirty years, and there has also been very extensive treatment of the forms of an ungendered lay piety, there has been very little attention to men's experience as men. Very often that piety has been simply normalised or universalised. It may, of course, be that that is appropriate, and that there was no specifically masculine piety in the later Middle Ages, in which case we would also need to consider whether there was a specifically feminine form of piety, but unless we ask the question, we will not discover the answer. In the event that we consider

---

[1] I would like to thank Nicole Harding for her work as a research assistant on this project.

[2] Caroline Walker Bynum, *Holy feast and holy fast: the religious significance of food to medieval women* (Berkeley, Los Angeles and London, 1987).

[3] W.M. Ormrod, 'The personal religion of Edward III', *Speculum* 64 (1989), pp. 849–77; Katherine J. Lewis, 'Becoming a virgin king: Richard II and Edward the Confessor', Samantha J.E. Riches, 'St George as virgin martyr', Patricia Cullum, 'Gendering charity in medieval hagiography', all in *Gender and holiness: men, women and saints in late medieval Europe*, ed. Samantha J.E. Riches and Sarah Salih (London, 2001); Becky R. Lee, 'Men's recollections of a women's rite: medieval English men's recollections regarding the rite of the purification of women after childbirth', *Gender & History* 14:2 (2002), pp. 224–41; Christina M. Fitzgerald, *Drama of masculinity and medieval English guild culture* (Gordonsville, VA, 2007); Katherine J. Lewis, 'Male saints and devotional masculinity in late medieval England', *Gender & History* 24:1 (2012), pp. 112–33.

that there was a feminised piety then there must have been some kind or kinds of masculinised piety, even if we do not necessarily tie those styles to sexed bodies.

In *Holy feast and holy fast* Caroline Walker Bynum was interested in exploring the significance of food and fasting to medieval women's experience of religion. It was a follow up to her earlier book on an aspect of male devotion, *Jesus as mother*, and was thus a further exploration of the interplay of gender and religion.[4] The book was also written contemporaneously with Rudolf Bell's *Holy anorexia* which suggests a broader cultural concern with women's relationship with food and its rejection.[5] Bynum argues that late medieval women's piety was predicated on their role as mothers and household providers. As mothers, women nourished children with their own bodies and as housewives they cooked for and fed their households. As devotees they desired or identified with the suffering body of Christ in the Passion directly or sought union through the medium of the bread and wine of the Eucharist. However priestly control of the Eucharist meant that access to the consecrated host was limited, and led to women hungering for it. Moreover cultural perceptions of women as particularly sinful led them to prioritise a penitential form of piety involving them in privation and self-deprivation, particularly of food, in an *imitatio Christi*, offering up the resulting suffering to God as an act of devotion.[6]

This enabled women to access God directly on the spiritual level and paradoxically acted as a source of power. Their humility could be seen as identical with Christ's, and could allow them to access similar power. Claims to direct contact with God were supported by phenomena such as prolonged fasting, trances, and absence of menstruation, and could bring spiritual influence over clergy. Control over food was one of the few powers that women had, and they could make choices about how it was to be used. Refusal of the role of wife and mother by adoption of chastity, or distribution of food and other family resources to the poor, disrupted the power of fathers, husbands and priests. Refusal of food could be used to bargain for access to the Eucharist, or for control of the woman's body by taking vows.[7]

Although much of the above could be seen as involving an essentialist reading of gender, Bynum argues that medieval deployment of gender ideas was more fluid and complex. Clergy distributing the food of the Eucharist could be seen to be performing a female role. Christ's body itself could be seen as feminised: covered in wounds, it bled like a woman; the wound in the side lactated like a mother. Mary could act as a priest, celebrating the Mass and priests could be pregnant with the Host. But Bynum argues that unlike men women did not think in terms of dichotomies and oppositions, but in unities, expressing

---

[4] Caroline Walker Bynum, *Jesus as mother: studies in the spirituality of the High Middle Ages* (Berkeley, Los Angeles, 1985).
[5] Rudolph Bell, *Holy anorexia* (Chicago, 1985); Hilde Bruch, *The golden cage: the enigma of anorexia nervosa* (Cambridge, MA, 1978) helped to establish the concept in public understanding and the death in 1983 of Karen Carpenter, the popular musician, after a well publicised battle with the eating disorder, created an interest in the wider American culture.
[6] Bynum, *Holy feast and holy fast*, pp. 277–9.
[7] Ibid., pp. 279–93.

spiritual matters through the body.[8] All of the above created a powerful paradigm of female piety in the Middle Ages that was mystical, eucharistically-focussed and penitential, with a particular focus on food denial. The implication of this for masculine devotion would presumably be that it would not be eucharistic, though it might well be focused on the person of Christ, that it would not be particularly penitential, and that it would relate to resources over which men had control and incorporate other conventional elements of masculine identity.

The book was generally very positively received at the time in a broad range of disciplines, and it has been very influential on subsequent work in the field.[9] There has been a very considerable body of work on women's religion published in the last quarter century, far more than there has been on masculine religion, and much of it focused on areas that Bynum signalled as important, though it has not all accepted her construction of female piety.[10] There has been some critique of aspects of Bynum's work. Kathleen Biddick has challenged the presentism of the model of gender used, and has also argued that numbers of the images which Bynum used as illustration have been misunderstood or taken out of context, and rather than demonstrating female eucharistic devotion are actually anti-semitic narratives of host desecration.[11] Karma Lochrie, too has been critical of the tendency to essentialise and ahistoricise the relationship between body, sexuality and gender.[12]

One of the issues for scholars seeking to address masculine devotion to the Eucharist and the person of Christ is the terms in which Bynum expressed the experiences of her female subjects. The erotic component of significant elements of that devotion can read very awkwardly to a modern audience when translated to male subjects as it appears to suggest a homoerotic relationship between the

---

[8] Ibid., pp. 294–6.

[9] Reviews include: Carole M. Counihan, *American Anthropologist*, new series, 90:1 (1988), pp. 230–2; Glenn W. Olsen, *Church History* 57:2 (1988), pp. 225–7; Retha M. Warnicke, *Journal of the American Academy of Religion* 56:3 (1988), pp. 562–4; Judith C. Brown, *American Historical Review* 94:3 (1989), pp. 735–7; Ann G. Carmichael, *Journal of Interdisciplinary History* 19:4 (1989), pp. 635–44; Rita Copeland, *Speculum* 64:1 (1989), pp. 143–7; Jack Goody, *English Historical Review* 105:415 (1990), pp. 429–31; Julia M.H. Smith, *Social History of Medicine* 3:1 (1990), pp. 107–8.

[10] An indicative and not remotely comprehensive list includes: *Women and power in the Middle Ages*, ed. Mary Erler and Maryanne Kowaleski (London,1989); *Woman is a worthy wight: women in English society c.1200-1500*, ed. P.J.P. Goldberg (Stroud, 1992); *Studying medieval women: sex, gender, feminism*, ed. Nancy F. Partner (Cambridge, MA, 1993); Elizabeth Alvilda Petroff, *Body and soul: essays on medieval women and mysticism* (Oxford, 1994); Gail McMurray Gibson, *Theatre of devotion: East Anglian drama and society in the late Middle Ages* (Chicago, 1995); David Aers and Lynn Staley, *The powers of the holy: religion, politics and gender in late medieval English culture* (Philadelphia, 1996); Jocelyn Wogan-Browne, *Saints' lives and women's literary culture, 1150-1300: virginity and its authorizations* (Oxford, 2001); Christine Peters, *Patterns of piety: women, gender and religion in late medieval and Reformation England* (Cambridge, 2003); Katherine L. French, *The good women of the parish: gender and religion after the Black Death* (Philadelphia, 2007).

[11] Kathleen Biddick, 'Genders, bodies, borders: technologies of the visible', *Speculum* 68: 2 (1993), pp. 389–418.

[12] Karma Lochrie, *Margery Kempe and translations of the flesh* (Philadelphia, 1991), p. 3.

male devotee and the figure of Christ. For those commentators committed religiously or culturally to a 'straight' reading of masculine devotion or indeed to the person of Christ, this is an area very difficult to negotiate. Leo Steinberg's *The sexuality of Christ* has made a convincing case that the body of Christ in much medieval art is to be understood as an explicitly sexed body and that the display of his penis is a device for emphasising Christ's incarnation, his manhood.[13] As Richard Rambuss shows, Steinberg is himself resistant to any non-heterosexual reading of these images, an approach which has been questioned by some scholars working from a queer theory perspective.[14] Much of the work done on queer readings of devotion to Christ has been by writers who position themselves as Renaissance or early modern scholars rather than as medievalists, and their work can therefore escape the attention of medievalists.[15] Nevertheless, Robert Mills has shown that Bernard of Clairvaux, Rupert of Deutz, Francis of Assisi and Richard Rolle had experiences of the crucified Christ which can be understood in homoerotic terms, involving addressing Christ as lover, embracing and kissing him and describing a penetration by his charity.[16] Garrett P.J. Epp argues that the (homo)sexually attractive body of Christ is not just an invention of modern scholars but a concern of the Lollard *Tretise of Miraclis Pleying*.[17] My purpose in this essay is not to engage in a debate about whether these devotional acts can or should be seen as erotic, whether hetero- or homosexual, or whether bodies and souls should be aligned to enforce or disrupt heteronormative readings, but to show both some of the difficulties that have confronted scholars seeking to explore masculine piety, and that medieval men could and did have devotional experiences which were expressed in terms very similar to those used by medieval women. Desire was, however, not the only way in which medieval men could relate to the person of Christ. Identification with the human Christ was also a possibility, which avoided the problem of desire, an approach which will be further discussed later in the essay.

In this essay I will not try to replicate for a male cohort of saints and holy men the kind of study that Bynum did of the religious women of late medieval Europe, not least because the mass of material involved would be too great to manage in a relatively short space. Despite the fact that there was a significant growth in the number and proportion of women who were canonised or considered for canonisation during this period, they were not a majority, whatever the impression given by the focus on female sanctity in recent historiography.[18] Instead I will

---

[13] Leo Steinberg, *The sexuality of Christ in Renaissance art and modern oblivion* (New York, 1983; revised edn. Chicago, 1996).

[14] Richard Rambuss, *Closet devotions* (Durham, NC, and London, 1998), p. 138.

[15] Or indeed be marginalised as belonging to an 'other' chronological period.

[16] Robert Mills, 'Ecce homo', in *Gender and holiness: men, women and saints in late medieval Europe*, ed. Samantha J.E. Riches and Sarah Salih (London, 2002), pp. 152-4.

[17] Garrett P.J. Epp, 'Ecce homo', in *Queering the Middle Ages*, ed. Glenn Burger and Steven F. Kruger (Minneapolis, 2001), pp. 236-41.

[18] While the majority of lay saints canonised during the period 1198-1431 were women (55.5%) and an even higher proportion after 1305, their numbers were significantly smaller than those of the clergy considered for sainthood, and taken together, over the period 1198-1431, 85.7% of

explore the practice of religion in one corner of late medieval Europe: England. In the process I will consider a range of individuals and groups, some of whom had a contemporary reputation for sanctity, others of whom simply participated in the dominant religious practice of their time and place. As a result I hope to be able to say something not only about the exceptional piety of the saintly but also the conventional piety of the majority.

In the cases which Mills cites there are clear parallels between the experiences of male and female devotees, and I want to explore the writing of one of these, Richard Rolle (c.1305x10–1349), the pre-eminent English mystic, as a helpful case for exploring masculine piety.[19] Rolle occupied a position that was at once marginal to the conventions of ecclesiastical life and was to become central to formulations of late medieval English mystical piety. Rolle's social background was of the upper levels of the peasantry and, like some of the monks discussed by James Clark in his essay in this volume, he was assisted to an education, though by the son of a local lord, Thomas Neville, archdeacon of Durham, rather than a monastic house. He gave up on a university career before completing his degree or being ordained, however, instead adopting the life of a hermit.[20] He was thus neither cleric nor entirely layman, and as such he can be seen to have rejected conventional forms of clerical masculinity, which focused on the ability to celebrate the Mass. However this adoption of a resistant form of masculinity, which may have been in part an *imitatio Christi or via unitiva*, was itself to be highly influential through his devotional writings in both English and Latin, which were to be hugely popular with both lay and clerical audiences and are among the most frequently copied of medieval texts in England.[21] As Michael Satlow has argued earlier in this volume, a rejection of hegemonic practice could lead

---

those canonised were male. André Vauchez, *Sainthood in the later Middle Ages*, trans. Jean Birrell (Cambridge, 1997; orig. pub. 1988), pp. 267–9.

[19] Although Hughes suggests he was born c. 1305–10, other writers have suggested that he was older, perhaps born around 1290. Rolle was considered a saint at Hampole priory which celebrated an office for him and where he was the object of pilgrimage and a thaumaturge, but possible ambivalence about some of his teachings among some senior clergy of the diocese meant that no attempt was made to have him formally canonised. Jonathan Hughes, 'Rolle, Richard (1305 x 10–1349)', *Oxford dictionary of national biography* [ODNB] (Oxford, 2004); online edn, May 2008 [http://www.oxforddnb.com/view/article/24024, accessed 13 November 2012].

[20] His description of himself as 'not a rector' is ambiguous, and could simply mean that he had been ordained but not beneficed, but the absence of reference to other aspects of priestly activity and his lack of any formal appointment, despite patrons who might have been able to provide a benefice, suggests that he never progressed beyond minor orders. See also James G. Clark, 'Why men became monks in late medieval England' in this volume, p. 174.

[21] Jonathan Hughes, *Pastors and visionaries: religion and secular life in late medieval Yorkshire* (Woodbridge, 1988), p. 90. In this book Hughes assumed that Rolle was priested but he had changed his mind by the publication of the ODNB entry above. The object of the mystical life was the union with God. While Rolle was only a beginner on the mystical journey at the point when he dropped out of university and became a hermit, he may well have seen the rejection of the conventional rewards of clerical masculinity as a necessary ascetic preparation on the road to union with God. In this he may have been imitating St Francis of Assisi, that other mystic who did not proceed to major orders, and who also dramatically rejected the demands and rewards of hegemonic lay masculinity.

in later generations to a reformulation of hegemonic discourse, and as Catherine Sanok shows, by the early fifteenth century an element of mystical devotion had become incorporated into the lives of both laymen and clergy.[22]

Rolle appears not to have had much time for attendance at Mass on the grounds that it interfered with his spiritual experience of *canor*, or heavenly song.[23] In this he may be seen to depart from eucharistically focussed forms of piety but this is a logical expression of his preference for the spiritual over the material forms of devotion. It may also of course relate to his own inability as a layman to celebrate Mass for himself, or even to the relatively undeveloped state of Corpus Christi devotions in England during Rolle's lifetime.[24] It has been argued that the eucharistic focus of much late medieval female piety was predicated on women's dependence on priests to receive the sacrament, and priests' reluctance to provide it on demand. As a layman, Rolle was presumably in a similar position and his privileging of spiritual experience may be a way of bypassing priestly control of the Eucharist as some women had by envisioning themselves receiving the Eucharist directly from Christ's hands, as Colette of Corbie did.[25] There is however no evidence that Rolle saw himself receiving the Eucharist in this fashion, not least because his experience of the presence of God meant that he did not need this mediated form of contact.

While Rolle's mystical experience has often been described as abstract, focusing on the heat, sweetness and song of God's love (and therefore by implication superior to the more embodied spirituality of female mystics such as Margery Kempe) that is not to say that he could not write in more concrete terms for a lay audience. He wrote a *Meditations on the Passion* in English which describes the suffering of Christ at the Crucifixion:

> þou lyst rowyd and reed streyned on þe cros, þe kene crowne on þin hede, þat sytteth þe so sore; þi is so bolnyd, þat first was so faire; þi synwes and þi bonys stertyn owte starke, þat þi bonys may be nowmbryd; þe stremys of þi reede blood rennyn as þe flood; þi woundys are for-bled and grisly on to se.[26]

It matters less whether this represents Rolle's own experience of mystical vision than that he thought it appropriate to a lay devotion, and thus it may tell us more about a popular understanding of devotion to the Passion than some of Rolle's more personal texts.

This text while focussed on the Crucifixion is not obviously eucharistic in form, and while it refers to the body and blood of Christ, it does not use that

---

[22] Michael Satlow, 'From salve to weapon', above, p. 16–17; Catherine Sanok, 'John of Bridlington, mitred prior and model of the mixed life', above, p. 152.
[23] '(Q)uando necessitas misse audiende exigeret, quam alibi audire non poteram, aut dies solempnis cogeret, propter obliquos morsus populorum', from Rolle's *Contra amatores mundi*: Rolle, *English writings of Richard Rolle, hermit of Hampole,* ed. Hope Emily Allen (Oxford, 1931), p. li.
[24] The feast of Corpus Christi was first promulgated in the diocese of York in 1322, but celebration of the feast does not seem to have become common until the 1360s, after Rolle's death.
[25] Bynum, *Holy feast and holy fast*, p. 139.
[26] Rolle, *English writings*, p. 24.

phrase and there is no reference to bread or wine. When, in the last part of the second meditation, he does describe the body of Christ metaphorically, it is as a heaven full of stars, a net full of holes to catch the fish of his soul, a dovehouse, a meadow, a book, and in a rare food image, a honeycomb: 'for hit is in euche way full of cellis, and euch cell ful of hony, so þat hit may nat be touched without yeld of swetnesse'.[27] Elsewhere he does refer to the crucified body as 'faire aungels fode' and 'when aungels brede was dampned to dede' but this makes it not bread for human consumption and so is again not eucharistic.[28]

In the introduction to his translation of the Psalter into English he writes in a more abstract fashion, describing the 'Grete habundans of gastly conforth and ioy comes in þe hertes of þaime þat says or synges devoutly þe psalms in lovyne of Jhesu Crist. Þai drop swetnes in mans saule ... and kyndelis þaire willes with þe fire of luf.'[29] The reference to sweetness is characteristic of his work and similar to the language used by female mystics. Although much of his writing in English focuses on the Crucifixion the majority of his writing describes the joy of the love of God.

Although Rolle does refer to penitential forms of behaviour, including fasting, he did not consider these particularly useful, despite suffering criticism when he returned to eating after periods of fasting.[30] Elsewhere he offers advice to the novice at meditation to remain 'indefatigably seated' while ruminating on the memory of sweetness.[31] To do otherwise was to risk fatigue of the body which might interfere with the ability to contemplate.[32]

Rolle's piety thus has some similarities with the female mystics who are Bynum's subjects but also notable differences: the focus on the person of Christ, the concern with the suffering of the Passion and the experience of sweetness are similar but this does not seem to have been eucharistically focussed: food images and practices, and penance are of limited interest. But equally it is not clear that there is anything specifically masculine about his piety. However one way in which his practice can be seen as specifically masculine is in his writing of didactic material, some of it in Latin. Both men and women wrote (or in the case of some female mystics, dictated) devotional literature, but explicitly instructional material, which involved claims to authority were much more commonly written by men. Rolle's writings in Latin were addressed primarily to a clerical audience, whereas his writings in English were in part for a lay audience which was not clearly gender differentiated, and in part for specific women religious. However the fact that his *Incendium amoris* was translated into English as the *Fire of love*

---

[27] Ibid., pp. 34–5.
[28] 'A song of love-longing to Jesus', ibid., pp. 42–4.
[29] Ibid., p. 4.
[30] 'Quippe sic carnem modo maceravi et caput contunditur dolore deducto quod consistere non queo, ita gravatur, nisi [corroborer] sanante cibario'. *The Melos Amoris of Richard Rolle of Hampole*, ed. E.J.F. Arnold, (Oxford, 1957), p. 106.
[31] '(M)editacionemque mellifluam in memoria retinens et ruminans, non pro modico mobilis quemadmodum stulti qui non stabiliuntur, sed sollicitus infatigabiliter sederit', ibid., p. 35.
[32] 'Sessio solatur sanctos. Contemplativi capiunt canticum quiescentes, canorum gaudium gerunt; nam, fatigato corpore, cor iam in canore non calet quietum', ibid., p. 12.

Feasting not fasting

by the Carmelite Richard Misyn in 1435 suggests that there was a lay audience for this text and that language, did not, at least by the 1430s, reflect a difference in practice between laity and clergy.[33] This would support the argument made by Catherine Sanok in her essay in this volume that religious masculinity was relatively undifferentiated by the 1430s, although that may not have been the case a century earlier.[34]

Bynum puts a lot of emphasis on the argument that women were particularly eucharistically focused and sought union with Christ through reception of communion, a desire which was heightened by the restrictions placed on frequent communication by clergy who feared its devaluation if it were too readily accessible. Those men in priestly orders however did not have the problem of gatekeepers restricting their access. Priests celebrated a daily Mass and so were able to receive the Eucharist whenever they chose. As such hungering after reception was less likely to be an issue for them. It may thus be difficult to demonstrate eucharistic piety for priests. However the existence of licences to celebrate Mass or to have it celebrated in their own home, and thus the ability to attend Mass on multiple occasions during the day, issued to clergy as well as to laypeople, such as the licences issued in 1437 in the diocese of Exeter to Sir John Wilet, rector of Trevalga, to celebrate in any suitable place in his house, and to the prior of St Germans, to have divine service celebrated by himself or others in his presence and that of his household, suggest a desire for the Eucharist or at least to be present at the making of the body of Christ, that could not be satisfied by a single daily encounter with the body of Christ.[35]

Given that celebration of the Mass was a central part of a priest's job description, piety and professionalism cannot easily be distinguished, and the tendency in much secondary literature on the clergy is to see them as professionally rather than piously orientated. However as Marita von Weissenberg argues elsewhere in this collection, appropriate performance of office could be an intrinsic element of masculine piety, and other licences issued to clergy, which are not about personal devotion but about provision of the Mass to parishioners who might otherwise be unable to access it, demonstrate the point.[36] In 1436, Sir Richard Kestell, vicar of Lowan, had a licence for divine service to be celebrated by himself or his parochial chaplain, in any chapel, oratory or other suitable place in the diocese, and Sir William Blygh, parochial chaplain of Bickington, had permission to celebrate twice in a day, in his own chapel and at Buckland-in-the-moor, on Sundays and holy days, until Michaelmas.[37]

---

[33] Richard Copsey, 'Misyn, Richard (d. 1462)', ODNB, online edn. [http://www.oxforddnb.com/view/article/18823, accessed 15 November 2012].

[34] Catherine Sanok, 'John of Bridlington, mitred prior and model of the mixed life', in this volume, pp. 153–5.

[35] *The register of Edmund Lacy, bishop of Exeter, 1420–55, Registrum Commune*, ed. G.R. Dunstan, Canterbury and York Society, II (1966), pp. 46–7.

[36] Marita von Weissenberg, '"What man are you?": piety and masculinity in the *vitae* of a Sienese craftsman and a Provençal nobleman', in this volume pp. 114–15.

[37] *Register of Edmund Lacy*, pp. 5, 33.

P.H. Cullum

In some cases commemorative brasses may give a clue to the devotional interests of clergy who have otherwise left no record of their personal devotion. The most frequently surviving brasses of East Anglia from this period are chalice brasses.[38] Chalice brasses are interesting because they may display the chalice alone or with a wafer; the former is particularly significant because although it signals the priest's function it also indicates that part of the Eucharist, the wine, which was reserved to the celebrant. The wafer, which can also be found displayed in clerical brasses, had to be shared (at least on some occasions) with the congregation, but the wine did not, so while the wafer is a sign of a professional role, the chalice alone may be more likely to indicate a personal devotion. Brasses for the parish clergy typically show them in Mass vestments but not all show them carrying the sacred elements. An anonymous late fourteenth-century brass from North Mimms in Hertfordshire shows a priest in prayer under a canopy, while the contemporary image of Simon de Wensley, of Wensley in North Yorkshire, shows him with a chalice but no wafer; and the mid fifteenth-century brass of Robert Lond at St Peter's, Bristol, shows him holding both chalice and wafer.[39] At Newton Regis, Warwickshire, the early fourteenth-century incised slab of a rector, possibly John de la Warde, shows a half-figure image accompanied by a chalice, a book, and acolytes with tapers. Saul suggests that the location of the monument, in a niche to the north of the altar, would have allowed it to be used as an Easter Sepulchre.[40] This would have meant that every Easter the rector would have shared the tomb of Christ. Here personal devotion, public performance as a priest and provision of a continuing liturgical resource for his parishioners were all bound up together. Even more than those priests who took chalice and paten into the grave so that they could return to ministering to their flock at the resurrection, this man's identity as pastor would continue to bind him and his parishioners together.

Food is central to Bynum's argument about women's piety but it played a role in men's religiosity and performance of masculinity too. However, for men it was not self-deprivation which was central (though there is a little evidence for that) but a combination of the display of generosity and *imitatio Christi*.[41] In the Luttrell Psalter, contemporary with Richard Rolle's writing, the most important set of images is the one that culminates in Geoffrey Luttrell at table with his wife and son, two Dominicans, and another couple, perhaps relatives, perhaps members of the household, or perhaps, and this is what I will suggest, guests.[42] In the

---

[38] Nigel Saul, *English church monuments in the Middle Ages: history and representation* (Oxford, 2009), p. 197.
[39] Muriel Clayton, *Victoria and Albert Museum catalogue of rubbings of brasses and incised slabs*, 2nd edn (London, 1929), plate 54.
[40] Saul, *Church monuments*, p. 204.
[41] Charles de Blois had a reputation for eating moderately and fasting on all the vigils of major feasts. Vauchez, *Sainthood*, p. 364.
[42] A high quality virtual Luttrell Psalter can be found at http://www.bl.uk/collections/treasures/luttrell/luttrell_broadband.htm. The feast is at fo. 208r. The food preparation scenes are fos. 206r-207v. Michael Camille argued that the diners represent the *familia* or household, and that the couple represent Geoffrey's younger son, and the wife of the older son. Michael Camille, *Mirror*

preceding pages there are scenes of the preparation of the meal in the kitchen, so food is important to this display. Camille interprets this as a feast, probably the Epiphany feast, on the basis of the presence of the Dominicans as guests, and the food that he identifies being served.[43] However there are problems with this identification. As he acknowledges, the feasters are remarkably serious, and there is not actually very much food on the table.[44] A more plausible argument is that this is not just a lord's table but it is the Lord's Table, that is it is both Geoffrey Luttrell feasting and also the Last Supper, for which a sober demeanour would be appropriate.[45] Emmerson and Goldberg point to the large silver dish in front of Sir Geoffrey marked with a cross like a wafer, and the cup in Sir Geoffrey's hand, which pose him like Christ in a number of Last Supper images.[46] Neither discussion refers to the prominence of bread on the table, which would also tend to support Eucharistic associations.[47] There are strong visual parallels with Dieric Bouts the elder's painting, *Altarpiece of the Holy Sacrament* (1464–67). This painting, commissioned to celebrate the two-hundredth anniversary of the institution of the feast of Corpus Christi by the Confraternity of the Holy Trinity Louvain, includes four fifteenth-century figures, generally considered to represent the senior figures of the guild.[48] These four are all stationed in service roles, around the table or in the next room, demonstrating their devotion to Christ but also their responsibility for provision of the meal.

The early fifteenth-century *Instructions for a devout and literate layman*, a rare survival of a devotional text written as a daily regimen for a specific but unknown layman, shares some features with the Luttrell Psalter.[49] While attendance at the parish church was an important part of the man's morning routine, a significant part of the text was taken up with dinner. Before and after dining he was to say grace standing, then to think on the words 'Hail Mary' during dinner, though this could only be intermittent as he was also to be busy with other acts: when he took a drink he was to say 'in the name of the Father' and to make the sign of the Cross; the household was to eat in silence and he was to

in parchment: the Luttrell Psalter, and the making of medieval England (London, 1998), pp. 83 and 95.

[43] Camille, *Mirror in parchment*, pp. 87–9.
[44] Ibid.
[45] R. Emmerson and P.J.P. Goldberg, '"The Lord Geoffrey had me made": lordship and labour in the Luttrell Psalter', in *The problem of labour in fourteenth-century England*, ed. James Bothwell, P.J.P. Goldberg and W.M. Ormrod (York, 2000), pp. 52–3.
[46] Ibid.
[47] The relative lack of other food on the table is explained by the need to emphasise this as a Last Supper, but the preceding pages make it clear that Geoffrey Luttrell is a generous host.
[48] The painting can be seen via the Web Gallery of Art at http://www.wga.hu/index1.html.
[49] W.A. Pantin, 'Instructions for a devout and literate layman', in *Medieval learning and literature: essays presented to Richard William Hunt*, ed. J.J.G. Alexander and M.T. Gibson (Oxford, 1976), pp. 398-401. The Latin text does not share the genre or the physical dimensions of the Luttrell Psalter, being a small roll, designed to be carried about in a purse, but it does provide a personalised devotional regime, as demonstrated by reference to named spiritual advisors. The survival of the manuscript at Coughton Court, Warwickshire, suggests a Midlands provenance but unfortunately it cannot be placed any more precisely. An English translation of the whole text can be accessed at http://www.yale.edu/adhoc/etexts/pantin.htm.

have a reading at the table, by various unspecified individuals, or by one of his children as soon as they were old enough. On other occasions he could 'expound something ... which may edify your wife and others', or meditate silently on 'Hail Mary', 'Thou who has made me, have mercy upon us and upon me' and 'In the name of the Father'. He could also make a cross out of five breadcrumbs (though only his wife should see this). While feasting is not a part of this discussion, as it would not be on an ordinary day, the meal was a focus for a mixture of Christocentric and Marian piety. The paterfamilias at the head of the table with his duly instructed and appropriately behaved *familia* about him was an expression of the ideal holy community, just as were Christ and the apostles or Christ and the faithful.

The hall was a masculine space in which the lord or master performed his authority to both his household and to the wider community through the guests he entertained, and the poor he aided. In discussing the January page of the *Tres Riches Heures* Michael Camille has described the hall where Jean de Berry hosts a great feast with many guests as a 'homosocial space'.[50] As various household accounts demonstrate, guests in the greater households were very numerous. Thomas Arundel, bishop of Ely, fed an average of twenty-three guests a day, over a quarter of those present. In 1507–8 nearly half of those fed by the household of the duke of Buckingham at Thornbury were guests.[51] Even smaller households, like those of Geoffrey Luttrell, might entertain a few guests on most days, and this was not just a matter of status or business, hospitality was as much a religious as a social duty. Like the stranger at Emmaus, any guest could be Christ in disguise.

More obviously identifiable with Christ were the poor, and even in the later Middle Ages numbers of aristocratic and episcopal households sustained resident almsfolk. Others practised the distribution of food from the table, and it was not uncommon for the filling of the alms dish under the direction of the master of the house to be a ceremonial event which took place during dinner, and even to be written into household ordinances.[52] Some men even continued to feed the poor from their household after death. Richard Carlell, butcher, of York (d.1453), directed that his wife should every Sunday for five years receive into the house five poor men or women to receive food and drink in return for prayers for his soul.[53]

---

[50] Michael Camille, '"For our devotion and pleasure": the sexual objects of Jean, Duc de Berry', *Art History* 24:2 (2001), pp. 169–94 at p. 180. Camille also argues that de Berry 'scandalously appropriates the feminine space of the hearth as his own' but only in much more low status homes was the hearth truly a feminine space. As the Luttrell Psalter demonstrates, in lordly households the kitchen was a masculine space. Perhaps more scandalous is de Berry's placement in front of a round firescreen like the one in the slightly later Master of Flémalle/Robert Campin's, *Virgin and Child before a firescreen* (1430). In the latter image the firescreen acts both as a halo for the Virgin and represents the sacramental wafer being baked. Christ's body superimposed on the screen makes the identification clear. In the same way, Jean de Berry presents himself identified with the sacrament and thus as Christ.

[51] C.M. Woolgar, *The great household in medieval England* (New Haven and London, 1999), p. 23.

[52] Woolgar, *Great household*, p. 14.

[53] P.H. Cullum, '"And hir name was Charite": charitable giving by and for women in late medieval Yorkshire', in *Woman is a worthy wight: women in English society, c.1200–1500*, ed. P.J.P. Goldberg (Stroud, 1992), p. 191.

Feasting not fasting

In the past I have argued that women's post-mortem charity was more likely than men's to focus on food and drink and that this reflected their life time domestic role, and I have not changed my mind about that; but one factor not taken into consideration in that analysis is that by the mid fifteenth century the two groups were significantly different. The women were overwhelmingly widows, while the majority of men had surviving wives. This meant that most of the men would leave households behind, whereas for the majority of widows the household would break up. It was therefore more important for men to leave foodstocks alone as they would be needed by the household. Men were more likely to distribute money, which could, of course, be used to buy food, as well as other things.[54] The provision and distribution of food within the household and beyond its door allowed men a demonstration of *imitatio Christi* which drew on and bolstered their social identities.

There is some evidence that higher status men had a specific devotion to the Cross. Charles de Blois could not pass a cross without stopping to greet it.[55] Henry VI too was devoted to the Cross, dropping his hat because he would ride bareheaded rather than risk coming upon a cross with his head covered, and having his crown encircled with crosses rather than flowers or leaves.[56] At the level of the guild too, the Cross and the Crucifixion were important objects of devotion. There were guilds of the Holy Cross at Beverley, Birmingham, Bishop's Lynn and Stratford upon Avon, among others. The mystery plays too, though temporally connected to Corpus Christi, were focussed on the Passion sequence. The devout and literate layman signed himself with the cross at head, hands, feet and side as soon as he got up in the morning, implicitly as a reminder of the Five Wounds. This allowed the male devotee a physical identification with the body of Christ, such as Charles of Blois' wearing of knotted cords which caused bleeding sores on his chest. To add to his suffering he would also wear a hair shirt.[57] As Katherine Lewis shows, Henry VI too adopted a hair shirt whenever he was expected to dress finely, lest he be tempted to stray from the path of humility, and encouraged an awareness of inferiority and sinfulness.[58] For kings and aristocratic men, training for war and the expectation of the suffering of wounds, even if not always fulfilled in adulthood, may have led to an identification with the wounded body of Christ. Even as conventional a king as Edward III had relics of a thorn from the Crown of Thorns and a fragment of the True Cross, which was called the Neith Cross. The latter he gave to his foundation of St George's chapel at Windsor, where every Good Friday an oblation was placed before the Neith Cross, and subsequently

---

[54] Ibid., pp. 182–90.
[55] Vauchez, Sainthood, p. 364.
[56] Henry the Sixth, a reprint of John Blacman's memoir, with translation and notes by M.R. James, (Cambridge, 1919), p. 28. I am grateful to Katherine J. Lewis for bringing this to my attention. In this volume she discusses the extent to which Blacman's memoir represents the actual practice of the king, but in accepting the constructedness of the account, I view this as what was considered appropriate to a king, whether it was Henry's actual practice or not. See pp. 130–31.
[57] Vauchez, Sainthood, pp. 364–5.
[58] Katherine J. Lewis, "'Imitate, too, this king in virtue, who could have done ill, and did it not": lay sanctity and the rewriting of Henry VI's manliness', p. 134.

melted down for cramp rings for the relief of epilepsy, in an expression of the belief that the king shared certain of Christ's healing powers.[59]

The devout and literate layman followed his crossing ritual with a visit to church where he engaged in the devotion known as creeping to the Cross: '(t)hen, plucking up some confidence, with Mary Magdalene throw yourself at the feet of the most sweet Jesus, and wash them with your tears and anoint them and kiss them; and if not with your eyes and mouth, at least do this in your heart. Do not climb up to the cross, but in your heart say with the publican: "Lord, be merciful to me a sinner".' This penitential form of piety could be expressed in quite emotive terms:

> At the door when you go out say: 'All the men of this city or town from the greater [or the mayor?] to the less are pleasing to God and only I am worth of hell. Woe is me. Welawey'; let this be said from all your heart so that the tears run; you need not always say it with your mouth; it is sufficient to say it with a groan. As far as the church, say no other word except: 'Thou who hast made me [etc.].' Yet sometimes if you meet a dog or other beast, you may say: 'Lord, let it bite me, let it kill me; this beast is much better than I; it has never sinned. I after so much grace have provoked you; I have turned my back to you and not my face, and I have done nothing good, but all ill. Woe is me. Welawey.' On entering the church, say: 'Lord, it is as a dog and not as a man that I presume to enter your sanctuary. Woe is me. Welawey.'[60]

This rather theatrical display of emotion was not so dissimilar to that evidenced by some female mystics, but while in them it has often been seen as an emotional lack of control, here it should be seen as performative (which is not to say that it was not heartfelt) and designed to let those around the devotee know of his penitence and humility. This kind of penitential behaviour often went alongside an avoidance of swearing. Oaths were often sworn on the person of Christ or God so 'God's body' or 'God's wounds' were common forms. Not only were they blasphemous but they had the capacity to re-enact the Crucifixion, just as labouring on the Sunday did. Wall-paintings of the 'Christ of the Trades' – that is, a figure of Christ surrounded by the tools of various trades, and sometimes accompanied by dice and playing cards – can still be seen at a number of English parish churches such as Hessett, Suffolk, and Duxford, Cambridgeshire. Those men who abhorred swearing and tried to prevent it in others were acting as defenders and protectors of Christ.

Something of the significance of the interaction of religion and masculinity at the very end of the Middle Ages can be teased out from an examination of the life of Sir Piers Legh (d. 1527). Sir Piers Legh was a member of a well-established Cheshire gentry family.[61] He probably married Ellen Savage, the daughter of a

---

[59] W.M. Ormrod, 'The personal religion of Edward III', *Speculum* 64:4 (1989), pp. 849–77, here pp. 855–6 and p. 864.

[60] Pantin, 'Devout and literate layman', pp. 400–1.

[61] An ancestor died supporting Richard II, another with Henry V in France. Sir Piers Legh himself served the Yorkist dynasty, but with his patron, Lord Stanley, to whom he was related, he backed Henry Tudor at Bosworth and Stoke. He flourished under Henry VII, being granted a

neighbouring knight, in 1468; the marriage produced six children who survived to adulthood, and nine are represented on their brass which survives in Winwick church near Ashton under Lyne.

The brass of Piers Legh and his wife Ellen is relatively small, about 60 cm high, and is now set into the wall of a side chapel in the church. This was the Legh family chapel and dedicated to the Trinity. It was intended that it should lie over the grave of Piers Legh in front of the altar.[62] It is likely that it did originally, but the chapel has been subsequently remodelled. Although it shows Sir Piers Legh, his wife and their children, it is clear from the inscription that Ellen lies elsewhere. The memorial is modest in scale and perhaps that, and its intended position on the floor, was to be understood as a signal of humility.

The representation of Ellen is very conventional, and similar brasses are to be found elsewhere of this date. The emphasis is on her knightly status, wearing a mantle carrying her natal arms of Savage on the left shoulder and a cross from the Legh arms on the right. She wears a large cross behind her praying hands, suggesting that Legh or his executor wanted her depicted as a pious lady. The image of Sir Piers is, however, very unusual. He is dressed both in armour, as befitted his status as a knight, but also in a chasuble, over, or upon the front of which, are his arms, and his hands are raised in the *orans* position of prayer. He thus shows the viewer, which is confirmed by an inscription, that after the death of his wife, he became a priest. The inscription says (in Latin): 'Pray for the soul of the worthy man Sir Peter Legh, kt, here buried and Lady Ellen (or Eleanor) his wife, daughter of John Savage, kt, the body of which Ellen was buried at Bewgenett,[63] 17 day of the month of May, Anno Domini 1491. The said Peter after the death of the said Ellen having been canonically consecrated a priest died at Lyne in Hanley 11 August Anno Domini 1527.' In the various versions of his will written around five years before his death, he also refers to himself as knight and priest.[64]

The six surviving children were named in his will: his heir, also called Piers, John, Richard, Margaret and Alice were all conventionally named. But the third son, Gowther, bore a rather unusual name. He may have been named after a godfather, but he may equally have been named after the hero of the romance *Sir Gowther*.[65] *Sir Gowther* survives in two late fifteenth-century manuscripts, both from the northeastern Midlands, which is not a great distance from the Cheshire/Lancashire border which was Piers' home territory. *Sir Gowther* is one of the so-called penitential romances and may be an indication that even during

---

Forestership in 1498–9, becoming Steward or Seneschal of Blackburnshire and adjacent wapentakes in 1505, and a collector of taxation for Lancashire.
[62] Will of Sir Piers Legh. John Rylands Library, Manchester, Legh of Lyme muniments. Box I bundle I No. 2.
[63] Near Petworth, in Sussex.
[64] I have discussed other cases of laymen, typically as widowers, becoming priests in '"Give me chastity": masculinity and attitudes to chastity and celibacy in the Middle Ages', paper given at the *Gender & History* colloquium, September 2012, at the University of York.
[65] *Sir Gowther*, ed. Anne Laskaya and Eve Salisbury (Kalamazoo, 1995). A digital version of the Introduction can be found at http://www.lib.rochester.edu/camelot/teams/gowint.htm and of the text at http://www.lib.rochester.edu/camelot/teams/gowthfrm.htm.

his married life Piers and/or his wife adopted a penitential form of piety. Sir Gowther in the romance was a wild figure who, after various sins, including in one version of the story the rape of a convent of nuns, had a conversion, fought the Saracen and was redeemed. Quite what Legh's intention in naming his son after this figure was, is unclear, but it may represent a sense of sexual sin which needed to be redeemed, or indeed a frustrated desire to go on Crusade. If it was the former, then the adoption of celibacy after his wife's death, at first informally and latterly formally, as a priest, may also have been intended penitentially.

Ellen's death in 1491 after some twenty years of marriage left Piers to widowerhood for the remaining thirty-six years of his life. This was quite unusual. Piers was probably in his mid-thirties at the time and some of the children may well have been still young. Remarriage was common for gentry in such situations. However, he may not have felt the need, given that he had heirs and to spare. Nevertheless the decision not to remarry may indicate that he was already thinking in terms of an aspiration to the priesthood. The last twenty years of the fifteenth century also marked a significant upswing in the number of gentry widows who chose to become vowesses, and it may be that their desire for a chaste life was shared by some of their male relatives.[66] It is possible that Piers was himself related to an Elizabeth Lee, a vowess from Ecclesfield who died about the same time as he did.[67] He was certainly related to Thomas Savage, brother to Ellen, who became bishop of Rochester in the year after Ellen's death, was translated to London, in 1496 and finished his career as archbishop of York.[68] It is possible that Savage encouraged Legh to be ordained though he was not ordained until after Savage's death. He was also to make Cuthbert Tunstall, from a Yorkshire gentry family, but by then bishop of London, one of the supervisors of part of his will.[69]

It was suggested above that the size and location of the Legh brass might indicate a sense of humility, but if so it was a very specific kind of humility. In the brass Legh still wore the armour which signalled his knightly status, as did the inscription. In his will he also required that his standard and his coat armour be carried before his body to the church and to remain there.[70] He did not reject the world. He may have given up public office but he held tightly to his knightly status, through his display of arms and his funeral, but like other high status men he sought to express a masculinity which drew on both secular and religious elements.

Legh is not known to have held a benefice, but he would presumably have wanted to celebrate Mass. It is not clear where he would have done that, perhaps at Disley chapel, which was a couple of miles from Lyme, possibly there was a chapel at the house. There was certainly one at Bradley Old Hall, his earlier

---

[66] P.H. Cullum, 'Vowesses and veiled widows: medieval female piety in the Province of York', Northern History 32 (1996), pp. 21–41 at p. 28.
[67] Borthwick Institute, University of York, Probate Register II, fo. 100f. (Lee).
[68] S.J. Gunn, 'Savage, Thomas (d. 1507)', ODNB, online edn, January 2008 [http://www.oxforddnb.com/view/article/24727, accessed 19 November 2012].
[69] Will of Sir Piers Legh (see above, note 62).
[70] Ibid.

residence near Winwick, where he was buried. We can therefore establish that Piers did not become a priest as a career move, nor did he acquire additional social status. However, given the prevailing view that priests had a higher spiritual status than laymen, it may be that he acquired spiritual stature from the choice. There is evidence of Legh's profound personal devotion to the Mass and specifically to the worthy celebration of the Mass. Not only did he build a chapel at Disley dedicated to the Virgin, but at Winwick too he established a Trinity chapel within the parish church, and was responsible for reroofing it.[71] In his will he wished that the twenty-four torches borne about his body to the funeral be divided equally between Disley and Winwick chapels. Although it is not explicitly stated here, the usual purpose of such bequests was to provide elevation torches at the Mass. He also specified that he wanted 100 masses and *diriges* said within a month of his burial upon a single day. These were to be: 20 Jesus masses; 20 Five Wounds masses; 20 masses of the Virgin; 20 masses of the Holy Ghost; 10 of the Trinity and 10 Requiem masses. This suggests a devotion focussed significantly on the crucified Christ. He also specified that every priest was to have 4d., 'and every prest to gitt hym a clerk to helpe hym say dirige and masse. And every of thame to have 2d. And at every masse aforesaid be offered a peny at the lavatory for me.'[72] These kinds of details are usually understood in the brief mention of payments to priests and clerks. The spelling out suggests a close concern with the performance of these masses. Finally he asked that he be buried in the Trinity chapel at Winwick, 'afor the myddist of the altar there wheras the prest sall always the tyme of consecracion stand even over and upon my harte'. The priest would thus be personating Legh, and Legh with his hands uplifted in the *orans* position is specifically reciting the consecration prayers for ever. Here we have a layman becoming a priest to facilitate his access to the Eucharist, and who was thus able to celebrate and communicate daily.

Legh's brass may be unique, but the practice was not. Through his brass and his will we can come to some sense of the inner motivations of a man who identified with wife and family, yet lived half his life as a celibate; a man proud of his status but also self-consciously humble; who as a layman acquired such a devotion to the Eucharist that he wished to spend eternity celebrating Mass.

CONCLUSION

Late medieval English masculine piety differed in significant ways from the paradigm of feminine piety constructed by Caroline Walker Bynum, but that is not entirely surprising. Bynum's subjects were saints, or near saints, and their sanctity was something that to a degree set them apart from other women, let alone men. However, the differences were not entirely clear cut, not least because much devotional practice was household or communal in nature, and these commonalties often involved both men and women. Indeed for many laymen the

---

[71] Ibid.
[72] Ibid.

engagement of wives and households in their religious practice was bound up in their identities as householders and members of local society.

Some men shared the mystical and eucharistic foci of holy women but these seem to have been inflected in different ways. Clerics and some elite men who were employers of clergy could access the Mass as often as they desired, even if the latter were probably still limited in the frequency with which they could receive communion. Nor was the Host as frequently identified with the suffering body of Christ, which seems to have been accessed more through images and representations of the Cross, to which there was clearly a masculine devotion. Moreover, the emotional or affective style of piety associated with Margery Kempe and some other holy women was clearly not just a feminine form of piety, whatever our modern associations of emotional utterance with a feminine lack of control. While a bodily penitential form of piety can be found among men it was not usually linked to food or fasting but to the use of hair shirts and other forms of mortification of the flesh, which more clearly drew on monastic and eremitical traditions of penance. While some men did use food abstinence to discipline the flesh, rather than as act of intercession, it was more common to use food to unite the practice of *imitatio Christi* with demonstration of the qualities of the good husband or provider, both at the table and through charitable activity, in the will or through the guild. For men feasting, not fasting, was a key route to the demonstration of pious masculinity.

INDEX

Aachen, Albert of 105, 108
   History of the Journey to Jerusalem 105
Abaye 22–3
abbot 68, 84, 89, 154, 155
Abel 19
acolytes 192
Adam 19, 37, 57
Adam, son of Henry of Huntingdon 67
Adhémar (d.1098) bishop of Le Puy 13, 99–111
   moral enforcement 107–9
   spiritual warrior 102–7
   vicar apostolic 103
adolescence *see* youth
adultery 53, 60
adulthood 87, 173, 182, 195
Aelfric 68
Aethelred, King 68
Agincourt 143
Aiscough, William, bishop of Salisbury 130 n.22, 131 n.31, 137
Alef, Prince 86
Alexander V, Pope 145
Alexander VI, Pope 130
Alexander, bishop of Lincoln 66
Alfred, King 142
alms and charity 114–15, 120, 124, 158, 194–5
anger 19, 122–3
Anglo-Saxon Chronicle 82, 83, 84
Anglo-Saxons 66, 73, 78, 79, 82–3, 85, 92, 141, 166
Anselm (of Bec), archbishop of Canterbury 48, 51, 52, 55, 62, 68–9, 91
   Cur deus homo 52
Antioch 162
   battle of (1097–8) 95, 103, 106–7, 108
ap Rhys (family of) 177
   Robert 174
arbalists 102
archdeacon 13, 67, 69–70, 108 *see also* Henry of Huntingdon, Nicholas, archdeacon of Huntingdon, Thomas Neville
archers 102
Ariano, county of 115, 121
aristocracy 4, 135, 170, 176, 195
Aristotle, grandson of Henry of Huntingdon 67
Armagnac, count of 136
armour 105, 197, 198
   breastplate 107
   hauberk 74–5, 105
   helmet 104–5
   spurs 104–5
Armstrong-Partida, Michelle 6

Index

army 73, 98, 100, 102, 103, 104, 105, 106–8
artisan 23, 112
  butcher 194
  comb-maker 116–19
Arundel, Thomas, bishop of Ely 194
asceticism 11, 12, 18–19, 22, 40, 47, 55, 56, 57, 59, 62, 150, 151, 164, 169
Ascheby, Nicholas, prior of Westminster Abbey 171
Ashley Psalter 165
Asser 142
Augustine of Hippo, see St Augustine
authority
  clerical 13, 35, 58, 80, 91, 92–3, 98, 110, 155
  episcopal 13, 36, 37, 40, 44, 100–1, 104, 110, 154
  masculine 8, 9, 15, 190, 194
  monastic 89, 150–2, 154
  papal 5
Autun, ecumenical council at 51
Avranches, John of, archbishop of Rouen 51

Babylonia 17, 25
Ballard, Thomas, monk 173
baptism 119
Barlow, Roger 174
Barlow, William 174
Barstow, Anne 49–50, 51 n.12
  Married Priests and the Reforming Papacy: The Eleventh-Century Debates 49
Bath 137
Battle Abbey 173, 179
bear 77–8, 86
Beauchamp, Richard, earl of Warwick 144, 155
Beaufort Hours 155, 156
Beaufort, Thomas, duke of Exeter 143–44
beauty 24–5, 36, 108
Beauvais 28, 32, 38

Bede 35, 74
Bell, Rudolph M. 9, 114, 185
Ben Zoma 16, 22
Benedictines 144, 160, 165, 178, 180
benefice 198
Benett, William 172
Beorn, king of Norway 77
Berkeley, James 179
Bernard of Clairvaux 97, 138, 187
  In praise of the new knighthood 97
Bernold 39–40, 42
Berry, Jean de 194
Bertha, wife of Count Gerhard of Vienne 38
bestiality 55, 62
Bewgenett 197
Bible 17, 23, 52
  Hebrew, or Old Testament 17, 53, 109
  Corinthians 54, 56–57
  Genesis 19
  Isaiah 23
  Jeremiah 24
  Job 53
  Joel 22
  Romans 56
  Timothy 53
Bickington, chapel of, diocese of Exeter 191
Biddick, Kathleen 186
bishops 13, 32, 36, 44, 71, 73, 91, 98, 99, 100–1, 103–4, 145, 154, 155
  see also Adhémar
  Anglo-Norman 48, 53
  as bridegroom 53
Blacman, John 14, 130–42
  Collectarium manusuetudinum et bonorum morum Regis Henrici VI 130–1
blasphemy 134–5, 196
Blois, Charles of, duke of Brittany (1319–64) 132, 134, 135, 138, 139–40, 195
Blygh, Sir William 191

Index

bodies 8, 19, 42, 47, 49, 55–7, 60, 62, 74–5, 78, 85, 133–4, 136, 139, 185–6, 189
   body of Christ 15, 64, 184–5, 186, 187, 189–90, 191, 195, 196
   feminised 185
   flesh 57, 59, 134, 139, 142
   genitalia 25, 56, 86, 187
Bokyngham, John, bishop elect of Lincoln 154
Bona Anima, William, abbot of St Stephen's of Caen and archbishop of Rouen 52
Bouillon, Duke Godfrey of 96–7, 104–5
Bouts, Dieric, the elder 193
   Altarpiece of the Holy Sacrament 193
Bowet Henry, archbishop of York 157, 158
Boyarin, Daniel 21, 24
Bradley Old Hall, near Winwick 198–9
Brand, Abbot, of Peterborough 88
brasses, commemorative 192, 197–9
Bredon, Simon 179
Bridlington, Augustinian priory of 143, 149, 150, 153, 154
Bridlington, John of *See* St John of Bridlington
Britons 73
Bruton Abbey (Somerset) 179
Brutus 166
Buckingham, duke of, *see* Stafford, Edward
Buckland-in-the-moor, diocese of Exeter 191
Bull, Marcus 98
Bullough, Vern 65
Bury, abbey of 141
Butler, Judith 147
Buttler (alias Pennant), Thomas, abbot of Basingwerk 177
Buttler, Nicholas, abbot of Basingwerk 177

Byker, Ralph de 181
Bynum, Caroline Walker 15, 184–6, 187, 190, 191, 192, 199
   Holy Feast and Holy Fast: the Religious Significance of Food to Medieval Women 15, 184, 185
   Jesus as Mother 185
Byzantium 95

Cain 19
Calixtus II, Pope 72
Cambrai, letter of 54, 58–9
Camille, Michael 193, 194
canon law 28, 29, 53, 68, 69, 70, 100
canonisation 126–7, 129, 132, 153, 142, 187
canor 189
Capgrave, John 141
   De illustribus Henricis 141
Carlell, Richard, butcher 194
Carolingian
   empire 12, 28, 29, 31, 32 40
   reform 31
Carthusian order 139, 181
   Hull charterhouse 181
   London charterhouse 130, 139
   Witham charterhouse, Somerset 130
Cassiodorus 50
Caxton, William 133, 134, 138
   Golden Legend 133
celibacy 4–6, 7, 11, 12–13, 32, 56–7, 60–3, 64–5, 68–70, 72, 75, 81, 94, 198
   enforced 47–56, 58–9, 108
chalice (and paten) 39, 192
Chanson de geste 105
charity, *See* alms and charity
Charles the Bald 30, 32, 35, 37–8, 40, 42
Charterhouse *see* Carthusian order
Chartres, Fulcher of 103–4
chastity 11, 40–1, 47, 55–6, 59, 67, 107, 128, 136–9, 148, 185

203

Index

Chaucer, Geoffrey 149
  Tale of Sir Topas 149
Chertsey Abbey 126
Cheshire 196
Chianti 119
Christ Church Cathedral Priory, Canterbury 173, 179, 180, 181
Christ 10, 15, 37, 53, 98, 123, 152, 185, 187, 193, 194, 196
  of the Trades 196
  Second Adam 37
churching 10
circumcision 21
Cistercians 160, 174, 176, 177
citizenship, civic-mindedness, civic duty 28–9, 114, 116–120, 148
Clark, James G. 188
Clermont, council of [1095] 95, 98, 100
clothes 8, 24, 133–4
  gown 133, 172
  cloak 133
  doublet 172
  boots and shoes 133, 155
  hood 133
  hairshirt 134, 195, 200
Clover, Carol 33, 40
Clovis, king of Merovingians 30
Cluniacs 160, 176
Cohen, Shaye 21
Colyer, Raynold, canon of Smithfield 168
concubine 48, 54–5, 57–8 *see also* wife
confession 44
Constable, Giles 96
Constance, council of 154
Constance, daughter of King Philip I 104
Constance, diocese of 50
continence 54–6, 57, 59, 61, 136
Coon, Lynda 43
Copland, Robert 130
Corbie, Colette of 189
Cornwall 78, 86
Corpus Christi 189, 193, 195
covenant 21

cramp rings 196
Crema, John of, papal legate 64–5, 67, 70–1
Cross 15, 95, 98, 193, 194, 195, 196, 200
  Crucifixion 187, 189–190, 196, 199
  devotion to 195, 200
  creeping to the Cross 196
  Neith Cross 195–6
  True Cross 195
Crusades
  gendered interpretations of 6–7, 96–7
  First Crusade 95, 106
Cunegund, wife of Emperor Henry II 141
Cushing, Katherine 95

D'Aguilers, Raymond 102
  Liber 102–103
Dalarun, Jacques 112
Dalton, Paul 79, 85
Danes 28, 66
Daniel, Walter 181
David 44, 137
de Jong, Mayke 41
demon 35
desire 16, 18, 19–23, 26, 33, 116, 187
  see also yetzer
  sexual 18, 22, 47, 55–7, 61, 137, 142, 147
Deutz, Rupert of 187
Diem, Albrecht 41
Disley, chapel of, (Lyme) 198, 199
Dol, Baldric of 107, 108
Domesday Book 82
Dominicans 192–3
Dore, abbey of, Herefordshire 175
Duby, Georges 86
Duda 33–34
Dunkeswell, abbey of 181
Dutton, Paul 42
Duxford, Cambridgeshire 196

Eadmer 69
Eadwine, monk of Ely 92

Index

East Anglia 192
Easter Sepulchre 192
Ebbo, bishop of Rheims 30, 40, 44
Ecclesfield 198
Edgar, king of England [d.975] 166
Edgington, S.B 6
education 51, 114, 142, 168–9, 174–5, 178–9, 188
  grammar school 165, 168, 174, 179
  song school 174
  charity 175
  monastic almonry 174, 178
  see also Eton College, university
Edward (the Confessor), King 85 *see also* St Edward the Confessor
Edward III, king of England 165, 195
Edward IV, king of England 126, 143
Edward, prince of Wales (d. 1471) 126, 135, 136
effeminacy, *mollitia* (softness) 33, 40, 43, 46, 57, 61, 96, 129, 133
Ely 79–80, 82, 84
Ely Abbey 13, 82, 90–2
Ely, Isle of 82, 89, 90
Emma, Queen 39
Emmaus 194
Emmerson, R. 193
epilepsy 196
Epp, Garrett P.J. 187
eremiticism 180 n.96
Ermenfrid, bishop of Beauvais 28
Ermentrude, wife of Charles the Bald 35, 38
ethnicity 18, 78–9, 82–3, 85, 92
Eton College 130, 135
Eucharist 15, 184–6, 189–91, 192–93, 199, 200
  Host desecration 186
Eugenius IV, Pope 154
Eve 20
Everton, William 181
Exeter Cathedral 179

family and household 6, 10, 15, 65, 77, 80, 112, 121, 134, 135, 137, 170–3, 176–7, 185, 192–5, 197
  childbirth 9
  fertility 9
  son 19, 20, 52, 54, 59, 87, 173–4, 179
  clerical 6, 12, 52, 109, 148
  foster-father 122
  uncle 176, 177
  brother 87–8, 99, 176
  cousin 176
  sister 24–5
  orphans 24–5, 108
  widow 24–5, 195, 198
  See also Father, Mother
father; fatherhood 4, 5, 15, 20, 67, 70, 109, 112, 113, 135 185
  spiritual fatherhood 109, 152
Fens 78
femininity, feminine 1–2, 5, 10, 15, 20, 44, 65, 184–5
Fitzgerald, Christina 10
Fitzjames, Richard, bishop of London 179
Flanders 78
Flanders, count of 87
Fliche, Augustin 50
Florence, bishop of 5
food 15, 23, 135, 185, 190, 193–4, 195, 200
  fasting 15, 107, 117, 123, 185, 189
  feasting 15, 192–93, 194, 200
  drinking 19, 135, 151, 193, 194
fornication 53–6, 58, 60, 61, 62, 71
Francis of Assisi, Franciscans 118
Frauenknecht, Erwin 49–50
  Die Verteidigung der Priesterehe in der Reformzeit 49
Freeman, Thomas S. 131, 140
free will 55–6
friends 24–5, 92

Gaimar, Geffrei 84
  L'Estoire des Engleis 84–5

Index

gender 1–4, 6–11, 20, 26, 33, 109, 110, 147
  single gender model 33, 40
  third gender 4, 32, 65
  ungendered 65, 158
  clerical gender 5, 12, 47, 49–50, 62–3, 65
generosity 90, 121, 192
Gentiles 21
Gent, Gilbert of 77–8
Gesta Francorum 101–3, 106, 108
Gesta Herewardi 13, 79–80, 82–3, 85, 89–93
Gesta Tancredi 109
ghost 102
Gilsdorf, Sean 100
Glastonbury, abbey of 166
Goldberg, P.J.P 193
Gregorian reform 5, 11, 12, 31, 65, 67, 75, 80, 94–5, 108
Gregory the Great 32–3
Gregory VII, Pope 50
Grosmont, Henry of, duke of Lancaster 141
  Livre de seyntz medicines 141
guilds 10
  Confraternity of the Holy Trinity 193
  Louvain 193
  Holy Cross: Beverley, Birmingham, Bishop's Lynn, Stratford upon Avon 195
Gylot, Pascal, abbot of St Mary Graces 176

hagiography 8, 14, 36, 96, 101, 114, 116–18, 120–5, 133, 138, 140, 142
hairshirt *see under* clothes
Hanley, near Ashton under Lyne 197
Haselbury, Somerset 74
Hastings, battle of 82
hawks 135
Henry I, king of England 71–2, 91
Henry II, Emperor 141
Henry II, king of England 66

Henry IV, king of England 181
Henry of Blois, bishop of Winchester 74
Henry V, king of England 143, 144
Henry VI, king of England (d. 1471) 14, 126–42, 143, 195
  appearance of 133–4
  character 128–9
  cult of 126–7
  morality of 134–6
  sanctity of 128–132, 139–42
  sexuality of 136–9
Henry VII, king of England 176
Herefordshire 72
Hereward (the Wake) 13, 77–93
  achieves manhood 88–90
  career of 77–9
  historical Hereward 82–5
  youth of 85–7
Herrenfrage 47, 65
hermit 74, 188
Hervey, bishop of Bangor and Lincoln 91
Hessett, Suffolk 196
heteronormative 147, 187
heterosexual 7, 147
hierarchy 12, 14, 26, 33, 34–7, 81, 96, 150, 164, 172
Hilduin, abbot of St Denis 30
Hill, John 99
Hill, Laurita 99
Hilton, Walter 145, 150
  Epistle on the Mixed Life 145, 150
Hincmar (of Rheims, d. 822) 12, 28–45
  archbishop 28, 30, 36, 38, 41, 44
  coronation *ordines* 29
  dealings with men 39–40
  dealings with women 37–8
  De cavendis vitiis et virtutibus exercendis 32–3
  uses St Remigius as a model 36–7, 41–2
  vita of Remigius 36–7
  Visio Bernoldi 39–40, 42
Hincmar of Laon 39, 43

Index

Holt, Andrew 97
Holy Lance 102, 104, 107
Holy Trinity 197
Homobonus of Cremona (d.1197) 132
homoeroticism 186–87
homosexual 7, 187
homosociality 7, 10, 15, 164, 179, 194
honour 53, 55, 57–9, 62, 64, 85, 135
horse 103, 105
Hugh, Augustinian canon 148, 149, 150, 151, 152, 158
   vita of John of Bridlington 148, 149, 150, 152, 153, 155, 157, 158
humanism 15, 158
humility 15, 36, 41–3, 115, 120, 123, 132, 133–4, 144, 151, 155, 157, 185, 195, 196, 197–8
hunting 78
Huntingdon, Henry of (d. c. 1157) 12–13, 64–76, 83–84
   archdeacon 13
   Historia Anglorum 66–7, 68, 70
   religious sexuality in his work 67–72
   violence in his work 72–5
   his son *see* Adam son of Henry
   his grandsons *see* Aristotle, grandson of Henry, Simon, grandson of Henry
   his father *see* Nicholas, archdeacon of Huntingdon
husband 5, 15, 35, 38, 53–4, 99, 115, 122, 185, 200
   clerical husband 48, 71

illegitimacy 57, 100, 174
illness 8, 35, 78, 142
imitatio Christi 123, 185, 188, 192, 195, 200
incest 55–6, 60, 62
inheritance 13
Instructions for a devout and literate layman 193
Ireland 78, 87
Irminsinde 38
Isaïa, Marie-Céline 36, 43
Israel 19–21, 22, 109

James, M.R 138
Jerusalem 23, 95, 98, 102
   battle of (1099) 95
   kingdom of 7, 95
   Temple 17
Jews 17, 21, 26–7, 40
   anti-Semitism 186
Job 142
John, abbot of Bury St Edmunds 171
Jones, Timothy S. 83
Jordan (river) 24
Judah 23
Justice 117–8, 122, 128

Kalendre of the New Legend of England 144, 153, 157
Karras, Ruth Mazo 4, 113, 116, 124
Kempe, Margery 157–8, 159, 189, 200
Kenilworth 166
Kestell, Sir Richard, vicar of Lowan, diocese of Exeter 191
king, kingship 19, 29, 32, 36, 40, 53, 71, 109, 128–9, 131, 133, 135, 139–42, 195
   rex justus, rex bonus 129
King's College, Cambridge 130
Kingswood Abbey (Gloucestershire) 179
knight 74, 78, 84, 86, 88–9, 90, 103, 104–6, 108, 117, 122, 197–8
   knighthood 13, 15, 77, 86
   belt and arms 77, 86, 88
   squire 117
Knighton, Henry 162
Knights Templar 97
Kynton, John 181

Lambert, Sarah 7
Lancashire 197
Lancaster, Thomas (earl) of 126
land, estates 38, 85, 119, 121, 150, 170–1
Lanfranc, archbishop of Canterbury 51, 68
Laon 39, 42, 43
Last Supper 15, 193

Index

Lateran
  Council I [1123] 48, 51, 72
  Lateran Council II [1139] 51
Latro 42–3
lay brothers 163, 168, 179
Lee, Becky R. 10
Lee, Elizabeth, vowess 198
Legh, Sir Piers 15, 196–9
  his children Piers, John, Richard, Margaret, Alice, Gowther 197, *see also Sir Gowther*
Lewis, Katherine J. 195
Libellus Æthelwoldi episcopi 91
Liber Eliensis 91
Life of John of Bridlington 144, 149–50, 152, 153, 155, 158
life
  active 14, 152, 159
  contemplative 152
  mixed 14, 145, 150, 151–3, 155, 158
Lisieux, decrees of 57
Lochrie, Karma 147, 186
Lond, Robert 192
London 71, 120, 173
  council of [1102] 67–9, 74
  council of [1125] 70
  council of [1129] 71
lordship 89, 121–3, 171
Lot 56
Lothar I, Emperor 30
Lothar II, King 44
Louis IX, king of France (1214–70) 132, 133, 134, 135, 136, 138, 139, 141
Louis the German, King 30
Louis the Pious, Frankish emperor 30
Lovatt, Roger 130, 131, 140
Lucius, King 166
Luttrell, Geoffrey 192–3, 194
  Luttrell Psalter 192, 193
Lydgate, John 141, 144

Maine 78
Malmesbury, William of 48, 62, 83

manhood, manliness 2, 3, 4–5, 9, 10, 11, 13, 14, 15, 16, 29, 32, 47–9, 55–9, 60–1, 65, 78, 85, 113, 120, 123–5, 129, 137, 139, 140, 173, 187
  clerical manhood 47–9, 56–9, 62
Margaret of Anjou, queen of England 136
market, market stall 116
marriage 4, 13, 19, 24–25, 31, 41, 54, 56–8, 114, 116, 121, 198
  clerical 6, 32, 46–63, 67–72
  married clergy 12–13, 46, 64, 67
  invalidated 48
  lay 13, 49, 54
  legislation of 47, 51–2, 54, 58, 62, 68, 72, 114
  virginal 115
  symbolism of 5
martyrdom 98, 106, 129, 131
Mary Magdalene 196
masculinity
  clerical 4–6, 12, 14, 31, 46–63, 67–76, 81, 113, 188
  crusader 97
  definition 2, 11, 124, 147
  emasculinity 10, 65, 169, 171
  hegemonic 5, 16–7, 21, 26, 34, 81, 188
  high status 15, 151
  husbandry 135
  hybrid 97
  insecure 34
  lay 10, 13, 14, 57, 80–93
  masculinities 2, 4, 8, 11, 34, 80, 97, 117, 120, 147, 148
  mature 86–9, 116–17
  monastic 5, 182–3
  Rabbinic 6, 11, 16–27
  secular 73, 113, 123–4
  spiritual 12, 14, 73–4, 113, 117, 120, 123–5, 129, 131–9
  crisis of 33–4, 47–9, 80, 81
  unmarked 147, 148, 150, 155, 158, 189–90

urban 10, 116
warrior 5, 12, 73–5, 97
Mass 88, 104, 185, 188, 189, 191, 192, 198–9, 200
(and dirige) 199
Jesus 196, 199
Five Wounds, of the Virgin, Holy Ghost, Trinity, Requiem 199
Matilda, Empress 74
mayor 196
McMurray Gibson, Gail 10
McNamara, Jo Ann 5, 31, 33, 47, 65, 80
mendicant 115, 169
merchant 118, 172, 173
Merton College, Oxford 179
midrash 17
Mills, Robert 187, 188
miracles 67, 126–7, 132, 143, 150–1, 157, 158
Mirrors for Princes 29, 139, 140, 141
Mishnah 17, 23, 24
Misyn, Richard, Carmelite 191
mitre *see under* vestments
monastery 96, 163–83
ad succurrendum profession 15, 163–4, 177–9, 180, 181
aliens in 175–6
entry to 168–75
family link with 176–7
laymen and secular clerics resident in 163–4, 168
monasticism 2, 7–8, 41
monastic population 160–3
progression from clerical life 175, 180
unstable 181–2
monks 4, 7, 32, 75, 88–9, 91, 92, 123, 138, 139, 160–83
sexual behaviour of 107–8
Monkton Fairleigh, priory of 172
Monte, Piero da 136
Montfort, Simon de 126
Monumenta Germaniae Historica 49
morality 132, 134

mother, motherhood 9, 34, 109, 181, 185
Mt. Sinai 20
Musard, John, monk 176
mystery plays 10, 195
mysticism 115, 185–6, 188–90, 196, 200

nakedness 108, 137–8
nature 20–1, 46, 60–1
Neal, Derek 4, 10, 30–1, 135
Neville, Alexander, archbishop of York 143
Neville, Thomas, archdeacon of Durham 188
Newton Regis, Warwickshire 192
Nicea, battle of (1097) 95, 102
Nicholas II, Pope 50
Nicholas, archdeacon of Huntingdon, father of Henry of Huntingdon 67, 68, 70
Nine Worthies 164
Nogent, Guibert of 106, 107–8, 109
The Deeds of God through the Franks 106
Norman Anonymous 50–7, 60–1
tract J22/26 *Apologia pro filiis sacerdotum et concubinarum* 50–2, 54
tract J25 *Scire velim quis primus instituit* 50–3, 55–6, 60–1
Normandy 6, 12, 46–7, 50, 51
Normans 48, 66, 78, 82–3, 87–9
North Mimms, Hertfordshire 192
Norwich Cathedral Priory 164–5
Nos uxorati ('We Married Clergy') 46, 61
novice 161, 163, 169, 172, 179, 190
Noyon, letter of 58–9
nun 35 *see also* Duda

oath 70, 119–20, 134, 196
occupation 168–9, 176, 177, 180–1
Odysseus 165
Orbais, Gottschalk of 29
Orcherd of Syon 164

Orderic Vitalis 48, 99, 182
ordination 32, 52, 160–2, 168, 172, 173, 177
Origny, convent of 37
Orkney 87
Ortner, Sherry 20

Palestine 25
papal legate 64–5, 70, 99, 173
Paris, Gilo of 107, 109
parish, parishioners 13, 15, 58, 69, 167, 191, 192
  church 144, 145–6, 157, 193, 196, 199
Partner, Nancy 68, 70–1
Paschal II, Pope 91
Passion 185, 189, 190, 195
  devotion to Five Wounds 195
paternalism 109–10
patience 116, 121–3, 128, 158
Patrologia Latina 31
Paul (the apostle) 53–7
Paxton, Jennifer 91
penance; penitence 29, 43–4, 75, 108, 196
Percy family (Wiltshire) 172
Peterborough 89
Peterborough Abbey 82, 84, 88, 89, 91
Peterson, Robert, prior of Lewes 176
Pettinajo, Pietro (d. 1289) 14, 114–20, 124–5
Philip I, French king 104
Picts 66, 73
Piers Plowman 164
piety 14, 128
  affective 1, 193–4, 199, 200
  Christocentric 1, 15, 124, 193–4, 199
  feminine 9, 10, 15, 184–6, 189, 199
  lay 1, 15, 95, 112–25, 128, 131, 132–9, 184–200
  Marian 193–4
  masculine 10, 15, 116–25, 145, 148, 150, 151, 153, 184, 187–90, 199–200

penitential 185–6, 190, 196, 197–8, 200
pilgrimage 98, 99, 108, 109, 143–4
pimp 107
Pippin (of Aquitaine), King 30
Podestà of Siena 117, 118
Poitiers, ecumenical council at 51
Pole, William de la, duke of Suffolk 137
poor 108, 134, 148, 185, 194
Porter, Sir William 144
postulant 160, 162, 168, 170, 172, 182
Pratt, David 142
priest, priesthood 15, 35, 36, 39, 46–63, 68, 70–1, 94, 98, 99, 107, 108, 136, 138, 162–3, 168, 169, 178, 179, 182, 185, 191, 197, 198, 199
prior 145, 148, 150–1, 152, 153, 157
  see also St John of Bridlington, William Wode, Nicholas Ascheby, Robert Peterson
prostitution, prostitutes 46, 60, 138
Provence, Margaret of 136
Pulton of Lydd (Kent), John 172
purity 54, 55, 68, 69, 98, 108, 116, 138
Purvis, J.S 157

queen 35, 38
queer theory 7, 187

rabbis 6, 11, 17–27
Rabbi Elazar ben Padat 24–5
Rabbi Yishmael 23
Rabbi Yohanan 24–6
Rachel 35
Rambuss, Richard 187
Ramsbury, Matilda of 48
Ramsey, abbey of 91
Rebecca 35
Reformation 2, 11
relic 102, 107, 195 *see also* Holy Lance
  Benedict's head 165
  Crown of Thorns 195
Remigius, bishop of Lincoln 68

Index

Resh Lakish 24–6
retinue 87
Reve, Roger, burgess of Bury St Edmunds 171
Rheims 30, 58
Rheims, Flodoard of 37–8
Richard III, king of England 127
Richard, monk of Ely 79
Richilde, Queen 37–8
Riley-Smith, Jonathan 96
Robert the Monk 96–97, 98, 106, 107
Robert the Wise, king of Naples 114, 121, 122
Roger, bishop of Salisbury 48
Rolle, Richard 152, 187, 188–9, 192
  Meditations on the Passion 189
  English Psalter 190
  Incendium Amoris (Fire of Love) 152, 190–1
Roman philosophy 16, 22
Romans 17, 66
Rosen-Zvi, Ishay 18
Rouen, archdiocese of 51
Rouen, Council of 51–2
Roxburgh 144
Rubenstein, Jeffrey 25–6

Sabran, count Elzéar de (also count of Ariano, d. 1323) 14, 114–15, 121–5, 132
St Albans Abbey 177
St Andrew's, church of, Hempstead, Norfolk 157
St Anne 9
St Augustine
  of Canterbury 166
  of Hippo 34, 54
St Augustine's Abbey, Bristol 175
St Æthelbert 141
St Æthelstan 141
St Æthelthryth 91–2
St Benedict 138, 165–6
St Bertin 87
St Dauphine de Puimichel 115, 122–3
St Denis, monastery of 30
St Dunstan 164
St Edmund of East Anglia 141
St Edward the Confessor 141
St Edward the Martyr 141
St Francis of Assisi 187
St Genebaudus, bishop of Laon 42–3, 44
St Germanus 73–5
St Germans, prior of, diocese of Exeter 191
St John of Bridlington, prior (d. 1379) 14, 143–59
  behaviour of 148–50
  canonization of 143
  miracle by 150–1
  model of mixed life 145, 151–3
  visual representations of 144–5, 153–7
St Katherine of Alexandria 9
St Kenelm 141
St Lawrence, church of, Ludlow 145, 153, 154–5
St Margaret 9
St Mary Graces, abbey of 181
St Mary's Abbey, York 173, 178
St Mary-in-the-Meadows, abbey of, Leicester 162
St Matthew's, church of, Morley, Derby 155
St Omer 87
St Oswald 141
St Oswine 141
St Osyth, priory of 174
St Patrick 153–4
St Peter 44, 89–90
St Peter's, Bristol 192
St Remigius 30, 36, 40–4
St Roche 127
St Wulfric 74–5
San Pier Maggiore, abbess and convent of 5
sanctity
  construction of 8, 13–14 *see also* Henry VI, St John of Bridlington, Pietro Pettinajo, Elzéar de Sabran

sanctity (*cont.*)
  clerical 36–7, 40–4, 144, 148–51
  confessor-saint 121–2
  female sanctity 8–9
  husband-saint 112–3
  kingly 127, 140–1
  lay 14, 112–15, 124–5, 128–32, 139–42
  living saint 118
  lord-saint 121–4
  male sanctity 9, 13–14, 112–25, 126–42, 143–59
  monastic 144, 164, 148–51, 164–5
Sanok, Catherine 189, 190
Saracens 96, 104, 198
Sarah 35
Sassoferrato, Bartolus of 119
Satlow, Michael L 188
Saul, Nigel 192
Savage, Ellen, wife of Sir Piers Legh 196–8
Savage, John, knight 197
Savage, Thomas, bishop of Rochester, archbishop of York 198
Saxons 66, 73, 82
Scots 66, 144
Scott, Joan 109
Scrope family (Bolton) 172
Scrope, Richard, archbishop of York 126
secular clergy 5, 12, 15, 32, 46–63, 160, 161, 162, 163, 173, 174, 175, 177, 180, 181
  married 12, 46–63, 71
Segar, Elizabeth 172
Segar, Stephen, abbot of Hailes 172, 176
self-mastery 14, 113, 116–17, 139
Sempringham, prior of 154
Serlo of Bayeux 54, 61
  Defensio 54
sermon 98, 105, 107
sexuality 4–5, 6, 7, 12, 25, 41, 46–56, 59–63, 65–72, 75, 107, 108, 136–9, 147, 186
  sterility 115

normative 147
  see also chastity, celibacy
Shropshire 73
Sicily, king of 115
Siena 114, 116, 117 *see also* Podestà
Simon, grandson of Henry of Huntingdon 67
simony 39, 69, 100, 172
sin 18, 19, 37, 39, 40, 41, 44, 50, 56–7, 60, 64, 107, 128, 142, 198
Sir Gowther 197–8
Sleightholme, William 157
social capital 170, 172–3
sodomy 46, 55–6, 60–3
soldier 23, 29, 73, 96, 97, 99, 103, 105
  of Christ 98
Song of Antioch, The 104–5, 106
South English Legendary 165
Spain 6
Stafford, Edward, duke of Buckingham 194
Stanley, James, bishop of Ely (d. 1515) 174
Stanley, Sir John 174
Staunton, William 153–4
Steinberg, Leo 187
  The Sexuality of Christ 187
Stephen, count of the Auvergne 41
Stephen, king of England 74, 79
Stone, John 173
Stratford 181
Stretch, John 166
Swanson, Robert 31, 65
Sweetenham, Carol 107
Swineshead, abbey of 181
Synods
  Douzy, synod of 33
  Fismes, synod of 36
  Tusey, synod of 41

tail-rhyme 144–5, 149
Talmud 11, 24
  Babylonian 17, 20–3, 25–6
  Palestinian 17, 22, 26
Taranto, Bohemond of 102, 104, 106

temple 22
Teutfrid, priest 39
Tewkesbury, Battle of 126
Theutberga, Queen 44
Thibodeaux, Jennifer D 4–5, 6, 147
Thomas, Hugh 85
Thornbury 194
Thwing 148, 149
Tobias 157
Torah 11–12, 16–17, 19–23
Tosh, John 34
Toulouse, Raymond of, count of St Gilles 102, 107
Tractatus pro clericorum conubio 50–1, 53–4, 57–8, 61
Traub, Valerie 147
Treatise on Grace 50–1, 55–7, 60
Tres Riches Heures 194
Tretise of Miraclis Pleying 187
Tudor, Edmund 136
Tudor, Henry *see* Henry VII
Tudor, Jasper 136
Tunstall, Cuthbert, bishop of London 198
Turfrida 87
Turold, abbot of Malmesbury 84
Twyning, Thomas 181
Tynemouth Priory 177

Ulric, bishop of Augsburg, bishop of Imola 49–50
  Rescripta 49–50, 62
  Pseudo-Ulrich 50
university 168, 170, 178–9
  education 168, 173, 174, 178
  exhibition 172–3
  Cambridge 173
  Oxford 148, 172 n.58, 173, 174, 179, 180
Urban II, Pope 13, 95, 98, 99, 110

vassals 121–2
Vauchez, André 114, 129, 135
  Sainthood in the Middle Ages 8–9
Vergil, Polydore 128, 142
vespers 64, 116

vestments
  chasuble 197
  cope 145, 154, 155
  stole 104–105, 145, 154, 155
  mitre 145, 153, 154
  crozier 145
Vikings 28
violence 13, 24–6, 72–5, 113, 116
  spiritual 73–75, 103, 106, 110
Virgin Mary 9, 117, 141, 199
  as priest 185
virgin, virginity 41, 61, 115
virility, *virilitas* 12, 32, 49, 81, 84, 138
virtue 21, 78, 116, 132, 135, 136, 138, 139–40, 141, 149, 150, 157–8, 164
virtus 78–9, 85–6, 88–90
via unitiva 188
vita 36, 91, 92, 112–14, 120, 122, 124–5, 148–53, 155, 157, 158
von Weissenberg, Marita 133, 191
vowess 198
Vulpecula 42–3

Wallingford, priory of 174
Wallingford, Richard of 174
Walsingham, Thomas 143, 144
Warde, John de la 192
warfare 31
  warrior 23, 84–5, 89–90, 107
  spiritual war 12, 21 73–75, 103–4, 110
  warrior-cleric 5, 73, 75, 102–4
Warwick, castle 144
weapons
  bow 104, 165
  dagger 24, 135
  lance 24–25 *see also* Holy Lance
  shield 104–5
  spear 105
  sword 24, 78, 88–9, 105, 135, 165
Weinstein, Donald 9, 114
Wellys, William, bishop of Rochester (*d.* 1443) 178

Index

Welsh 73
Wensley, North Yorkshire 192
Wensley, Simon de 192
Werner, Janelle 6
Wertheimer, Laura 6
Westminster
  abbey of 165, 166, 171
  council of [1102] 48, 62, 89
  council of [1125] 64
Whalley Abbey 172
Wheathampstead (family of) 177
Wheathampstead, John, abbot of St Albans 177
whore 54, 58, 64, 70–1
wife 20, 35, 42, 46, 47, 48, 53, 57, 63, 68, 70–2, 115, 122, 138, 185, 194, 199
Wilet, Sir John, rector of Trevalga, diocese of Exeter 191
William de Corbeil, archbishop of Canterbury 71
William I (the bastard), king of England 78, 82–4, 89, 90, 92
William Rufus, king of England 72
Winchcombe, abbey of, Gloucestershire 181

Winchester, council of 51
Windsor, St George's chapel 127, 195
Winwick, near Ashton under Lyne 197, 199
witch 79, 89
Wode, William, prior of Bridlington 144
wolf 89, 90
Wolffe, Bertram 130, 131
womanhood, women 1–2, 4, 9, 10, 12, 15, 16–21, 22, 24, 32–5, 37, 38, 39, 40, 42, 44, 57–8, 64, 70–1, 80, 96, 98, 107–8, 113, 114, 136, 138–9, 158, 185, 189, 191, 194, 195, 199
  see also wife
Worcester 73
Worcester Priory 176, 179
Worcester, John of 83–4
Wulfstan, bishop of Worcester 73–5

yetzer 18–19, 21, 23
yetzer ha-ra 18
York (monastic recruitment) 162
youth, youthfulness 78, 80, 85–7, 89, 133, 136, 137, 162, 168, 170, 174, 181, 182

GENDER IN THE MIDDLE AGES

I   *Gender and Medieval Drama,* Katie Normington, 2006
II *Gender and Petty Crime in Late Medieval England: The Local Courts in Kent, 1460–1560,* Karen Jones, 2006
III *The Pastoral Care of Women in Late Medieval England,* Beth Allison Barr, 2008
IV *Gender, Nation and Conquest in the Works of William of Malmesbury,* Kirsten A. Fenton, 2008
V   *Monsters, Gender and Sexuality in Medieval English Literature,* Dana M. Oswald, 2010
VI *Medieval Anchoritisms: Gender, Space and the Solitary Life,* Liz Herbert McAvoy, 2011
VII *Middle-Aged Women in the Middle Ages,* edited by Sue Niebrzydowski, 2011
VIII *Married Women and the Law in Premodern Northwest Europe,* edited by Cordelia Beattie and Matthew Frank Stevens, 2013
IX *Religious Men and Masculine Identity in the Middle Ages,* edited by P. H. Cullum and Katherine J. Lewis, 2013
X   *Reconsidering Gender, Time and Memory in Medieval Culture,* edited by Elizabeth Cox, Liz Herbert McAvoy and Roberta Magnani, 2015
XI *Medicine, Religion and Gender in Medieval Culture,* edited by Naoë Kukita Yoshikawa, 2015
XII *The Unspeakable, Gender and Sexuality in Medieval Literature, 1000–1400,* Victoria Blud, 2017

www.ingramcontent.com/pod-product-compliance
Lightning Source LLC
Chambersburg PA
CBHW070803230426
43665CB00017B/2474